Seeds
Proceedings of the Oxford Symposium on Food and Cookery 2018

Seeds

Proceedings of the Oxford Symposium on Food and Cookery 2018

Edited by Mark McWilliams

Prospect Books
2019

First published in Great Britain in 2019 by Prospect Books, 26 Parke Road, London SW13 9NG.

© 2019 as a collection Prospect Books.
© 2019 in individual articles rests with the authors.

The authors assert their moral right to be identified as authors in accordance with the Copyright, Designs & Patents Act 1988. No part of this publication may be reproduced, stored in a retrieval system or transmitted in any form or by any means, electronic, mechanical, photocopying, recording or otherwise, without the prior permission of the copyright holders.

ISBN 978-1-909-248-65-6

The front cover illustration shows Native American men tilling the earth and women planting seeds. '*Wie sie ire äcker bauwen und beseen*', hand-coloured engraving on paper (Frankfurt am Main: Johann Feyerabend for Theodor de Bry, 1591) pt. 2, plate XXI; Courtesy of the John Carter Brown Library).

The back cover shows the Svalbard Global Seed Vault.

Title page shows a new invention notification for an apple parer, corer and slicer, from the 10 May 1856 issue of *Scientific American*.

Design and typesetting in Gill Sans and Adobe Garamond by Catheryn Kilgarriff and Brendan King.

Printed and bound in Great Britain.

Contents

Foreword
Mark McWilliams … 9

Plenary Papers

Svalbard Global Seed Vault: Noah's Ark for Seeds in the Arctic
Åsmund Asdal … 11

Saving the Future: Conservation in Action – The Millennium Seed Bank of the Royal Botanic Gardens, Kew
Elinor Breman … 18

Muriel Howorth and the Atomic Gardening Society: Writing Food Futures
Molly MacVeigh … 30

Symposium Papers

Reclaiming Diversity of Taste
Isaura Andaluz … 41

Eating Life Force: The Meaning of Seeds in the German Alternative Food Movement
Volker Bach … 49

'Thorebygg' in Farmhouse Ale Brewing in Norway
Hans Olav Bråtå … 58

Seeds in the Story of the Paradise of Pleasure and the Myth of the So-Called Mediterranean Diet
Adrian Bregazzi … 67

Neapolitan *Pastiera* and the Religious Significance of Wheatberries
Anthony F. Buccini … 79

The Sesame Seed and 'Japaneseness'
Voltaire Cang … 89

How Coffee Killed a Town: Investigating the Nineteenth-Century Rise and Fall of Coffee in Lipa, Batangas
Bel S. Castro … 99

Seeds

From Peasant Food to Posh Ingredient: A History of Buckwheat in Brittany
Mary Margaret Chappell — 108

Field Selection in Plant Breeding: Different Ways to Make a Variety
Renata Christen — 118

Preparing Seeds for Palatability: Chicken Guts and Chefs' Tools
Len Fisher — 125

Fenugreek: Seed of a New History of Modern North Africa
Anny Gaul — 129

A Land of Wheat: In Search of the Lost Grain of Israel/Palestine
B.Z. Goldberg and Ronit Vered — 137

The Long and Simple History of the Dibble and its Cousins
Peter Hertzmann — 148

'The answers to our ancestors' prayers': Seeding a Movement for Health and Culture
Elizabeth Hoover and Sean Sherman — 160

Fruits of Empowerment in Grazia Deledda's *The Church of Solitude*
Eilis Kierans — 171

The Seed of Hope: Acorns from Famine Food to Delicacy in European History
Andrea Maraschi — 177

Sacralized Grains in the Americas: The Culinary Preparations of Maize and its Symobolic Use in Religious Rituals
Sandra Melchior, Marcella Sulis, and Carolina Sulis — 186

Bittersweet Coffee and the Seeds of Hope: European Immigrants' Memories of Vegetable Gardens in Early Twentieth-Century São Paulo, Brazil
Sandra Mian — 197

The Impact of Seed Laws on Agricultural Biodiversity
Katharina Mojescik — 207

Growing and Eating God: The Mental Image of Wheat in Traditional Romanian Communities
Raluca Parfentie — 217

Seeds

In a Sense, Imperfect: Seedlessness and the American Quest for Convenience in Fruit
Jeffrey Rubel — 226

Chocolate and Vanilla: Seeds of Taste
Kathryn E. Sampeck — 240

Replenishing the Seeds that Made Southern Cookery
David Shields — 257

Traditional Crops: The Case of Bambara Groundnut
Hanna Simonsen — 267

Zoochory
Ray Sokolov — 274

Revisiting the Acorn Eaters: The Case of the Arkadians in Greek Antiquity
Corey Straub — 281

Amaranth: Food of the Gods, or Seed of the Devil?
David C. Sutton — 286

The English Quest for Novelty: Kitchen Garden Seeds from Abroad from the Sixteenth to the Early Eighteenth Centuries
Malcolm Thick — 297

Seed-Time: Back-to-the-Land Sex and Politics at the Fin de Siècle
Kate Thomas — 308

"Throw away your *gogo*'s seed": The Centrality of Traditional Seed in KwaZulu-Natal, South Africa
Jaci van Niekerk and Rachel Wynberg — 318

Mustard in the Talmudic Literature
Susan Weingarten — 328

Karakilçik Wheat and its Promise for a Better Food World
Zafar Yenal — 337

Contributors — 346

8

Foreword

The sights could not be more different. In one, curved greenhouse-like buildings rise gently from the wildflowered English countryside; in the other, an angular metallic shape juts starkly out of a snowbound Norwegian mountainside. And yet both – the Millennium Seed Bank at Royal Botanic Gardens, Kew, and the Svalbard Global Seed Bank – serve at once as witness to the widespread destruction of the Anthropocene and as ark-like hope for surviving those same collective acts of self-harm.

This year the Oxford Symposium on Food and Cookery took as its theme Seeds. We alternate annually between consideration of large or theoretical subjects – Authenticity, say, or last year's Landscape – and smaller, more focused topics. Seeds are indeed typically small: as Bee Wilson noted in our call for proposals, 'you could fit enough seed for an acre of wheat in a single large shopping bag'. That portability has been crucial in human history: almost every large-scale movement of people has included its share of Johnny Appleseed-minded folks, whether sailors carrying corn across the Atlantic on Columbus's ships or enslaved peoples smuggling okra in the opposite direction through the horrors of the Middle Passage.

The papers presented this year explored the topic with the Symposium's unique mix of intellectual rigour and quirky creativity. Authors explored topics ranging widely from what was once seen as the promise of irradiated seeds to the many threats to indigenous species, from the way individual grains shape communal identity to the role of seeds in religious symbolism, from seeds' role in economic boom and bust cycles to prehistoric and high-tech ways of planting seeds. And yet these papers often share an unexpected similarity: though many explore the specific context of seeds in the past and others lament that loss in the present, both approaches share a sense of the way landraces – individual species carefully adapted to specific geographies and climates – capture a sense of place. What's added, especially in juxtaposing them, is an unavoidable sense of doom.

After all, next to portability, seeds' most important attribute is durability. In the right conditions, seeds can last almost indefinitely, and yet that crucial attribute is clearly endangered. As this volume goes to print, the United Nations has released a dire report from the IPBES Global Assessment that predicts the extinction of up to a million species of plants and animals. With over a quarter of the species on our planet threatened, the potential devastation dwarfs humanity's already disastrous impact on Earth. In this context, 'innovations' from transnational agribusinesses seem especially ominous. When forcing farmers to sign technology agreement contracts do not seem enough to stop the age-old practice of saving seed, seed varieties have now been genetically engineered with 'terminator technology' to prevent them from being productive in the second generation. No wonder some have called these varieties 'suicide seeds'.

Seeds

Such developments make the work of the seedbanks at Kew and Svalbard that much more important, but the meaning of these efforts seems difficult to pin down. Recently, for example, the Global Seed Bank had its first withdrawal: the International Centre for Agricultural Research in the Dry Areas (ICARDA) needed their seeds to re-establish their local collection that had been damaged by fighting around their headquarters in Aleppo, Syria. That ICARDA could draw on its reserves in Svalbard seems terrifically hopeful; that they needed to seems a terrifying glimpse into a turbulent future.

Debate over how to think of such developments filled symposiasts' conversations over three astonishingly hot July days in Oxford. Weather is not climate, of course, but the heatwave seemed especially insistent given the topics we were considering. In the end, many of us found our fears balanced by promising efforts to save, reestablish, and popularize threatened seeds around the world: to restore a whole range of seeds taken from Indigenous peoples in America, to nurture buckwheat in Brittany, to expand access to landrace wheat varieties in Turkey and in the western United States.

Here I would like to thank everyone who helped me with this volume, particularly Elisabeth Luard, Ursula Heinzelmann, Cathy Kaufman, Peter Hertzmann, Catheryn Kilgarriff, and Brendan King – and, of course, the many symposiasts who enact the Oxford Food Symposium's vision: change the conversation, expand the table, improve the plate. The committed scholarship and activism of such people is, itself, a kind of hope.

Mark McWilliams
Editor, Oxford Symposium on Food and Cookery

Svalbard Global Seed Vault: Noah's Ark for Seeds in the Arctic

Åsmund Asdal

Seeds contain DNA and genetic combinations, making it possible to conserve plant varieties and valuable traits of crop plants. Plant genetic resources are conserved in gene banks, and the Svalbard Global Seed Vault offers free-of-charge space for conserving security copies, like a bank box in the Arctic.

Seeds are wonderful structures, created by nature to make plants able to survive critical conditions and unfavourable seasons. Seeds have a huge and fascinating diversity of forms, sizes, and colours, adapted to life forms, spreading mechanisms, and growing conditions.

Seeds are the most important human food source. They are nutritious, and they can be stored until the next growing season or for longer periods, which is very useful for modern civilization. Further, seeds are adapted to modern farming. Or more correctly, seeds have properties that allow the mechanization and development of modern farming methods.

Even more ingenious and important for the topic of this article, seeds hold genetic material. The natural mode of crossings between male and female plants through generative reproduction allows for new genetic combinations, plant breeding, improved varieties of cultivated plants, and the development of agriculture and food production.

This potential for evolution has been the precondition for the development of agriculture and also the evolution of civilization. Crop plants that can be cultivated have, over millennia, been derived from wild plants, thanks to an interior genetic diversity that has allowed the development of landraces through the crossing and selection of favourable and farmable genotypes.

Well known examples are bread wheat (*Triticum aestivum*) derived from an accidental cross between emmer wheat (*Triticum dicoccum*) and goatgrass (*Aegilops tauschii*); vegetables like cabbage, broccoli, Brussels sprouts, and cauliflower, all originating from wild *Brassica oleracea*; and maize (*Zea mays*) originating from the quite modest wild growing plant teosinte (*Zea spp.*).

The Pioneer Nikolai I. Vavilov
Collecting and conserving genetic resources as seeds in gene banks started at the

beginning of the twentieth century. The first gene bank in the world was established by the Russian pioneer Nikolai I. Vavilov in St. Petersburg. The N.I. Vavilov All-Russian Research Institute of Plant Industry (VIR) still exists in the same buildings and still holds one of the largest collections of seeds in the world.

Slowly, more countries founded national or regional gene banks, and today we have a worldwide net of international, regional, and national gene banks that conserve millions of seed samples covering large parts of the global diversity of crop plants.

The Nordic Gene Bank for plants (NGB), now the Nordic Genetic Resource Centre (NordGen), was founded in 1979 as a regional plant gene bank for the five Nordic countries Finland, Sweden, Denmark, Norway, and Iceland, as well as three autonomous territories in the Baltic Sea: Greenland, Faroe Islands, and Åland Islands.

Today, the Nordic seed collection at NordGen consists of approximately 35,000 unique accessions (seed samples) of around 530 different plant species. Conserving dried and frozen seeds is a favourable and relatively cheap method for the conservation of plant genetic resources. In addition, seeds are perfect for distributing genetic resources, just by sending some seeds by ordinary mail. Every year NordGen distributes thousands of seed samples from its gene bank stocks to plant breeders and researchers all over the world. Seeds are even sent directly to farmers and hobby growers, mainly in the Nordic countries.

Unfortunately, not all horticultural and agricultural plants have seeds that can be used for the conservation of their genetic material. Some plants do not produce seeds at all, while others have so-called non-orthodox seeds, which are seeds that do not stand heavy drying and freezing. Many tropical plants have non-orthodox seeds.

Furthermore, many crop plants are clones, and the propagation of new plants is done by tubers (potato), cuttings (many berry species), or grafting (fruit trees). Most of these species produce seeds, but the seeds are a result of sexual crossing and do not contain the genetic combinations that constitute the variety with the desired qualities and properties. The seeds contain the parent plant genes, but not in the combination that characterizes the variety that we want to conserve or use for food production.

In these cases, genetic resources as plant varieties are conserved by other methods, for example in field gene banks, or in laboratories (as in vitro-cultivated seedlings or as plant cells cryo-conserved in liquid nitrogen at -196° C).

Conserving Seeds in Svalbard

However, this article is about seeds. Quite soon after the establishment of the Nordic seed collection at the Nordic Gene Bank headquarters in Alnarp, Sweden, in 1979, the need for a secure back-up facility in permafrost was discussed. Different options were considered before deciding to take advantage of an abandoned coal mine gallery in Longyearbyen, Svalbard, that maintained a stable temperature of -3.6° C.

Peaceful Svalbard turned out to be a perfect place for this kind of secure storage for seeds. In addition to permafrost, Longyearbyen, despite its remote location, offered public services and good infrastructure, including an airport with frequent flights to the mainland. And, not least, the mining company Store Norske Spitsbergen Kulkompani showed significant interest in cooperation and was very helpful during the establishment. The first seeds were brought into the coal mine in November 1984.

This Nordic solution to secure its seed collection by conserving duplicates in the Artic permafrost received significant attention worldwide. Appreciation for this approach led to the idea of making a similar arrangement for seeds from other gene banks being discussed quite soon after the first Nordic seeds were in place.

The International Treaty on Plant Genetic Resources for Food and Agriculture (ITPGRFA) established an international legal framework for the conservation and access to plant genetic resources. This framework was also an important precondition for a global back-up facility for genetic resource conservation, and the Food and Agriculture Organization of the United Nations (FAO) formally requested a facility study from the Norwegian government in 2004.

The resulting report was positive, and the Norwegian decision to fund and build the Seed Vault was announced by the five Nordic prime ministers in June 2006. Offering a facility like this to the global plant genetic resource community aligns with the Norwegian commitment to an international endeavour to maintain biological diversity in general and genetic resources in particular. The initiative received extensive support from relevant international bodies, gene banks, national plant genetic resource programs, and governments worldwide.

Construction was completed in 2007. The Seed Vault was opened, and the first seeds were brought into one of three storage halls on 26 February 2008. The Svalbard Global Seed Vault celebrated its ten-year anniversary in February 2018.

The Construction

The Seed Vault is carved out from, and built into, virgin solid rock in the hillside of Platåfjellet (the Plateau Mountain); it is not built in a coal mine, which is a common misunderstanding. The entrance is located 130 metres above sea level, which is well above the worst case scenarios for sea level rise due to climate change. Permafrost in the mountain massive provides a temperature around -3 to -4° C. Additional artificial cooling brings the temperature down to -18° C, which is the recommended temperature for long-term conservation of dried seeds adopted by the majority of gene banks.

The seed store facility consists of three storage halls embedded in geologically-stable solid rock. The entrance to the halls goes through a 100 metre-long tunnel from the outside portal in the hillside. The portal itself is adorned with a piece of artwork – *Perpetual Repercussion* by Dyveke Sanne – which has become a landmark for visitors to Svalbard.

The Svalbard Global Seed Vault aims to conserve duplicates of all unique seed accessions that are conserved in national, regional, or international gene banks and other holdings. Current FAO estimates indicate that there are approximately 2.2 million unique seed accessions conserved in gene banks globally. The dimensions of the seed vault allow for deposits of approximately 4.5 million accessions.

The Seed Vault is owned by the Norwegian government, which also guarantees the long-term maintenance of the facility and the secure conservation of the seeds. The Norwegian Ministry of Agriculture and Food is the liable and legal national authority for the Seed Vault.

The Seed Vault is managed through an agreement between the Ministry, the Global Crop Diversity Trust ('Crop Trust'), and NordGen. Crop Trust partially funds Seed Vault operations as part of the global conservation system. Crop Trust also financially supports the multiplication of seeds and shipment costs to Svalbard for gene banks that lack resources in their own budgets. NordGen is responsible for the operation of the Vault, and also contributes to the management budget.

Statsbygg (the Norwegian directorate for the management of state-owned buildings) is responsible for both service and the continuous surveillance of the facility and its technical installations. An International Advisory Panel with representatives from all parts of the world meets regularly to oversee the operation of the Vault, anchor the Seed Vault mission internationally, and act as ambassadors for the Seed Vault.

Conserving Seeds in the Seed Vault

In its first ten years of operation, the Seed Vault has been an indisputable success. By the end of 2018, seventy-six gene banks from all over the world have deposited more than one million seed samples. In addition, the Seed Vault has unexpectedly become an iconic symbol of the importance of conserving plant genetic resources. The partners use the Seed Vault in public awareness campaigns and in communication with politicians, media, and other stakeholders designed to increase not only commitments to conservation, but also to create an understanding of, and support for, the research and plant breeding activities that are carried out by institutes, breeding companies, and gene banks all over the world.

Seed deposits require a standard depositor agreement signed by the depositing institute and the Norwegian Ministry for Agriculture and Food. The main issue in the agreement is that deposited seeds remain the property of the depositing gene bank. Seeds are packed and shipped by the gene bank and stored under 'black box' conditions, which means that boxes are never opened in Svalbard and that seeds can only be sent back to the depositing gene bank. The depositing gene bank can reclaim their seeds at any time, for any reason. The agreement also includes a clause ensuring that genetic material conserved in the Seed Vault is made available by the depositing seed bank for breeding, research, and education, in accordance with ITPGRFA or other relevant international regulations. Depositing seeds in the Seed Vault is free of charge; however, the depositor has to cover shipping costs.

Viability monitoring and regeneration of seed samples when needed remains the responsibility of the depositor. As the Seed Vault offers similar or better storage conditions than that available in most gene banks, testing seeds from the same yield in the home gene bank generally indicates when seeds loose viability and thus need to be replaced by fresh seeds.

NordGen is responsible for the operation and management of the Seed Vault. The most important part of this effort is maintaining contact with potential depositor institutes and facilitating the shipment and transfer of seeds to Svalbard. Normally, the Seed Vault is opened three times a year for receiving seeds. Seed boxes are shipped by air cargo, and NordGen staff receive the seed boxes in Svalbard and bring them inside and onto the shelves in the Vault.

In the Seed Vault Today

NordGen maintains a publicly-accessible seed database on the Internet that lists details of the seeds held in the Vault, including species, depositor institutes, and the origin of seed accessions.

At the end of 2018, the exact number of seed accessions in the Seed Vault was 983,524, deposited by 76 gene bank institutes. The total number of deposited seed samples was 1,075,954. These numbers differ because a depositor gene bank has withdrawn seeds for the first time: the International Centre for Agricultural Research in Dry Areas (ICARDA) has retrieved part of its seeds deposit from the Seed Vault.

The former ICARDA gene bank was located at its headquarters in Aleppo, Syria. Because of the Syrian conflict, the seed bank was partly damaged and partly inaccessible. In 2015 ICARDA decided to establish new gene bank collections in Lebanon and Morocco, and seeds from the depot in the Seed Vault have been withdrawn to support this effort. ICARDA is the first gene bank to request seeds to be returned from the Seed Vault. Despite the sadness of the situation in Syria, this transaction demonstrates the importance of having a global facility like the Svalbard Global Seed Vault. Since the first withdrawal of seeds in 2015, ICARDA has already twice deposited new seeds to replace the retrieved accessions in the Seed Vault.

Depositors in the Seed Vault are mainly international, regional, or national gene banks and research centres. A couple of NGOs have also deposited seeds. Most gene banks have seeds originating from a large number of countries in their collections; consequently, the Seed Vault holds seed samples from almost all countries in the world. The collection comprises seeds of about 5000 species, which are crops or plant species related to crops that could be used as gene donors in plant breeding and research.

Some of the Consultative Group for International Agricultural Research (CGIAR) centres are in charge of the largest numbers of deposited seed samples. These centres aim to duplicate at least 90% of their seed collections in the Seed Vault. Four of them have deposited more than 100,000 accessions each: the International Maize and Wheat Improvement Centre (CIMMYT), the International Rice Research Institute (IRRI), the International Crop Research Institute for the Semi-Arid Tropics (ICRISAT), and ICARDA. Four other CGIAR centres are major depositors: the International Centre for

Tropical Agriculture (CIAT), the International Institute of Tropical Agriculture (IITA), the Africa Rice Centre, and the International Potato Centre (CIP). The international World Vegetable Centre in Taiwan is also among the larger depositors. Eighteen gene banks have deposited more than 10,000 accessions each. The major depositor countries on the national gene bank level are USA, Germany, Canada, Australia, The Netherlands, South Korea, Taiwan, and Switzerland. NordGen itself has deposited 24,864 accessions as of December 2018.

As gene banks for PGRFA are aiming to conserve the maximum diversity of important food crops, the number of accessions and genotypes within several crops are significant. Eighteen crops have more than 10,000 different accessions. Wheat and rice each have more than 160,000 accessions conserved in the Seed Vault. Other important and well represented crops include barley, sorghum, beans, maize, cowpea, alfalfa, soybean, chickpea, kikuyu grass, *Triticosecale*, potato, groundnut, oat, pigeon pea, and mustard.

Public Awareness about PGR Conservation

In addition to its primary objective of conserving crop diversity, the Svalbard Global Seed Vault also seeks to advance the larger cause of conservation of crop diversity through increased public awareness, and through building political and scientific support. As a symbol of this important task, the Seed Vault has received significant attention from the media and politicians. Visitors to the Seed Vault include policy makers from international organizations, governments, businesses, and plant breeding and research organizations.

As many tourists are interested in the Seed Vault and its mission, a separate exhibition section is an integrated part of the permanent exhibitions at Svalbard Museum in Longyearbyen. A tour to the entrance of the Seed Vault has become a must for many tourists. Especially in the dark season, the front part of the Seed Vault and its illuminated piece of art offers a quite spectacular view. If you are lucky, you will also see the northern lights, aurora borealis, covering large parts of the sky above the Vault.

Unfortunately, Svalbard and the Arctic is one of the places on Earth experiencing the most rapid climate change. For the conservation of the frozen seeds, higher temperatures in Svalbard mean that more electricity has to be used to maintain the temperature at -18° C. At the same time, higher temperatures, more rain, and the resulting lack of permafrost in the top soil above the Seed Vault's entrance tunnel have occasionally caused water to intrude into the outer part of the tunnel. In order to increase the long-term security of the seeds, the Norwegian government has decided to rebuild parts of the tunnel to make it completely waterproof. This construction will be completed by May 2019, making the Seed Vault an even more secure place for the conservation of this vital natural resource needed for future food supplies.

More information

More information about the Svalbard Global Seed Vault and its operations can be seen on the web pages of the cooperating partners:

- The Norwegian Ministry of Agriculture and Food operates the official Seed Vault webpage: <https://www.seedvault.no>
- NordGen operates a webpage that contains the Seed Portal and information for depositors: <http://www.nordgen.org/sgsv>
- NordGen also offers general information and instructions for depositing seeds: <https://www.nordgen.org/en/global-seed-vault/>
- Crop Trust offers information about their work for global PGR conservation in general and use of the Seed Vault in particular: <https://www.croptrust.org/our-work/svalbard-global-seed-vault/>
- The documentary *The Backup Copy* (Snowball Films) offers a useful summary of the Seed Vault's mission and activities: <https://vimeo.com/62688049>

Saving the Future: Conservation in Action – The Millennium Seed Bank of the Royal Botanic Gardens, Kew

The Jane Grigson Memorial Lecture

Elinor Breman

For the majority of the public, the first images that spring to mind when thinking of the Royal Botanic Gardens, Kew, are iconic glasshouses – either the curves of the Palm House or the newly-restored grandeur of the Temperate House. They may then think of the amazing and beautiful plants that are housed within, and the world-class horticulture that supports these displays. Few know of the science that goes on at this renowned institute to increase knowledge of the world's plants and fungi – or that Kew manages a second botanic garden, Wakehurst, nestled in the Sussex Weald countryside.

It is at Wakehurst that you find the Millennium Seed Bank, or MSB, the largest ex situ conservation programme on the planet. The work that goes on in this building is helping to ensure a future for plant life on Earth by preserving seeds from wild plants, making them available to future generations. Kew cannot do this in isolation and so works with partners around the world to help conserve plant life. Since 2000 we have worked with more than ninety-five countries, and the partnership continues to expand. There are currently MSB conservation projects active in fifty-four countries. More than

Figures 1 and 2: The Millenium Seed Bank of the Royal Botanic Gardens, Kew, nestled in the Sussex Weald countryside at Wakehurst, Kew's wild botanic garden.

The Millennium Seed Bank of the Royal Botanic Gardens, Kew

39,000 plant species, represented by over two billion seeds, are stored in a vault beneath the building, making this corner of England the most biodiverse place on the planet. The building was designed to last 500 years and has space to store up to 75% of the world's bankable flora.

Seeds arrive at the MSB almost daily from all corners of the globe. This is just one of the stages in a journey from the seed being collected in the wild through to its being banked in this state-of-the-art facility. There have already been many steps along the way before the seeds reach this stage. The first is to ensure that all material is legally collected and that partners who work with Kew to conserve wild plant diversity and duplicate their collections with Kew enter into access and benefit-sharing agreements. The terms of these agreements define what can and cannot be done with collections and enable prior-informed consent under the terms of the Nagoya Protocol and the International Treaty on Plant Genetic Resources for Food and Agriculture.[1]

Once the legalities have been addressed, projects can be started. These range from bilateral to multinational at the regional or global scale. All begin with the identification of a need to conserve plants. These may be plants that are threatened in the wild, for example from over-exploitation or habitat loss, or those that have limited ranges or small populations and, as such, are at greater risk from extinction. They could be useful plants used either locally or globally. Kew and its partners bring to bear all of their taxonomic expertize in devising targeted collection lists and identifying potential collection sites for each species. The hard part is then to find these plants in their natural environment in order to collect seeds. We work on all continents and in some very remote areas, and we rely heavily on our partners' knowledge and expertise in locating and identifying target plant species in the field. Reaching the plants is not always easy – you may need to trek into an area for a day or more to find your site, or up a mountain if working on alpine plants. In some cases, helicopters or even dug-out canoes are used to reach remote areas. The seeds themselves may also be inaccessible: for example in our Global Tree Seed Bank Project we have had to change the way we collect – and the equipment

Figures 3 and 4: It can be challenging to reach collecting sites in the field.

we take – in order to reach seeds that can be as much as thirty metres overhead.[2]

Once the population has been identified and assessed we can collect the seeds, ensuring that there is no impact on the regeneration of the wild population and that as much genetic diversity as possible is captured from the population. This means collecting less than 20% of the seed available on a given day and collecting from across the population. A collection consists of not just the seeds, but also a dried pressed plant from which the seed was collected (a herbarium specimen), as well as data collected in the field. The herbarium specimen is used to ensure the correct identification of the plant – crucial if the seeds are to be of use. Collections are stored in the country of origin and sent to the MSB for safety duplication. Should something happen to the in-country seed bank collection, Kew can repatriate material from this duplicate.

Let me take you on a journey with a newly-arrived seed collection. All collections are given a unique identification number. The herbarium specimen is lodged at Kew's herbarium, joining more than seven million vouchers from around the world collected over the past 170 years. These vouchers provide a lasting record of plant distribution and changes in phenology (changes in a plant's life cycle in relation to the seasons, e.g. flowering time) through time. The seeds are unpacked and placed in a dry room, at 15% relative humidity and 15° C, where the seeds will stay until they reach equilibrium with the conditions inside the room. Drying the seeds helps to conserve them. For every 10% drop in relative humidity the lifespan of the seeds doubles. Seed collections are cleaned to remove debris, and then a portion of the collection is x-rayed to provide an initial quality check for the collection. By looking at the internal structure of the seeds, it is possible to determine the number of healthy, potentially viable seeds, something that can't be told from looking at the outside of the seed. Seeds are placed in air-tight containers and banked at -20° C, a temperature that is optimum for extending the lifespan of the seeds during storage. For every 5° C drop in temperature the lifespan of the seeds doubles. This means that seeds stored at the MSB could survive for tens to hundreds of years.

Germination tests are carried out on all collections. These not only show the quality of the collections but also provide useful information on how to turn the seeds back into plants – a vital step if these species are to be used. This process is harder than it might at first appear, as material comes to the MSB from all corners of the globe, and so requires all kinds of different conditions to enable germination, from specific temperature and light regimes to the addition of growth hormones or smoke treatments. In addition, very little is known about the conditions required for wild plants as often the germination tests represent the first time they have been grown by people.

So why is this work important? There are some 400,000 plant species known to science, and more are discovered and described each year, many by Kew scientists. This is good news as all life is dependent on plants, and diversity has been shown to aid ecosystem function. Yet one in five plants are currently faced with extinction.[3] Plants have always gone extinct – it is part of the cycle of natural selection and evolution – but the problem is that the current rate of extinction is a thousand times greater than that in the fossil record. This means that plants are currently going extinct 1000 times faster than they have in the past. We live in the Anthropocene, a geological period during which human activity is the dominant influence on climate and the environment. The current rate of plant loss is driven by human causes – land conversion, climate change, over-exploitation, pollution, invasive species, and urbanization. Humans, therefore, have a responsibility not only to reduce these threats, but also to halt these losses before the ecosystem services provided by plants collapse. These services are generally split into four groups: supporting, provisioning, regulating, and cultural – and we are dependent on them all.

If we look in more detail at the provisioning services, these include those covering basic human needs for food, shelter, medicine, fuel, and fibres. Around 8% of plants have a documented use under provisioning services, and there will be many more yet to be recorded. Human food falls into this category and is the focus of the second of the United Nations Sustainable Development Goals calling for zero hunger.[4] Food security is, however, vulnerable. The human population is forecast to approach 9.7 billion by 2050.[5] In order to meet the global food demand by 2050, production will have to increase by 60% relative to 2005.[6] This cannot be achieved simply by increasing the area under production due to competing land uses, the need to maintain ecosystems, sustainability issues, and available land quality.

The world has around 30,000 edible plants, with the potential for up to half of the known species of plants (some 200,000) to be useful for sustenance, but only 150 are in regular cultivation although up to 7000 are collected for food.[7] Even more striking is the fact that 80% of the world's calorific intake comes from just twelve plant species (barley, maize, millet, rice, rye, sorghum, sugar cane, wheat, cassava, potato, sweet potato, yam), and 60% from just three (rice, wheat, maize).[8] Dependence on such a small food base is a further vulnerability to our food security.

Our small food base is not the only challenge. Climate change scenarios suggest that by the middle of this century growing season temperatures will bear little resemblance to those experienced from 1900 to 2000 for any given location, with the coolest growing season being hotter than any prior to 2000. The occurrence of four to six month-long droughts is also set to increase two- or three-fold.[9] These changes will directly impact the world's crops. Increased sterility occurs in rice flowers at raised temperatures; maize is highly sensitive to drought at the time of flowering; wheat senescence (deterioration with age) comes earlier and faster at higher temperatures.[10] It has been predicted that for every 1° C increase in average temperature during the growing season 6-10% of productivity will be lost as a result of impacts on the physiology of crops.

A further issue is the way in which we grow much of our food. Monocultures of crops are highly susceptible to pests and diseases, a problem exacerbated by climate change and which could contribute to food shortages in the coming decades. For example, aggressive new strains of stripe rust disease have decimated wheat yields in recent harvests. In 2010, a global epidemic destroyed some 400,000 hectares of wheat in Ethiopia, and losses of more than 80% were witnessed in some parts of the Middle East and North Africa. Climate change is making stripe rust management more unpredictable than a decade ago, as shifting climate patterns bring higher temperatures and increasingly variable and intense rainfall – optimal conditions for the development and spread of rust diseases. Combined with limited funding and the need for transborder surveillance and coordination between countries and regions, this situation could spell disaster for farming communities and wheat-producers worldwide. The solution is a combination of sustained crop improvement research to ensure a steady supply of stripe rust-resistant wheat varieties and coordination between countries to facilitate improved surveillance and early warning systems.

Not only do we need to adapt crops to climate change, improving their performance under stress, but we also need to increase yields to meet the needs of population growth. The key to crop improvement is to recapture the genetic diversity that has been lost by decades to millennia of selective breeding. In the process of domestication of wild plants through landraces to modern varieties, a large amount of genetic diversity has been lost as plants have been bred to be more and more specialized for the agricultural environment and to maximize production yields. For example, bread wheat has lost 69% of its genetic diversity in this process, cotton 60%, maize 35%, and soybean 34%.[11] Wild relatives that have not been subjected to domestication by and large contain more genetic diversity than their cultivated cousins and could hold the key to the required improvements. In addition, these wild relatives often grow in conditions that would be considered marginal for crops, or even outside of that range, meaning that they have the potential to expand the environmental range of current crops. Their shape and form often differs from the cultivated crop, and can provide traits that are likely to be of use in combating the effects of climate change.

The importance of crop wild relatives, or CWR, has already been demonstrated by a number of studies. The contribution of CWR is growing, largely through the donation of useful genes that determine pest and disease resistance, abiotic stress tolerance, and higher nutritional value.[12] The need to act to conserve CWR has never been greater as they too are under threat from habitat degradation and climate change. A case in point is a wild relative of aubergine, *Solanum ruvu*, now thought to be extinct in the wild. This rare, African spiny aubergine was collected once as part of a general survey in 2000. Unfortunately, by the time it was identified as a new species by a Kew botanist in 2010, its native habitat had been destroyed. Attempts to re-collect it were made that year, but the plant could not be found and is now considered to be extinct.

Species Case Study: Finger Millet Conservation in Africa
Ruth Eastwood

Finger millet is popular in dry areas of Africa and Asia. It is one of the most nutritious of all the world's cereal crops, containing high levels of starch, calcium, iron, and methionine, an amino acid that is absent from the diets of millions of the poor who live on starchy foods such as cassava and plantain.

Seeds can lie dormant for weeks in the soil, and as soon as the rains come, the grain springs to life and is ready for harvesting in just forty-five days. One of the drawbacks of finger millet production is that it is labour intensive, leading farmers to favour the production of maize, sorghum, and cassava instead. In addition to this, finger millet is stigmatized as a food for the poor, a perception which has had serious health implications. In households where rice has replaced finger millet as the staple diet, nutritional deficiency and anaemia are widespread.

Wild crop relatives of finger millet are an important source of genetic diversity which can improve the yield of the crop and provide resistance to diseases, such as blast, which is the most serious disease of finger millet. Blast-resistance genes have been found in crop wild relative *Eleusine africana*, commonly known as African finger millet. Some varieties of this wild relative exhibit a high protein content and are nutritionally rich in calcium. The potential of the wild relatives of finger millet to improve the crop is huge. As a result of the Adapting Agriculture to Climate Change project, collections of this important CWR have been made in Nigeria and are available from the MSB for use in developing new varieties of finger millet. Work is also under way at the India-based International Crops Research Institute for the Semi-Arid Tropics (ICRISAT), again funded by the Crop Trust, to use CWRs of finger millet with tolerance to blast and introduce these traits to cultivated varieties and get these out into farmers' fields.

The Adapting Agriculture to Climate Change Project is helping to address food security by focusing on the wild relatives of some of our most important crops. Collecting and storing seeds from these plants will provide material for expanding the genetic diversity of our key crops, helping them adapt to current and future challenges. Funded by the Government of Norway for ten years, this project is managed by the Global Crop Diversity Trust, and Kew is a major partner. The three main aims of the project are to conserve CWRs, to start pre-breeding and evaluation for climate change adaptation, and to make the resulting information widely available.

The MSB was asked to manage the initial stages of this project because of its expertise in wild species seed banking and capacity building. An initial prioritization assessment, or gap analysis, was carried out to identify which crop wild relatives existed, where they occurred, and which were currently under-collected.[13] The analysis was based on Annex I species from the International Treaty on Plant Genetic Resources, which recognizes the interdependence of countries for food. The Treaty aims to: establish a multilateral system to provide farmers, plant breeders, and scientists with access to plant genetic materials; ensure recipients share benefits they derive from the use of these genetic materials with the country of origin; and use a single agreement for the use and transfer of plant genetic resources. The analysis resulted in a list of twenty-nine major crops for

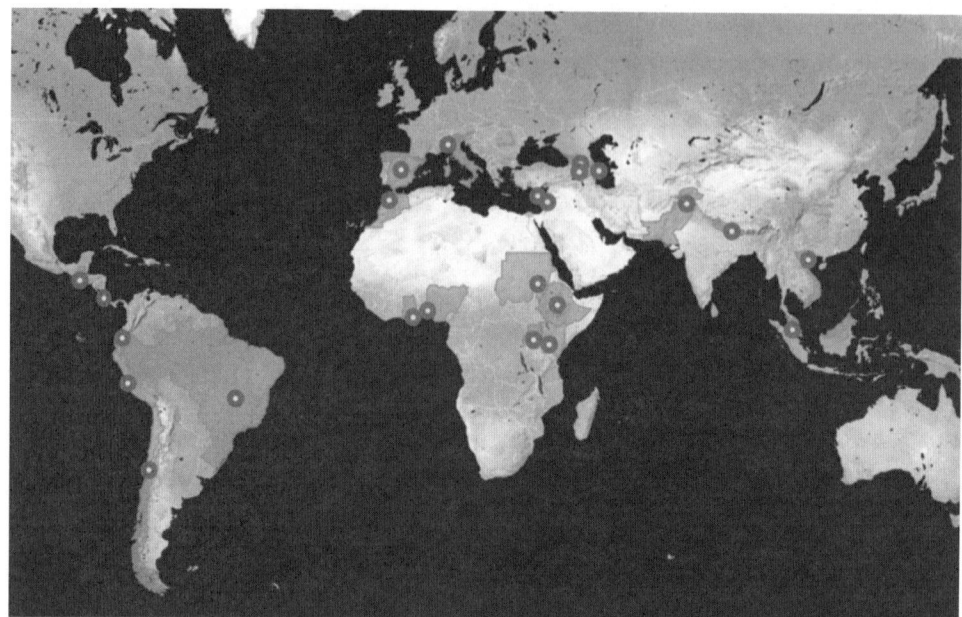

Figure 5: Seed collecting partner countries in the Crop Wild Relative project: Armenia, Azerbaijan, Brazil, Chile, Costa Rica, Cyprus, Ethiopia, Georgia, Ghana, Guatemala, Ecuador, Italy, Kenya, Lebanon, Malaysia, Nepal, Nigeria, Pakistan, Peru, Portugal, Spain, Sudan, Uganda, Vietnam.

collection (food and fodder), represented by around 350 crop wild relative species. Three criteria were used when devising the list: the relative socio-economic importance of the related crop, the potential use for the crop improvement (i.e. ease of crossing with the related crop), and the threatened status of the CWR.

Twenty-four countries have been involved in this project, all of whom are signatories to the Treaty. Due to the geographic spread of the target CWR, fifteen new partners joined the MSB Partnership as a direct result of this project. While many of these partners had a wealth of experience working with seeds from agricultural settings, collecting seeds from wild plants was new to them. The MSB provided capacity building and technology transfer in the form of training courses and field guides. In addition to two sessions at the MSB, seven in-country training courses were held, covering everything from planning a collecting trip through to gathering seed, processing it at the seed bank, and storing it safely. In addition, nine technical lab-based courses were held at the MSB. Overall, more than 174 partner staff were trained, including staff from each CWR collecting organization. Field guides were developed for the majority of partners following an easy-to-use format incorporating species descriptions, distribution maps, images of the species and their seeds, and infographics on collecting techniques and time of seed dispersal. In addition, seed collecting, cleaning, and drying

The Millennium Seed Bank of the Royal Botanic Gardens, Kew

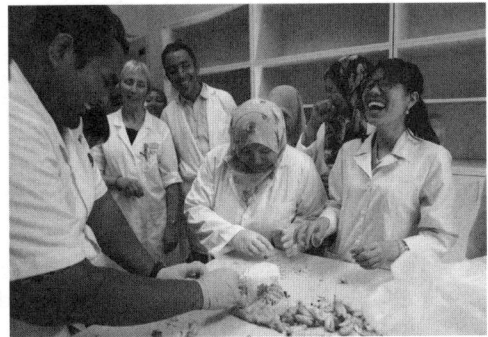

Figures 6 and 7: Capacity building is a key part of the Crop Wild Relative project, both in the field in partner countries and in the laboratories at the Millennium Seed Bank..

equipment was purchased by the project for shipment to partner organizations. Using the MSB's experience of working with partners and our knowledge of developing low technology solutions, the content of these kits was refined to essentially form a mini seed bank in a sixty-litre blue drum.

By the end of 2018 the collection phase was almost complete, with twenty-two of the countries involved having finished their fieldwork and seed collection. More than 3000 seed collections of target genera have been made, representing over 280 species and sub-species. As with all our collections, these are stored in the country of origin and backed up at a geographically distinct location, the MSB.

Partner Case Study: Collection Success in Nigeria
Ellie Wilding

Co-ordinated by the National Centre for Genetic Resources and Biotechnology (NACGRAB), the collecting project in Nigeria ran from 2015-2017 and was a great success. The work in Nigeria focused on the crop wild relative genepool of finger millet, pearl millet, rice, sorghum, groundnut, sweet potato, cowpea, and eggplant – all fundamental crops to the livelihoods of people worldwide. Working in collaboration with extension agents, senior government officials and local people in the rural communities they managed to make 205 collections across 22 taxa in all six geopolitical zones in Nigeria – surpassing the target. This was quite an achievement given that the North-East zone was inaccessible prior to 2017 due to the Boko Haram insurgency, and three of the taxa occurred here. In addition, the predicted distribution of the target CWR was highly variable, with some predicted to occur across the country, and others only in tiny remote areas. The altitude of collection sites was also variable, with collections made from 18 m above sea level (*Elesuine indica*) up to 1,695 masl (*Solanum anomalum*).

Collecting the ideal recommended number of 10,000 seeds per collection to enable use as well as conservation of the taxa has been a real challenge for our partners, due to the rare nature of many CWR. However, some collections of wild relatives of oat, carrot, barley, alfalfa, and finger millet were notably large, with one collection of wild carrot, *Daucus carota*, containing 179,377 seeds and one of wild finger millet, *Eleusine indica*, reaching 217,169 seeds. In addition, it would be useful to increase the multiprovince origin for widespread species. Research shows that to capture the genetic diversity of a species material from at least five populations should be collected.[14] To date, 17% of taxa have been collected more than twenty times across the global scope of the project, but single population collections have been made for 42% of the species.

An important element of the project was producing conservation threat assessments using the International Union for Conservation of Nature's (IUCN) criteria, which were undertaken for a sub-set of the species collected. Since 2016, full assessments have been completed for ninety-two species. Seventy-one were classified as least concern, three as endangered, and five as critically endangered; fourteen were classified as being data deficient. Assessing the conservation status of CWR through this globally recognized scheme helps conservation efforts to be directed towards their conservation both in their natural habitat and ex situ in seed and field banks. Assessments continue and help to inform future conservation actions for the species assessed.

Red Listing Case Study: The Critically Endangered Madagascan Banana
Richard Allen

The Madagascar Banana (*Ensete perrieri*; *Musaceae*) is a wild relative of the Abyssinian Banana (*E. ventricosum*) and has recently been included on the IUCN Red List. It was assessed by Kew researchers based in the UK and Madagascar as part of the CWR project. This species is endemic to the dry tropical forests of western Madagascar and is under pressure from deforestation. Only 5 mature individuals of *E. perrieri* are known and a recent survey (2017) has suggested that only 3 individuals may be left. Therefore, it was categorized as critically endangered (CR).

Most of the world's cultivated bananas are genetically identical, leaving them vulnerable to diseases (e.g. Panama Disease which is caused by a fungus). The banana market is dominated by a variety known as the Cavendish Banana (*Musa acuminata*). Cavendish Bananas are triploid, meaning that they have three sets of chromosomes instead of the two sets found in normal diploid plants. This means that they are sterile which has three main effects: firstly they have no seeds, which makes them more palatable; secondly they can only be cultivated clonally via cuttings; and thirdly they are unable to develop any resistance to disease. Therefore, although *E. perrieri* is not commercially viable due to large seeds being spread throughout its fruit, the rescuing of this CWR from the brink of extinction could one day prove critical for the survival of its commercial cousins.

Germination tests have been performed on 60% of the collections held at the MSB. Of these, 75% pass our germination test standards, indicating that the quality of these collections is very high. At the end of 2018, over 2000 germination tests had been carried out. This is an important step in our care of seed collections: in addition to providing information about the quality of the collections, it provides us with a protocol for turning the seeds back into plants – both vital factors if the collections are to be of use.

The final step for the MSB in the project is to send material out to international centres who will be able to genetically identify traits that will be important for protecting our crops in the future. A first step is often taken by international gene banks which grow plants from a small number of seeds to multiply the collections, making the material more widely available. This distribution process began in 2015, and to date over 2650 collections have been sent to seven international centres: 263 Medicago collections to SARDI in Australia; 144 banana collections to the International Transit Centre in Belgium; 89 Solanum collections to the World Vegetable Centre in Taiwan; 51 rye collections to IPK in Germany; 187 oat collections to Plant Genetic Resources Canada; 1721 collections of cereals to ICARDA in Lebanon; and 198 collections of finger millet, pearl millet, sorghum, and pigeon pea to ICRISAT in India. Traits being investigated include heat, drought and salinity tolerance, pest and disease resistance, waterlogging and rot resistance, and yield. CWR still to go out for testing include: *Ipomoea ramoissima*, a relative of the sweet potato tolerant to waterlogging; *Oryza nivara*, a relative of rice with resistance to Grassy Stunt virus; and *Solanum brevicaule*, a relative of the potato with resistance to Fusarium Wilt. A recent shipment organized by the Crop Trust consisted of aubergine wild relatives that have been sent to facilities in Spain, India, and the Ivory Coast to develop new strains adapted to the future climate of South-east Asia and West Africa. Upcoming shipments from the MSB include rice to the International Rice Research Institute (IRRI) in the Philippines, and carrot and pea to the United States Department of Agriculture (USDA).

Seed Supply Case Study: Alfalfa Pre-Breeding Project
Chris Cockel

Alfalfa is an important forage crop planted for hay, pasture, and silage in more than eighty countries. Production of livestock and forage is being shifted to more marginal, less fertile agricultural soils as the world population increases. Climate change is predicted to further stress alfalfa production in areas where the crop is most important, such as the desert regions of Central Asia and northern Chile. As water becomes scarcer in these regions, the development of improved, drought-tolerant alfalfa varieties will be essential.

Alfalfa pre-breeding work is being conducted by a team co-ordinated by the South Australian Research & Development Institute and includes scientists from Australia, Chile, Kazakhstan, and Inner Mongolia. Their goal is to evaluate wild alfalfa species collected from Kazakhstan, Azerbaijan, Chile, Peru, and Bolivia for drought stress tolerance, with a focus on germplasm found in the Atacama desert and northern Andes. The germplasm is being evaluated in target environments in southern Chile, Kazakhstan, Inner Mongolia, and South Australia. Overall, the alfalfa pre-breeding work aims to identify new sources of drought tolerance in wild alfalfa for use in already existing breeding programs in Chile, Kazakhstan, and China.

We have come a long way following the journey of the seed from the wild, through collection and processing, storage at the MSB and partner institutes, and its onwards trajectory into use – certainly a long way from the perception of many that Kew is just a nice day out in a beautiful garden. The science carried out at Kew, and in collaboration with our partners, is key to underpinning our conservation work. All of the seeds stored at the MSB hold the potential highlighted through the CWR project – some may house medicinal compounds, some beauty for horticultural display, others answers to pressing plant health issues like ash dieback. Next time you are looking for a day out, come and visit Wakehurst and learn more about the work happening at the Millennium Seed Bank.

Acknowledgements

I would like to thank all my colleagues at the Millennium Seed Bank who are involved in the Crop Wild Relative project for their help and support in providing material for this paper. Special thanks to Ruth Eastwood, Chris Cockel, Ellie Wilding, Richard Allen, and Oriole Wagstaff.

Notes

1. The Nagoya Protocol on Access to Genetic Resources and the Fair and Equitable Sharing of Benefits Arising from their Utilization to the Convention on Biological Diversity, also known as the Nagoya Protocol on Access and Benefit Sharing, is a 2010 supplementary agreement to the 1992 Convention on Biological Diversity (see <https://www.cbd.int/abs/>). The International Treaty on Plant Genetic Resources for Food and Agriculture, published by the Food and Agriculture Organization of the United Nations, aims to guarantee food security through the conservation, exchange, and sustainable use of the world's plant genetic resources for food and agriculture; it is in line with the Nagoya Protocol and Convention on Biological Diversity in calling for the fair and equitable benefit sharing arising from the use of these genetic resources (see <http://www.fao.org/plant-treaty/en/>).
2. For more information on the Global Tree Seed Bank project which is conserving some of the world's rarest and most threatened tree species, see 'Global Tree Seed Bank Project', Millennium Seed Bank Partnership <http://brahmsonline.kew.org/msbp/Projects/Trees> [accessed 9 May 2019].
3. RBG Kew, 'The State of the World's Plants', 2016 <https://stateoftheworldsplants.org/2016/> [accessed 9 May 2019].
4. The 17 Sustainable Development Goals (SDGs), adopted by all United Nations members in 2015, are a call for action by all countries to promote prosperity while protecting the environment (<https://www.un.org/sustainabledevelopment/sustainable-development-goals/> [accessed 9 May 2019]).
5. 'World Population Prospects', FAO, 2017 <https://population.un.org/wpp/> [accessed 9 May 2019].

6. 'Food Security', Research Program on Climate Change, Agriculture and Food Security <https://ccafs.cgiar.org/bigfacts/#theme=food-security> [accessed 9 May 2019].
7. S. Sethi, *Bread, Wine, Chocolate: The Slow Loss of Foods We Love* (New York, NY: HarperCollins, 2015).
8. L.E. Grivetti and B.M. Ogle, 'Value of Traditional Foods in Meeting Macro- and Micronutrient Needs: The Wild Plant Connection', *Nutrition Research Reviews*, 13 (2000), 31-46
9. 'The Intergovernmental Panel on Climate Change' IPCC <https://www.ipcc.ch/> [accessed 9 May 2019].
10. T. Ishimaru and others, 'A Genetic Resource for Early-Morning Flowering Trait of Wild Rice Oryza Officinalis to Mitigate High Temperature-Induced Spiklet Sterility at Anthesis', *Annals of Botany*, 106.3 (February 2009), 515; A. Jarvis, A. Lane, and R.J. Hijmans, 'The Effect of Climate Change on Crop Wild Relatives', *Agriculture, Ecosystems & Environment*, 126.1-2 (2008), 13-23.
11. S.D. Tanksley and S.R. McCouch, 'Seed Banks and Molecular Maps: Unlocking Genetic Potential from the Wild', *Science*, 277.5329 (22 August 1997), 1063-66.
12. R. Hajjar and T. Hodgkin, 'The Use of Wild Relatives in Crop Improvement: A Survey of Developments over the Last 20 Years', *Euphytica*, 156 (2007), 1-13.
13. N.P. Castañeda-Álvarez and others, 'Global Conservation Priorities for Crop Wild Relatives', *Nature Plants*, 2 (2016), article 16022 <https://doi.org/10.1038/nplants.2016.22>.
14. A.H.D. Brown and J.D. Briggs, 'Sampling Strategies for Genetic Variation in Ex Situ Collections of Endangered Plant Species', in *Genetics and Conservation of Rare Plants*, ed. by D.A. Falk and K.E. Holsinger (Oxford: Oxford University Press, 1991), pp. 99-122.

Muriel Howorth and the Atomic Gardening Society: Writing Food Futures

OFS Rising Scholar Award Winner

Molly MacVeigh

In the March of 1959, atomic advocate Muriel Howorth received four pounds of irradiated North Carolina peanuts in the mail. After roasting and salting the nuts, Howorth invited several of her scientific friends over for dinner in order to try them. To Howorth, these unusually large nuts were exciting – a token of the way nuclear energy might help to feed the undernourished people of the world. Her guests, however, were less impressed. 'The British scientists present,' she wrote in a later account of the evening, 'did not […] seem to appreciate that this nut was, in fact, the outcome of an immense achievement.'[1] To alleviate some of her post-party frustration, Howorth decided to plant the remaining nuts and see what happened.

The results were shocking. The seeds germinated in four days and quickly grew to four feet tall, a feat that landed Howorth on numerous television and radio programs. Beverley Nichols, an influential garden writer at the time, got wind of Howorth's plant and reported in the *Sunday Dispatch* that it was the 'most sensational plant in Britain'. 'It is a lush, green plant,' Nichols continued, that 'gives you a strange, almost alarming sense of thrusting power and lusty health. It holds a glittering promise in its green leaves, the promise of victory over famine.'[2] Inspired by the experience, in 1960 Howoth founded the Atomic Gardening Society (AGS), a group designed to crowd-source research on irradiated plant mutations. 'I knew,' Howorth wrote, 'that there were, in this country, too few plant geneticists and laboratories. I deduced that a few thousand assistants […] would greatly assist the scientists to speed up this humanitarian and scientific work.'[3]

To promote the organization, Howorth self-published a book called *Atomic Gardening* and reached out to big names in atomic science and horticulture to try to get support for her cause. She offered six free irradiated peanuts upon membership, and distributed careful instructions as to how to grow the plants and assess the resulting mutations. She also partnered with C.J. Speas, an American dentist who ran the world's only private seed irradiation facility, and by October of 1960 Speas had shipped over three million seeds to England. The list of gardens experimenting with irradiated seed included such prestigious locales as the Royal Botanic Gardens at Kew, the Royal Horticultural Society's Garden at Wisley, and Wannock Gardens in Eastbourne. There were even claims of member reports coming in from as far as Greece and Australia.

Still, for all of the hopeful rhetoric and rapidly proliferating organizational infrastructure, by 1963 the AGS was largely inactive. This was in part because Howorth had to step down due to failing health, but it was also because atomic gardening as a method never lived up to its promise. Mutations were unpredictable and largely undesirable. Home gardeners were frequently faced with plants that didn't germinate, or bore poorly, and the failures were even more frustrating in the context of the society's utopian promise. While a cohort of citizen scientists accelerating the irradiation research effort has a certain compelling logic, in the face of the minute odds of a productive mutation, AGS membership seems laughably small. Despite all of Howorth's creative atomic discourse, the society was more or less a failure in terms of concrete scientific production.

So it is perhaps unsurprising that when Howorth's story is told at all, she is largely framed as a charming historical eccentricity. Sophie Forgan, one of the first historians to discuss Howorth in a scholarly context, both cites her projects as illustrative early attempts to write science for the layman and dismisses Howorth's books as 'certainly of no lasting significance'.[4] While Paige Johnson's scholarly work and public-facing website argue for Howorth's importance in understanding British post-war nuclear culture, even Johnson's loving biographical account closes with the concession that Howorth's legacy must 'be acknowledged to be a minor one, her efforts notable more for their uniqueness than for their impact'.[5] While I share the general reservations about Howorth's unabashed nuclear enthusiasm, as well as the sense that much of her appeal lies in anecdotal oddity, here I want to focus less on her scientific foibles and more on the rich variety of her literary production. While the science-fictional rhetoric of Howorth's non-fiction rendered atomic agriculture both awesome and accessible, her final novel provides the imaginative infrastructure for questioning the easy valorization of techno-fixes.

Howorth's life and writing exist at the complex intersection of food, fiction, and popular science. Her story is not only about atomic potential and agricultural developments, but also deeply entangled in the processes of literary production and reception. Equal parts gardener, author, and enthusiastic purveyor of scientific facts and scientific fictions, Howorth is uniquely situated for considering the novel's contributions to crafting more just and sustainable food systems. Borrowing from the contemporary ecocritical discussion around the novel's capacity to represent climate change, this paper asks a set of related questions about the relationship between food futures and science fiction. What kinds of resources might novels provide in thinking diachronically, or in terms of networks, or in mapping the systems of everyday life? How might speculative fiction structure or anticipate the food relations to come?

This essay is itself working in a speculative mode insofar as it asks questions and raises possibilities without coming to a comprehensive articulation of the links between food systems and novelistic capacities. After describing the contemporary ecocritical turn toward science fictional rhetoric, I begin by situating Howorth's early written work in the context of both this growing conversation and mid-twentieth-century British nuclear culture. I then shift attention to Howorth's last major work, a science-fiction novel called *Impact of a Million Stars*, in order to consider the temporal resources of science fiction as a genre and the ongoing power generated by its engagement with imagined futures, even those created in Howorth's time. I argue that *Impact*'s narrative structure and cross-cultural diegetic space allow it to both espouse and expose possible flaws in techno-optimist futurities.

Atomic Science and Genre

Considering the uses of literature in thinking through future food systems invokes a long-standing debate in literary study about the tension between utilitarian and aesthetic value. As Rita Felski suggests, a significant strain of literary criticism mistrusts the idea of use value, seeing assessments of utility as 'an alienating reduction of means to ends'. This mistrust has been voiced in many different registers: 'the language of Romantic aesthetics, the neo-Marxist critique of instrumental reason, the poststructuralist suspicion of identity thinking. What distinguishes literature, in this line of thought, is its obdurate resistance to all calculations of purpose and function'.[6] While the rise of ideology critique offered a counter-narrative about literature's role as a 'medium of political enlightenment and social transformation', recent developments in the environmental humanities offer a still more directly utilitarian framework. On an institutional level, Arizona State University's Imagination and Climate Futures Initiative explores how climate fiction 'shapes our imagination, how it relates to climate science, and how it might affect social and political life'.[7] Stockholm Resilience Centre's Radical Ocean Futures Project is even more explicit in their instrumentalization of fictional stories. The project, 'founded on the belief that sometimes science fiction might succeed where scientific papers fall short', uses a method called 'science fiction prototyping' to craft multi-media narratives of potential future oceans. These short fictions, they claim, help us 'assess how unexpected changes, along with human responses to those changes, may play out in a complex world that is, at its heart, surprising'.[8] In both projects, as in ecocriticism writ large, fiction is explicitly leveraged for environmental activist aims.

In the last few years, ecocritics have been increasingly convinced that genre fiction is the literary form best suited for achieving these aims. The *longue durée* and planetary scale of the climate crisis, one version of the argument goes, are unpresentable within the confines of realist fiction. What we need instead are the generic resources of science fiction and horror, books that 'set themselves the task of scaling our vision dramatically up or down, or both, blasting through ordinary perception to the most surprising vistas we can imagine'.[9] Long dismissed in literary scholarship as insufficiently concerned with individual character development and complex interiority, science fiction's concern with the planet as a whole seems uniquely suited for the scalar challenge of representing global warming. As Ursula Heise notes, 'It therefore makes sense – though it remains generically surprising – that science fiction motifs and structures keep cropping up in environmental non-fiction, books whose principal concern is to drive home the *reality* of current ecological crises.'[10] One might point to Alan Weisman's 2008 *The World Without Us*, for instance, a text that describes a post-apocalyptic possible future where humans have already disappeared. Or there's Naomi Oreskes and Erik M. Conway's *The Collapse of Western Civilization*, a pseudo-history of the present written by a fabricated future historian. Following Frederic Jameson, Heise argues that both texts make the reader 'see the present anew as the past of societies yet to come'.[11] The temporal structures of genre fiction offer a unique resource for attempting to articulate the imaginative enormity of change spanning billions of years.

One might find an analogous discursive moment in the mid-twentieth century, when journalists and non-fiction writers were faced with the task of explaining atomic science. In addition to the challenge of rendering impossibly small atomic particles and impossibly large explosive impacts, mid-century science writers were also navigating shortages and rationing. As Sophie Forgan points out, despite 'significant images in exhibitions and museum displays', the immediate post-war period is striking in its 'lack of visuality, and [...] reliance on old established textual representations'. In Britain, film and paper supplies were strictly rationed, so 'books were printed on cheap, poor quality paper, with few illustrations if any'.[12] Instead, authors turned to figurative language and allusions, harnessing characters like Alice in Wonderland to make technical writing less threatening and more attractive to the lay public.[13] Just as contemporary climate writers have turned to the forms of speculative fiction, science writers in post-war Britain harnessed a variety of literary modes to capture the challenging scales of nuclear progress.

True to the discursive predilections of her era, Muriel Howorth frequently flipped between fictional and non-fictional arguments for the peaceful potential of atomic science. In 1950, she wrote and staged *Isotopia: An Exposition on Atomic Structure*. Designed for fourteen players including such figures as 'Knowledge', 'Atom Man', 'Isotope', and 'Cow', Howorth's play opens with a bespangled narrator ventriloquizing Roman philosophers. After citing Democritus and Lucretius, the narrator skips forward to Isaac Newton and John Dalton, their respective contributions to atomic science represented through Atom Man's *glissés* and *relevés*. Following a dancing exegesis of the basic components of atomic structure, the play turns to more recent applications of atomic potential. Knowledge explains that 'radio-active isotopes can keep bananas fresh without refrigeration', 'keep apple blossoms closed till the frost is over', and 'sterilise tinned fruits and vegetables'. She also covers the isotope's industrial and medical capabilities, the dramatic climax coming in a scene where the 'Cow mimes to be ill and leans over table. As Geiger clicks Cow pulls up, smiles, rubs stomach, and retires to semi-circle smiling'. After this triumph of radioactive tracing technology, the narrator makes a plug for Howorth's Atomic Energy Association, whose meetings disseminate this kind of information. The topic is enormously complicated, the narrator explains, as she asks the audience to 'forgive…our humble attempt at visual information regarding the peacetime uses of atomic energy in the realms of Isotopia'.[14] The play's explicit didacticism, emphasis on concrete example, and attention to gendered audiences would go on to characterize many of Howorth's subsequent publications.

Shortly after *Isotopia*, Howorth published *Atoms in Wonderland*, a narrative pamphlet aimed at children. *Atoms in Wonderland* touches on many of the same themes as *Isotopia*, though here Howorth trades dancing women for an imaginative landscape of protons and neutrons with 'bright little fingers which shone like glow worms' and 'very piercing eyes'.[15] These subatomic particles live in a castle underground until invited up to play with 'the Biggies', in a laboratory called 'Wonderland'. In Wonderland, the personified particles learn about curing the sick and working in factories. A few of the particles go on to become land girls, and have 'great fun looking right through the soil and the roots to see if the plants were getting enough food, and the right food'.[16] To some extent, the particle personification in both *Isotopia* and *Atoms in Wonderland* does the work of 'scaling our vision dramatically up or down' that McGurl cites as the vital skill of genre fiction. While neither text is science fiction working in a conventional mode, re-casting atomic science at the familiar scale of persons and families renders the minute interactions of protons and electrons legible to a general public. In emphasizing tangible outcomes like cow-curing and plant-feeding, Howorth reins in the massive power of atomic isotopes even as she grants them outsize personalities.

Howorth's next two publications, *Atom and Eve* and the AGS manual, *Atomic Gardening*, even more effectively render atomic science as simultaneously awesome and accessible. In Howorth's introduction to *Atomic Gardening*, for instance, she couches science-fictional rhetoric in a relatively folksy style. 'I have always loved gardens,' she begins one section. 'Not perhaps the vast, classic gardens such as Chatsworth boasts… nor the niceties of Cleve Prior Manor, with its famous apostles, carved in yew.' She looks instead 'at gardens as things of character, as personalities. My garden would speak of me, yours of you; they are the outcome of our imagination'. The tone here is charming, a chatty meditation on gardening that would seem at home in any number of mid-century horticulture texts. But in the paragraphs that follow the tone shifts into a much grander register. 'But [...] let us look at our "garden of the future",' Howorth writes, 'this is something new indeed. Something in which not only our imagination works, but something engrossing, impelling. It is we who are going to assist in horticultural and agricultural investigations for the inducing of mutations which will be beneficial to humanity, of world concern.'[17]

Even beyond the science fictional resonance of a phrase like 'gardens of the future', visible here is the shift to planetary scope that characterizes the genre. Howorth's commanding 'we' casts the reader as a co-protagonist in a narrative of 'world concern' – a horticultural project beneficial to all humanity. *Atomic Gardening* moves effortlessly from gardens as reflecting individual imaginations to gardens as representative of the contemporary zeitgeist.

While it's possible to read this rhetoric as a product of Howorth's unique approach to atomic organizing, or even a product of the print-culture restrictions of her time, there is a clear through line from Howorth's formal innovations to the science-fiction climate writing of today. As Ursula Heise writes, 'in adopting strategies of speculative fiction, environmentalist writers [...] seek to open readers' eyes to the futures they already inhabit'.[18] Howorth's play, children's story, and informational pamphlets each operate in similar modes. Through careful manipulation of scale, tone, and familiar material references, Howorth's multi-generic writing performs speculative fiction's trick of casting the future as always already present.

Impact of a Million Stars and Novel Messages

If Howorth's informational pamphlets depict atomic science in shades of futuristic wonder, Howorth's actual science-fiction novels often appear to use atomic science as a marker of the quotidian real. In 1963's *Impact of a Million Stars*, her novel most explicitly concerned with radiation and isotopes, atomic science emerges as a comparatively plausible piece of a highly improbable plot arc. *Impact* tells the story of a nuclear scientist named Radcliffe traveling through Asia. He attends an ichthyologic conference, uses his Geiger counter to discover unsafe radiation levels, and then saves a village from radiation-tainted fish before going on to prevent an atom bomb explosion in Paris with a giant laser. While Howorth's previous non-fictional projects deployed literary forms to make nuclear science legible, here the dynamics are reversed. *Impact* has an overtly science fictional premise, but sprinkled throughout are factual traces of Howorth's atoms for peace activism.

When Radcliffe gives his presentation at the fish conference, for instance, he reminds the audience that 'we must not forget the radiation and tracer technique can boast a very high percentage of success for the common good [...]. Agriculture now uses radioisotopes to sterilize and eliminate pests'. Sounding very much like Howorth herself, Radcliffe continually emphasizes atomic science's world-feeding potential, explaining that isotopically doctored raw, sliced bacon, sealed in large cans, has been treated and is already being supplied to army units in the tropics and Arctic where it's edible for at least two years. This new method of food preservation by the peaceful uses of atomic energy could lead, in the not too distant future, to the elimination of famine and the more even distribution of food throughout the world.[19]

This passage is striking partially because of the range of tenses. If, following Heise, science fiction is notable insofar as it opens readers' eyes to the futures they already inhabit, here Howorth enacts that dynamic on a grammatical level. Flowing seamlessly from the possible (tracer technique *can* boast...) to the actual (Agriculture now *uses*...), Howorth collapses the space between the future and the present. She also locates this collapse within a linear temporal unfolding: raw bacon has been treated with radioisotopes in the past and is already being distributed, a development which 'could lead, in the not too distant future, to the elimination of famine'. Even while rendering the future as already present creates a temporal disjunction, Radcliffe's speech maintains a comforting sense of inevitable progress.

It's notable, too, that this discussion of atomic potential is framed as a non-fictional lecture. Using the device of an academic talk embedded within a fictional matrix renders the delivered information comparatively plausible. The novel's titular allusions to stars and lasers immediately announce its status as speculative fiction – a genre in which aliens and intergalactic journeys are unsurprising narrative moves. In this genre-novel context, pest control and food preservation seem comparatively mundane. Where Howorth's informational pamphlets treated atomic science as fantastic and futuristic technology, in *Impact* these developments seem unremarkable – narrative filler establishing context for the unfolding of plot.

By couching atomic science as simultaneously mundane and fantastic, Howorth's novel complements the explanatory efforts of her non-fiction. Not only does the novel present atomic science as both already present and inevitably progressing, but it also gives the impression that these new developments are part of a deep and continuous history of thought. As he introduces his lecture, for instance, Radcliffe explains that Frederick Soddy and Ernest Rutherford might be located in a lineage of experimenting men stretching back through the alchemists. While the old alchemists were 'toiling and broiling to change base metals into more precious ones', Radcliffe expounds, recently 'a young Englishman of twenty-three found that the earth we live in is not the inanimate matter we'd supposed, but a storehouse packed with explosives more powerful than yet known [...]. Transmutation is taking place under our very feet!'.[20] Radcliffe's language both evokes the alchemical discourse of days of yore and prefigures contemporary discourse around new materialism.[21] And after his talk, when he exits the lecture hall to see a 'company of youthful thinkers' under the acacia trees, he continues to suggest an extensive and de-periodized intellectual chronology. Through the early hours of the morning these youthful thinkers discuss 'the problems of this new conception of the atomic theory of matter, mind and soul, as the disciples of Democritus had done two thousand five hundred years ago on the far-off clover hills of Thrace'.[22] While it might be something of a stretch, reading Howorth's novel in relation to Wai Chee Dimock's understanding of 'deep time' – as 'nonstandard time' that loosens 'the chronology and geography of the nation' – offers a productive lens.[23] The young thinkers under an acacia tree in the Philippines are deep in a discussion that began 'two thousand five hundred years ago' in Greece – a conversation that both owes a debt to early alchemy and prefigures contemporary scholarship on lively matter. If Radcliffe's speech grammatically collapses present and future, the contexts of its delivery also work to push intellectual progress into a deep-rooted, non-national chronology.

Yet for all the novel portrays peaceful atomic power as the culmination of thousands of years of progress, *Impact*'s pro-technology message is quite nuanced compared to

Howorth's more celebratory non-fiction. Along with Radcliffe's sermonizing, there's a bleak portrait of a village poisoned by irradiated fish and the fact of the near-catastrophic explosion on the river in Paris. Radcliffe's mother, a nuclear scientist herself, explains her horror at some previous radiation research: 'Experiments were conducted on human guinea-pigs – prisoners from a concentration camp. Some were turned into monsters, into unknown species of humanity. It made me sick; I just couldn't carry on.'[24] Despite Radcliffe's final triumph, the reader is left with the impression that atomic power is something dangerous and difficult to control. Radiation technology's very transformative potential also pushes it quickly into troubling ethical territory. So perhaps as a consequence of the novel form's ability to simultaneously present fixed and systemic perspectives, paying close attention to *Impact* reveals a tale of techno-optimism that cannot help but undercut its own utopian claims.

Reading *Impact* half a century after its publication also destabilizes the novel's utopian imagining. If science fiction often performs the neat trick of bridging the present and the future, older science fiction serves to index structures of thought carried over from past-presents. Howorth's depictions of Hong Kong and the Philippines are notably orientalist, full of lazy stereotypes and racist descriptions. And these dated portraits of national character are often carried out through allusions to inappropriate appetites. When Radcliffe and Mac Noo visit the village with tainted fish, Radcliffe observes that the villagers all look as though they're dying. 'And so they are,' says Mac Noo, 'and yet the island's full of good stuff like ginseng.' The dangers of radiation, here, are subsumed into the poor food choices of the island inhabitants – food choices that often serve as shorthand for savagery. Telling the story of the Boxer Rebellion, for instance, Brownrigg describes how ten-year-old Yu Pi 'fell into the hands of the T'ai ping gang' who promptly 'took his pony for food as they swarmed down to Hong Kong'.[25] The anecdote, totally incidental to the plot, reads as gleeful exoticizing. Eating pony! The horror! In Edward Said's classic formulation, 'European culture gained strength in identity by setting itself off against the Orient'.[26] Here, the consumption of horse becomes a cultural boundary marker, a mode of 'setting off', explicitly tied to what crosses the boundary of the body.

Brownrigg's description of desperate pony-eating and the general depiction of Philippine dining stand in sharp contrast to the description of the wholesome British appetite – an appetite vigorous in exactly the right measure. Early in the conference the chairman apologizes for his inability to serve a proper Christmas dinner as it's an 'austerity year'. The chairman explains, 'The Nutritions Council Convention has indoctrinated us with the slogan "*Good nutrition is simple living*", but I have no doubt our kitchens could be at your disposal for Christmas tit-bits.' This apology is quickly followed by an extensive description of the dinner served the next night, a 'nutrition year for simple living' carnival week menu. The dinner includes over thirty dishes: sliced pumelo on suha relish, braised beef in kalamansi syrup, vanilla budo delight, oyster consommé, and on and on. This kind of feast, detailed under the explicit heading of 'simple living' and falling close on the heels of a conference discussing food scarcity, serves as a caricature of excessive appetite. Yet the next day, when Radcliffe receives a room service order of 'Kalamansi juice, two mackerel surrounded by prawn wafers, toasted beancakes, and coffee', Brownrigg looks over approvingly. 'I told them to make it a good one,' he chuckles, 'They don't understand that an Englishman likes to eat well in the morning.'[27] Radcliffe is politely dismayed at the breakfast's size, but Brownrigg brushes off his concern. As long as the hunger is English, and the right lip-service to moderation is performed, hearty appetites are a sign of national virtue.[28]

These scenes of excess, framed respectively as nutritional hypocrisy and a quirk of British character, help demonstrate the questions unaddressed by Howorth's Malthusian logic. Looking back at *Atomic Gardening*, Howorth's 'success story of atomic energy and peanuts' prizes the nuts primarily for their capacity to create 'more and better food for the world'. A successful layman experimenter 'would […] have added his quota of food to a population which is going to double in the next thirty-five years'.[29] Despite Howorth-by-way-of-Radcliffe's prediction that 'the peaceful uses of atomic energy could lead, in the not too distant future, to […] the more even distribution of food throughout the world', the bulk of her project focuses on increased production, not redistribution. Considered in light of appetite's cultural and racial nuances, this optimistic faith in technologically-increased food quantities seems misplaced. Whose appetites are sanctioned? What are the politics of waste? How does colonial history inflect the dynamics of scarcity and excess? Strictly production-oriented solutions skip these questions entirely.

To be clear, I am not asking a laser novel to articulate a coherent plan for ending world hunger. This seems, at the very least, unfair. But I do think it's useful to point out that these questions – so familiar to the contemporary discussion around global food systems – are largely absent in the non-fictional context of *Atomic Gardening* yet loom large in the subtext of *Impact of a Million Stars*. Encountered with half a century of distance, *Impact* rehearses a tired white-saviour narrative: white male scientist, spouting the rhetoric of technologically-increased production, saves small fishing village from radiation poisoning and the world from another nuclear explosion. The trick of opening readers' eyes to the already-present future gets skewed when encountered at temporal remove. Yet ultimately this sense of discomfort is part of what makes Howorth's story so useful in the contemporary context. Radcliffe's imperial arrogance and orientalist microaggressions, so visible fifty years after the fact, serve to undercut the simple confidence of his techno-optimist claims. *Impact*'s narrative infrastructure of travel, danger, and cross-cultural communication implicitly raises those questions of appetite and colonial history that get so thoroughly cast aside in Howorth's non-fiction work. Attending to her final novel serves both to illustrate the inevitable failures of imagination and unforeseen complexities of future projection, and to demonstrate the value of the novelistic form in capturing those complexities without explicitly articulating them as such.

Conclusion: Rambunctious Gardening

Howorth's enthusiasm, both in object and intensity, is hard to match. But one could nonetheless draw a line from her nuclear convictions to the future-oriented strain of environmental thought that began this essay. While the predominant scholarly affect of the Anthropocene might be characterized as gathering dread, some scholars see anthropogenic climate change as evidence of the human capacity to change the earth. Though this is by no means an unequivocal good, the techno-optimist line of thinking sees this evidence of human power as worthy of celebration. Diane Ackerman, perhaps most prominently, has claimed that these days 'we're not passive, we're not helpless. We're earth movers. We can become Earth restorers and Earth-guardians'.[30] Or as Emma Marris suggests in her most recent book, 'We've forever altered the Earth, and so now we cannot abandon it to a random fate. It is our duty to manage it. Luckily it can be a pleasant, even joyful task if we embrace it in the right spirit. Let the rambunctious gardening begin.'[31]

In light of the often nostalgic or elegiac tone of dominant environmentalist thought, there is something refreshing about this future orientation. The injunction to joyful management has the appeal of a call both concrete and uplifting. But if Howorth – a rambunctious gardener of the first order – is any indication, it is worth both holding onto and carefully examining our own futuristic enthusiasms. What are the logics and assumptions that structure the food futures we're imagining? Who are the protagonists and minor players in these stories? Which of these narratives would we like to see germinate?

Acknowledgments

I am grateful for the financial support provided by the Cherwell Studentship of the American Friends of the Oxford Symposium on Food and Cookery, as well as the research assistance provided by the staff of the British Library.

Notes

1. Muriel Howorth, *Atomic Gardening* (London: New World Publications, 1955), p. 77.
2. Howorth, *Atomic Gardening*, p.16.
3. Paige Johnson, 'Safeguarding the Atom: The Nuclear Enthusiasm of Muriel Howorth', *British Journal for the History of Science*, 45 (2012), 551-57 (p. 569).
4. Sophie Forgan, 'Atoms in Wonderland', *History and Technology*, 19 (2003), 177-96 (p. 189).
5. Johnson, p. 571.
6. Rita Felski, *Uses of Literature* (Malden, MA: Blackwell, 2008), p. 7.
7. Imagination and Climate Futures Initiative, 'About', Arizona State University <https://climateimagination.asu.edu/about/> [accessed 4 November 2018].
8. Stockholm Resilience Centre, "Project', Radical Ocean Futures <https://radicaloceanfutures.earth/home#about-project> [accessed 4 November 2018].
9. Mark McGurl, 'The Posthuman Comedy', *Critical Inquiry*, 38 (2012), 533-53 (p. 541).
10. Ursula Heise, *Imagining Extinction: The Cultural Meanings of Endangered Species* (Chicago: University of Chicago Press, 2016), p. 215.

11　Heise, p. 218.
12　Forgan, pp. 177, 178.
13　See Forgan for a more extended discussion of *Alice in Wonderland*.
14　Muriel Howorth, *Isotopia: An Exposition on Atomic Structure…Written in the Form of a Mime to be Produced by Fourteen Players* (n. pub.: Eastbourne, 1949), pp. 8-9.
15　Muriel Howorth, *Atom in Wonderland* (Sheffield: Loxley Brothers Limited, 1950), p. 2.
16　Howorth, *Atom in Wonderland*, p. 12.
17　Howorth, *Atomic Gardening*, p. 27.
18　Heise, p. 220.
19　Muriel Howorth, *Impact of a Million Stars* (London: New World Publications, 1963), pp. 62-63.
20　Howorth, *Impact*, p. 60.
21　This segment in particular resonates with Isaac Newton's discussion of alchemical transmutation in Query 31: 'And by these Experiments compared with the great quantity of Sulphur with which the Earth abounds, and the warmth of the interior Parts of the Earth, and hot Springs, and burning Mountains, and with Damps, mineral Coruscations, Earthquakes, hot suffocating Exhalations, Hurricanes and Spouts; we may learn that sulphureous Steams abound in the Bowels of the Earth and ferment with Minerals' (*Opticks: Or, A Treatise of the Reflections, Refractions, Inflections and Colours of Light* (London: Sir William Innis, 1730), p. 354).
22　Howorth, *Impact*, p. 65.
23　Wai Chee Dimock, *Through Other Continents: American Literature Across Deep Time* (Princeton: Princeton University Press 2008), p. 4.
24　Howorth, *Impact*, p. 186.
25　Howorth, *Impact*, pp. 93, 57.
26　Edward Said, *Orientalism* (New York: Vintage Books, 1979), p. 3.
27　Howorth, *Impact*, pp. 47, 50.
28　As Annette Cozzi notes, however, traditional 'masculinized British identity is constructed as wholesome and unadulterated, bolstered by a moderate appetite immune to both the raging desires of the undisciplined female and the corrupting lure of the feminized colonies' (*The Discourses of Food in Nineteenth-Century British Fiction* (New York: Palgrave MacMillan, 2010), p. 106). For all Brownrigg and Radcliffe are performing masculine Britishness, the boundary marking registers the danger of corruption-by-consumption.
29　Howorth, *Atomic Gardening*, pp. 12, 21.
30　Diane Ackerman, *The Human Age: The World Shaped by Us* (New York: Norton, 2014), p. 311.
31　Emma Maris. *Rambunctious Garden: Saving Nature in a Post-Wild World* (New York: Bloomsbury USA, 2011), p. 171.

Reclaiming Diversity of Taste

Isaura Andaluz

It tastes like the earth. This is how people in New Mexico describe the taste of red *chile nativo*. Pure, with no salt or spices added, the sun-dried chilli pods are pureed with a bit of water, resulting in a thick, red sauce that can have a bite, which gently subsides. The soils where these chillis are planted dictate the saltiness. Local daytime temperatures regulate the level of heat or sweetness imparted by the chillis. The plants direct us to how they wish to be used and preserved.

Chile nativo is a staple food crop in New Mexico, not a condiment. It is the vitamin C of the desert. At the immature stage, chillis are green and edible, providing an early crop beginning in August. Venture to a local farmers' market and you will be greeted by a steel cage standing high above the ground, its handle extending out in anticipation of the chilli roaster's gloved hands. The chilli roaster must discern the thickness of the chilli's skin, timing how long the propane flames hit the cage to avoid shreds of green pulp. The chillis are tossed into the cage, which is spun around and around, roasting them to perfection.

They are then transported home for sharing, freezing, or immediate consumption. Immediate consumption means peeled green chillis, without the stem and seeds, laid on top of a nice warm flour tortilla, spread with sour cream, sliced fresh garlic, and salt – smoky flavours of the coming autumn. When the *chile nativo* turns red, it is strung up into *ristras* to dry for winter storage. The dried chilli pods are later added to stews and soups like *chicos* with beans or made into a sauce for enchiladas, *carne adovada*, or *huevos rancheros*. In early spring, leftover pods, including the seeds, are cooked with wild *quelites* (local chenopods).

Chile Nativo
The word *chile* is Spanish for peppers (*capsicum annuum*). The *chile nativo* of New Mexico is considered a landrace crop, as the seeds have been saved and replanted for over 400 years. Several varieties still contain genetic traits related to the Mexican wild chillis from which they were derived. In northern New Mexico, the women would gather and toss a handful of their chilli seeds into a community basket. Handfuls of fresh, mixed seeds were gifted back to the women for planting at home. The incorporation of genes specific to surrounding communities into their original seed stock prevented inbreeding, thus ensuring continuous adaptation. When one is gifted

seed, it is not a commodity to be resold. The seed no longer bears the name referencing the area from which it was gifted, as it will evolve in its new place, welcomed by a new seed community.

The names of the chilli varieties usually reference the locality where they are cultivated; a watershed, mountain, or other geographic landmark such as Chimayo (a village), Embudo (a river), or Isleta (a pueblo). The chillis are identified by the specific pod shape and texture, taste, and size. They range from two to seven inches long with small shoulders of up to one and three-quarter inches long. These chillis have thin to medium skins making them excellent varieties for dried chilli, as they will not lose weight or flavour due to excess water in the cell walls.

Seeds are the memory of life. Each time a seed is planted, it continues evolving together with the local climate, soil, insects, and many other species. New Mexico's unique bioregions create prime conditions for genetic diversity. Through traditional breeding practices, the *chile nativo* has developed traits critical for growing in the South-west, such as drought and salinity tolerance, and resistance to pests and disease. The efficacy of these traits puts the *chile nativo* at high risk for cultural and biological appropriation by seed and biotech corporations.

Querencia

In New Mexico, you will sometimes hear the word '*querencia*'. *Querencia* means a sense or love of place. *Querencia* requires knowledge, respect, and ethics for the use of the commons. Yet, increasingly it feels like this word is at risk of extinction, as is the local language of the commons.

The use of water for agriculture is often demonized. Industry in New Mexico continually argues that water for development has a higher value than for agriculture. New Mexico has two types of water rights: surface and underground. The surface water rights can be bought and 'transferred', giving the new owner the right to pump water at another location, which can be used for industry or municipalities rather than agriculture.

Traditionally crops were watered by surface water through *acequias* (traditional community waterways). Still in use only in certain parts of New Mexico, the water is shared through *repartimientos* to *acequias*. The water in each *acequia* is then shared among *acequia parciantes* (users of the water). Many *parciantes* in New Mexico still use the Spanish vocabulary specific to *acequias*. When water is scarce, an *hilo de agua* (thread of water) is given to wilted plants, just enough to sustain them.

The Spanish and Native American names given to geographic areas provide a planting guide for what is to be planted, where, and when. The wild *quelites* arrive early in the spring without irrigation, filling any barren place. They temporarily hold the soil and moisture until other crops are planted, growing exponentially as their leaves are dried for winter spinach. Next, the *huerta de chile nativo* is planted, offering two harvests: green and red. A *milpa* (cornfield) is planted to one side. Dryland beans and

Reclaiming Diversity of Taste

wheat hide in the soil, waiting for the monsoon rains. Excess crops are dried and stored for winter. Absent this geographical knowledge base, the capacity for survival in an arid place ceases to exist.

Commodification of Chilli

In 2008, phones started ringing and emails were furiously sent when it was discovered that New Mexico State University (NMSU) was developing a genetically engineered (GE) chilli for the chilli industry, also known as the New Mexico Chile Association (NMCA). 'Why?' was the first question everyone asked. This development would put our *chile nativo* at risk of contamination from cross-pollination! The state is known for its chillis! Then everyone realized that there are now two types of chilli in New Mexico: the *chile nativo* and the commercial, commodity varieties.

The first commercialization of chilli in New Mexico was started by NMSU in 1888 by Dr Fabian Garcia. His goal was to develop a canning chilli that was larger and fleshier with less heat and smoother skins. The breeding lines he used included two Mexican chillis: the *chile pasilla* (long and dark brown) and *colorado* (a red chilli). In 1921, Dr Garcia released the New Mexico No. 9 that became the first standardized variety of a new pod type called the 'New Mexican'. New Mexico became the leader for industrialized chilli farming, processing, and canning. A milder chilli called NuMex 6-4 was released in 1958, which remains the industry standard. NMSU has developed a total of twenty-one modern chilli cultivars for commercial growers.

Green Chilli

Before the advent of frozen green chilli, the traditional processing method for the chilli was drying. While still in limited use, these older methods are also time consuming. *Chile rescaldado* or *chile pasado* are two names for green roasted chilli that is preserved by hanging the fruits to dry with seeds and stems intact. Once stored, it can later be used by reconstituting it in warm water, before it is sautéed with onions, garlic, and spices and added to meat or a soup. Small, immature green chillis (no longer than two and a half inches) are sliced open to remove the stems and seeds before being strung to dry for use to season cooking oil, thus the name 'push arounds'.

In 1951, a company called Bueno Foods (El Encanto, Inc.) was established to produce frozen green chilli. More consumers now had freezers, and restaurants could now begin offering green chilli year-round. The market for frozen green chilli led to the development of larger chillis with thicker skins by NMSU. But yield, not flavour, became the driving factor. Commercial producers chemically peel the chilli and add chilli resin to their products for a consistent heat standard. Thus the true flavour of the chilli varieties has become inconsequential.

Frozen chilli products opened markets outside of the state, which required increasing acreage planted to chilli. The resulting increase in monocropping led to the inevitable weakening of the commercial chilli plants due to industrial agricultural practice. Issues with phytophthora (chilli wilt), salinity, and pests intensified.

The NMCA's response was to urge development of a GE chilli to combat these problems. Efforts were started in 1993 by NMSU, which will own the patent along with a biotech company. Prior research on local chillis had indicated possible resistance to diseases, leading NMSU to re-examine and accelerate their research on *chile nativo* traits such as pigmentation and resistance to drought, salinity, and disease.

Technology now exists that allows for isolation of genes with specific traits, such as disease resistance. Although these traits are present in seeds belonging to the commons, corporations are claiming ownership through utility patents. This practice results in nothing less than the theft of the commons. No one can create a seed – only nature. The traits within these seeds can be strengthened through selective breeding, but they are not being invented. The focus on one trait can lead to genetic erosion, as the seeds have the biological memory of the microclimates from where they come, and more importantly the cultural memory of the seed stewards who nurtured them till the present time. Seeds are part of a living system where nothing functions in isolation.

Licensing agreements and patents prohibiting seed saving or plant propagation are becoming more prevalent on seed packets and plants. A utility patent can be applied to a single trait such as drought resistance for twenty years. Corporations already hold utility patents on such traits as peppers resistant to whitefly, drought-resistant corn, and lettuce with a red centre. These traits are well known among farmers and small seed producers, yet they did not obtain a patent for them. To whom does this intellectual property belong? The first corporation to patent the trait? Or the commons from which it was taken?

The GE chilli has yet to be released, but its release will likely be the end of New Mexico's *chile nativo*. Cross-pollination with a GE chilli will destroy the integrity of the landrace chillis. There is no way to breed out the GE traits. As *chile nativo* is a staple food crop, GE contamination will mean that the patent holder would own and control our seeds and food, since all parts of a GE plant are patented – seed, plant parts, and pollen. Currently there are hybrid seeds that have bred in male sterility to prevent people from replanting their new varieties. This approach does not involve the use of terminator technology. If biotech companies were really concerned about protecting their patented traits, they too could have used this method. Instead, their strategy has been to 'contaminate and conquer'.

Corporate Subjugation

Before 1980, life forms were not patentable. The case of Diamond v. Chakrabarty opened the doors for patenting live, human-made microorganisms. The result was an unprecedented number of mergers and acquisitions of seed businesses by chemical, agricultural, and pharmaceutical corporations with an emphasis in biotechnology. This trend has continued with the world's plant genetics now concentrated in the hands of a few corporations. The top ten seed companies controlled 40% of the seed market in 1996; this increased to over 75% in 2012.¹ Between 2008 and 2013, the top eight corporations acquired more than seventy seed companies. Currently, the top three companies control almost 60% of the world's seeds and germplasm. These three companies are the result of the following mergers in 2017 and 2018: Syngenta and China Chem, Dupont and Dow, and Monsanto and Bayer.

The possible introduction of a GE chilli in New Mexico was the first realization that the people's food and seed were at risk of corporate takeover. Community members formed a coalition, Save New Mexico Seeds (SNMS), to work to protect the *chile nativo*. The first thing SNMS learned was that a GE chilli would have an impact both locally and nationally. In fact, farmers and consumers in other states faced similar issues with other crops. The next thing SNMS learned was that GE alfalfa had been trialled in New Mexico several years earlier. Alfalfa is planted in all but one New Mexico county. As a result, farmers located next to GE alfalfa fields were potentially at risk of being sued by Monsanto for unknowingly possessing GE alfalfa traits. Thus began SNMS's path into the political world.

Theft of the Commons

SNMS's first effort was to get legislation introduced that would protect anyone from lawsuits for unknowingly possessing patented plants. A bill called the Farmer Protection Act was introduced three times (2008, 2010, and 2011). In the end Monsanto, BIO (lobbyist for international and domestic biotech companies), the NMCA, and NMSU were successful in stopping the bill: it barely failed in the House floor vote in 2011. During this time, SNMS begin conducting chilli tastings at farmers markets throughout New Mexico to bring attention to the GE chilli and its potential impact on *chile nativo*.

In 2011, the NMCA successfully introduced the New Mexico Chile Advertising Act. It requires compulsory registration of farmers who label their chilli 'New Mexico Chile'. Many farmers ignored this law since the *chiles nativos* are called by the locale where they are grown. In 2012, the law was amended to include the name of any city, town, county, village, pueblo, mountain, river, or other geographic feature or features located in New Mexico. This law is an attempt to force local growers to relinquish their vernacular, erasing the existence of the *chile nativo*. Why should New Mexicans have to register to call their crops by their rightful names?

The NMCA argued that this law was necessary because people were selling Hatch chilli that was not from Hatch, New Mexico. Hatch chilli has been a major marketing campaign for the commercial growers. But at a hearing that was held after opposition to this law, the New Mexico Department of Agriculture conceded that if a farmer was registered, they could call their chilli by any name, even Hatch, regardless of where it was grown in the state.

Efforts have been made to have this law repealed, but due to the current political scene everything is at a standstill. Farmers are still using their chillis' rightful names without registering, but when the chilli is being sold, it is simply called 'local'. When consumers see the term 'local chilli' at a restaurant, they know that the business supports the *nativo* farmers.

In January 2018, a bill was introduced at the behest of BIO, with support from the NMCA and the Farm Bureau. Called the State Seed Pre-emption Act, it would have given the state complete control over any seed planted in New Mexico. The 'State of New Mexico' in this case meant the Board of Regents for NMSU, which oversees the New Mexico Department of Agriculture. NMSU, although a state-funded university, has much to gain financially from development of patented seeds.

The people successfully fought against this Act. According to New Mexico's Attorney General, '[t]he result is that decisions on what can be grown locally will be taken away from local control and exist exclusively in the state domain [...]. "Vegetable seed" includes the seeds of those crops which are grown in gardens [...].'[2] This law would have affected every person planting a seed in New Mexico.

Reclaiming Taste

New Mexico's agricultural history is based on exchange. Crops, livestock, and seeds are still exchanged or gifted. Once a crop is for sale only, it becomes a commodity and is grown with different intentions. The biotech companies have systematically introduced legislation in New Mexico intended to deny access to those things that are basic to a community's ability to be self-sufficient. When the commons is enclosed, legislated, and regulated, the people's awareness of their connection to it is lost. So when we lose control of our own language, such as calling our chillis by their names, the connections to our very sustenance begin to disintegrate, along with the ethics that bind us to them. The loss of New Mexico's vernacular is the loss of the commons.

But something else is disappearing. Through genetic engineering, hybridization, and elimination of crop varieties, the diversity of taste is narrowing. This industrial approach has led to a monocrop of taste, masking real, authentic flavours with food-science flavours. For example, say you go into a major supermarket and purchase a simple chilli salsa. Along with chilli, onions, tomatoes, and herbs, it may also contain sugar, xanthan gum, undisclosed spices, and additional flavouring. Then you might sample a few other salsas that taste almost identical, except for the level of heat. Industrial salsas are convenient, yet the price is a lack of authentic taste.

If you eat at a restaurant that offers 'New Mexican' food, you are asked, 'Red or green?' Which means, what type of chilli sauce would you like poured over your food? The green is usually commercial chemically-peeled and frozen green chilli. It is watery and tasteless except for the chilli resin added for the industry-specific levels of spiciness: mild, medium, or hot. The red is usually industrial dried red chilli that has turned reddish-brown and often tastes bitter. Both are thickened with corn starch or flour, creating a gravy-like sauce. Ask for Christmas, and you get both red and green sauce. If you want the same taste, just buy the commercial frozen chilli in the grocery stores.

Reclaiming Diversity of Taste

Reclaiming Taste

Up until the late 1980s, chilli farmers would line up along north 4th Street in Albuquerque. People would walk from one truck to the next, taking a small bite out of a chilli to taste its freshness, flavour, and heat level. Hands would be full of one or two chilli peppers, as the people walked back and forth from different trucks until they found their favourite chilli. Then one year the trucks vanished, and no one has been able to say what happened to the farmers.

Over the years, farmers markets became established in New Mexico. Through our work at local farmers markets, we knew that tastings and sharing were among the best approaches to help forgotten or neglected crops reappear on our local tables. Therefore, the farming communities' response through the SNMS coalition was to conduct chilli tasting events across the state at local farmers markets. Farmers market managers were contacted to see if they had farmers selling green chilli who would like to participate. Each farmer then sold us roasted green chilli for the tastings.

At each market, chillis were laid out for sampling from the local farmers, *chile nativo* growers across the state, and the industrial chilli growers. There were usually no more than seven varieties tasted at a single time. On a small paper plate, bite-size amounts of chilli were placed clockwise, with the top of the plate (noon) being the mildest chilli and moving clockwise in the direction of the hottest chillis. Each chilli had a number next to it. Tasters were provided a few organic corn chips and a toothpick. After each taster had sampled the chillis, they then placed their toothpicks into a cup bearing the number of their favourite chilli. Then the farmers' names were revealed.

Comments by the tasters for the *chile nativo* were usually, 'Where can I buy this?' and 'This reminds me of my grandfather's/grandmother's *chile*.' Comments on the industrial chilli were always, 'This tastes watery.' No one ever voted for the industrial chillis – ever.

To demonstrate how seriously our New Mexicans took the tastings, at one event a mother and daughter tasted all the chillis. The women left, then returned with a small bottle of garlic salt secured from a local food vendor. They wanted to retest the chillis again, but this time with garlic salt. Before they purchased the chilli, they wanted to make sure that it had the full flavour of what they commonly regarded as the 'best' chilli.

One weekend we conducted a smaller tasting at an event where tourists were in the audience. That day there was only a choice between a commercial red and a *nativo* red. Interestingly, the commercial red was liked almost as much as the *nativo*, because that was the only flavour of chilli that most tourists had ever tasted in local restaurants. They neither recognized real chilli flavour nor disliked the commercial chilli. We felt that this was an example of how easy it is to eradicate tastes from our palates.

The tastings were exceedingly successful. The following year we continued to hold more tastings, and some of the markets went on to make it an annual event, without the industrial chillis. Consumers began to seek out the *chile nativo* and have continued to do so. This success has enabled farmers to raise their prices significantly over those of industrial chillis. There has also been a revival in local pride for a crop that had been treated as inferior because the chillis were smaller, varying in size and taste. But the key ingredient was the flavour. The tastings helped to educate consumers by letting them experience once again the real flavours of their local chilli – the taste of the earth.

Notes

1. New Mexico State Legislature Legislative Finance Committee, 'New Mexico Legislature Fiscal Impact Report for Agriculture & Vegetable Seed Law Preemption'. New Mexico State Legislature, 18 January 2018 <https://www.NewMexicolegis.gov/Sessions/18%20Regular/firs/HB0161.PDF > [accessed March 30 2018] (para. 1 and 3 of 2).
2. Phillips McDougall, 'Putting the Cartel before the Horse…and Farm, Seeds, Soil and Peasants etc: Who Will Control the Agricultural Inputs?' ETC Group, 4 September 2013 <http://www.etcgroup.org/putting_the_cartel_before_the_horse_2013 > [accessed April 15 2018] (para. 4 of 6).

Eating Life Force: The Meaning of Seeds in the German Alternative Food Movement

Volker Bach

'Think of the fierce energy concentrated in an acorn! You bury it in the ground, and it explodes into an oak.'

George Bernard Shaw's famous quotation continues to inspire, despite the fact that we no longer tend to think of seeds as repositories of energy. To him, it was probably no figurative expression. Prior to the discovery of DNA and the mechanisms of heredity, the function of seeds was poorly understood and many scientific theories filtering into the common consciousness embraced the thought of a vital force that could be concentrated, expended, and renewed. Uncertainty and speculation met with great interest, almost a fascination with heredity that gave rise to many misapprehensions. The legacy of scientific racism is the most thoroughly researched and debunked, but the years between the rise of Darwinism and the scientific understanding of genetics also saw the emergence of an alternative food culture in which seeds, germs, and the idea of life energy (*Lebenskraft*) played a significant role. This essay will look the way that a particular life-giving quality was ascribed to grains in their intact state, and how as a result entire grains and seeds came to be a staple ingredient in breads marketed as healthy.

Lebensreform

According to contemporary literature, Germany was experiencing a crisis of nutrition in the final decades of the nineteenth century. It would have been difficult for an outside observer to see exactly what constituted this crisis: food security was improving, people were eating a more varied and richer diet, wage growth outstripped food prices for the first time in over a century, and life expectancy was rising.[1] Yet reading a certain kind of publication, you would hardly know things were improving. The picture was dire, the situation desperate: people were being poisoned en masse. Nothing less than the future of the German people was at stake, and only the most comprehensive intervention could save it from destruction. This, in a nutshell, was *Lebensreform*, probably the most influential non-political movement in the recent history of Germany.[2]

There was never a founding father or organized body of the *Lebensreform*'s teachings. The movement seems to have arisen in response to a perceived need rather than through any individual inspiration or organized propaganda. Many individual writers and practitioners developed it over the course of many decades.[3] Their beliefs and teachings could vary greatly, and not many of them would have considered themselves part of the same movement. Observed from the outside, though, the reform movements appeared united in the same general thrust towards a brighter, better future in harmony with nature and in the conviction that modernity was getting it wrong – whatever 'it' was. The leaders of this disparate phenomenon, often avid readers and correspondents fluent in several languages, were strongly influenced by each other and by works from abroad. A growing concern with health, diet, and a natural lifestyle was universal through much of the Western world from the 1850s on, but *Lebensreform* was still in many ways a specifically German phenomenon, and its heritage continues to shape modern Germany.

One thing that characterized *Lebensreform* was ambition: the name itself means the reform of life in its entirety, a project that encompasses every aspect of human existence. Overreach was written into the cultural DNA of the Kaiserreich, a state that could seriously think itself destined to lead the civilized world on a good day, so this should not come as too great a surprise. At the same time, the *Lebensreform* movement was, in the tradition of German bourgeois intellectualism, *unpolitisch* – apolitical, concerned only with the pursuit of understanding for its own sake.[4] This lofty philosophical stance had helped generations of professors, scientists, and publicists survive the attentions of government censors. It was deeply embedded in the culture of *Bildungsbürgertum*, the class of people whose professional and social status depended on their academic credentials. Embracing idealism, dismissing politics as trivial and sordid while extolling pure knowledge and high culture, and eschewing open conflict became the mental habits of the perfect academic functionary. This is the atmosphere in which much *Lebensreform* flourished and the reason why it had so little contact with the great political reform efforts of its time.

Its social roots in the educated bourgeois milieu also explain the single-minded pursuit of depth – philosophical, religious, or (pseudo-)scientific – that added to the German specificity of *Lebensreform*. Few teachers were willing to stop at explaining how to live a healthy life. The question why, by derivation from what universal principles, something was healthful needed answering. Entire theories of the living universe were proposed, developed and subscribed to by eager followers in the pursuit of a healthier breakfast.

Science and the Scope of Ignorance

While the nineteenth century saw the birth of both the scientific study of nutrition and heredity in the modern sense, the state of knowledge at the time offered little certainty. Nutrition was still in its infancy. Debates raged over the importance of recently-discovered proteins while the role of minerals and vitamins was as yet almost entirely unknown, at best guessed at.[5] The results of a diet composed on these scientific

Eating Life Force

principles would not have been encouraging.[6]

Even less was known about the mechanisms by which a seed or egg produced a copy of the parent organism. It bears remembering that all of this was a new and exciting field of study at the time. The fact that plants reproduced sexually – that biologically speaking there was no difference between the egg of an animal and the seed of a plant – had only become established in the late eighteenth century. Charles Darwin had proposed the theory that explained evolution through heredity in 1859, and Gregor Mendel, unrecognized in his time, was the first to systematically observe natural laws governing the inheritance of certain traits. His study, published in 1866, only became widely known after his results were reproduced independently by other scientists decades later. Yet even while the functions of heredity were being studied, nobody until the 1960s knew how these traits were passed on to the next generation. This meant that while generations of dietary reformists tried to formulate their ideas about the proper role of seeds in their food, they had no idea what exactly a seed was, and neither did anyone else.

This is not to say there were no attempts to explain the mechanism involved. Charles Darwin himself developed an entirely materialist model of heredity in which gemmules circulated through each organism. These tiny particles recorded the characteristics of each organ and were concentrated in the seed or egg, to be passed on to future generations. Francis Galton followed Darwin with the idea of particles as information bearers. He assumed that these units – he called them 'stirps' – were used up in forming functional body cells, but not in making seeds. A seed thus carried the supply of stirps that would last an organism for its lifetime. A more dynamic idea was proposed by Ernst Haeckel, a biologist, gifted artist, and popularizer of Darwinist ideas in Germany. He envisioned *Lebensteilchen* (particles of life) he called 'plastidules'. These were incorporated into each cell and contained the blueprint for the entire organism. Plastidules were alive in a way: they encoded their information and copied themselves by oscillating movements (*Plastidulbewegung*), an image that resonated with traditional views of natural harmony.

Materialist explanations were not yet dominant, though. The concept of a vital force, an *èlan vital*, that animated all of nature still had currency in the late nineteenth century. The idea of a ubiquitous force that could not be detected or measured must have seemed less dubious when electromagnetism was a newly-discovered phenomenon, but its popularity in Germany likely owed much to the fact that it matched ideas proposed by the natural philosophers of the romantic era, among them the revered poet Goethe. Seeing nature as infused with a shared purpose, a harmonious intent that would be realized if it were left to itself, was a recurring topos of the deistic religion that many German intellectuals espoused.

Under all of these explanations it seemed perfectly reasonable to assume that there was something – a force, a material, or a unique repository of qualities – concentrated in a seed and that the seed as a whole was in some way alive, more than the sum of its parts. These ideas would prove very influential in the emerging health food culture of

Lebensreform and ultimately in German bread as we know it today.

The Importance of Language

It should be pointed out here that all of these explanations are wrong, albeit in different degrees. There is no way any of them can stand up to scientific scrutiny. Some of them were already proven wrong at the time, others only in the course of the twentieth century. Nobody could be convinced of their rightness by observing the facts. Nonetheless, tens of thousands of people embraced lifestyles and diets based on some variations thereof, mainly, I would argue, because of the emotive language that tied into existing preconceptions.

That this could work is not least due to the particular social structure of the *Lebensreform* movement. It spread mostly among urban, educated people. Eva Bärlösius reconstructed the social context of the movement and found two common threads: the starting point of an individual epiphany, and the desire to communicate it through writing.[7] People who became converts to reform diets often credited them with saving their health or wellbeing in a crisis and proceeded to write about it. The most successful leaders in the movement were known above all for their books.

To briefly look at the language they used, I will focus on the words used to describe seeds – something they wrote a great deal about. Before we enter into the details, though, we need to recall that they were writing German, and German does not really have a word for 'seeds'. Rather, it has several.

The first translation that suggests itself is '*Samen*'. *Samen* can refer to seeds in a botanical or agricultural context, but also to semen (which only has limited culinary use in North Germany). Some more traditionally prudish distributors have opted for the unequivocal '*Sämereien*' in a gardening context. It is unusual for *Samen* to be used in a culinary context, though it does show up in compounds such as *Leinsamen* (linseed). A related word is '*Saat*', which can refer both to seeds in themselves and the seed that is put into the ground, but rarely to food.

More commonly used to describe seeds is the word '*Kern*' which can mean specifically seeds of e.g. sunflowers (*Sonnenblumenkerne*) or apples (*Apfelkerne*), but also more generally mean the centre or core of something. It can be used figuratively to refer to the heart or nub of an issue and tends to have positive associations in frequently used expressions such as '*kernig*' (roughly translated as hearty, solid, or sound). When the German nuclear industry tried to improve its image, they decided on the expression '*Kernkraft*' for nuclear fission power. Related to *Kern*, but typically used for cereals, is the word '*Korn*'. *Korn* corresponds fairly well to the English word grain, and it was used frequently in health food discourses.

Finally, a word that recurs again and again as we look into the culinary use of seeds in *Lebensreform* diets is '*Keim*'. It translates literally as germ or sprout, but has very different associations. Outside of medical parlance, a *Keim* is not a disease-causing microorganism, but a promising beginning or early stage, the origin of life. Its prevalence points to the focus of *Lebensreform* diets on seeds as bearers of life.

Eating Life Force

The choice of words here is never coincidental. The writers of reform diet theories were acutely aware of fine distinctions in language and consciously coined new terms to further their agendas. The most famous such coinage is the word '*Lebensmittel*' (literally 'the means/remedies of life'). Diet guru Werner Kollath created it in conscious opposition to the then current term '*Nahrungsmittel*' which described foods as they were sold to consumers. According to Kollath, *Lebensmittel* were healthy because they were intact and alive: '*Lebensmittel* still have their own metabolism, *Nahrungsmittel* do not.'[8] If we did not know *Lebensreform* diets were strictly vegetarian, statements like these might conjure up rather grisly images.

The Origins of *Vollkorn*

The most important quality in seeds to most *Lebensreform* adherents was their wholeness. Industrially milled flours, with the germ and hull removed, were considered deficient in the way most 'unnaturally' processed food was. Most Germans today know the word *Vollkorn* – whole grain – as a ubiquitous designation for a type of flour or bread, but it originated in the *Lebensreform*'s catchphrase incubator. Alternatives like *Ganzkorn* or *Ganzmehl* were considered, but rejected in favour of the connotative richness of '*voll*' – whole, full, entire, signalling plenitude and completeness. The pioneer of dietary reform Gustav Schlickeysen promoted the idea of completeness in his system of *Vollwertkost*, food that retained the whole worth or value, though he did not coin the term *Vollkorn*, instead advocating *Schrotbrot* made from coarsely ground wheat. The word *Schrot*, too, has positive connotations that Schlickeysen himself evokes in a poem praising men – '[…] *von echtem Schrot und Korn* […]'[9] – and describing the bread that gave them their nature as made from coarsely ground wheat and water alone: ' […] *Sieh auf dem Feld die Aehren wogen, im Brode liegt des Lebens Kraft. Nur in dem Schrot und Korn verzehren, wir das, was die Gesundheit schafft.*' (Behold the ears of corn waving in the field, the strength of life lies in in bread. Only through Schrot (coarse-ground meal) and grain do we eat that which gives us health.)[10]

This is as good a summary of the belief behind *Vollkornbrot* as we are likely to find. It reflects the widespread conviction that when you ate food, you ate life, as fresh and concentrated as possible. How to ensure this happened was contested; several methods of producing the most life-giving bread competed. Gustav Simons (1861-1914) took inspiration from Russian baking traditions when he proposed soaking whole grains and integrating them into the bread to ensure their nutritional value went undiminished. His *Simonsbrot* was produced industrially by the 1920s and is still available. Stefan Steinmetz (1858-1930), a milling engineer, developed a method of hulling grains that left the outer shell of the grain intact. The *Steinmetzbrot* made from this flour, too, remains available to this day.[11] A different approach was taken by Volkmar Klopfer (1874-1943) who sought to broaden the appeal of whole-grain bread by making it more palatable to the average consumer. He wrote in 1930 that only bread that contained the 'dormant germ of life' (*den schlummernden Keim*) should rightly be called *Vollkorn*.[12] Though his work on milling techniques formed the basis for further development to today's *Vollkorn* products, *Klopferbrot* is no longer sold under that name.

Bread remained an important part of most reformist diets despite the fact that the need to bake it was manifestly at odds with the desire to eat food as alive, fresh, and unprocessed as possible. One attempt to combine the two was *Keimbrot*, a loaf produced from sprouted, soaked grains that is cooked slowly at a very low temperature. In the case of *Essenerbrot*, it is sometimes just sun-dried. Simons was careful to insist that proper germination was short, only just awakening the dormant germ (*schlummernden Keim*), and quite unlike the malting used to make beer. *Keimbrot*, too, is still available, though it is most popular when closest to conventional bread.[13]

Another approach was to add whole grains, seeds, and nuts to bread, though these, too, were baked in the process. In this case, the idea seems to have arisen as a way to signal authenticity. With no legal definition of *Vollkorn* in existence until 1927, consumers could not be sure what they got in the loaves for which they paid a premium. If, as Schlickeysen taught, 'every grain [was] a loaf', the presence of entire grains in or on the bread showed that at least some of these micro-loaves were provided intact.[14] Many nuts and seeds could also be decorative and could add attractive flavours, but that was not the case with the frequently used soaked grains. Their point was to be seen to be entire.

Some advocates of *Lebensreform* bought mills to produce fresh, unadulterated meal for baking at home, though producing palatable *Vollkornbrot* was a difficult process. Many more used them to make *Frischkornbrei*, an uncooked porridge of freshly-ground grains. This was first proposed by Schlickeysen and popularized by Werner Kollath (1892-1970) and the Swiss dietician Maximilian Bircher-Brenner (1867-1939), who claimed that he saw the original dish prepared by mountain farmers in remote Alpine valleys. The modernized version provided in the Wendepunkt-Kochbuch based on his diet goes:

> *Apple-Diätspeise*:
> 2-3 small or one large apple, cleaned by rubbing with a dry cloth, but without removing the skin, core, or seeds. 1 tablespoon walnuts, hazelnuts or almonds, grated. One level tablespoon rolled oats, soaked for twelve hours in three tablespoons of water. Juice of half a lemon. 1 tablespoon condensed, sweetened milk.
>
> The condensed milk and the lemon juice are first mixed in with the oats, then the apples are grated with their skin, cores and seeds pressing down firmly on the apple grater and mixed into the porridge thoroughly during the grating process, i.e. during frequent breaks. This way the porridge covers the apple pulp (*Apfelfleisch*) and protects it from exposure to the air which preserves the appetizing white appearance of the dish. The grated nuts are strewn over it at the table (1 tablespoon) to increase the fat and protein content.[15]

Variations with blueberries, bananas, and dried fruit follow. This is of course the preparation that became known throughout the world by its Swiss-German name muesli.[16]

Eating Life Force

Sprouts, Seeds, and Nuts

Aside from bread grains, nuts and seeds played an important role in many aspects of the *Lebensreform* diet, especially its vegetarian variations. Early vegetarian restaurants often served raw foods – again reflecting a common concern of the reformist diet with freshness and life – as platters of vegetables, fruit, and nuts. Rich in fat and protein, portable, and pleasant to eat raw, nuts enjoyed high status among vegetarians and raw-foodists. An extreme case was that of August Engelhardt (1875-1919), a mystic and social reformer, who embraced a diet comprised almost entirely of coconuts in his eremitic existence on the then German-owned island of Kabakon.[17] Cocovorism never caught on, though imported coconut did.

The life-producing property of seeds was endlessly fascinating to the *Lebensreform* dieticians, and many recipes call for germinated or sprouted seeds for their particular invigorating qualities. Simon described the germination that characterized his bread as 'a first initiation of growth without removing any substance in actuality, thus only a first rearrangement of the nutritive substances within the grains themselves'.[18] In conjunction with Klopfer's idea of a sleeping germ, this could be described as awakening the life of the seed. He was careful to distinguish it from traditional malting to produce beer, a beverage rejected by the *Lebensreform* movement. Germination was not only used on cereals; Emil Drebber (1873-1943) invented and marketed a healthy high-energy food made from malted nuts and almonds he called *Nussprana*. The name is interesting because, unlike later nonsense brand names such as the Nutella clones Nusspli and Nusskati, it links the German word *Nuss* (nut) with the Sanskrit *prana*, which means life, breath, or animating force. That he expected his customers to understand this reference illustrates what we would call the movement's nerdiness today.

The Legacy of *Lebensreform*

The dietary ideas of the *Lebensreform* era continue to be influential in many aspects of Germany's alternative eating scene, and I would contend this is not due to their insight, but to their intuitiveness. Where its proponents embraced scientific fact, they often went badly wrong. Bircher-Brenner, for example, identified newly-discovered vitamins as 'generative substances' (*Zeugungsstoffe*) in the 1930s.[19] This resonates well with the way the transmission of life mystified and fascinated people at the time, but of course it is completely wrong. It is not even clear how it fitted into Bircher-Brenner's broader theory that nutrition was provided by ingesting quanta of sunlight accumulated in plants, but only available in a denatured form in meat or processed foods. Yet despite the obvious problems modern science causes this idea, it remains popular because it is intuitive.[20] Other writers never ventured this far into the realm of actual science, instead making evocative and blurry statements that appealed to an intuitive understanding of nature. Sabine Merta's study collected expressions such as '*Spannkraft der Natur*' (Schlickeysen, a word that translates as tensile strength and carries overtones of vitality, alertness, and mobility) and '*eigene Vitalität*' (Lahmann, claiming this inherent vitality for mineral compounds found in plants). Arguably the most successful of these German prophets of an alternative life, Rudolf Steiner (1861-1925), wrote of preserving nature's *'elementare Bildekräfte'* (nature's elementary powers of creation, where the word *bilden* connects to a wide semantic field that includes anything from emergence to character education) by growing and treating food in harmony with nature's dynamic rhythm.[21]

The great strength of these phrases lies in the fact that they are difficult to pin down, but feel right. In our observation, nature by and large works, and it is easy to believe that it should and indeed wants to. The scientific argument that nature is not telic, that there is no inherent purpose to things and that therefore no perfect diet can be expected to exist, not only runs counter to much of our everyday experience, it is also contrary to millennia of theology and philosophy. We want things to exist for a reason. If they do, it should logically be possible to understand their purpose and follow it. It is as true of dietary pseudoscience as it is of political rhetoric: the emotions and desires that are conjured up by words can matter more than the bare facts they refer to.

However, we should not dismiss one important point Bärlösius made: before they became preachers, many dietetic writers experienced the healing powers of the diet they espoused in themselves. This is entirely believable: not only can a conscious change of almost any kind lead to positive health outcomes through a placebo effect, but the reform diet advocates of the early twentieth century actually turned out to be correct in many details. Following the diet advice of a mystic like Rudolf Steiner or a pseudoscientific quack like Max Bircher-Brenner would have produced better health outcomes than eating the traditional food of the German middle classes or even a diet designed by the leading lights of nutritional science. It is worth remembering that it is always possible to be right for the wrong reasons.

Notes

1. Judith Baumgartner, *Ernährungsreform – Antwort auf Industrialisierung und Ernährungswandel*, Europäische Hochschulschriften series III vol 535 (Frankfurt (Main): Peter Lang Verlag, 1994), pp. 63 ff. and the pioneering Wolfgang R. Krabbe, *Gesellschaftsveränderung durch Lebensreform. Strukturmerkmale einer sozialreformerischen Bewegung im Deutschland der Industrialisierung* (Göttingen: Vandenhoeck & Rupprecht, 1974).
2. The study of the *Lebensreform* movement has become fashionable lately: two of the leading scholars of food history in Germany, Sabine Merta and Eva Bärlösius, both wrote their doctoral theses on it, and the popular history magazine *Zeit Geschichte* dedicated an entire issue to it in 2013. With new source material unearthed and additional work published, the field's expansion has yielded very interesting insights into a subculture with remarkable staying power in the face of history's tribulations.
3. A fascinating study of how this development happened at the microscale in a slightly later period is Brunhilde Bross-Burkhart's *Der private biologische Gartenbau in Süddeutschland seit 1945 – Die Rolle der Pioniere und Veränderungen im Wissenstransfer* (PhD dissertation Berlin, self-published 2011). Individuals could become influential in formative times even through private contacts or publications of very limited circulation.
4. This is the topic of an entire volume of essays: Marc Cluet and Catherine Repoussard (eds.), *Lebensreform – Die soziale Dynamik der politischen Ohnmacht/la dynamique sociale de l'impuissance*

politique (Tübingen: Francke Verlag, 2013).

5   For example, in 1896, Fannie Merritt Farmer stated, 'The salad plants […] contain but little nutriment, but are cooling, refreshing, and assist in stimulating the appetite. They are valuable for the water and potash salts they contain' (*The Boston Cooking School Cook Book* (Boston: Little, Brown, 1896; repr. New York: Hugh Lauter Levin Associates, 1996), p. 287).

6   Testing new dietetic theories was attended with difficulty not least because the diets they produced were so unsatisfying. It is no coincidence that the experiments that disproved Justus von Liebig's theory of protein as a source of energy took place in prisons, with inmates serving as guinea pigs. See Peter Higginbotham, *The Prison Cookbook* (Stroud: History Press, 2010), p. 83 f.

7   Eva Bärlösius, *Naturgemäße Lebensführung. Zur Geschichte der Lebensreformbewegung um die Jahrhundertwende* (Frankfurt (Main): Campus Verlag, 1997).

8   Qtd. in Sabine Merta, *Wege und Irrwege zum modernen Schlankheitskult. Diätkost und Körperkultur als Suche nach neuen Lebensstilformen 1880-1930*, Studien zur Geschichte des Alltags, vol. 22 (Stuttgart: Franz Steiner Verlag, 2003), p. 131. Today, while *Nahrungsmittel* is still used in legal and technical contexts, the positive connotations of the term *Lebensmittel* have made it the standard word to describe any food sold by retailers.

9   This idiomatic expression is hard to render adequately. It refers to genuineness, honesty, and the strength of convictions. Today, it is associated automatically with bread, but its origins lie with coinage, *Korn* referring to the precious metal content of an alloy and *Schrot* to the weight of the coin. See Lutz Röhrich, *Lexikon der sprichwörtlichen Redensarten* (Freiburg im Breisgau: Herder Verlag, 2010), p. 1405

10 Merta, p. 107.

11 Baumgartner, p. 81 f. and Merta, pp. 107 ff.

12 Volkmar, *Klopfer Brot* (Dresden: 1930), p. 4 f.

13 E.g. '*Bettinas Keimbackstube*' <http://www.lebenskeimbrot.de/> [accessed 20 May 2018]. Instructions for making sun-dried Essene bread are found at Von Henning Müller-Burzler, '*Echtes Essener-Brot selbst gemacht – eine Rohkost-Spezialität*' <www.mueller-burzler.de/echtes-essener-brot-selbst-gemacht-eine-rohkost-spezialitaet.html> [accessed 20 May 2018]. Most *Essenerbrot* and *Keimbrot* sold today is conventional wholemeal bread enriched with malt.

14 Merta, p. 107.

15 Berta Brupbacher-Bircher, *Das Wendepunkt-Kochbuch*, 17th ed. (Zurich: Wendepunkt-Verlag, 1937), p. 155 (recipe 576).

16 Merta, pp. 119 ff.

17 Angelika Jacobs, 'Der Apothekenhelfer August Engelhardt', *Spectrum der Wissenschaft*, 20 June 2008 <https://www.spektrum.de/quiz/der-apothekenhelfer-august-engelhardt/959520> [accessed 20 May 2018].

18 Qtd. in Merta, p. 111.

19 Maximilian Bircher-Brenner, *Geleitwort*, in Brupbacher-Brenner, *Wendepunkt-Kochbuch*, p. 10.

20 The theory of biophotonics – the idea that light energy is the animating force directly underlying all life on earth – received a new lease on life with the discovery that biological processes can cause organisms to emit photons. Spearheaded by German physicist Fritz-Albert Popp, this idea has been popularized by many avid and business-savvy adherents, e.g. '*Biophotonen*', *Licht des Lebens* <http://www.lichtdeslebens.de/biophotonen/> [accessed 20 May 2018].

21 Merta, pp. 95, 108, 137.

Seeds

'Thorebygg' in Farmhouse Ale Brewing in Norway

Hans Olav Bråtå

Naked barley (now labelled *Hordeum vulgare*, ssp. *distichon*, var. *nudum* or *Hordeum vulgare*, ssp. *vulgare*, var. *coolest*) was one of the dominant groups of grains in Norway in the Bronze Age (1400-800 BC), and was well suited to the relatively warm climate at the time. In the Iron Age, it was replaced by ordinary barley (*Hordeum vulgare spp.*), which is adapted to a colder, wetter climate and requires less nutrient-rich soils. Naked barley is known from a Celtic brewery dated to 500-400 BC in southern Germany and from a thirteenth-century brewery near Berlin. Although naked barley was cultivated throughout Europe, the largest cultivated areas were in the Alpine region, Belgium, and Norway.[1]

However, while it is clear that naked barley was used in European brewing, little is known about its use in brewing in Norway. In this paper, I examine the history and terroir of one such barley, named 'Thorebygg', which now seems to be extinct. Thorebygg was used for brewing traditional farmhouse ale, but only in small amounts and particularly when the best quality ale was required. According to Mitterpacher, it was most frequently used in Norway, where it gave an '*ottima birra*' (excellent beer). In general, traditional farmhouse ale brewing in Norway ended at the beginning of the twentieth century, which broke the linkages between brewing and the use of Thorebygg.[2]

Thorebygg was cultivated mainly on burned plots as part of swidden agriculture, but also on ordinary farmland. The advance in craft brewing has led to renewed interest in ingredients used in the past, such as old species and varieties of grains, and their history. Fundamentally, this interest focuses on *terroir* understood in the broad sense and the recreation of *terroirs*, which necessarily are fictive *terroirs*. This paper may be considered a contribution to a wider discussion about the elements needed to reconstruct *terroirs* in their historical context.[3]

In this paper, I first describe the historical and geographical distribution of Thorebygg in Norway and then describe how the grain was cultivated, why it was cultivated, and how it was used. Thereafter, I analyze the relationship between the aforementioned factors, and particularly why Thorebygg was used for brewing.

Types of Swidden Agriculture

Swidden agriculture is an old form of agriculture dating back to the Neolithic. It has a long history in Norway. Despite limited sources from the Middle Ages, in 1490 there were regulations concerning *rugbråter* (swidden plots used to grow rye). Many

Norwegian words and surnames are derived from *bråter*, including my own surname. Most of them probably date from the sixteenth and seventeenth centuries. The practice of *bråtebruket* (forest cut for burning and later cultivation of the land) expanded particularly in the seventeenth century in south-eastern Norway. A royal commission in 1630 declared that farms practising *bråtebruk* had to take care to preserve the forest. Due to the increased value of the forest, the practice of *bråtebruket* ceased in Kristians amt (present-day Oppland County, in the north-central area of southern Norway) in the 1860s to 1870s.[4]

By the time Finnish settlers, who based their agriculture on the swidden method, moved into the forest in south-east Norway from Sweden in the mid-seventeenth century, swidden cultivation was already established in the country. The settlers introduced *svedjerug*, a species of rye adapted for sowing in the warm ashes from burnt large spruce trees. They also introduced barley varieties that were suitable for swidden farming in deciduous forest, mixed forest, and young forest. One of these varieties, named Maskin, was selected from farmland in the forested areas in 1916 for further commercial cultivation. Since Maskin could be sown in warm ashes, it was a valuable malt grain and was developed into the Canadian Harrington barley – one of the most popular malt barleys today.[5]

The Finnish tradition of swidden farming differed from the Norwegian one of *bråtebruket*. The Norwegian tradition of swidden agriculture is described by different words, which partly have their origins in different periods in history. The words also describe differences in the practice regarding the type of forest, brushwood, or twigs that were burned as well as how the burning was done. *Vål* is the oldest name for swidden agriculture and refers to a type that was practised from the first centuries AC. The names *koss/kase* and *bråte* for swidden agriculture date back at least to the Middle Ages. The words *sve/svi* were used in the Middle Ages to some extent, but in general they were relatively more recent words. *Koss/kase*, *bråte*, and *sve/svi* are not indicative of types of forest that were burned, as is the case for the various Finnish words.[6] The word *vål* is not mentioned in the written sources, whereas *koss/kase*, *bråte*, and *sve* are frequently mentioned and to some extent indicate how the burning was done as well as the type of trees, brushwood, and twigs that were burned.

Thorebygg Compared with Other Varieties of Barley

The origin of the name Thorebygg is unknown, but Pontoppidan speculates that it derives from the mythological god Thor (frequently also spelled Tor in the literature) or Walhalla because it was the grain of gods and heroes.[7] This may indicate that the grain gave a very good ale. Another possible origin is that, since the grain most often was cultivated in burned fields, it could have been associated with lightning and fire, which in Nordic mythology is often associated with Thor.

One potential problem when analyzing the historical use of Thorebygg is that the literature, particularly eighteenth- and early nineteenth-century literature, may confuse

Thorebygg with other grains or use different names for the same varieties of grain. As an example, a description dated 1745 from the Stavanger region refers to the grain as '*Thorebygg eller himmelkorn*' (Thorebygg or grain from the sky). In 1793, Schlegel wrote that the grain that Norwegian farmers called Thorebygg was the same as 'Davids Byg' and 'Himmel-korn'. In 1812, Floor noted that the barley Himmelbygg (*Hordeum vulgare celeste*) had two varieties – two-row and six-row – and that the latter was Thorebygg. The appearance of Thorebygg may to some extent have been confusing, as it is described as looking like 'wheat' or as a grain that has similarities with both wheat and barley, with a loose husk. Some confusion is easy to understand. For example, in 1937, agriculture professor Knut Vik wrote that the naked barley had similarities with wheat and rye because the grain easily fell off during threshing.[8]

Other authors quite early on distinguished between Thorebygg and other grains. For example, in 1761 Essendrop described Himmelbygg as being twice as large as Thorebygg. Experiments in the 1820s and 1830s distinguished between Thorebygg and other varieties of barley, such as Himalaiabygg. Experiments conducted at the end of the nineteenth century and early twentieth century, from 1889 to 1917, and in the early decades of the twentieth century, from 1917 to 1935, revealed a clear distinction between two-row and six-row barley and different varieties within each group, such as Thorebygg in the six-row group. The results from the experiments showed that Thorebygg was the largest and heaviest grain of the different varieties compared (74.1 kg per hl in 1889-1917). Thorebygg needed longer to ripen (103 days) than other barleys and had the lowest yield per m^2 (181 kg per 1000 m^2), compared with the barley with the highest yield (241 kg per 1000 m^2).[9]

Historical and Geographical Distribution of Thorebygg in Norway

Thorebygg is mentioned as different from barley and a subject for taxation in 1661 at Sørum, in 1688 and 1695 at Vang, and in 1686 at Ringerike. Vang is a present-day municipality in the mountains in the county of Oppland, whereas Sørum and Ringerike are present-day municipalities located in the best lowland grain areas in Norway, which are to the north of Oslo. These records document that Thorebygg was cultivated in a geographically large part of south-east Norway in the second half of the seventeenth century. In 1715, Ramus reported the cultivation of Thorebygg from the same lowland grain area.[10]

Statistics from 1809 give an interesting picture of the geographical distribution of Thorebygg, but it is important to note that Thorebygg and other high-quality grains and seeds were not sown every year and never in large amounts. Consequently, the statistics are less reliable for these species and varieties of grain and seeds than for others, and probably underestimate the production of Thorebygg and similar kinds of grain.[11] Statistics from 1809 show that 2093 barrels of Thorebygg grain were sown that year, of which 55% was sown in the county of Hedmark. Hedmark borders Sweden, and the lower lying central western part of the county has traditionally been a very good area for growing grains. According to the same statistics, only 1.6% of the total amount of Thorebygg was sown in Kristians amt (i.e. Oppland), to the north-west and in a more mountainous area. In the other main grain-growing area in Norway, the county of Trøndelag, 19% of the total amount was sown. In general, less Thorebygg was grown along the coast in the south, west, and north-western parts of southern Norway, except for Stavanger amt. That regions in which Thorebygg was grown differed in size hinders a precise comparison. Nevertheless, the main picture is that Hedmark, or parts of it, was a core area, together with Trøndelag.[12]

A comparison of the total number of barrels of Thorebygg sown in 1809 and 1835 revealed that much the same amount was sown in each year: 2093 barrels in 1809, and 2126 barrels in 1835. However, this was less than 1% of all the grain sown, and might have been decreasing in contrast to oat, barley, and rye.[13] The year 1809 was one of famine in Norway, due to a British blockade during the Napoleonic Wars. Therefore, the statistics may indicate either that the conditions for cultivating Thorebygg were limited or that the amount used for sowing was stable since it was probably an indigenous grain and not subject to import blockades, unlike other grains. Still, according to many authors, it was only cultivated to a minor extent and often not regularly. Thorebygg was a fragile crop and did not tolerate much rain in the autumn. It was therefore recommended that only minor amounts be sown and that in many cases farmers ought to prefer other kinds of barley.[14]

An interesting consideration is when the cultivation of Thorebygg ceased. In the mid-nineteenth century, in Røyken Municipality in the lowlands south-west of Oslo, the municipal executive board each year decided the prices of different species of grain. The prices are documented in annual records from 1837 to 1861. According to the board's records, Thorebygg was not traded there in subsequent years. However, it must have existed at the beginning of the twentieth century, since experiments related to productivity of Thorebygg were conducted at Vollebekk (near Oslo) in 1905.[15]

Cultivation Methods

Thorebygg was predominantly cultivated as part of swidden farming and sown together with vegetables such as turnips or peas, or grains such as rye. The *kase*, *bråte*, and *sve* methods of burning the fields were applied during the eighteenth and nineteenth centuries. This was the case in mountain communities in the valleys of Valdres and Gudbrandsdalen and in lowland grain areas such as Toten, Hadeland, and Hedmarken. According to Haslund, the *kase* method, based on burning deciduous forest, was most frequently used for cultivating Thorebygg and turnips. Aschehoug emphasizes that *bråter*, based on burning alder, gave a very good yield. Thorebygg was sown in the ashes, often the day after burning twigs and small trees, or while the ashes still were warm. The swidden land could be harvested for one or two years, but seldom more. In some places during the nineteenth century, rye and Thorebygg were sown in the ashes, and Thorebygg ripened in the first year and the rye the second year.[16]

Thorebygg requires a long growing season and ought to be sown before other species and varieties. In the southernmost part of south-east Norway, the growing season in the eighteenth and nineteenth centuries was from mid-May to mid-September. Farther north, at Aker (close to Hamar in Hedmark), grain was apparently sown at the end of May or early in June, while harvesting was done at the beginning of September.[17] However, since Thorebygg is sensitive to moisture, the crop often failed if the autumns were too wet.

Although sowing in ashes was preferred, Thorebygg could be sown on farmland or on soils where swidden agriculture was not practised. A diary covering the period from 1749 to 1772, kept in the area with the best soils in Hedmark – the probable core area of Thorebygg – documents that Thorebygg was sown on cultivated land.[18] It was often sown together with other grains and always in lesser quantities than ordinary barley.

Thorebygg grew well in dried bogs. Floor emphasizes that it grew best in dried bogs where the upper part had 'rotted' and in other types of soils that retained the moisture well. According to both Elieson and Floor, Thorebygg was a more suitable grain than other species and varieties of grain for growing in such places.[19] Other authors describe how Thorebygg was cultivated in nutrient-rich soil or well fertilized soil consisting of clay mixed with 'good' earth and sand, while soil that was too wet had to be avoided.[20]

Primarily a Malt Barley

Thorebygg was primarily used as malt and was supposed to have given a superb malt. Unfortunately, none of the sources explains the process more closely. However, the process described in 1779 for Spydeberg, a present-day municipality in the county of Østfold, south-east Norway, may give some clues: there, the most common malt was made of oat, but to improve the ale one barrel of oat malt was mixed with one quarter of barley malt, which might have been Thorebygg since it was cultivated there.[21] This suggests that the two types of malt were prepared independently. Malting oats and barley separately would have preserved the quality of the barley malt during the preparation.[22]

Few descriptions exist of ale made of Thorebygg. Pontoppidan refers to a contemporary source that described the ale as '*sund og liflig*' (healthy and agreeable), whereas Mitterpacher describes it as an '*ottima birra*' (excellent beer).[23] Still, Thorebygg was mainly used as a supplement to other malts, and consequently the total blend and processing probably would have had more influence on the ale than a single malt.

Thorebygg was also appreciated for cooking. Its flour was fine, white, and tasty and was used instead of wheat. It was also excellent for baking and for porridge.[24]

During the nineteenth century, Thorebygg was considered more valuable than ordinary barley, and this was reflected in the prices paid for it. In 1812, a barrel of Thorebygg cost 70 *riksdaler* (the same price as rye, wheat, and peas), while a barrel of ordinary barley cost 46 *riksdaler*. At Røyken during the 1850s, wheat, rye, Thorebygg, and peas were regarded as equal in value in general, and on average they were priced 40% higher than ordinary barley.[25] Thorebygg was announced for sale in Norwegian newspapers in the 1800s.[26]

Discussion

Thorebygg was used for brewing because it provided a very good malt and an excellent ale. Primarily, it was added to other grains to improve the quality of the ale. Wilse's description from Spydeberg in 1779 indicates that oats and barley (which might have been Thorebygg) were malted separately before being mixed during the mashing process. This seems plausible, given the superior quality of Thorebygg compared with other malting grains.

What was the ale made from Thorebygg like? The descriptions are vague, other than it was very good. Wilse's description from Spydeberg may give some idea, because barley (such as Thorebygg) should improve the quality of ale brewed from oats. The latter type was frequently considered a pale ale and inferior to ale made from barley. Oats were therefore often mixed with barley.[27] Generally, a dark strong ale was preferred at Christmas and on special occasions such as weddings and funerals, whereas a paler and less strong ale was preferred during the hay making season. Since Thorebygg was a high-quality grain, it probably was used to improve ale made for Christmas and specific occasions, particularly in terms of strength, taste, and colour. However, it is difficult to characterize the ale on the basis of written sources, not only because taste and smell are subjective, but also because the processing (the brewing) itself would have strongly influenced the product.[28]

An interesting question is which properties made Thorebygg so attractive for the production of ale. Apparently, it was much larger than other barley grains, which would have made it favourable for malting since each grain would have had more starch in proportion to the husk and hence more energy for the yeast. Large grains, preferably barley, were selected by the traditional method of *veggjeronde* after the threshing.[29] After grinding, too, large grains would have been favoured because they would not have obstructed the filtering of the wort through the filter vat to the same extent as smaller grains. Furthermore, Thorebygg might have had specific qualities related to tolerate the high temperatures necessary to stop sprouting during the malting process. This possible attribute could be related to an adaptation to being sown in ashes, which might be warm, like the one mentioned before for barley Maskin.

However, it would have been risky to cultivate Thorebygg because a long growing season was needed, and it easily suffered when conditions became too wet. Additionally, rich soil was preferred. These aspects (i.e. high quality of the grain, difficult cultivation, and relatively low yields) resulted in higher prices for Thorebygg than for ordinary barley.

Written sources document that Thorebygg was cultivated over large areas in Norway in the second half of the seventeenth century. The wide distribution indicates a much older history, probably dating back to the Middle Ages. It is therefore unlikely that Finnish settlers, who entered Norway in the mid-seventeenth century, introduced Thorebygg to Norway. Moreover, different types of swidden agriculture were old established cultivation methods in Norway, at least since the Middle Ages. At these swidden plots, which expanded the cultivated land, Thorebygg was frequently sown together with other kinds of grains and vegetables.

It seems that Thorebygg was suitable for taking advantage of swidden agriculture because the burning would have released large amounts of nutrients, from which grain production in the first or second year after burning would have benefited. Swidden agriculture, reflected in the words *kaser, braater,* and *sveer*, might often have been based on deciduous forest and brushwood. The preferred use of alder for swidden farming is interesting because the soil in which it grows, and hence the alder itself, is rich in nitrogen, thus making alder a natural fertilizer. Thorebygg might originally have been based on swidden agriculture, but was such a valuable grain that farmers who had rich, good quality soils might have decided to sow it in their other fields. The 1809 data relating cultivation show that most Thorebygg was sown in the areas with the best soils, such as Hedmark and Trøndelag.

The final part of this story concerns why farmers ended the cultivation of Thorebygg. There are many probable reasons, one of which is that in the last decades of the nineteenth century Norway shifted from a society based on labour-intensive agriculture to an industrial society. This shift increased focus on grains with high yields and emphasized simplification of the species and varieties of grain grown. Modern transportation allowed the importation of cheap barley and wheat of good quality.[30] Another probable reason for the end of Thorebygg cultivation is that traditional Norwegian farmhouse brewing started to decline in that period, and in general ended during the first decades of the twentieth century. Consequently, there was no market for Thorebygg for brewing, and better and finer grains were entering the market for baking and making porridge. On the contrary, the fact that farmhouse brewing lasted for so long may have contributed to the existence of Thorebygg until the beginning of the twentieth century.

Final Remarks

Thorebygg was a naked barley cultivated in southern Norway at least from the seventeenth century, and probably from the Middle Ages. It was primarily used as a grain for brewing ale, among other reasons because it was large and therefore provided much energy for the yeast. Thorebygg was primarily cultivated on swidden plots, together with other grains and vegetables, as part of expanding the cultivated areas. Since it was a high energy grain, the ashes and the natural fertilizers obtained from burned forest and shrubs probably were a prerequisite for its cultivation. Deciduous forests with alder might have been particularly important. If Thorebygg was among the species and varieties of grain sown in warm ashes, its use as a malt barley might have been improved by that origin and practice. Probably the existence of the grain ended due to societal changes that influenced agriculture and because traditional Norwegian farmhouse brewing ended at the turn of the twentieth century.

'Thorebygg' in Farmhouse Ale Brewing in Norway

Notes

1. Sverre Bakkevig, '*Problemer i bronsealderens korndyrking på Forsandmoen, Rogaland, SV-Norge*', *Ams-Varia*, 33 (1998), 55-62; Åsmund Bjørnstad, *Vårt daglege brød. Kornets kulturhistorie* (Ås: Vidarforlaget, 2010), pp. 93-95; Anna Michalová, 'Minor Cereals and Pseudocereals in Europe', in *Report of the Network Coordinating Group on Minor Crops, First meeting, 16 June 1999 Turku Finland*, ed. by. L. Maggioni (Rome: International Plant Genetic Resources Institute, 2000), p. 59; Hans-Petter Stika, 'Early Iron Age and Late Mediaeval Malt Finds from Germany – Attempts at Reconstruction of Early Celtic Brewing and the Taste of the Celtic Beer', *Archaeological and Anthropological Sciences*, 3 (2011), 41-48.
2. Ludvig Mitterpacher, *Elementi D'Agricoltora* (Milano: Giuseppe Galeazzi, 1784), p. 228. Although this brewing in general ended at the beginning of the twentieth century, farmers and others in some communities continued traditional brewing in subsequent decades. In some communities they follow the main principles of this brewing even today. In this paper I use the term 'ale' for the Norwegian farmhouse beer because that beer was based on the traditional yeast called *kveik*, which was mostly taken from the top of the fermentation tub (see Odd Nordland, *Beer and Brewing Traditions in Norway* (Oslo: Universitetsforlaget, 1969), preface; Hans Olav Bråtå, 'Local Traditions as a Means for Commercial Production of Historical Beers: The Case of Vossaøl, Norway', *Norsk Geografisk Tidsskrift-Norwegian Journal of Geography*, 71 (2017), 301-12 (p. 304) <10.1080/00291951.2017.1395909>; and S. Haslund, '*Bygget som ølkorn i det vestlandske havreområdet*', in *Or Noregs Bondesoge*, ed. by S. Haslund (Oslo: Norges Boklag, 1942), p. 223).
3. Bråtå, pp. 301-12; M.W. Patterson and N. Hoalst-Pullen, 'Geographies of Beer', in *The Geography of Beer*, ed. by M.W. Patterson and N. Hoalst-Pullen (New York: Springer, 2014), pp. 1-5; S.M. Schnell and J.F. Reese, 'Microbreweries, Place, and Identity in the United States', in *The Geography of Beer*, ed. by M.W. Patterson and N. Hoalst-Pullen (New York: Springer, 2014), pp. 167-87.
4. Kåre Lunden, *1350-1814 Frå svartedauen til 17. mai. Norsk landbrukshistorie II* (Oslo: Samlaget, 2002), pp. 188-89; N. Ødegaard, *Kristians amt 1814-1914* (Kristiania: Grøndahl & Søn boktrykkeri, 1918), p. 134.
5. Bjørnstad, p. 154; Ingunn Holm, '*Skogfinsk og norsk svedjetradisjon*', *Heimen*, 50 (2013), 162-77.
6. S. Haslund, '*Det norske landbruks historie*', in *En samlet fremstilling av læren om landbruket, dets forskjellige grener*, ed. by N. Ødegaard (Kristiania: Aschehoug, 1919), p. 87; Holm, pp. 170-72.
7. Erich Pontoppidan, *Det første forsøg paa Norges Naturlige Historie* (København: Berlingske Arvingers Bogtryggeri, 1752), p. 169.
8. B.C. de Fines, '*Stavanger Amptes udførlige Beskrivelse 1745*', in *Skrifter og optegnelser angaaende Norge og forfattere efter reformationen*, ed. by N. Nicolaysen (Christiana: Johan Dahls Forlag, 1870), p. 119; P.P. Flor, *Oekonomisk Reise til Lister og Jedderen foretagen i Efteraaret 1810* ([n.p.]: Norges Vel, 1812), p. 88; Joh. Fredrik Wilhelm Schlegel, *Statistisk Beskrivelse av de fornæmste europeiske stater* (Kjøbenhavn: Boghandler Mallings Forlag, 1793), p. 207; Knut Vik, *Åker og engdyrking* (Oslo: Aschehoug & Co, 1937), p. 99; J.N. Wilse, *Physisk. Oeconomisk og Statistisk Beskrivelse over Spydeberg Præstegield og Egn i Aggershuus-Stift i Norge* (Christiania: C. E. Schwch, 1779), p. 207.
9. Jens Essendop, *Physisk Oeconomisk Beskrivelse over Lier Præstegield i Aggershus stift i Norge* (Kjøbenhavn: [n.pub], 1761), p. 57; Andreas Vevelstad, *Aust-Agder Landbruksselskap gjennom 150 år* (Kristiansand: Fædrelandsvennens trykkeri, 1981), pp. 25-26; Vik, p. 104. Although Vik's table is supposed to present experiments in the years 1914-1935, one column in the table refers to 1905 as the year of experiments with Thorebygg; Nils Ødegaard, *Jordbrukslære* (Kristiania: Aschehoug & Co, 1924), pp. 386-87.
10. Tore Ey, *Vang og Slidre* (Kristiania: Nikolai Olsens Boktrykkeri, 1916), p. 51, p. 88; Thor Hexeberg, '*Gardshistorie for Sørli*', *Sørum-Speilet*, 11 (2005). p. 13; Jonas Ramus, *Norriges Beskrivelse* (Kjøbenhavn: [n.pub], 1715), p. 69; Thorleif Solberg, *Tingbok for Ringerike, Bok 33, 1686* < http://ringerike-slektshistorielag.com/images/Tingbok/1686.pdf> [accessed 30 April 2018].
11. T.H. Aschehoug, *Statistiske studier over folkemængde og jordbrug i Norges landdistrikter i det syttende og attende aarhundrede* (Kristiania: H. Aschehoug, 1890), p. 167; Haslund (1942), pp. 222-23; Olav Klokk, *Oversigt over det norske landbruks utvikling siden 1750* (Kristiania: Helge Erichsen, 1920), pp. 42-43.
12. Klokk, pp. 42-43.

Seeds

13   Klokk, p. 43.
14   Peter Elieson, *Haandbog for begyndene Landmænd i Norge* (Christiania: Jacob Lehmann, 1835), pp. 28-29.
15   Røyken Historielag <http://historielaget.no/global/upload/NBPPQ/files/Formannskapsprotokoller.pdf> [accessed 30 April 2018]; Vik, p. 104.
16   Ascheoug, pp. 140-41; Yngvil Beyer, *Christiane Koren Dagbok 1809* (Oslo: Nasjonalbiblioteket/bokskap.no, 2017) <http://www.bokselskap.no/boker/koren1809/junj> [accessed 30 April 2018]; Hans Glømme, *Jordbunden I Buskerud fylke* (Kristiania: Grøndahl & Søn Boktryggeri, 1921), p. 156; Haslund (1919), pp. 86-88; Amund Helland, *Topografisk-Statistisk Beskrivelse over Kristians Amt* (Kristiania: Aschehoug & Co, 1913), p. 500; Klokk, p. 11; Simen Skappel, *Træk av Det Norske Agerbrugs Historie i tidsrummet 1660-1814* (Kristiania: Grøndahl & Søns Bogtrykkeri, 1904), pp. 19, 53; Ødegaard (1918), p. 114; Kristian Østberg, *Norsk Bonderet* (Kristiania: Johan E. Schoubyes Boktrykkeri, 1918) p. 114; Wilse, pp. 207-08.
17   N. A. Dahl, *Aas Herred* (Kristiania: Grøndahl & Søn Boktrykkeri, 1916) p. 12; Elieson, p. 28; Jens Kraft, *Topographiske-Statistiske Beskrivelse over Agershuus Amt* (Christiania: Chr. Grøndahl, 1820), pp. 255-58; Stange Historielag, *Generalmajor Peder von Todderud sin annotiationsbog fra Aggrgaard 1749-1772* (Stange: Stange Historielag, 1998), pp. 1-77; Vik, p. 104.
18   Stange Historielag, pp 1-77; Wilse, pp. 207-08.
19   Elieson, pp. 28-29; Flor (1812), p. 88.
20   Essendrop, p. 57; Christian Sommerfeldt, *Agerdyrknings-katekismus, eller Grundregler for et Retskaffent Jordbrug i Norge* (Kiøbenhavn: R. Møller, 1779), p. 86; Hans Jacob Wille, *Beskrivelse over Sillejords Præstegield i Øvre-Tellemarken i Norge* (Kiøbenhavn: Gyldendals forlag, 1786), p. 183.
21   Essendrop, p. 58; Pontoppidan, p. 169; Anton B. Rustad, *Skogerboken. Herredets Historie mv* (Drammen: Fremtiden trykkeri, 1931) p. 641; Schlegel, p. 207; Sommerfeldt, p. 86; Wilse (1779), pp. 373-76. One barrel is equivalent to 138.97 litres, and one quarter is equivalent to 34.71 litres (Ødegaard (1918), p. 134).
22   Nordland, p. 21. Nordland refers to sources which explain that if oat and barley were mixed and left for sprouting together, the barley would have developed sprouts that were too long because it sprouted more easily than oat. This might have given the ale an unwanted, bad taste.
23   Mitterpacher, p. 228; Pontoppidan, p. 169.
24   Essendrop, p. 57; G. Graarud, *Holmestrandiana, 3die Del av Holmestands Historie* (Holmestrand: Jarlsbergs Bok og Akcidens Trykkeri, 1929), p. 267; Bartholomæus Herman von Løvenskiold, *Beskrivelse over Bradsbierg Amt og Scheens Bye med fine Forsteder* (Christiana: Bogtrykker Bergs Forlag, 1784), p. 59; Stange Historielag, pp. 48, 61.
25   '*Side:Norges land og folk - Hedemarkens amt 1.djvu/874*', *Wikikilden* <https://no.wikisource.org/wiki/Side:Norges_land_og_folk_-_Hedemarkens_amt_1.djvu/874> [accessed 22 April 2018]; '*Formannskapsprotokoller*', *Røyken Historielag* <http://historielaget.no/global/upload/NBPPQ/files/Formannskapsprotokoller.pdf> [accessed 24 April 2018].
26   Examples are found in the newspapers *Morgenbladet*, 28 May 1823 (No. 148) and 31 May 1823 (No. 151), and *Den Constitutionelle*, 13 September 1843 (No. 256).
27   Anders Christophersen Hammer, *Norske Calendarium Oeconomicim* (Grans præstegård: the author, 1724; repr. Oslo: Norsk Folkemuseum, 1957) p. 94-97; Nordland, p. 2.
28   Bråtå, pp. 301-12.
29   Norwegian farmers used to sort the grain into two or three categories by throwing the grain towards a wall. The heaviest grains flew the longest distance and landed close to the wall (*veggen*). That grain was called *veggjeronde* and was used for brewing or for making the best porridge (see, for example, K. Tjønnås, *Gransheradsoga. Del II Kulturhistorie* (Notodden: Notodden kommune), pp. 822-23.
30   Hans Olav Bråtå and Merethe Lerfald, *Maten og matproduktene i Gudbrandsdalen. Historiske hovedtrekk siden steinalderen* (Lillehammer: Østlandsforskning, 2012), p. 137.

Seeds in the Story of the Paradise of Pleasure and the Myth of the So-Called Mediterranean Diet

Adrian Bregazzi

This paper explores the functions of seeds in the story of the paradise of pleasure (St Jerome's preference to 'a garden in Eden', and the descriptor used in Catholic bibles until the late twentieth century), and the myth of the so-called Mediterranean Diet, rather than seeds in a primarily agricultural or culinary context. It then explores the conceptual and ideological similarities between the paradise of pleasure and the aspirations embodied in the so-called Mediterranean Diet.[1]

The paper acknowledges the mutually exclusive polysemy of seed as both a begetter of more seeds and itself destroyed as a source of nutrition, and refers to seed in metaphorical uses derived from interpretations/employment of seed defined as an embryonic plant enclosed in a protective outer covering, a unit of reproduction of a flowering plant, capable of developing into another such plant. For this paper 'seeds' will include grains; peas, beans and other legumes; nuts; and seeds themselves.

The paper will draw comparisons between interpretations of life in the paradise of pleasure and the so-called Mediterranean Diet's projections as authentic and traditional, as a panacea, of 'living the life', and dreamy sun-drenched places where nothing ever happens.

A Paradise of Pleasure

St Jerome's late fourth-century Latin Bible, the *Versio Vulgata*, was composed from Hebrew and Greek sources, and was the official Latin text for the Western Church until the late twentieth century. It mentions neither a Garden nor an Eden, which were both integral to the original Hebrew text.[2] Instead, the literal translation of his Genesis 2.8 reads, 'And the Lord God had planted a paradise of pleasure from the beginning: wherein he placed man whom he had formed' ('*plantaverat autem Dominus Deus paradisum voluptatis a principio in quo posuit hominem quem formaverat*' (*Versio Vulgata*)).[3] Decisions at Vatican II (1962-1965) meant that Jerome's text was replaced in 1979 by the *Nova Vulgata*, which reverted to the more familiar '*paradisum in Eden*'.[4]

However, in the Douay bible, which for Catholics was the English source of the scriptures from 1609 BCE until the late twentieth century, the generative function of seeds appears early in the first chapter of Genesis:

> And he said: Let the earth bring forth the green herb, and such as may seed, and the fruit tree yielding fruit after its kind, which may have seed in itself upon the earth. And it was done
> And the earth brought forth the green herb, and such as yieldeth seed according to its kind, and the tree that beareth fruit, having seed each one according to its kind. And God saw that it was good. (Genesis 1.11-12)

And:

> God created man to his own image, to the image of God he created him. Male and female he created them. [...]
> And God said, Behold, I have given you every herb bearing seed upon the earth, and all trees that have in themselves seed of their own kind, to be your meat. (Genesis 1.27-29)[5]

Thus, the diet ('meat') of the occupants of paradise was based wholly on fruit, the previously mentioned good seeds and herbs, and food from the miracle Tree of Life; all of which are indicators of the eternal fecundity of paradise and its occupants.[6] As the Qur'an succinctly states, 'It is Allah Who causeth the seed-grain and the date-stone to split and sprout. He causeth the living to issue from the dead, and He is the one to cause the dead to issue from the living. That is Allah: then how are ye deluded away from the truth?' (Qur'an 6:95 Sūrat Al-Anām).[7]

The Tree of Life makes a second appearance in Douay towards the very end of Apocalypse, providing an insight into later thinking and to the possibility of seasonality in paradise, and ways plants could overcome such restrictions to be continuously available:

> And he shewed me a river of water of life, clear as crystal, proceeding from the throne of God and the Lamb.
> In the midst of the street thereof, and on both sides of the river, was the tree of life, bearing twelve fruits, yielding its fruits every month; and the leaves of the tree were for the healing of the nations. (Apocalypse 22.1-2)

However, from a twenty-first century perspective, the fascinating implication of verse 29 is that all the Earth's plant life had been created for all climates and on all continents, whether these were known or unknown to the authors and early audiences of the Torah.[8] Thus, all the New World ingredients that would become integral to foods of countries of the Mediterranean littoral after their 'discovery' in the fifteenth century, those that could flourish in local climates and in the ideal climate of paradise, were, within the narrative of the Creation, already available to the original inhabitants of the paradise of pleasure.[9] Furthermore, while the early audiences of the Torah would have had vivid ideas on what paradise could be like, the availability of as yet unknown foods along with the fruits of the two enchanted trees prompts the possibility that these

Seeds in the Story of the Paradise of Pleasure

audiences, and even the authors, could imagine the existence of other fabulous foods in paradise that could sustain the inhabitants beyond the limited means of its indicative raw veganism. This fabulousness is further enhanced by one of the rivers flowing out of paradise and watering 'all the land of Hevilath, where gold groweth' (Genesis 2.10,12).

Genesis 2.9-10 continues:

> And the Lord God brought forth of the ground all manner of trees, fair to behold, and pleasant to eat of; the tree of life also in the midst of paradise: and the tree of knowledge of good and evil.
> And a river went out of the place of pleasure to water paradise, which from thence is divided into four heads.

And Genesis 2.15-17:

> And the Lord God took the man and put him in the paradise of pleasure, to dress it and to keep it.
> And he commanded him, saying; Of every tree of paradise thou shalt eat;
> But the tree of knowledge of good and evil, thou shalt not eat. For in what day soever thou shalt eat of it, thou shalt die the death.

While 'to dress it and to keep it' ('*custodiret illum*' = to maintain/preserve it) could be interpreted as implying that tools were made available, improbably even fashioned by Adam himself, it is more feasible that this should instruct conceptually that some form of labour was integral to paradise, that life could not be fulfilled by lounging around, however appealing that may seem to be. Sloth was stigmatized from the very beginning.[10]

It is also fascinating to consider that while the nomothete Adam gave names to all living creatures 'the same as its name', and these animals resided outside the walls of the paradise of pleasure, the elements of the plant kingdom within (and without) remained nameless (save for the two miracle trees), and thus all food was nameless in this paradise of namelessness.[11]

The first instance of any form of cookery in the bible is in the curse uttered on the expulsion of Adam and Eve from paradise, that, 'In the sweat of thy face shalt thou eat bread till thou return to the earth' (Genesis 3.19). The lengthy and arduous processes essential to making bread, from sowing seeds, through gathering and milling grain, to baking, were all understood first-hand by many of the original audiences of the text. And this comparatively grim outlook had itself been preceded by 'cursed is the earth in thy work; with labour and toil shalt thou eat thereof all the days of thy life. Thorns and thistles shall it bring forth to thee; and thou shalt eat the herbs of the earth' (Genesis 3.17-18). Those previously benign herbs of the earth that were 'meat' in paradise have themselves now become cursed with thorns.

These terse passages, first cast in the earliest Torah in the fifth century BCE, are based on significantly redacted written and oral narratives and provide little but for the imagination that would not have been difficult for the original intended audience, many of whom demurred urban life in favour of pastoral or agrarian lives in an often arid environment.[12] The Torah's *Gan ʿEden* (גַּן עֵדֶן) would have been seen as the epitome of a self-sufficient sanctuary of sweet running water, with copious seed-bearing plants and fruitful shade-giving trees offering unlimited fresh food in a perfect climate. In the long view, this was a wholly vegan precursor to the post-Fall land flowing with milk and honey in Exodus.[13]

The very absence of any detailed description in Genesis was seized upon and employed by the Western Church to create rich seams of guilt in all its believers. It also spawned energetic elaboration by religious scholars, and in the arts popularly demonstrated in the left-hand panel of Hieronymus Bosch's *Garden of Earthly Delights* (1490-1510) and in John Milton's *Paradise Lost* (1667-1674).[14]

Seeds come from fruit that come from seeds – the eternal cycle of life. But seed also has a fundamental and mutually exclusive polysemy – a seed is something that is both planted to generate more seeds/fruit containing seeds, but also something that is eaten by humans and generally destroyed in cooking and/or digestion, echoing the Fall. Whence, having been driven from paradise into the thorns and thistles, the fabled holotypes, no longer innocent and amoral, laboured making bread, released their own seeds, and the begetting began.

The Mediterranean Diet

From the outset the so-called Mediterranean Diet was an American invention primarily for an American audience seen to be in need of dietary improvement.

The so-called Mediterranean Diet has its ideological genesis in one man's preconceptions and flawed research undertaken in Crete, Corfu, and Calabria in the early 1960s, when Ancel Keys determined that apparent longevity in working communities was attributed to diets heavy in olive oil.[15] (Olive oil is essentially a fruit juice pressed from the mesocarp of a pit/seed-bearing drupe.) Indeed, the source data referenced thereafter for the entire burgeoning Mediterranean Diet business were based on selected data relating to less than seventy men across Crete and Corfu.[16]

After a long period of gestation, the Diet was realized and quickly rose to fame in the USA after the 1993 launch of the Mediterranean Diet Pyramid, created by an alliance of Oldways (a Boston-based advocacy organization), the Harvard Medical School, and the World Health Organization.[17] This graphically displayed the Diet's original commandments. The Diet subsequently became a fully commodified cultural phenomenon in affluent Western societies world-wide after saturation promotion organized by Oldways, aided by substantial financial backing from the (then) International Olive Oil Council and a plethora of media attention, books, and diverse food products.[18] The Oldways pyramid underwent a significant overhaul in 2009.[19]

So successful was the Oldways promotion of the Mediterranean Diet that it eclipsed the Whole Food/Natural Food movements formed in the Rachel Carson and anti-Big

Seeds in the Story of the Paradise of Pleasure

Food-inspired counter cultures of the USA in the 1960s – whose popularity had realized the whole food/health food shops and sections in supermarkets across the USA that were crucial in providing the whole grains, legumes, nuts, and seeds essential to the foundation food layer of the Oldways pyramid.[20] Indeed, it is difficult to understand how the Oldways Mediterranean Diet could ever have taken off without the precedence of those Whole Food/Natural Food movements.

Ironically, those movements were more concerned with seeking out the values of old ways than Oldways would ever be. In 1971, Jean Hewitt waxed lyrical about natural foods:

> In Grandmother's day, fresh home-grown fruits and vegetables gave seasonal flavor and food value to soups, stews and desserts and were lovingly canned or turned into jams, jellies and pickles for year-round enjoyment. The cookie jar was always filled with homemade oatmeal and raisin cookies made with honey from the hives in the hollow and eggs from chickens scratching in the yard. [...] Sacks and barrels at the general store were filled with unrefined and unprocessed ingredients that had a short shelf-life but lots of flavor.[21]

Crucially, in contrast to the conceptually locative Mediterranean Diet, Hewitt does not describe Natural Foods exclusively in terms of what might then have been considered as American food – Natural Foods are not geographically delimited in that sense. Indeed, she is keen to point out that many of the ingredients used in her cookbook would be unknown to 'Grandmother', highlighting grains and seaweeds that were now available: 'The Chinese mastered the glories of soybeans, bean curd and fermented bean pastes in cooking; Indians and other Far-Eastern peoples have used millet; seaweeds are standard in the traditional Japanese diet.'[22] And she is not describing nor promoting a Diet, nor attributing curative/preventative powers to Natural Foods, rather:

> Above all, the dishes made from these recipes can furnish a varied, well-balanced diet based on four main groups: fruits and vegetables; dairy products; meat, fish and other protein sources; grains and cereals. The emphasis is on the flavor potential and nutritional value of the ingredients, and not on any specific benefits that may be attributed to them. No claims are made here for natural and organic eating as miracle cures for any disease or condition.[23]

This refusal to claim 'miracle cures' is in marked contrast to Oldways' developing list of the health promises of the traditional Mediterranean Diet. Since the birthing of its pyramid, it claims that 'hundreds if not thousands' of scientific studies show that 'eating the Med way may':

- Lengthen your life
- Improve brain function
- Defend you from chronic diseases

- Fight certain cancers
- Lower your risk of heart disease, high blood pressure, and elevated 'bad' cholesterol levels
- Protect you from diabetes
- Aid your weight loss and management efforts
- Keep away depression
- Safeguard you from Alzheimer's disease
- Ward off Parkinson's disease
- Improve rheumatoid arthritis
- Improve eye health
- Reduce risk of dental disease
- Help you breathe better
- Lead to healthier babies
- Lead to improved fertility.[24]

The current full-colour (2009) Mediterranean Diet Pyramid provides the delivery system for these impressive health promises in its eight, often ambiguous, commandments:

- Base every meal on fruits, vegetables, grains (mostly whole), olive oil, beans, nuts, legumes and seeds, herbs and spices
- Eat fish and seafood at least twice a week
- Eat moderate portions of poultry, eggs, cheese, and yoghurt daily to weekly
- Eat meats and sweets less often
- Drink [red] wine in moderation
- Drink water
- Be physically active
- Enjoy meals with others.[25]

The simplistic and colourful iconography of this diagram suggests that the health and lifestyle benefits of the Diet are limited to, or maybe lead to, idealized heterosexual sports- and dance-loving families (two adults, two children), probably monogamous, and not engaged in jobs involving physical labour.

Those commandments compare with these from the monochrome 1993 Oldways Optimal Traditional Mediterranean Diet:

- Eat daily: breads and grains including pasta, rice, couscous, polenta, and bulgur; fruits, vegetables; beans, other legumes and nuts; cheese, yogurt & other dairy products; olive oil and olives.
- A few times a week eat fish, poultry/eggs; sweets.
- Eat lean red meat a few times a month.
- Take physical activity daily.
- You can drink up to two glasses of wine per day.[26]

Seeds in the Story of the Paradise of Pleasure

And these guidelines from the 2010 Fundación Dieta Mediterránea Piràmide:

- Every main meal should include 1-2 servings of fruit, 2 servings of vegetables (variety of colours/textures, cooked/raw); olive oil; bread, pasta, rice, couscous, other cereals (preferably whole grain) 1-2 servings
- Every day: 1-2 servings of olives, nuts, seeds; herbs, spices, garlic, onions (less added salt, a variety of flavours; 2 servings of dairy produce (preferably low fat)
- Weekly: 2 servings of white meat; 2 servings of fish/seafood; 2 servings of legumes; 2-4 servings of eggs; 3 servings of potatoes; 1 serving processed meat; 2 servings of red meat; 2 servings of sweets.
- Drink water and herbal infusions; drink wine in moderation and respecting social beliefs.
- Regular physical activity; adequate rest; conviviality.
- Biodiversity and seasonality; traditional, local and eco-friendly products; culinary activities.[27]

The Madrid-based Fundación's quantified, broadened regime reflects its being the currently most active and enthusiastic promoter of the Diet, having taken a lead role in the successful application for UNESCO Intangible Cultural Heritage status for the Mediterranean Diet (for Croatia, Cyprus, Greece, Italy, Morocco, Spain, and Portugal).[28] Unlike Oldways, the Fundación is quite open about its sponsors, who include the wine, dairy, sweets (torron), olive oil, fresh fruit, agricultural industries, and the multinational Danone.[29] Indeed, sponsors are essential for the Fundación's existence.[30]

Thus cereals ('mainly wholegrain'), unprocessed legumes, nuts, fruits, and seeds consensually reside in the foundation food layers of the icon of a Mediterranean Diet Pyramid – as such they are at the conceptual and devotional heart of the Diet ('base every meal on these foods' is the Oldways commandment). This raw, whole, unprocessed nature evinces, but does not realize, a *cuisine pauvre*, the epitome of artisanality in the simulated poverty of eating only what is available locally and in season. In a sense, it serves as an unwitting precursor to the twenty-first century upmarket celebrations of authenticity and tradition in indigenous food and cooking typified by Alex Atala, Rodolfo Guzmán, Virgilio Martínez, Enrique Olvera, and others.[31] This cultural rawness also encourages participants to believe that they can experience what is intended to be seen as the simple, delicious Good Life of Mediterranean coastal communities, however improbable this nostalgia may be. Indeed, this gastronomic transportation to a diaphanous Mediterranean is essential to the cachet of the Diet, as without this illusion the Diet would simply be an anonymous aura-free lifestyle regime. Ironically, in most instances the regime of the stylized Mediterranean Diet Pyramids cannot be afforded by poorer people who can only eat what is available and affordable.[32] Similarly, it is not the diet of the actual peoples of the vast Mediterranean littoral, where a universal diet does not exist.[33] In fact, the Oldways pyramid ignores the majority of Mediterranean littoral countries and was loosely based on aspects of snapshot research into the diets of just parts of Crete and southern Italy, wherein the chosen dietary model could be found.[34]

Ignoring the harsh realities of life (employment or the lack of it, financial stress, war and terrorism, familial dysfunction, among other things – including even the simple realities of acquiring and preparing food), the wide, ambiguous base layer of the pyramid in the current Oldways model is prescriptive of the good-lifestyle elements of the Diet – play, physical activity, team sports, family, social eating, multiculturalism – and simultaneously little short of descriptive of the benefits of the long good life promised by the Diet itself, a secondary myth of a paradise of pleasure, partly delivered by seeds, and in which nothing ever happens.

The Mediterranean Diet as a Paradise of Pleasure

The dominant climate of the Mediterranean littoral is a recognized climate type in its own right: one characterized by warm wet winters influenced by westerly winds, and calm, hot, dry summers. This Mediterranean climate can also be found in parts of Afghanistan, Argentina, south and south-west Australia, California, Chile, Ethiopia, Iran, Iraq, Pakistan, and South Africa. For many, this is the classic, idyllic climate, and – with imagination – the ideal climate of a comfortable paradise of pleasure.

The UNESCO inscription of the Intangible Cultural Heritage of the Mediterranean diet takes the vicissitude-free life much further, creating an abstract vision simply by dissociating the diet from the physical labours of food production. In this idealized world vision those labours just happen, and nobody gets their hands dirty:

> [The diet] involves a set of skills, knowledge, rituals, symbols and traditions concerning crops, harvesting, fishing, animal husbandry, conservation, processing, cooking, and particularly the sharing and consumption of food. Eating together is the foundation of the cultural identity and continuity of communities throughout the Mediterranean basin. It is a moment of social exchange and communication, an affirmation and renewal of family, group or community identity. The Mediterranean diet emphasizes values of hospitality, neighbourliness, intercultural dialogue and creativity, and a way of life guided by respect for diversity.[35]

Clearly this inspirational manifesto is much more than a description of a diet, and while its aims appear to be laudable, if lofty, the motivation behind acquiring the inscription may be more associated with economic development in its nominated countries than with actually achieving any of its cultural aims. Certainly Palestinians in Gaza, Syrians caught up in civil war, immigrants sweltering in the fruit and vegetable poly tunnels of Almeria, and refugees and forced migrants undertaking perilous crossings of the Mediterranean Sea may not see much evidence of values of hospitality, neighbourliness, intercultural dialogue and creativity, or a way of life guided by respect for diversity. Nevertheless, like a spell, the vision is cast.

Seeds in the Story of the Paradise of Pleasure

In 1994, Nancy Harmon Jenkins also painted a romantic view of rustic life in southern Tuscany from the elevated position of her 'rugged stone farmhouse':

> When we first came to live in the valley, our neighbors, like most of their neighbors, had no electricity, no plumbing, no telephone, no tractor or other mechanized means of transportation. A profound and appealing stillness pervaded the valley, broken only by human voices and the rooster's crow. Terraces of wheat, studded with gnarled olive trees and edged with grapevines, marked the contours of the steep hillsides, and around them climbed forests of oak, chestnut, and Aleppo pine.[36]

And later, the food her neighbour dutifully sets out before her family twice a day:

> much of it still grown and harvested on the farm – bread baked in the outside oven, pasta with fresh vegetables from the gardens, chickens and rabbits from the farmyard and pork from the pig that is slaughtered every Christmastime, mushrooms and chestnuts from the forest, and above all olive oil and wine that they still proudly make themselves. They eat, in fact, an almost perfect Mediterranean diet [...].[37]

There is something quite Dolmio-like about this vision of charming bucolic familial simplicity: the 'appealing stillness' of that almost pre-industrial valley may only have been enthralling to the writer who could fly in and out at her leisure.[38]

We are encouraged to conjure up these images of happy families gathering around venerable wooden tables to eat a hearty feast of homemade pasta with homemade tomato sauce, fresh-foraged salad, and homemade robust country bread anointed with their own olive oil, all washed down with a little of their own red wine, in a whitewashed house set against a verdant hillside, topped with an azure sky. These images are what the commodified Mediterranean Diet is all about: 'The temperate isles of the Mediterranean are home to sun, sea and delicious dishes thought to hold the key to good health.'[39] They are where it is hoped that we will imagine ourselves basking and wandering.

Though in the cases of Crete and Calabria, where subsistence farmers provided some of the data employed to realise Oldways Optimal Traditional Mediterranean Diet in 1993, the reality (literally) on the ground was quite different. Shortly before Ancel Keys first visit to Crete in 1953, Leland G. Allbaugh found Cretans openly miserable with their diet – 'we are hungry most of the time' – and meat alone or with cereal was mentioned as a favourite food by 72% of the families questioned.[40] In Calabria in the early 1990s, smallholders and farm labourers thought their diet to be the scourge of poverty and scorned the monotony of vegetables they considered not very nourishing.[41] Subsistence farming is, by definition, all about growing crops that are optimal in both nutrition and yield, with flavour as an additional criterion. Thus, while it is clear that life must have been extremely hard for these folk, it is astonishing that this hardship did not feature in the formative research for the Diet.

Nevertheless, in spite of the harsh realities of life in some of the territories of the Mediterranean littoral, even some of its simple realities, and in spite of the harsh realities of one's own life as an outsider to these territories, the Mediterranean Diet itself relies on a level of acceptance of an idealized, illusory, and diaphanous place whose formative epicentre is itself bound up in historic myth. Full subscription to the Diet – its authentic, sanitized, and gentrified confection of simple carbohydrate-rich traditional 'peasant' foods founded on seeds in the form of whole grains, peas, beans and other legumes, nuts, and seeds themselves; its aspirations and its apparent promises – is, in its mythic way, a latter day interpretation of a bounteous paradise of pleasure in which food just is (sans shopping, preparation and cooking, cleaning up), all is wonderful (including the weather), there is no issue with money, and nothing ever happens.

Of course, this is unattainable: this is the essence and purpose of myth.

Notes

1. I will be referencing two primary sources of iconographic and ideological foundations for the so-called Mediterranean Diet: the Fundación Dieta Mediterránea <https://dietamediterranea.com/en/nutrition/> and Oldways Preservation and Exchange Trust <https://oldwayspt.org/traditional-diets/mediterranean-diet> [both accessed 20 May 2018].
2. There is no mention of paradise as such in the Torah (ScriptureforAll.org <http://www.scripture4all.org/OnlineInterlinear/OTpdf/gen2.pdf> [accessed 20 May 2018]).
3. Unless otherwise stated the Douay bible (1609) will be the source for English translation (Imprimatur Bernardus Cardinalis Griffin, 1955); *Versio Vulgata* <http://vulgate.org/ot/genesis_2.htm> [accessed 20 May 2018].
4. Latin-English Interlinear (*Nova Vulgata*) Bible, Archive.org <https://archive.org/details/INTERLINNovaVulgata> [accessed 20 May 2018]. The 1985 New Jerusalem Bible, claiming to be the most widely used Roman Catholic Bible outside the United States, omits paradise entirely, favouring: 'Yahweh God planted a garden in Eden, which is in the east, and there he put the man he had fashioned.' <https://www.catholic.org/bible/book.php?id=1&bible_chapter=2> [accessed 20 May 2018].
5. Both Douay (1609) and the King James Bible (1611) render 'meat' here, though the *Versio Vulgata* and *Nova Vulgata* both cite *escam* (food): '*ut sint vobis in escam*' ('as food for you').
6. This passage is annotated in Douay as '[t]he tree of life' – so called because it had that quality, that by eating of the fruit of it, man would have been preserved in a constant state of health, vigour, and strength, and would not have died at all.
7. Abdullah Yousuf Ali translation <https://quran.com/6/95?translations=18,21,84,85,17,19,22,101> [accessed 20 May 2018].
8. By oral tradition the Torah (הָרוּת) has Mosaic origins and thus dates from the fourteenth century BCE. It forms the first five books of the Hebrew bible.
9. I am employing 'Mediterranean littoral' as shorthand for 'Mediterranean Sea littoral'.
10. Christian authors took a different view of physical inactivity. Gregory of Nyssa (c. 332-395 BCE) wrote, 'Contemplating the glory of God – boundless, incomprehensible, and utterly overwhelming – was what filled his days and night. […] God was everywhere and everything. […] When Eve offered him the forbidden fruit […] Adam immediately took it and ate it. Why? "I am exhausted," he said to himself. "I want to return now to the clay from which I was made. I want to die"; Martin Luther (1483-1546) took this a stage further, suggesting that Adam may have answered 'why?' with 'An eternity in this

condition is unendurable. I hate the contemplation of the One who made me. I hate the overwhelming debt of gratitude. I hate God' (qtd. in Stephen Greenblatt, *The Rise and Fall of Adam & Eve* (London: Bodley Head, 2017), pp. 305-09.

11   See Umberto Eco, *Languages in Paradise, in Serendipities, Language & Lunacy* (London: Weidenfeld & Nicolson, 1999), pp. 23-52.
12   For a discussion and further references on redaction in the Torah, see Greenblatt, pp. 35-38, 329-30.
13   Exodus 3.8: 'and to bring them out of that land into a good and spacious land, into a land that floweth with milk and honey'.
14   For a summary of scholarly debate, see Greenblatt, pp. 303-11.
15   Ancel Keys, qtd. in Nina Teicholz, *The Big Fat Surprise* (London: Scribe, 2015), pp. 176-78.
16   Teicholz, pp. 217-18. Keys's findings are summarized by Sara Baer-Sinnott: 'When the data were examined, it was clear that people who ate a diet where fruits and vegetables, grains, beans, and fish were the basis of daily meals were healthiest. Topping the chart were residents of Crete. Even after the deprivations of World War II – and in part, perhaps, because of them – the cardiovascular health of Crete residents exceeded that of US residents. Researchers attributed the differences to diet' ('How the Mediterranean Pyramid Came to Life', *Oldways Cultural Food Traditions*, 2 May 2017 <https://oldwayspt.org/blog/how-mediterranean-pyramid-came-life> [accessed 20 May 2018]).
17   Like the USDA Pyramid of 1992, the Oldways Pyramid is a two-dimensional triangle <https://oldwayspt.org/traditional-diets/mediterranean-diet> [accessed 20 May 2018]. For a detailed history of the Oldways pyramid from an Oldways perspective, see K. Dun Gifford and Sara Baer-Sinnott, *The Oldways Table* (Berkeley, CA: Ten Speed Press, 2007), pp. 1-13.
18   Teicholz, pp 193-97. For an example of how commodification occurs, the baby food company Piccolo links its Mediterranean Goodness products to '[t]he temperate isles of the Mediterranean [that] are home to sun, sea and delicious dishes thought to hold the key to good health' ('Mediterranean Goodness', *Piccolo*, 25 February 2017 <https://www.mylittlepiccolo.com/blogs/news/124533191-mediterranean-goodness> [accessed 20 May 2018].
19   'Mediterranean Diet', Oldways Cultural Food Traditions <https://oldwayspt.org/traditional-diets/mediterranean-diet> [accessed 20 May 2018].
20   Rachel Carson's *Silent Spring*, first published in 1962, helped initiate global environmental movements and the appreciation of organic farming by highlighting the effects of the then indiscriminate use of pesticides on the environment.
21   Jean Hewitt, *The New York Times Natural Foods Cookbook* (London: Souvenir Press, 1972), p. i.
22   Hewitt, p. i.
23   Hewitt, p. ii.
24   'Mediterranean Diet'.
25   'Mediterranean Diet'.
26   Teicholz, p. 187.
27   'What's the Mediterranean Diet?', *Fundación Dieta Mediterránea* <https://dietamediterranea.com/en/nutrition/> [accessed 20 May 2018]. A serving size is 'based on frugality and local habits'.
28   'Mediterranean Diet', UNESCO, 2013 <https://ich.unesco.org/en/Rl/mediterranean-diet-00884> [accessed 20 May 2018].
29   'What Is the Foundation?' *Fundación Dieta Mediterránea* <https://dietamediterranea.com/en/fundacion/> [accessed 20 May 2018]. Oldways remains quiet about its relationship to Big Sugar: it convened a conference in Mexico City on 'Sweetness, Sugar, and Health', sponsored by Coca-Cola and other sugar-related companies. The conference concluded that the 'biological preference for sweetness is universal' and that 'sugars and all approved lo-caloric and non-caloric sweeteners are safe, and they offer useful options that help consumers manage sweetness' (Thomas O. McGarity and Wendy E Wagner, *Bending Science: How Special Interests Corrupt Public Heath* (Cambridge, MA: Harvard University Press, 2010), p. 198).
30   Teicholz, pp. 211-12.

31 It is noteworthy that these dietary regimes largely ignore honey, fungi, foraging, game, offal, and religious dietary restrictions.
32 Marialaura Bonaccio and others, 'High Adherence to the Mediterranean Diet Is Associated with Cardiovascular Protection in Higher but not in Lower Socioeconomic Groups: Prospective Findings from the Moli-sani Study', *International Journal of Epidemiology*, 46.5 (1 October 2017), 1478-87 <10.1093/ije/dyx145>.
33 Teicholz, pp. 180-81.
34 Teicholz, p. 185.
35 'Mediterranean Diet', UNESCO.
36 Nancy Harmon Jenkins, *The Mediterranean Diet Cookbook* (New York: Bantam Books, 1994), p. xii.
37 Jenkins, p. xii.
38 For fifteen years the Mars-owned Dolmio brand employed a cast of stereotyped Italian family members in its advertising (Rebecca Smithers, 'When'sa Your Dolmio Day? "Occasionally", New Labels to Say', *The Guardian*, 14 April 2016 <https://www.theguardian.com/money/2016/apr/14/dolmio-pasta-meal-kits-mars-occasional-food-warning-health> [accessed 20 May 2018].
39 'Mediterranean Goodness', *Piccolo*.
40 Leland G Allbaugh, *Crete: A Case Study for an Underdeveloped Area* (Princeton, NJ: Princeton University Press, 1953), pp. 100, 105.
41 Vito Teti, 'Food and Fatness in Calabria', in *Social Aspects of Obesity #1* (Amsterdam: Gordon and Breach, 1995), qtd. in Teicholz pp. 220-21.

Neapolitan *Pastiera* and the Religious Significance of Wheatberries

Anthony F. Buccini

Introduction

Little known outside Italy, one of the most beloved dishes of Naples and Campania is a sweet preparation that traditionally is closely, almost exclusively, associated with the celebration of Easter: *pastiera* is a pie made with a pastry crust and filled with sweetened and well-scented ricotta, eggs, candied fruit, and, in its most prized and presumably most traditional version, cooked whole wheatberries. This inclusion of whole wheatberries is striking, for their use in Italy's cuisines is very limited and typically has decidedly rustic associations. Yet *pastiera* is a dish that has belonged to the culinary repertoire of elite circles associated with Naples at least since the Angevin period (1266-1442), a relationship clearly reflected in the origins of the dish's usual name. Direct textual evidence for the cookery of the non-elite is typically lacking before the nineteenth century, but earlier indirect, literary evidence shows that *pastiera* has for centuries been a dish popular with the lower echelons of society and, as I demonstrate here, its ultimate origins surely lie in their culinary culture. Indeed, the characteristic use of whole wheatberries fits into a pattern with other dishes all bearing religious significance in various places in southern Italy, the ancient *Magna Graecia*, and in turn these dishes have close analogues in Greece and other lands which through the Orthodox religion have undergone Greek cultural influence. The history of *pastiera* thus offers us a striking instance of the role of solemn festivities as a contact point between high and low socio-cultural strata in a strongly hierarchical society.

Pastiera in Naples and Campania in Recent Times

A central part of the traditional culinary culture of Naples is acceptance of communally established and generationally transferred recipes, and the generally accepted limits on variation which a given recipe admits. This attitude does not stifle culinary creativity, which always has room for expression in many contexts, but it does make it possible to maintain a core culinary base with which the community identifies and takes deep pride in; in this way, culinary change is hardly precluded, but it is slowed down. As argued in previous work, nowhere in a cuisine are the brakes on change stronger than in the area of foods associated with solemn festivities (Buccini 2013: 97, 2015a:

334). In general – and especially for the lower ranks of society – joyous festivities strongly tend to be occasions where a cuisine is particularly open to innovation and the incorporation of new or alien foodstuffs and dishes. *Pastiera* is a dish associated with Easter, the most important and joyous of holidays in southern Italy, but, as I demonstrate below, it is an extraordinary dish in that it is also closely tied to the last days of Lent, the most solemn days of the Christian calendar. It is worthwhile to bear these points in mind during the following discussion.[1]

Pastiera in its 'Classic' Form

As one would expect, there is a core recipe for *pastiera tout court* (also referred to as '*pastiera napoletana*') which admits relatively little variation if it is to deserve the name in the eyes of most Campanians.

The pie is made with a *pasta frolla* crust, traditionally with lard, though butter has gradually entered into the recipe as an acceptable alternative. One of the three principal ingredients of the filling is fresh ricotta, typically made with the whey from sheep's milk though in areas where ricotta is produced from other kinds of milk (e.g. buffalo milk), that is also used. Eggs reinforced with a couple of extra yolks are another central ingredient. The third main ingredient is the most characteristic one, namely cooked whole wheatberries (*grano cotto*) of the common variety (*grano tenero, triticum aestivum*). A fairly recent accommodation to the pace of modern life is the use of *grano cotto* purchased in jars, but to be true to tradition one prepares the grain oneself, a process which involves two to three days of soaking and cooking the grain until it is tender but still whole; the soaking is long, with multiple changes of water, and the cooking is then reasonably short, though with dry grains of wheat the times vary according to various factors. Some recipes call for soaking and then cooking in two stages, first in water and then in milk; the cooking in milk sometimes includes also other ingredients such as lard, sugar, and vanilla. If one purchases pre-cooked grain, one proceeds directly to cooking the wheatberries in milk.

Preparation of the filling involves beating the ricotta with a good dose of sugar until it is smooth, further mixing with the eggs and cooked grain and the flavourings. Of these the essentials are grated lemon and/or orange zest; candied fruit, especially *cedro* (citron), orange, and/or *cucuzzata* (squash); and a dose of orange blossom water. A pinch of cinnamon is included by many cooks. A recent development employed by some is the further addition to the filling of some *crema pasticcera* (custard) made with milk/cream, flour, egg yolk, sugar, and vanilla, which is acceptable to traditionalists as a supplement to, but not as a replacement for, the ricotta.

The pie is decorated with strips of the same dough used for the base, arranged most often to form a diamond-pattern lattice top (a straight cross pattern is sometimes used) before it is cooked in an oven. A widespread final touch to the cooked pie is a dusting of powdered sugar.

Neapolitan *Pastiera* and the Religious Significance of Wheatberries

For many Campanian families the preparation of *pastiera* and other (especially savoury) pies that are part of the Easter celebration is very much part of the overall holiday experience. Of course, one can also buy traditional versions from pastry shops, and, not surprisingly, many shops offer *pastiera* not just at Easter but also at other times of the year. Professional pastry chefs commonly offer versions that are less traditional, for example, adding chocolate bits to the filling or using *crema pasticcera* as a principal element in the filling.

Other variants on the classic recipe include replacing the wheatberries with rice or farro (which refers actually to three 'ancient' grains: spelt, emmer, einkorn). Barley is also used nowadays to make otherwise traditional *pastiere* in many emigrant communities, e.g. in the United States.

Related Dishes Bearing the Name '*Pastiera*'

Throughout Campania there exists alongside *pastiera napoletana* a closely related family of dishes: *pastiera di pasta*, though that appellation is relatively rarely encountered. More usual are names in which the qualification specifies the form of pasta used: *pastiera di tagliolini, tagliatelle, maccherone, fedellini,* etc.

The most striking difference between the two families of *pastiere* is the use of whole grain (wheat, rice, barley) in the one and the use of a boiled form of dough in the other, a change which not only renders the two very different with regard to flavour and texture but also, as discussed below, alters the symbolic character of the dish. Ricotta is not used in the pasta-based *pastiere*; rather, the boiled pasta sits in a bath of milk and beaten egg which is largely absorbed before the final baking. The flavouring agents, however, are generally similar to those used in the classic *pastiera*: an ample amount of sugar, candied fruit, lemon and/or orange zest, vanilla, cinnamon, and a flower-based essence (orange blossom water or millefiori).

Grano cotto: A Matter of Life and Death

As mentioned above, the use of whole grain – wheatberries and farro – have long been associated with rustic cookery or cookery of the poor; one thinks, for example, of the dish *mesc-ciua* of the mountainous area of eastern Liguria.[2] Use of whole grains has surely survived in some dishes in part because their flavour and texture are highly appreciated, but, from a practical point of view, the energy saved in not milling the grain is offset by the longer preparation times required for soaking and cooking. In Italy, a land where porridges of cracked or milled grain, bread, and pasta have been staples since classical antiquity, the choice – in effect – to go back in time and consume whole grain, especially the more slowly prepared wheatberries, is in some sense an extraordinary act. While some wheatberry dishes, such as *mesc-ciua*, may owe their survival primarily to aesthetic considerations or their value in representing local identity, others have or once had (in addition) a strong religious motivation, and in southern Italy the religious connection is particularly strong.

Other Wheatberry Dishes of Southern Italy

A wheatberry dish still popular in parts of Puglia (especially in and around Foggia) is called *grano dei morti*, 'grain of the dead', or in dialect *cicc cuott*, 'cooked kernels'. Typically this dish contains boiled wheatberries, pomegranate seeds, walnuts, and bits of chocolate, and is dressed with sugar and sweet, syrupy *vincotto* (greatly reduced and caramelized grape juice). *Grano dei morti* is traditionally consumed on All Souls' Day.

Another sweet dish featuring cooked whole wheatberries is associated most often with Sicilian cuisine and called *cuccìa*, but dishes bearing the same name are encountered in many communities in the continental south, throughout Calabria and on into Basilicata to the northeast and southern Campania to the north. In Sicily there are several sweet variants, ranging in richness from just wheatberries sweetened with sugar and grape must to a preparation in which the grain is cooked in milk or cream to a version, popular in Palermo, in which ricotta is a central ingredient. Savoury versions bearing the name '*cuccìa*' that are traditional in some communities are in essence wheatberry and legume soups. On the continent, both sweet and savoury versions are found in Calabria, but in southern Campania and in Basilicata it seems the savoury preparations (resembling the aforementioned Ligurian *mesc-ciua*) are the norm.³ In this connection, we should also note that in the surviving Greek dialects of southern Italy (today all moribund), such wheat and legume soups bear a different but clearly very old name, namely, '*purvìa*' or '*porgìa*' which derives from πολφία (Rohlfs 1930: 133, 208); cf. Classical Greek πολφός 'farinaceous food', πολφοφάκη 'soup of *polphós* and lentils' (Montanari 2015: 1719), where '*polphós*' was almost certainly a form of pasta.

In the east of southern Italy, we find that the term '*cuccìa*' there does not designate any cooked dish but is found in some of the surviving Greek dialects of Otranto province in the south of the Salento peninsula as the word for 'fava bean' (Rohlfs 1930: 133). In southern Puglia, we do, however, find sweet preparations with wheatberries that resemble some of the sweet versions of *cuccìa* in Sicily and Calabria and are very much the same preparation described above for northern Puglia, '*grano dei morti*'; in Salento, the dish is called *colva*, while in Bari and Foggia the form of the name is *coliba*, though it seems in Foggia this name is dying out (Gasparetto 2013).⁴

We have already noted that in Puglia, *grano dei morti* or '*colva/koliba*' is a dish eaten on All Souls' Day. In Sicily, *cuccìa* is closely tied to the Feast of Saint Lucy on December thirteenth and so falls on a holiday traditionally associated with the winter solstice and thus with the start of lengthening days, the return of the sun that brings renewed life. In Calabria, *purvìa/porgìa* is also traditionally consumed on Saint Lucy's Day, though in some places it is part of the celebration of Saint Nicholas's Day the week before (6 December); finally, in at least some places in Basilicata, the savoury *cuccìa* with wheatberries and legumes is eaten on May Day and thus surely can be regarded as a food associated with fertility (see Rohlfs 1930: 133, 208).

Taken altogether, these various wheatberry dishes generally show association with days of overt (Christian: All Souls', Saint Lucy's, Saint Nicholas's) or covert (residual pagan: May Day) religious significance and are all associated with commemorations/ celebrations of death or the renewal of life after death – in this regard, Campania's Easter dish of *pastiera* fits in very well. But the other southern Italian wheatberry dishes all have through their names clear connections to Greek culture, whereas *pastiera* does not.

The Relationship between Southern Italian and Greek Wheatberry Dishes

Though many Italian writers have mentioned the ties between Italian and Greek symbolic uses of wheatberries in relation to specific dishes, I am aware of no broader treatment of the topic. Outside of Italy, the Greek facts are relatively well-known and, while ties between Greek culture and the cultures of the Middle East, Balkans, and eastern Europe in this regard have been discussed by many, the southern Italian evidence seems to have gone largely under scholarly radar.[5]

The occurrence of the names '*coliba*' and '*colva*' in Puglia represents the most obvious connection to Greek tradition and the composition of these dishes is strikingly close to that of Greece's *kollyva* (κόλλυβα): with many variations in details, the basic recipe for the Greek preparation includes cooked whole wheatberries, sweetened with honey or sugar and augmented with whole and crushed nuts, dried fruit, sesame seeds, parsley, and pomegranate seeds. The dialect names of the dish in Puglia are clearly and straightforwardly derived from the Greek name just cited: with the accent on the initial syllable, the southern Pugliese form '*colva*' shows syncope of the unstressed medial vowel and the form '*coliba*', with -b-, may reflect the partial b/v merger that obtains in some southern Italian dialects (further research here is required). Comparing the occasions on which the Greeks and other Orthodox communities consume wheatberry dishes (e.g. Bulgaria, Serbia, Romania; Feeley-Harnik 2015: 160) the match continues: while the Orthodox tradition famously uses *kollyva* in connection with funerals, the dish is also consumed on other occasions that commemorate the dead, including All Souls' Day, as in Puglia.

While derivatives of Gr. '*kollyva*' ('*koliva*') appear only in Puglia, '*cuccìa*' (with some variant forms) is found as the name of wheatberry dishes in a much larger area, extending from Basilicata westward to southern Campania and Calabria and on across all of Sicily. As noted above, there is at once greater variation in the Italian dishes so named and also greater deviation in the recipes from the Greek and Pugliese *kolliva/coliba*. The *cuccìa* family of dishes are, it seems, also not associated with All Souls' Day but in many cases are linked to the Feast of Saint Lucy, bearing an unmistakable though less direct association with the dead and death. It should also be noted that whereas Pugliese *coliba/colva* is a dish suitable for the strictest fast days, including by Greek standards where even the use of olive oil is prohibited on the most solemn occasions, the dishes bearing the name '*cuccìa*' vary in this regard, from extremely (no animal products nor olive oil) to less austere (with dairy in sweet preparations and olive oil in the savoury dishes).[6]

'*Cuccìa*' derives from an old Greek word (sg. κουκκίον, pl. κουκκιά) meaning both 'kernel' and 'bean' (especially 'fava') and in the plural took on a collective sense of 'a dish of kernels/wheatberries' or, as in the savoury versions discussed above, 'a dish of wheatberries and beans'. Regarding the historical relationship between the two Greek-derived names of wheatberry dishes in southern Italian dialects, Rohlfs provides a precious piece of data. In his entry for '*cuccìa*' he notes: '*Brei aus Weizenkörnern ist in Griechenland eine weitverbreitete Speise; dieser Brei (sonst* τα κόλυβα) *heißt auch in Arkadien* τα κουκκιά' (1930: 133). This Greek dialect evidence viewed together with the Italian evidence gives us an insight into the relative chronology of the spread of the Greek names for wheatberry dishes into Italy. The simplest explanation is that the Arkadian κουκκιά represents a relictal form, likely replaced elsewhere in Greece at some point by the innovation κόλυβα, a word which also spread on across the sea to Puglia but not further; the rest of southern Italy maintained the older '*cuccìa*' < κουκκιά. The distribution of reflexes of κουκκιά and κόλυβα in Orthodox lands seems to reinforce this view: the innovation κόλυβα spread to the Balkan lands but the further-flung Ukraine and Russia (as well as Catholic Poland) have forms of the *kutia* type, reflexes of the older name κουκκιά.

A more detailed study of this material is needed, but for now we can suggest that southern Italian '*cuccìa*' most likely dates to, at the latest, the early Middle Ages – probably before the Arab conquest of Sicily in the ninth century and possibly dating further back to antiquity, when much of Sicily and all of the coast and much of the interior of continental southern Italy was a zone of prolonged and intimate contact between Greeks (with many Greek settlements dating back to the eighth and seventh centuries B.C.) and the local Italic peoples.[7]

As with many elements of Christian practice, the symbolic use of wheatberries in Greek Orthodox tradition is widely recognized as an adaptation of older pre-Christian practice. Specifically, the basic form and use of *kolyva* and *kutia* undoubtedly continues the form and use of *panspermia*, 'all seeds', in pre-Christian Greece. The *panspermia* was an offering that was prepared with boiled grain, but it was not consumed, being instead reserved for symbolic consumption by the dead. Though it was associated with several occasions in the Greek religious calendar, it was a central part of the *Anthesteria*, a three-day festival celebrated in what for us would be late February; *panspermia* was offered by the celebrants specifically on the third day of the festival; the parallel in Roman religion was the Ferelia, also celebrated in February (Harrison 1912: 326). In Harrison's view, *Anthesteria* was, in effect, the pre-Christian All Souls' Day, and the *panspermia* was not just an offering to the dead but also given to them so that they could take the offering back into the earth and bring the whole seeds and grain to fruition for their return in the autumn, as represented by the *pankarpia*, 'all fruits'. She describes this festival thus: 'The *Anthesteria* was then a feast of the revocation of souls and the blossoming of plants, a feast of the great reincarnation cycle of man and nature' (1912: 294).

Nilsson explicitly connects the ancient *panspermia* to the modern Greek *kolyva* and adds that the modern term, well attested in the Middle Ages, is recorded already in late antiquity 'as an offering of cooked wheat and fruit' (1972: 31). If my suggestion above is correct that southern Italian *cuccìa* represents an older term, replaced in Puglia by a new name emanating from Greece in Byzantine times, it seems possible that *cuccìa* dates back to at least very early Christian times, when there were still enclaves of Greek speakers in southern Italy and a larger Greek community in Sicily, or back even further to the pre-Christian period when Greek was still widely spoken in both southern Italy and Sicily.[8]

The Religious Symbolism of Pastiera Napoletana

In light of the preceding discussion, it is clear that *pastiera* in its classic form fits well into the widespread use of wheatberries in southern Italy and Greece. Its relationship to the *coliba/colva* dishes of Puglia and the similar simple sweet *cuccìa* preparations of Calabria and Sicily is to stand at the opposite end of a continuum: the simple dishes, much closer to the Greek *kolyva*, are sober, strict fast-day foods, contrasting with the more celebratory and richer versions from Sicily which employ dairy products (milk/cream or ricotta). At the far end of the continuum, we have *pastiera napoletana*, which not only includes dairy products (butter, milk for the cooking of the grain, and ricotta) but also eggs and, at its most traditional, even lard: *pastiera* is then a full-blown festive fat-day dish, befitting the celebration of Christianity's most joyous holiday.

And yet *pastiera* has in my view an essential tie to the simpler, sober versions at multiple levels. First, at its core it is a wheatberry and fruit dish, with the fruit present in the citrus zest and the candied fruit; the orange blossom water also calls to mind the transformational process from seed to new life. Overlooked in discussions of *pastiera* is, however, the fact that, at least when the pie is made in the traditional way, starting with dry grain, the process spans the whole three-day process of Christ's death and rebirth: the cooking of the grain, first in water, starts on Holy Thursday (Last Supper, betrayal) or Good Friday (trial and crucifixion); the final cooking of the grain in milk and the preparation of the other ingredients and assembly of the pie take place on Holy Saturday, and consumption of the pie can occur only after the resurrection on Easter Sunday. Thus encapsulated in the dish is the entirety of the passion and resurrection, and with it a reflection of the old practice of *Anthesteria*, also a three-day period, bringing together the commemoration of the dead and the celebration of rebirth.

The History of Pastiera

Though *pastiera*, both the dish and the name, are now known throughout Italy, both the dish and the name are clearly a long-standing part of regional culinary culture only in Campania (and to some degree neighbouring Molise). As we have shown above, the essence of the dish fits perfectly into the cultural and culinary landscape of southern Italy and Sicily with their very old but still clear ties to Greece: Naples and many of Campania's coastal towns trace their history back to Greek settlements founded long before the rise of Rome. Yet, unlike the majority of southern Italian wheatberry preparations, the dish does not bear a Greek name. Rather, the name '*pastiera*' is a coinage that dates to the Angevin period in southern Italy.

What we can say for certain about this name is that its suffix, *-iera*, is a borrowing from a language of France, either French itself or Provençal, into Neapolitan (appearing also in other Italian dialects). The royal court of the Kingdom of Sicily under the Angevins was located in Naples and, given that the Angevins were themselves French-speakers with holdings in northern France, French was one of the languages employed at court. But the Angevins were at this time also the Counts of Provence, and so many of the trusted administrative and military figures in Naples were native speakers of Provençal; the court was then a place where French, Provençal, and Neapolitan (and other Italian dialects) were all spoken. This court was also a place in which culinary matters were certainly taken seriously, as can be seen from the *Liber de coquina* which, in the version we have, was surely at least in part composed under the Angevins.[9]

No recipe for *pastiera* appears in the *Liber de coquina*, but the dish as known today would certainly not have been out of place in the final section of the book in which a number of elaborate pies are described. That *pastiera* dates back to this period is, however, demonstrated by the very first attestation of the word in reference to a food: it appears in a text produced by the *Curia Romana* – the papal administration – in 1337, when the Pope resided in the Provençal city of Avignon. That the papacy moved to Avignon was itself very much the work of the Angevins of southern Italy, and there were extremely close ties between the papal court and royal court of the Angevins in Naples and their Provençal court in Aix.

It is impossible today to determine who coined the name '*pastiera*' or even in which language the coinage took place; that in later times the word is known as a name of a dish only in Campania makes it likely that from the start it was in essence a Neapolitan word. There is, however, good reason to think that the name was invented in the course of interactions between Neapolitan speakers and speakers of Provençal. In Old Provençal, there already existed a well attested word *pastiera* which was one of the terms used in southern France to refer to the wooden trough used in kitchens and bakeries in which one would form and knead dough. Though '*pastiera*' could be a parallel but new formation bringing together pasta, 'dough', and the suffix *-iera*, 'tool pertaining to, container of', it seems plausible that the word in the sense of dough-making trough was extended poetically to refer to a new and elite take on an old Campanian holiday dish: in effect, it was a version of *cuccìa*, enriched with ricotta and eggs and scented with costly spices, prepared as a filling for an elite-style pastry crust made from fine flour. The new coinage would then perhaps be something of a joke, with the enriched *cuccìa*, with its totally unprocessed wheatberries, being the 'dough' prepared in a '*pastiera*', a poetic reference to the pie crust.

The circumstantial evidence that *pastiera napoletana* finds its origins in the humble but religiously important *cuccìa* is extremely strong. But the dish as we know it now, especially in light of the etymology of its name, is surely the product of an elite kitchen which we can say with confidence was most likely one where Neapolitan and Provençal speakers met.[10] Over time, the ennobled *cuccìa* gradually became established as one of the central dishes for the celebration of Easter in Campania and for a long time has been enjoyed by all classes of society in the region.

Notes

1. This section is based on direct personal knowledge of Campanian culinary traditions as well as extensive reading of a wide-range of relevant cookbooks of different styles (e.g. Francesconi 2013, Bracale 2016, De Crescenzo 2016, Santasilia 2015) and of many on-line recipes posted by people in Campania and Molise.
2. *Mesc-ciua* is a dish comprised only of cooked wheatberries or farro, chick peas, and beans, seasoned with salt and olive oil.
3. For more details, see Rohls 1930: 133. Further research is needed for southern Campania and Basilicata.
4. Compare Sada, who gives a recipe for the version of '*grano dei morti*' a.k.a. '*coliba*' from Bari as a dish traditional on All Souls' Day; he also mentions an almond-based confection, *fave dei morti* 'favas of the dead', shaped like favas, for the same occasion which points to the conceptual connection: All Souls' Day – *coliba* – favas – *cuccìa* (2013: 159).
5. For example, Tan gives a fine overview of the use of wheatberries in Orthodox and Muslim lands, as well as in some other places further east, but mentions only briefly Sicilian *cuccìa* (2015); Feeley-Harnik, in an article on the use of sweets in relation to Christian beliefs, also only refers to Sicilian *cuccìa* among Italian sweet wheatberry dishes with religious significance (2015). It is striking how little known Neapolitan *pastiera* is. The following discussion is based on Buccini (2015a).
6. For a detailed discussion of the contrasts between fasting in Greek and Italian traditions, see Buccini (2012).
7. See most recently McDonald (2015: esp. 224ff).
8. The fact that southern Italian *cuccìa* has a fairly wide range of meanings – sweet vs. savoury, with different kinds of sweet preparations so named – bespeaks relatively greater age over-against the great similarity of all *kolyva/coliba* recipes. Note too that savoury dishes of wheat and legumes can also be quite old and are completely consistent with the symbolic function (relating to death and rebirth) under discussion here. For the related symbolic value of beans and particularly favas in Greek and perhaps specifically in a southern Italian (*Magna Graecia*) context, see Andrews (1949).
9. Some of the recipes may well go back to the rule of Frederick II in the first half of the thirteenth century, as argued by Martellotti (2005), but the collection of manuscripts in which this cookbook is preserved dates to around 1300, when Charles II of Anjou ruled in Naples. See also Maier (2005).
10. Culinary influences between Campania and Provence in the Middle Ages were noteworthy and travelled in both directions, an exchange which bespeaks a considerable amount of face-to-face interaction of people from both places; see further Buccini (2013, 2015b, 2017).

References

Andrews, Alfred C. 1949. 'The Bean and Indo-European Totemism', *American Anthropologist* 51: 272-92.
Bracale, Raffaele. 2016. *Comme se magna a Ppasca e a Carnevale* (Napoli: Cultura Nova).
Buccini, Anthony F. 2017. '*Un Vrai Jambalaya* – "A Real Mess": The Complex Western Mediterranean Origins of Louisiana's Famous Dish', in *Offal: Rejected and Reclaimed Food: Proceedings of the Oxford Symposium on Food and Cookery 2016*, ed. by Mark McWilliams (London: Prospect Books), pp. 105-20.
—— 2016. 'Defining "Cuisine": Communication, Culinary Grammar and the Typology of Cuisine', in *Food and Communication: Proceedings of the Oxford Symposium on Food and Cookery 2015*, ed. by Mark McWilliams (Totnes: Prospect Books), pp. 105-21.

—— 2015a. 'Holiday Sweets', in *The Oxford Companion to Sugar and Sweets*, ed. by Darra Goldstein (Oxford: Oxford University Press), pp. 333-36.

—— 2015b. 'The Merchants of Genoa and the Diffusion of Southern Italian Pasta Culture in Europe', in *Food and Markets: Proceedings of the Oxford Symposium on Food and Cookery 2014*, ed. by Mark McWilliams (Totnes: Prospect Books), pp. 54-64.

—— 2013. 'Lasagna: A Layered History', in *Stuffed and Wrapped Foods: Proceedings of the Oxford Symposium on Food and Cookery 2012*, ed. by Mark McWilliams (Totnes: Prospect Books), pp. 94-104.

—— 2012. '*Chi vuol godere la festa, digiuni la vigilia*: On the Relationship between Fasting and Feasting', in *Celebration: Proceedings of the Oxford Symposium on Food and Cookery, 2011*, ed. by Mark McWilliams (Totnes: Prospect Books), pp. 66-75.

De Crescenzo, Luciano. 2016. *Frijenno magnanno* (Giuliano in Campania: Magic Book).

Feeley-Harnik, Gillian. 2015. 'Christianity', in *The Oxford Companion to Sugar and Sweets*, ed. by Darra Goldstein (Oxford: Oxford University Press), pp. 158-62.

Francesconi, Jeanne Caròla. 2013 [1965]. *La cucina napoletana* (Napoli: Grimaldi).

Gasparetto, Damiano. 2013. '*La Coliba o Grano Dei Morti*', Alessandria News <http://www.alessandrianews.it/societa/la-coliba-o-grano-morti-48495_p.html> [accessed May 2018].

Harrison, Jane Ellen. 1912. *Themis: A Study of the Social Origins of Greek Religion* (Cambridge: Cambridge University Press).

Maier, Robert (ed.). 2005. *Liber de coquina* (Frankfurt: F.S. Friedrich).

Martellotti, Anna. 2005. *I ricettari di Federico II* (Firenze: Olschke).

McDonald, Katherine. 2015. *Oscan in Southern Italy and Sicily* (Cambridge: Cambridge University Press).

Montanari, Franco. 2015. *The Brill Dictionary of Ancient Greek* (Leiden: Brill).

Nilsson, Martin P. 1972 [1940]. *Greek Folk Religion* (Philadelphia: University of Pennsylvania Press).

Rohlfs, Gerhard. 1930. *Etymologisches Wörterbuch der unteritalienischen Gräzität* (Halle: Max Niemeyer).

Sada, Luigi. 2013. *La cucina della Terra di Bari* (Mulazzo: Traka).

Santasilia di Torpino, Franco. 2015. *La cucina aristocratica napoletana* (Napoli: Grimaldi).

Tan, Aylin Öney. 2015. 'Wheat Berries', in *The Oxford Companion to Sugar and Sweets*, ed. by Darra Goldstein (Oxford: Oxford University Press), pp. 784-85.

The Sesame Seed and 'Japaneseness'

Voltaire Cang

Introduction

The sesame seed is one of Japan's oldest foods, having entered the Japanese archipelago and the diets of prehistoric Japanese in the early Jomon period (*c.* 5300-3600 BCE).[1] The seed and its by-product, sesame oil, have been part of the Japanese diet ever since and are now ubiquitous in Japanese cuisine. Sesame seeds are sprinkled over rice and noodles, ground and mixed into vegetable dishes, made into paste for sauces and dressings, and pressed into oil for deep-frying tempura.[2] Sesame seeds are also used in traditional sweets as decorative accents or the main ingredient, such as for sesame seed crackers and sesame paste-filled buns.

Aside from Japanese food, sesame is also often used in other cuisines popular in Japan – especially Chinese – making the country one of the largest consumers of sesame in the world. Japan was the biggest sesame seed importer until 2010, when China largely abandoned local production and turned to importation. China now claims 42% of the global share in import volume for sesame seeds, with Japan owning 8%.[3]

China's expanding imports, however, have not affected Japan's appetite for sesame. While the world's sesame growers and suppliers managed to keep up with increasing global demand, Japan continues to maintain its import levels at a steady rate of around 150,000 tons each year.[4] Media reports indicate this amount as representing 99% of Japan's domestic consumption, although major Japanese companies directly involved in the seed's trade peg the figure at 99.9%.[5]

The sesame plant is not native to Japan, and the country's geographic and climatic conditions are not conducive to its cultivation. Sesame farming is also labour-intensive, a critical problem amidst Japan's falling birth rates and ageing demographics, not to mention its even more rapidly ageing farming population. However, a few regions in Japan persist in growing sesame, contributing a mere 0.1 to 1% of the country's needs. These regions are mainly sustained by the premium prices Japanese companies and the general public pay for their produce, even if their seeds are not necessarily higher quality than imports from countries where agricultural conditions are more favourable to the sesame plant. Japanese are willing to pay high prices simply because the product is 'made in Japan'.

By being 'made in Japan', sesame seeds acquire a 'Japaneseness' that in turn grants them prestige or, borrowing from French sociologist Pierre Bourdieu, 'symbolic capital', which supersedes other qualities such as taste, appearance, or health benefits often superior in imported seeds.[6] Although the concept of 'Japaneseness' is usually applied to people – as is symbolic capital – it is also often employed for food in Japan, and becomes a major criterion in establishing value, quality, or desirability despite its irrelevance for evaluating food.

This paper considers 'Japaneseness' in food. It uses the sesame seed as a case study to discuss how 'Japaneseness' is created, enacted, and utilized – or exploited – through food in Japan.

A Cultural History of the Sesame Seed: Becoming Japanese

The sesame seed has not merited a book on its cultural history, at least in the English language, as far as investigated by this author. As for works on the sesame as plant, seed, or oil in all other academic fields, resources are paltry. An outstanding and perhaps the only exception would be the scientific compendium, *Sesame: The Genus Sesamum*, edited by ethnobotanist Dorothea Bedigian, who writes in the tome's introduction that sesame has been 'ignored as a research subject' in much of the world. She also laments that no university in the United States has a scientist who researches sesame, while the few elsewhere who do 'have undermined progress by being more competitive than collaborative'.[7]

There are few Japanese language resources, either. While recipe books, health manuals – many advocating sesame for hair loss and greying issues – and scientific works appear intermittently, hardly any work has covered sesame's cultural history in Japan. There is, however, one noteworthy exception, as with the literature in English: *Goma no kita michi* (*The Road Travelled by Sesame*) by Teisaku Kobayashi.[8] Kobayashi, who died in 2001, was an authority on the agricultural production and genetics of sesame. He first published *Goma no kita michi* (*Goma* below) in 1986; it has since been reprinted six more times, most recently in 2007, and is frequently cited in Japanese scientific papers and other sources. The brief history of sesame in Japan, which follows immediately below, will thus be based on *Goma*; updated and supplementary – sometimes conflicting – data are included from other sources as necessary.

Goma contends that the sesame's journey to the Japanese islands began in the tropical savannas of Africa; this assertion is repeated several times in the book and is frequently quoted by producers, food writers, and scientists in Japan. Bedigian, however, reveals that although the Sesamum genus is native to Africa, there is no botanical evidence of its domestication in the continent.[9] Rather, recent research on the taxonomy of cultivated sesame has shown that they derived from wild populations in the Indian subcontinent. After domestication in ancient India, sesame was introduced to Mesopotamia where it was commonly grown by the early Bronze Age (c. 3300 BCE).[10] As this era overlaps with the middle to late Jomon Period (c. 3600-1000 BCE) in Japan – when sesame was already found in various regions stretching from the Kanto area in the east all the way to the Ryukyu (Okinawan) islands in the south – it appears that sesame travelled out of India through several routes, with those destined for Japan passing through Central

The Sesame Seed and 'Japaneseness'

Asia to China and the Korean peninsula, places where sesame has also been consumed since ancient times.

Although sesame was grown in Japan more than 3000 years ago, it did not become a major crop and food until after the sixth century. *Goma* indicates that the introduction of Buddhism to the country in 538 – 552 according to others – promoted extensive use of sesame seed and oil in the Japanese diet, spurring sesame cultivation throughout the country.[11] The shift in diet is attributed particularly to the first of the five basic precepts in Buddhist teaching, that is, abstinence from harming or killing living things, which was faithfully observed by the religion's followers in Japan. The Buddhist faithful avoided meat and subsisted on plants, of which sesame became an essential food for its flavour, aroma, and nutritional value. In 675, the first Buddhist precept became the law of the land, as the consumption of animal meat was completely banned by Emperor Temmu (*c.* 631-686), who encouraged the spread of Buddhism while utilizing the religion's ordinances to strengthen and expand his political control.

With meat banned, even more people turned to sesame and soybeans to compensate for the absence of animal protein in their diets. Sesame, however, was less procurable than soybeans, and it was consumed mainly among the ruling and priestly classes. Its consumption by the elite is evidenced in the first written record of sesame in Japan: the Taiho Code, the system of administrative laws and ethics enacted in 701, lists sesame oil among other oils to be offered as annual tributary taxes (from an unspecified province) to the court in the then capital of Asuka near Nara. Sesame oil is listed first and, along with hempseed oil, is stipulated at 7 *shaku* (one *shaku* is approximately 18 millilitres), the largest amount.[12]

Although sesame production grew considerably in the sixth and seventh centuries, farmers could hardly cope with the ever-increasing demand, and the imperial court resorted to encouraging and offering incentives to sesame farmers, beginning from the reign of Emperor Temmu's successor, the Empress Jito. Historical texts record the empress regnant as having issued an order in 693 for increasing sesame seed production all over the country. Similar orders were issued by other regents in the succeeding centuries; by 927, the *Engishiki* code of laws completed in this year stipulated tributes of sesame seed and oil from thirty-four (out of then sixty-eight) provinces in Japan – excluding all northern regions – attesting to the spread of sesame farming throughout the country. Sesame remained a valuable crop: a tax code from Izu Province (present-day Shizuoka Prefecture) in 739 indicated sesame oil's value to be forty times more than its volume in rice, designating one *shō* (about 1.8 litres) of sesame oil as equivalent to 45 *shō* (more than 80 litres) of rice.

There are very few written records of the various ways sesame was actually consumed in these early centuries, although available texts from the Nara (710-794) and Heian (794-1185) Periods indicate that these were mostly in the form of oil, usually added to food for aromatic purposes. Japanese food historian Ayao Okumura has described one such dish from the Nara Period called *aburaii* (*abura*=oil; *ii*=rice), which a Heian

Period dictionary, *Wamyoruijusho* (c 931), explains is made by boiling rice in sesame oil-flavoured water.[13] The same dictionary also includes an entry for a pastry called *buto* made from rice flour dough that is shaped like rabbit ears and cooked in oil which is unspecified but likely to be sesame.[14] Kasuga Shrine in Nara, built in 768, still makes *buto* in a similar manner – rice flour and water is kneaded into dough, which is steamed and shaped into a twelve-centimetre half-moon with scalloped edges, then fried in sesame oil. The shrine uses *buto* in its formal food offerings, which shrine officials maintain has always been the case since its establishment more than 1200 years ago.[15]

Nevertheless, it was in the succeeding Kamakura Period (1185-1333) when the sesame seed came into its own as food in Japan. In this chaotic era, Buddhism offered people solace so that it flourished further as it also spread among the lower social classes. Several new sects, such as Jodo (Pure Land), Nichiren, and Zen, now the largest schools of Buddhism in Japan, were also established.[16] Consequently, Buddhist vegetarian cuisine became popularized and developed into the culinary practice called *shōjin ryōri* (literally, 'devotion cuisine').

During this era, sesame was considered one of the essential 'five major grains' in Buddhist priests' and laypeople's vegetarian diets, along with rice, barley, wheat, and beans.[17] As the most flavourful and aromatic, sesame was used profusely and often mixed with other grains and vegetables. It eventually became the chief ingredient of *shōjin ryōri*'s signature and indispensable dish, *goma dōfu* (sesame 'tofu'), made by grinding roasted sesame seeds into a paste mixed with water and arrowroot to be cooked slowly, then cooled in a mould and finally cut into small, square tofu-like pieces. Although it is uncommon for sesame seeds to be used as the main ingredient for savoury dishes in many parts of the world, Japan's *goma dōfu* is 'one notable exception' to the repertoire.[18]

Shōjin ryōri was developed into a sophisticated vegetarian cuisine by Zen Buddhist monks who studied its philosophy and basic cooking techniques through training and cultural exchanges with China during Zen's early years in Japan.[19] Although sesame seed is used more often than oil in *shōjin ryōri*, one form of the cuisine that developed in Kyoto requires oil in copious amounts. Also called *fucha ryōri*, many of its dishes are stir- or deep-fried in sesame oil. Since frying was an uncommon cooking method in pre-modern Japan, the practice is attributed to Chinese influence. Today, the custom of deep-frying vegetables in sesame oil for tempura is sometimes called the *shōjin*-style of frying ('*shōjin a-ge*'), borrowed specifically from *fucha ryōri*.[20]

Zen Buddhism was also a strong, and possibly the strongest, influence on the Way of Tea (aka 'tea ceremony') practice established in the sixteenth century, whose earliest proponents were Zen priests. The cuisine in the practice, called *kaiseki*, accordingly developed along *shōjin ryōri* principles. *Kaiseki* in turn greatly influenced the development of Japanese cuisine, and is now described as 'a trademark of modern Japanese cuisine, the defining feature of culinary "Japaneseness"'.[21]

Sesame seeds are found in all kinds of *kaiseki* dishes. The 'founding father' of the Way of Tea practice, Sen Rikyu (1522-1591), was known for his fondness for white sesame seeds, and they appear in many of his *kaiseki* menus. In Japanese cooking today, any dish described as '*Rikyu* style' would refer to its use of sesame seeds, mainly white.

Using the example of *shōjin ryōri*, food scholar Alan Davidson declared that 'it is probably in Japan that the use of sesame seeds has been most highly developed'.[22] Indeed, through *shōjin ryōri* and subsequently through *kaiseki*, the sesame seed became a common ingredient in the Japanese kitchen, with many now calling it indispensable to Japanese food. The classic Japanese cooking 'bible', Shizuo Tsuji's *Japanese Cooking: A Simple Art*, lists the sesame seed among the most essential ingredients of the cuisine. *Japanese Cooking* was published in 1980, in an era when sesame seeds were not easily available to consumers in North America and Europe; its author did not propose any substitution, however, instead encouraging his readers to search for the ingredient in Asian food shops.[23] Another work, Richard Hosking's pioneering and much-praised *A Dictionary of Japanese Food: Ingredients & Culture*, also views sesame in the same manner, that is, as an essential ingredient in the cuisine.[24]

The Sesame Seed and 'Japaneseness'

Despite the importance of sesame seed and oil in Japanese homes and restaurants today, these are very rarely sourced in the country. Japan resorted to importing sesame when its economy accelerated after and despite defeat in World War II, as purchasing sesame abroad was cheaper than growing it domestically. Farmers also shifted to more profitable and less labour-intensive crops, especially rice, which was granted hefty subsidies from the national government and was much easier to grow thanks to increased mechanization. In contrast, sesame farming 'has not been modified to suit mechanized agriculture' and requires much manual labour, making the crop suitable for farmers with limited plots and economic resources, who now constitute a majority of the world's sesame farmers.[25] Sesame quickly became a minor crop in Japan.

The lack of mechanization makes sesame particularly difficult to harvest: although mature sesame plants could be cut by machines, the later processes of tying them into bundles, drying, and threshing are all done by hand. Drying and threshing takes ten to twenty days on average: once the plants are dry, they are threshed (i.e. beaten by hand) to release the seeds in the capsules, a process that is repeated again after several days. The seeds are then sieved to remove residue such as soil, stones, and other parts of the plant, some of which are picked out by hand. In many cases there is a final winnowing process, again a manual operation, to completely remove extraneous matter. Finally, the seeds are dried for several days more.

There are, however, some areas in Japan that persist in farming sesame. Most are in outlying regions with comparatively warmer climates, spread out in eighteen of Japan's forty-seven prefectures. Latest available government statistics show minimal output in almost all of them: except for four prefectures (Kagoshima, Kumamoto, and Okinawa all in the south, and Ibaraki in the east), the rest produced one ton, many even less, out of the nearly 100 tons harvested in the year. Among the biggest producers, Ibaraki and Kumamoto contributed three tons each and Okinawa five tons, while Kagoshima produced a massive seventy-three tons, placing its share of the domestic sesame seed production at more than 70%.[26] Remarkably, more than 90% of Kagoshima sesame is produced in Kikaijima, a small island in the Amami island chain (still part of Kagoshima) just north of Okinawa.

Kikaijima measures less than fifty-four square kilometres, its population slightly above 7100. In the most recent five years, sesame production in the island fluctuated greatly, yielding about sixty tons in 2013 and 2016, but only twenty tons in 2014, 2015, and 2017, when devastating typhoons and series of 'guerilla rainstorms' (sudden, heavy, and localized rainfall) caused crop damage.[27] Kikaijima was not a traditional sesame-producing region until recently: while sesame had been planted in the island for home consumption, it was only in the 1990s after organic sesame farming was introduced – it made for efficient use of land in the short but warm season before sugarcane planting in the summer – that commercial farming actually took off.[28] The 1990s also saw a 'health boom' in Japan, and sesame was widely touted as a natural health food. The demand for domestically grown sesame seeds rose rapidly, as health-conscious consumers perceived them to be 'safer' than foreign-grown seeds.[29] In other words, the timing was right for Kikaijima's farmers who rode the boom: from an annual output of 200 kilos in the late 1980s, they now produce most of Japan's domestic supply, averaging sixty tons or more in a good, typhoon-free season.

Much of Kikaijima's sesame is grown under contract with sesame seed and oil manufacturers, with a small portion of the harvest processed into roasted seeds or salad dressings and sold on the island. Kikaijima sesame command high prices: a 50-gram package of white sesame seeds sells for 600 yen (£4), while a similar pack of imported seeds, also white, is priced at 120 yen (£0.80) at company K, Japan's biggest sesame seed and oil manufacturer.[30] The same company also sells imported sesame by the kilo, at 1200 yen (£8) per bag, corresponding to twice the price of Kikaijima sesame but with twenty times more seeds.

The huge price gap may be blamed on labour costs and the relative rarity of Kikaijima seeds, but it cannot be explained on account of seed quality: there is no clear quality difference between domestic and imported seeds, with a few more vocal entities in the sesame industry declaring imported products to be even better than seeds from Japan. Freshness is not an issue, since sesame seeds retain their flavour and aroma in storage after they are dried. Sesame also grows best in tropical climates, which encourage the growth of larger and more aromatic seeds than in sub-tropical Kikaijima and more temperate regions in Japan.[31] One major Japanese manufacturer that sells both domestic and imported seeds explicitly declares that the 'most delicious' white sesame seeds – the type grown in Kikaijima – come from Guatemala, while the 'best' brown (or gold) seeds, which are grown in other regions in Japan, are from Turkey. The manufacturer, perhaps to avoid being the proverbial 'nail that sticks out' only to get hammered down, takes pains to emphasize that its evaluations are based on company standards, not of the industry as a whole. (It also sells black sesame seeds, the third major type, mostly from Myanmar, which it describes as of 'good quality.')[32]

Japan-grown sesame is often described as 'safe' by producers. Like the health-food consumers above, they, too, perceive safety as a Japanese quality: the more 'Japanese' the food, that is, the higher its level of 'Japaneseness', then the safer it is. Aside from safety, 'Japaneseness' has also become a standard for deliciousness: Japan-produced food is often chosen by consumers over imported products, as it is perceived to be better-tasting. Local sesame as well as other domestically grown food are thus prized for their 'Japaneseness', out of which are drawn totally arbitrary notions of safety and deliciousness, even if the food may have lower levels of quality, aesthetic value, or nutritious merit than those from elsewhere. One author calls this tendency a common consequence of the 'prevailing food discourse in Japan' that believes in domestic food as 'safer and more delicious' on the grounds that it is made in the 'beautiful country' of Japan.[33]

Japanese food producers accordingly exploit the discourse in different ways to obtain higher prices for their products. For example, 'Japanese beef' – meaning meat from cows grown in Japan, different from 'wagyu' which also means 'Japanese beef' but referring to the breed of cattle – is regularly sold at higher prices than imported beef. The government, however, allows beef from cattle born overseas but raised in Japan to be labelled and sold as 'Japanese beef' as long as the period of the cattle's life in Japan is longer than its life abroad. Many beef farmers in the country today import live cattle and simply raise them some years or months, even just days, longer than their time outside Japan, making them 'Japanese'. A parallel case is found in sesame: one of the more popular brands of sesame seeds, *Kyo iri goma* (literally, 'roasted sesame seeds from Kyoto'), is sold at select food and health shops, including online, at prices higher than seeds of similar quality. It is not sesame grown in Kyoto, however: the seeds are imported from Turkey, although they have been roasted using so-called traditional 'Kyoto' methods and otherwise processed in the Kyoto area.[34]

Aside from the association with country (Japan), the link to people (the Japanese), is also crucial to the perception of food in Japan. Food made by Japanese, whether in or outside the country, is more often desirable than food produced by non-Japanese hands; this is reflected in Japanese importation trends for sesame seeds.

For the past ten years, Japan has regularly sourced its seeds mainly from six countries: Tanzania, Myanmar, Nigeria, Burkina Faso, Guatemala, and Paraguay. While the first four are among the world's top ten producers of sesame seeds (ranked first, second, sixth, and eighth, respectively, in 2016) and Guatemala is ranked seventeeth, Paraguay ranks but only twenty-eighth. (Japan is seventy-first.)[35] Twenty years ago, Paraguay was not even a major supplier to Japan or any other country. Ten years ago, however, it suddenly became the largest exporter to Japan, although it dropped down in the list after 2008 due to periodic discovery of chemical residue in its products. Paraguay recovered quickly, however, gaining ground in recent years and becoming Japan's third largest supplier in 2016.[36]

Paraguay's outsize role in Japan's sesame trade can be attributed to its cultural association with Japan: Paraguay is home to more than 7000 descendants of some 300 Japanese farmers and their families who immigrated to the country in the 1930s, most of whom continue to engage in agricultural work. A Japanese government report explicitly declares that the 'existence of Nikkei (Japanese immigrated to Paraguay), who have acquaintance of both markets, has contributed to the increase of Paraguayan sesame to Japan'.[37] More importantly, sesame production in Paraguay is recorded to have been started in the 1990s by a first-generation immigrant Japanese, Toshikazu Shirosawa, who shifted from cotton farming after cotton's value as a cash crop declined.[38] Shirosawa and other Nikkei farmers actively sought and eventually gained access to the Japanese sesame seed market, so that from about 5000 farm units in 1999, more than 40,000 farms in Paraguay engage in sesame farming today.[39] Indeed, despite the chemically-tainted supplies that would have permanently damaged Paraguay's position as chief exporter to Japan, the Japanese government has continued to buy the country's sesame while also giving technological and economic aid through JICA (Japan International Cooperation Agency) and ODA (Overseas Development Assistance) projects with Paraguayan sesame farmers to improve production and maintain, as well as increase, exports to Japan.

The fate of Paraguayan sesame in Japan brings to mind the contrasting case of California rice, which Japan had resisted importing until recently, despite its similarity to domestic rice; indeed, California rice was originally cultivated from seeds brought from Japan. However, because 'symbolically it [was] just as different as any other food that represents the other [since it] is grown on foreign soil', Japan repeatedly rejected California rice.[40] Which begs a rhetorical question: if California rice was grown by Japanese immigrants, would it have met a different fate? Although California rice has entered the Japanese market, today it is consumed primarily in local food chains, not in haute cuisine restaurants, and is rarely found in supermarkets.

Concluding Thoughts

A thorough discussion of 'Japaneseness' in food, if even only through the example of the sesame seed, is beyond the scope of this paper. Although studies on 'Japaneseness' have been pursued by scholars on Japan for centuries, most academic literature in English is confined to the most recent century. As for research on 'Japaneseness' in food, the literature is even more limited, though steadily increasing. One paper by prominent Japanese anthropologist Harumi Befu was among the first works to bring attention to 'Japaneseness' in food, even as it used food as only one of several instances in Japanese culture through which the concept could be analyzed and observed.[41]

In his paper, Befu notes that the 'origin of the material [food…] is not at issue in the designation of "Japanese"', as the discussion here has shown: the sesame seed acquired 'Japaneseness' through its long and sustained use in Japanese cuisine despite its foreign origins.[42] However, origin can be a powerful issue in establishing 'Japaneseness' in food, as it can grant the food a prestige above and beyond its inherent qualities, as observed

The Sesame Seed and 'Japaneseness'

in the case of locally-grown Kikaijima sesame.

Befu also indicates that the process of production 'is not so much criterial as are the final products themselves' in attributing Japanese traits or personality to the object concerned. He considers the examples of *sake* and sushi to make his case, stating that although they may utilize robot and other foreign technology, 'no one would dream of calling [them] "Western"'.[43] The example of 'Kyoto roasted sesame', however, shows otherwise, as it revealed how the process of production can actually be exploited to create if even an artificially wrought 'Japaneseness'. It is the same for Paraguayan sesame, wherein the actual process of production – how it is made – does matter, especially when tied to the identity of who made it.

Notes

1. Nelly Naumann, *Japanese Prehistory: The Material and Spiritual Culture of the Jomon Period* (Wiesbaden: Harrassowitz Verlag, 2000).
2. This paper uses 'ō' and 'ū' to represent the long 'o' and 'u' sounds in the Japanese language, except in proper nouns (Jomon, not Jōmon) and familiar terms in English (tofu, not tōfu), which are also not italicized.
3. 'Commodities', *Oil World*, 2017 <https://www.oilworld.biz/t/statistics/commodities> [accessed 20 May 2018].
4. Ministry of Finance Japan, *Trade Statistics of Japan* <http://www.customs.go.jp/toukei/info/index_e.htm> [accessed 20 May 2018].
5. 'Wadaman of Japan', *Wadaman Co., Ltd.* <http://wadaman.com/english/> [accessed 20 May 2018].
6. Symbolic capital is simply defined here as a form of leverage held by an individual on account of characteristics held in high regard within a culture; see Pierre Bourdieu, 'The Forms of Capital', in *Handbook of Theory and Research for the Sociology of Education*, ed. by John G. Richardson (Westport, CT: Greenwood, 1986), pp. 241-58.
7. Dorothea Bedigian (ed.), *Sesame: The Genus Sesamum* (Boca Raton, FL: CRC Press, 2011), p. 25.
8. Teisaku Kobayashi, *Goma no kita michi* (*The Road Travelled by Sesame*) (Tokyo: Iwanami Shoten, 1986/2007). All translations from Japanese are by this author.
9. Bedigian, *Sesame: The Genus Sesamum*, p. 49.
10. Dorothea Bedigian, 'History and Lore of Sesame in Southwest Asia,' *Economic Botany*, 58.3 (2004), 329-53 (p. 331).
11. The reasons for the conflicting dates, as yet unresolved, are explained in William E. Deal and Brian Ruppert, *A Cultural History of Japanese Buddhism* (Malden, MA: Wiley Blackwell, 2015), p. 19. Briefly, the confusion is due to divergent accounts of Buddhist missions to Japan in two important historical texts.
12. Teisaku Kobayashi, '*Goma no shokumotsu gaku to dentōteki riyō*' ('Food Science and Traditional Use of Sesame'), in *Goma no kagaku* (*Sesame Science*), ed. by Mitsuo Namiki and Teisaku Kobayashi (Tokyo: Asakura Shoten, 1989), p. 96.
13. Ayao Okumura, '*Nihon no shokubunka to shokubutsuyu*' ('Plant Oils in Japanese Food Culture') (Public lecture) <http://www.oil.or.jp/info/29/29_1.html> [accessed 20 May 2018].
14. Tatsuru Sagai, '*Shinsen toshite no tōgashi*' ('Chinese Pastries as Offerings'), *Wagashi*, 12 (2005), 47-57.
15. '*Nara ken buto manjū*' ('*Buto* Buns in Nara Prefecture'), *Nisshin Oillio* <http://www.nisshin-oillio.com/report/kikou/vol13.shtml> [accessed 20 May 2018].
16. Kazuo Osumi, 'Buddhism in the Kamakura Period,' in *The Cambridge History of Japan, Vol. 3: Medieval Japan*, ed. by Kozo Yamamura (Cambridge, UK: Cambridge University Press, 1990).
17. Hiroshi Ito, 'Japan's Use of Flour Began with Noodles, Part 2: The Proliferation of Quern-Stones,' *Food*

Culture, 16 (2008), 1-4 (p. 3).
18 Alan Davidson, 'Sesame', *The Oxford Companion to Food*, Third Edition, ed. by Tom Jaine (Oxford: Oxford University Press, 2014), p. 733.
19 Ayao Okumura, *Nihon ryōri to wa nani ka* (*What Is Japanese Cuisine*) (Tokyo: Nobunkyo, 2016).
20 Naomichi Ishige, *Nihon no shokubunkashi* (*History of Japanese Food Culture*) (Tokyo: Iwanami Shoten, 2015), p. 282.
21 Katarzyna J. Cwiertka, *Modern Japanese Cuisine: Food, Power and National Identity* (London: Reaktion Books, 2006), p. 112.
22 Davidson, p. 733.
23 Shizuo Tsuji, *Japanese Cooking: A Simple Art* (Tokyo: Kodansha International, 1980).
24 Richard Hosking, *A Dictionary of Japanese Food: Ingredients & Culture* (North Clarendon, VT: Tuttle, 1996)
25 Bedigian, *Sesame: The Genus Sesamum*, p. xi.
26 Ministry of Agriculture, Forestry and Fisheries (MAFF), *Tokubetsu nōsakubutsu no seisan jisseki chōsa* (*Production Survey on Special Agricultural Products*) <http://www.maff.go.jp/j/tokei/kouhyou/tokusan_nousaku/> [accessed 20 May 2018].
27 Kikai Town, '*Goma*' ('Sesame'), <http://www.town.kikai.lg.jp/tougyo/sangyo/nogyo/nosanbutsu/goma.html> [accessed 20 May 2018].
28 Koji Kitazaki, 'Current State of Sesame Production in Kikaijima and its Future Potential,' *Amami Newsletter*, 12 (2004), 15-20.
29 *Goma no subete ga wakaru hon* (*Everything You Need to Know about Sesame*) (Tokyo: Ei Publishing, 2008), p. 33.
30 The company's full name is not disclosed.
31 *Goma no subete*, p. 39.
32 '*Shōhin no shōkai*' ('Product Information')', *Kingoma honpo* <http://kingoma.co.jp/info/produce/> [accessed 20 May 2018].
33 Hiroko Takeda, 'Nationhood and Nationalism in Discourses on Food in Contemporary Japan,' *Studies in Ethnicity and Nationalism*, 8.1 (2008), 5-30.
34 '*Jidai no saki e: Josei keieisha funtō*' ('Taking Lead in the Era: The Struggles of Women Managers), *Fuji Sankei Business*, 26 July 2013, p. 17.
35 '*Sekai no goma: Seisan ryō kunibetsu rankingu* (The World's Sesame: Country Production Rankings)', *Global Note* <https://www.globalnote.jp/post-5789.html> [accessed 20 May 2018].
36 Ministry of Finance Japan, *Trade Statistics of Japan* <http://www.customs.go.jp/toukei/srch/indexe.htm> [accessed 20 May 2018].
37 Ministry of Foreign Affairs, Wadaman Science Co., Ltd., Summary Report: Republic of Paraguay 'Project Formulation Survey for Adding Value to Products of Small-Scale Farmers through the Introduction of Sesame Processing Technology' <http://www.mofa.go.jp/mofaj/gaiko/oda/seisaku/kanmin/chusho_h25/pdfs/5a01-3.pdf> [accessed 20 May 2018].
38 JICA (Japan International Cooperation Agency) News, 'Sesame Seed Production Effort Led by Japanese Descendants (Nikkei) Helps Small Farmers in Paraguay and Consumers in Japan', 20 February 2015 <https://www.jica.go.jp/english/low/news/field/2014/150220_02.html> [accessed 20 May 2018].
39 United Nations, *Study on Inclusive Development in Paraguay: International Cooperation Experiences* (Santiago, Chile: United Nations, 2014) <https://www.cepal.org/publicaciones/xml/5/52625/StudyonInlusiveParaguay.pdf> [accessed 20 May 2018].
40 Emiko Ohnuki-Tierney, *Rice as Self: Japanese Identities Through Time* (Princeton, NJ: Princeton University Press, 1993), p. 109.
41 Harumi Befu, 'Civilization and Culture: Japan in Search of Identity', *Senri Ethnological Studies 16* (1984), 59-75.
42 Befu, p. 62.
43 Befu, p. 62.

How Coffee Killed a Town: Investigating the Nineteenth-Century Rise and Fall of Coffee in Lipa, Batangas

Bel S. Castro

Every article dealing with the history of Philippine coffee mentions the grandeur that was Lipa, a prosperous period that began with a coffee boom in the late 1800s and ended with the coffee blight of *c.* 1889.

In most contemporary sources, the history of coffee at the end of the colonial era in the Philippines can be condensed into a single paragraph basically as follows:

> A Franciscan friar brought three trees (or three cans of beans) from Mexico (if not directly then transhipped from Africa or Brazil) and planted them behind a convent in Lipa (or Laguna) in 1740. In the early 1800s, Lipa Mayor Don Galo (also Galleo) de los Reyes required all residents to plant coffee trees. His son, Don Santiago de los Reyes, continued his father's efforts upon succeeding Don Galo as town mayor in 1832. By 1859, with the assistance of Augustinian friars including Fray Elias Nebreda (also Lebrado or Lebrada) and Fray Benito Varas, up to two-thirds of Lipa planted coffee. Lipa became the centre of the Philippine coffee industry, which reached its apex in the late 1880s. Soon after, an airborne fungus (*Hemileia vastatrix*) destroyed all the coffee plantations in neighbouring Ceylon, Java, and Sumatra as well as in India and Brazil. For a brief period, Lipa was the world's sole supplier of coffee beans. In 1886, the Philippines was ranked as fourth largest supplier of coffee in the world. Lipa continued to profit from the coffee trade until about *c.* 1889 when the same *Hemileia vastatrix* fungus that had devastated the coffee plantations in neighbouring coffee-producing countries finally reached Philippine shores and destroyed all the plantations in the Southern Tagalog region. By the late 1890s coffee no longer bloomed in Lipa.

With minor variations and omissions, this version of coffee history is the most popular and widely disseminated. Like the story of Kaldi and the dancing goats and the discovery of coffee, it is difficult to know where the factual ends and the apocryphal begins. The persistence of this version of the history of coffee in Lipa is astonishing, as even a cursory examination of published materials from the period offers little to support what seems to be more folklore than fact.

For instance, most references adopt a monocausal approach to the late nineteenth-century rise and fall of coffee in Lipa: the claim that a late 1880s blight on Southeast Asian coffee plantations supposedly left Lipa as the sole supplier of coffee beans to the world, allowing Lipa to profit greatly until the same fungus infected the Lipa plantations as well. This view has remained unchallenged for almost a century.

However, by viewing coffee in the broader context of the world economy, this paper dismisses this supposed late-nineteenth-century monopoly as myth and argues that the coffee boom towards the end of the Spanish colonial era can better be understood by examining a series of global events from the same period. The evidence suggests that the end of the coffee era in Lipa was not so much a consequence of pestilence but was ultimately a response to the pressures of global demand. It also argues that the seeds of the collapse of the industry were planted long before the coffee crisis of 1889-1892. The arrival of the coffee blight may have accelerated the inevitable, but it was not the prime cause.

Coffee is a unique commodity to study in the Philippines context, as it was not a substance that was initially produced for domestic consumption. As stressed by historian John Larkin, nothing dictated the pace of Philippine economic expansion as much as the demands of world commerce.[1] For decades, coffee was cultivated solely as an item of international exchange, its entire production destined for export to consuming countries in Europe and North America. As coffee cannot survive in colder latitudes, it was a natural choice for the exploitation of the land and labour of the Philippines in pursuit of profit. In such a manner, in the words of historian Steven Topik, coffee was the 'social motor' that sucked peripheral areas into the world economy.[2]

Yet a review of contemporary sources fails to capture these complexities. The true story of Lipa, if told from a sober perspective, is less a romantic recollection of memories of the good old days and more a cautionary tale of the hazards of trading in the world market from a position of weakness.

This new approach to the rise-and-fall of coffee in Lipa reveals a history more complex than previously understood and dramatically demonstrates the transforming power of gourmandism and nineteenth-century globalization.

About the Town

Lipa City is located about eighty-five kilometres south of Manila in the Southern Tagalog province of Batangas. Although the town of Lipa was formally organized and officially came under Spanish rule in 1702, the first Lipaeños can trace their roots to pre-Spanish trading communities that may have settled in the area as early as the 1400s. Within range of the Taal Volcano, the town moved several times in the 1700s. But when volcanic eruption destroyed the settlement in 1754, Lipa completed its final relocation to its present site in 1756.[3]

Modern-day Lipa is an agri-urban city with over 300,000 inhabitants in slightly under 50,000 households.[4] The pueblo that was re-established by Spanish authorities still bears traces of the urban design typical of the Hispanic colonial settlements of the era. The Lipa Cathedral, with its colonial baroque-style cupola, massive walls, and balconies,

How Coffee Killed a Town

still stands at the heart of the city. But other than that, little remains of the vaunted boom time of the late 1800s. It would be difficult to convince present day visitors that less than two hundred years ago, Villa de Lipa was the richest municipality in the country, a model community and one of the most affluent towns in Spain's colonial empire. And the source of all this prosperity was that which they called 'brown gold'.

Nineteenth-century Lipa was unique in that it was a town that was literally made and unmade by coffee. For more than fifty years, from 1840 to 1890, coffee was a significant source of commercial exchange. As the main trading point for coffee, Lipa at one point provided up to 96% of the country's coffee exports, and therefore was the centre of all the changes that the coffee trade wrought. Whatever debates there may be today, no discussion of the history of Philippine coffee can take place without including the role of the friars, farmers, traders, and landowners of nineteenth-century Lipa.

'The Grandeur that Was Lipa'

The early 1880s was a boom time for coffee. If in 1882 the average price per *picul* was ten pesos and twenty-five centavos, the same picul in 1888 fetched nearly thrice that at thirty-one pesos.[5] Accounts vary, but it is thought that the town of Lipa may have earned anywhere from two and a half to four million pesos that year. As this windfall was concentrated in the hands of less than a dozen families, what followed was a rise of consumerism and a display of wealth that was unprecedented, and since unparalleled. Local lore is full of stories of this age of abundance, of the opulent lifestyles of the Lipa aristocracy. Awash in cash, the wealthy coffee barons of Lipa built palatial homes and filled them with imported goods from the West: curtains from Paris, mirrors from Austria, stuffed chairs from Vienna, chandeliers from Germany, the finest porcelain from France. In Lipa, an individual's relationship to coffee defined his place in society.

A favourite tale of the Lipa folk relates how, at fiesta time, it was customary for wealthy coffee families to have their servants bring out of the storerooms sack upon sack of gold coins and silver Mexican pesos, which may have become mouldy and tarnished during their months of storage. Servants then washed and polished these before spreading them out on mansion balconies to dry in the sun. The menfolk of Lipa, when they took to the streets, rode astride imported Arabian stallions, better than any that could be found in Manila. When young men visited the cockpits to bet on their favourite fighting cocks, they required the services of strongmen who would walk behind them, each with a heavy sack of coins slung over their shoulders.[6] Wealthy matrons washed their faces in silver basins and ate off gold plates. Young women took to wearing slippers heeled with gold and embroidered with diamonds, and '[i]f they deigned to walk the streets, they were sheltered from the sun by servants bearing parasols'. The legend went that a favourite party game of young bachelors was 'to toss their diamond rings into the darkness and then search for them by the light of burning bank notes'.[7]

By 1894 the halcyon years of coffee were over. So dominant was Lipa in the national coffee trade that the death of the city's coffee industry was synonymous with the demise of the industry in the entire country.

The Rise and the Fall

Local historians have stated repeatedly that the Philippines was the fourth largest exporter of coffee and that, sometime in 1886-1888, Lipa became the sole supplier of beans to the world. This monopoly is thought to be the main reason that the price of Lipa coffee soared, giving birth to millionaires virtually overnight. Many continue to insist that this monopoly was due to a coffee blight that allegedly eliminated the coffee exports of competitors Java, Sumatra, Ceylon, and even India and South America, and all cite the same single source, *Southeast Asian Exports since the 14th Century: Cloves, Pepper, Coffee, and Sugar, Sources for the Economic History of Southeast Asia* by David Bulbeck and others.[8]

Viewing coffee in the broader context of the world economy, available statistics do suggest that 1886-1888 was indeed a crucial period for the world coffee market. While the same statistics validate that Lipa did in fact enjoy a coffee boom in the late 1880s, it also seems clear that the proverbial world coffee monopoly supposedly enjoyed by Lipa in the late 1880s simply did not occur. Even at its peak, the highest recorded quantity of coffee the Philippines produced in the 1880s never exceeded 8000 tons. And a closer examination of the same Bulbeck text offers contradictory information. Citing Dutch records, Bulbeck records that Philippine production of coffee for the period was less than 1.5% of the world's total production of coffee, and never more than 12.2% of Indonesia's production for the same period.[9] The facts that the United States alone imported well over 200,000 tons of coffee a year from 1886 to 1889 and that both Indonesia and Brazil continued to export significant amounts during that same period contradict that notion, even as proponents of Philippine coffee continue to cling to this fiction.[10]

This monocausal approach to Philippine coffee history leaves out critical world events that conspired to produce a worldwide shortage of coffee in the late 1880s. Addressing all these events in detail is beyond the scope of this paper, but a couple of indicators will be mentioned.

Export records from the period indicate that there was a drop in the volume of exportable coffee from Indonesia, from 100,065 tons in 1884 to almost half that, 51,724 tons in 1887.[11] This dramatic drop in production could be partially attributed to the calamitous effects of the oft-mentioned *Hemileia vastatrix*, although it has been hypothesized by William Clarence-Smith that there may be a relationship between the collapse of the Javanese production of coffee and the abolition of a brutal and much hated cultivation system – the end of labour coercion leading to the wholesale abandonment of coffee during that period.[12]

Coincidentally, at about the same time, the coffee fields in the Paraiba Valley of Brazil were also in decline. The *Hemileia vastatrix* fungus would not find its way to Brazil for another one hundred years so the loss in productivity is mostly attributed to slave riots, which eventually led to the abolition of slavery in 1888. As intensive farming had also already stripped and depleted the soil and pushed the trees to exhaustion, large farm owners abandoned their Paraiba Valley coffee fields, and the centre of Brazilian coffee production moved across the country to the Sao Paolo region.[13] Even though local Paraiba Valley smallholders never truly abandoned coffee, the industry in Brazil would take a few years to recover, and the disruption in Brazil's coffee production during this transition in 1886 did account for a dramatic drop of more than 100,000 metric tons.[14] Taken together, the shortfall from Brazil and Java alone reduced global coffee supply by 150,000 tons for the period from 1886 to 1887. This number does not even reflect reductions in coffee production in other crisis-affected areas such as Ceylon and Africa.

This deficit occurred at a time when global demand was trending upwards, fuelled by the United States' seemingly unquenchable thirst for coffee. These combined events, the reduction in world supply due to plant disease and the loss of slave labour, would have been enough to drive coffee prices up, but there was one more factor – scarcely mentioned in the most often cited Philippine resources – that likely caused the market disruption.

What is generally described by the Lipaeños as 'the great boom', which occurred in 1886-1888, was probably triggered not by global demand for Philippine coffee nor the alleged monopoly with the accompanying power to dictate prices, but by something else entirely: market manipulation in the West. By the late 1800s, Brazil was already a dominant supplier of coffee to the world. Plagued by myriad problems, it was estimated that the projected crop of 1887-1888 would be extremely small; one estimate quoting 3,033,000 bags. These low estimates led to the formation of a 'bull' clique, comprised of operators in New York, Chicago, New Orleans, Brazil, and Europe, who set a price of twenty-five cents for December forward contracts as their goal. Toward the end of June 1886, when this campaign started, coffee in the New York Exchange was trading at about seven and one-half cents. A year later, with discouraging crop news continuing to come out of Brazil, the price for December contracts had tripled to twenty-two and one-quarter cents, a new high price record. After peaking at that price, however, in less than a month the price of coffee futures dropped to sixteen cents. This sharp reversal would later be traced to what were, at first, just rumours of a greater than expected harvest. By the time the actual Brazil crop estimates became public – the 1888-89 coffee crop was estimated to be 6,827,000 bags, more than double the previous year – the market was already in freefall. After reports were received that various European coffee firms had failed, by March 1888 the price of future contracts in the American market went for as low as nine cents.[15]

Looking at the evidence, it is more likely that the sharp rise and fall in prices that triggered Lipa's 1888 coffee boom and bust had nothing to do with a supposed coffee monopoly or Lipa's market dominance. Rather, it was an indication of the coffee buyers' and traders' appetite for risk in speculating on a volatile commodity, a commodity whose price was being manipulated by traders and operators in at least three countries, thousands of miles away. The story of the rise and fall of coffee in Lipa was less a romantic pastoral story of agribusiness success, and more – like many boom and bust stories – a cautionary tale of greed and the flight of reason.

The Role of the Coffee Leaf Rust Epidemic of 1889

The conventional description of the *Hemileia vastatrix* epidemic of 1889 gives the impression that the devastation was sudden and devastating. This is not entirely accurate. Coffee rust causes premature defoliation, which weakens the tree and reduces yields. The fungus rarely killed trees, and even in cases of severe infestation trees could survive for months before dying. In Ceylon, from the time the fungus was discovered in 1867, coffee plantations remained viable for another twenty years before they were finally destroyed and production ceased entirely. In comparison, the decline of Lipa's coffee industry was complete in less than five years. How to account for the rapidity of the decline?

Testimony from the era reports that the coffee leaf rust was not the only biological attack that the planters had to endure, but was the last of a string of pests and diseases that tried their fortitude. The bulk of the damage to the plantations in the late 1880s was caused by two species of wood-boring worms. Farmers were familiar with these pests, and although reductions in the harvests were noticed since 1881 no real effort to control the infestation was recorded. The 1889 infestation, however, was particularly severe, prompting several of the wealthiest coffee-owners to plough up their lands and plant sugarcane in place of coffee.[16] It is possible that the Lipa farmers did nothing for so long because steadily rising coffee prices and increased plantings more than compensated for the losses and masked the actual impact of the damage that the pests were creating in the plantations.

The available evidence seems to confirm the theories of other coffee historians, that while leaf disease may have accelerated the inevitable, it was probably not the prime cause of the failure of coffee industries in Asia in the nineteenth century.[17] Other factors such as market manipulation, monoculture, poor agronomy, ignorance of sound practices of cultivation, diminishing virgin forest, falling prices, and competition with other agricultural products should also be considered.

The End of an Era: An Alternative Theory

If disease and soil exhaustion did not end the coffee industries of Indonesia, India, or Africa, why did it end Lipa's? A facile answer might be that the Lipa farmer simply gave up. Under pressure from the falling profits from the coffee trade, hectares of coffee trees were uprooted and then replanted with sugarcane, corn, and rice. Even if these agricultural products did not provide the same bonanza that coffee did at its peak, steady trade in these commodities was enough to sustain the lifestyles to which the landed gentry had become accustomed.

The Lipa farmers' rejection of coffee was also made easier because of their financial capacity to consider alternatives. As economically devastating as the loss of the coffee revenues may have been for the landed class of Lipa, it did not bankrupt them, and while they could have persisted in cultivating coffee against all odds, the then profitable sugar trade made the shift attractive, attracting financial investments to the detriment of the coffee trade.

Also, overlooked in most accounts is the impact of the political upheaval caused by the Revolution of 1896 and the Spanish American War, which disrupted all economic activity for nearly a decade. Deeply involved in the struggle against Spain and the United States, Lipa paid a dear price in life and property for its role in the war. It was in Lipa where Miguel Malvar, the last general still fighting the Americans, formally surrendered in April 1902. At the end of the hostilities, coffee farmers in Lipa wanting to revive the industry found that there were several fundamental changes to the marketplace. Foremost was the low price of coffee exacerbated by the low demand for Philippine coffee by its new occupying power, the United States of America.

In the same year the revolution against Spain began, 1896, the decade-long coffee crisis in Brazil ended. With Brazilian coffee flooding the market with cheap beans, coffee prices began to fall. Prices dropped even further in 1897 and remained low for the following ten years. With low prices and a soft market, local farmers found that coffee was no longer the gold mine that it had been in previous years. As the United States grew interested in Philippine tobacco, sugar, and hemp, the cultivation of these commodities was actively pursued instead – again, to the detriment of the coffee industry.

In sum, the demise of Lipa's coffee industry cannot be blamed solely on the coffee blight. Rather, its failure to recover should consider the absence of the necessary elements for its recovery, including access to land, access to capital and credit, availability of labour, access to markets, direct investments into research and development, etc.

Lessons from History

In his landmark book, *Uncommon Grounds: The History of Coffee and How It Transformed Our World,* Mark Pendergrast writes, 'Coffee provides one fascinating thread, stitching the disciplines of history, anthropology, sociology, psychology, medicine and business, and offering a way to follow the interactions that have formed a global economy.'[18] And what is woven in is sometimes less interesting than what is left out. From Kalaw to Villa, the inclination of Lipa historians has been to rhapsodize about their past, embellishing their accounts with phrases like 'the grandeur that was Lipa', 'a taste of utopia', and 'the legacy of a glorious past'. Lipa's riches continue to be the stuff of bedtime stories, a tale retold to the young Lipeño so that as he 'basks in that glorious past' he may be aware of his history and inheritance.

Certainly, memory and nostalgia have their place, but as has been shown, the colonial history of coffee in Lipa – as conventionally told – trivializes a history that is neither simple nor straightforward. The acceptance and perpetuation of the myths that have surrounded the history of coffee in Lipa by generations of writers has, for many years, stood in the way of comprehensive analysis of the factors that led to the growth and decline of Lipa's export economy in the nineteenth century. In its popular form, the tale of 'the grandeur that was Lipa' leaves out the contributions of other historical actors and falls short in examining the complexities that accompany the integration of a subsistent non-capitalist economy into the world economy.

This perspective is made even more relevant in the present day when the orientation of Philippine agriculture has shifted from production based on meeting needs to production driven by profit, a shift accelerated through the agency of agribusiness transnationals and the pressure to produce export-oriented cash crops to earn foreign exchange, sometimes even at the expense of staple foods. Over one hundred and fifty years after the golden age of Lipa ended abruptly, the Philippines again finds itself in familiar straits … perhaps repeating the errors of the past? A more thorough examination of the history of coffee in Lipa could shed light on the little analyzed Third World paradox: that of truncated development, or as Norman Owen put it, 'prosperity without progress'.[19] As barriers to free trade continue to be brought down and foreign interests are allowed to dictate the course of the country's agricultural development, Filipino farmers find themselves as powerless to control prices or exert any influence over the links in the commodity chain as they were one hundred and fifty years ago.

At the turn of the century, the population of Lipa stood at less than forty thousand. Of these, less than four thousand lived within the *poblacion*, or town proper. The vast majority of the Lipeños lived in the forty or so barrios that radiated out – some for many miles – from the centre of town.[20] The golden age described in local histories was hardly the history of these forty thousand citizens of Lipa but that of only a few families. These families, who belonged to the economic elite, composed a very small group – a group so small that they are all known by name: Solis, Luz, Katigbak, Africa. As such, the fortunes amassed by these families were enough to last several lifetimes.

The 'Class Two' families, or the middle class – to which professionals like doctors and lawyers belonged – also enjoyed sizable incomes at the height of the coffee boom. Some merchants and speculators even made incomes equal to the large landholders of the town. But for the rest on the lower rungs of the socio-economic ladder, which May estimated to be 98-98.5% of Lipa's population, theirs was a life of relative poverty.[21] Little is known about the lower classes, primarily because the historians of the day were unconcerned with the conditions of the poor. Anecdotal accounts relate uneven progress: as the economic elite continued to raise their stock, the extremes of great wealth and grinding poverty moved further and further apart. There is little evidence that the city of Lipa itself benefited from the revenues generated by the coffee trade. What this history could probably reveal, in fact, is that 'the grandeur that was Lipa' may be the biggest myth of all.

This paper argues that a better understanding of the present globalization trends and pressures on the coffee industry today begins with a better understanding of external demand as the fundamental variable which has driven local production of coffee to be a leading export at different points in time. It is essential that the true factors that drove the export economy in the nineteenth century be understood, because those factors may also be behind the coffee crisis facing Filipino coffee farmers today and may possibly hold the answers to the question of its sustainability.

Notes

1. John A. Larkin, 'Philippine History Reconsidered: A Socioeconomic Perspective', *The American Historical Review*, 87.3 (1982), 612.
2. William Gervase Clarence-Smith and Steven Topik, *The Global Coffee Economy in Africa, Asia and Latin America, 1500-1989* (Cambridge: Cambridge University Press, 2003), p. 6.
3. Jose Alex Katigbak, 'Lipa Yesterday', *Tambuling Batangas: A Monthly Supplement 1977*.
4. Census of Population (2015). 'Region IV-A (Calabarzon)'. Total Population by Province, City, Municipality and Barangay, *Philippine Statistics Authority* <https://psa.gov.ph> [accessed 20 June 2016].
5. A *picul* is a traditional Asian measure of weight, equivalent to approximately 60 kg; John Foreman, *The Philippine Islands*, 2nd ed. (New York: Charles Scribner & Sons, 1899), p. 337.
6. Maria Kalaw Katigbak, 'When Coffee Bloomed in Lipa', in *Filipino Heritage: The Making of a Nation*, ed. by Alfredo Roces (Manila: Lahing Pilipino Publishing, Inc., 1977-78), p. 1762.
7. Benito J. Legarda, *After the Galleons: Foreign Trade, Economic Change & Entrepreneurship in Nineteenth Century Philippines* (Quezon City: Ateneo de Manila University Press, 1999), p. 214.
8. David Bulbeck and others, *Southeast Asian Exports since the 14th Century: Cloves, Pepper, Coffee, and Sugar, Sources for the Economic History of Southeast Asia* (Singapore: Institute of Southeast Asian Studies, 1998).
9. Bulbeck and others, p.157.
10. Bulbeck and others, p. 157.
11. Bulbeck and others, p. 157.
12. William Gervase Clarence-Smith, 'The Spread of Coffee Cultivation in Asia, from the Seventeenth to the Early Nineteenth Century', in *Le Commerce du café avant l'ère plantations coloniales: espaces, réseaux, societies, XV–XIX siècle*, ed. by Michel Tuchscherer (Cairo: Institut Français d'Archéologie Orientale, 2001).
13. Gail L. Schumann, 'Why Europeans Drink Tea', *Plant Diseases: Their Biology and Social Impact*, 1998 <http://www.apsnet.org/online/feature/biodiver/coferust.html> [accessed 23 September 2003].
14. Stanley J. Stein, 'The Passing of the Coffee Plantation in the Paraiba Valley', *The Hispanic American Historical Review*, 33.3 (1953), 331-64.
15. William H. Ukers, *All About Coffee* (New York: The Tea and Coffee Trade Journal Company, 1922), pp. 463-64 <http://www.gutenberg.org/ebooks/28500> [accessed 9 April 2011].
16. John Foreman, *The Philippine Islands*, 2nd ed. (New York: Charles Scribner & Sons, 1899), p. 337; Simeon Luz, 'Cultivation of Coffee', in *Census of the Philippine Islands: 1903, Agriculture, Social and Industrial Statistics* (Washington: Government Printing Office, 1903), p. 82; Dean C. Worcester, *The Philippine Islands and Their People: A Record of Personal Observation and Experience, with a Short Summary of the More Important Facts in the History of the Archipelago* (New York: Macmillan Company, 1899), pp. 505-15.
17. William Gervase Clarence-Smith, 'The Coffee Crisis in Asia, Africa, and the Pacific, c. 1870 to c. 1914', in *The Global Economy in Africa, Asia and Latin America, 1500-1989*, ed. by Steven Topik and William Gervase Clarence-Smith (Cambridge: Cambridge University Press, 2003), pp. 100-19; A. E. Haarer, *Modern Coffee Production*, 2nd revised edn (London: Leonard Hill, 1962), p. 452.
18. Mark Pendergrast, *Uncommon Grounds: The History of Coffee and How It Transformed Our World* (New York: Perseus Books, 1999), p. 410.
19. See Norman G. Owen, 'Abaca in Kabikolan: Prosperity without Progress', in *Philippine Social History: Global Trade and Local Transformations*, ed. by Alfred W. McCoy and Ed. C. de Jesus. (Quezon City: Ateneo de Manila University Press, 1976).
20. Glenn Anthony May, *Battle for Batangas* (Quezon City: New Day Publishers, 1993), p. 8.
21. May, pp.19-23.

Seeds

From Peasant Food to Posh Ingredient: A History of Buckwheat in Brittany

Mary Margaret Chappell

If you were to name one food that both unifies and symbolizes the Brittany peninsula in France, it would be the *galette de blé noir/galette de sarrasin*, or buckwheat crêpe. There, the thin, savoury pancake made by swirling buckwheat batter over a large, round griddle has made its way into every aspect of daily life. Crêperies dish them out to customers for lunch and dinner. Crêpe trucks sell them on markets throughout the region. Supermarkets, small groceries, butcher shops, and bakeries stock them. And no local event would be complete without its crêpe or *galette* stand (Figure 1). *Galettes*, as they are fondly called, are such a big part of the collective experience in Brittany that in Rennes, the region's historic capital, Le Stade Rennais Division One football fans have taken the song '*Galette-saucisse, je t'aime*' ('*Galette* with sausage, I love you') for their unofficial anthem. That beloved Breton *galette* is a modern-day vestige of the long buckwheat tradition in Brittany that dates back to the late Middle Ages.

Figure 1. Galettes-Saucisses stands outside the Rennes football stadium, 1961. Musée de Bretagne archives.

From Peasant Food to Posh Ingredient

Brittany

Brittany is the westernmost region of France, a wide, wet, windy peninsula that stretches along the English Channel and into the Atlantic. The area's oceanic climate makes for mild winters, cool summers, and plenty of precipitation – an average of a hundred centimetres of rain each year. Compared to the rest of France, which is compact and crisscrossed by large, navigable rivers, Brittany has always been remote, so remote in fact that the department at the far western tip of Brittany is called le Finistère – the end of the earth. Until the sixteenth century, the Celtic Duchy wasn't part of France at all. It took a strategic marriage between Louis XII and Anne de Bretagne (the duchess regnant of Brittany), plus some intense negotiating to secure a treaty's worth of local privileges, before Brittany was brought into the Gallic fold. Still, the province remained defiantly separate in its customs and its language. Breton, a Celtic language similar to Welsh, was the predominant language in the western half of the region until the twentieth century.[1] To this day, Bretons maintain and rejoice in a reputation of being proud, resilient, stubborn, separate ... and a little remote and wild.

Buckwheat Takes Root in Brittany

Sarrasin or *sarrazin*, the most common of the two French expressions for buckwheat (the other is *blé noir* or 'black wheat'), is also the term coined during the Crusades (eleventh to thirteenth centuries) to describe Muslims or Arabs. Legend has it that buckwheat arrived in Brittany during the Crusades, ostensibly by the *Sarrasins* or Saracens, though both the timeframe and origin are difficult to authenticate. Elsewhere in Europe, buckwheat was also believed to have been introduced by Saracens; the English originally dubbed buckwheat Saracen corn, the Germans called it *Heidenkorn* (heathen corn), and to this day buckwheat is *grana de saraceno* in Italian. (The modern English word comes from the Dutch *bokweit* – beech wheat, after the beechnuts that buckwheat groats resemble.)[2] All etymology aside, buckwheat's origins can be traced much further east as the plant is native to Northern China. It was introduced to Europe via trade routes through Turkey, Russia, and the Netherlands, and did not become an established crop in France until almost 200 years after the last Crusade, a date that corresponds more closely to the crop's widespread arrival in Europe.[3]

The first mention of buckwheat cultivation in France dates back to a charter written in 1460 by a priest in Avranches, a town in Normandy just twelve kilometres from the Brittany border. A reference to buckwheat in Brittany appears in 1503, but perhaps the most significant reference can be found in the *Grandes Heures d'Anne de Bretagne*.[4] The illuminated manuscript, commissioned between 1505 and 1510 by Anne de Bretagne while she was Queen of France, is filled with illustrations of flowering plants, including *blé de turquie* (Turkish wheat), or buckwheat.[5]

The inclusion of buckwheat among the other flower illustrations in the *Grandes Heures d'Anne de Bretagne* is a far better indication of its botanical properties than any of the names it has been given in French or English. Common buckwheat (*Fagopyrum esculentum*) is, in fact, a flowering seed plant with heart-shaped leaves, whitish-pink flowers, and long red stems reminiscent of those of its two closest botanical cousins, rhubarb and sorrel. As a crop, buckwheat thrives in poor and acidic soils in which many grains cannot grow. It does especially well in cool, damp climates. Quick to germinate, the short-season crop requires little work before harvest. It attracts few pests and its dense canopy of leaves chokes out most weeds. After the harvest, the fast-decomposing stems and leaves can be ploughed under for green manure that replenishes a field's soil. And if all that weren't enough, buckwheat's melliferous flower clusters are highly attractive to bees, making it one of the highest-yielding honey plants.[6]

Fifteenth-century Bretons couldn't have found a better food crop for their fields than buckwheat. The cool, damp climate of the Brittany peninsula was just right for the plants, as were the poor soil conditions, particularly inland. Here was a crop that could be sown in plots where nothing else would grow. A crop that could convert untilled land into arable fields. A crop whose season was so short, it could even be sandwiched between winter and summer plantings to both replenish the soil and produce an extra harvest. Moreover, this 100-day plant (as it was nicknamed) yielded eleven to fifteen groats, whereas a head of wheat only yielded five to ten kernels.[7]

The small, trigonal groats could be easily milled into flour that was exceptionally nourishing – we now know that buckwheat is high in protein, fibre, and trace nutrients. (The only thing buckwheat didn't have going for it was gluten, so it couldn't be used to make bread.) By the late sixteenth century, buckwheat had become such a staple grain in Brittany that in 1587 the Breton writer and jurist Noël Du Fail declared, 'Without this grain [*le bled noir*], introduced to us sixty years ago, the poor would greatly suffer.'[8]

Buckwheat held another major advantage for Breton peasants: because it had been introduced to the region well after most other cereal grains (wheat, rye, oats), it was exempt from church tithing (*la dîme*) and seigneurial mill dues (*les droits de banalité*), two taxes levied on all farm products up until the French Revolution.[9] Farmers staunchly defended the exemption, and records show that in 1641 and 1643, two different groups took the matter to court at the *Parlement de Bretagne* – and won both cases.[10] Over a hundred years later, the tithe exemption remained a particular source of contention between peasants and clergy: in 1774, the priest of Plounévez in the centre of Brittany complained that his church wasn't earning enough because his parishioners primarily grew tithe-exempt buckwheat.[11]

From Porridge to Pancakes

There is little record of how buckwheat was prepared or served during the first 300 years of its cultivation in Brittany, even though it was the primary foodstuff on most farms. A true peasant food, buckwheat wouldn't have been found on a noble's table or included in a banquet menu, especially since its most common form of consumption was as *la bouillie*, a rudimentary porridge made of flour and water. Bretons made porridges out of all the grains they grew, including oats, millet, and rice. Although most were cooked like polenta in a

From Peasant Food to Posh Ingredient

large pot over a fire, they could also be simmered in a fabric bag submerged in a cooking liquid to make a *farz*, a sliceable dumpling similar to Scottish haggis. Today, *farz* are better known to cooks than *la bouillie*, thanks to *le kig-ha-farz*, a meat stew from northwest Brittany that was popularized as a festive, family-style dish in the twentieth century.[12]

Ultimately, it took the French Revolution – and the new republic's urgent need to re-establish food production in the decimated French countryside – for any formal attention to be paid to buckwheat's attributes and culinary uses.

In 1795, the newly formed *Commission d'Agriculture et des Arts* (the equivalent of the Ministry of Agriculture) published *Instruction sur le sarrasin*, a seven-page pamphlet to promote buckwheat. The pamphlet explains in great detail the best practices for cultivating buckwheat, and concludes with an enthusiastic list of all the ways to prepare it: 'The buckwheat groat (*la graine du sarrasin*) contains a flour which can be made into different types of porridges (*bouillies*), soups, very tasty and nourishing *galettes*, crêpes, frying batters, etc. Whole buckwheat groats cooked in water and served with butter make a good dish.'[13]

Not everyone might have agreed with this high recommendation of buckwheat's gustative properties. Among the dissenters would have been Madame la Marquise de la Rochejaquelein, a member of the deposed French aristocracy who published her memoirs of surviving the French Revolution in the early nineteenth century. As the young wife of a Royalist, Madame la Marquise was forced to hide out on a farm in Brittany in 1795, the same year *Instruction sur le sarrasin* was published. She found the Bretons and their buckwheat distinctly unsavoury, recounting, 'The poor Bretons are extremely dirty. They smoke tobacco, they drink straight from the jug and eat out of bowls, do not own plates or forks; cabbage soup and buckwheat porridge (*bouillie de blé noir*) served with buttermilk are their only food. Happily, their butter is very good: it was our solace.'[14] In those few lines, Madame La Marquise neatly (if not very kindly) summarizes the Breton peasant condition from the fifteenth century until the French Revolution: uncouth, inexorably poor, and subsisting on a diet of soup and buckwheat porridge.

Over a century later, the buckwheat porridge Madame la Marquise described had changed very little. In *Coutumes populaires de la Haute Bretagne* (1882), folklorist Paul Sébillot collected a recipe for *la bouillie de blé noir* which called for mixing buckwheat flour into water with a little salt, then cooking and stirring the mixture for fifteen minutes, or until nine thick, gloppy bubbles had formed and popped on the surface. Sébillot goes on to explain that '[l]ike all porridges, buckwheat porridge is usually eaten straight from the pot in which it was made [...]. A pat of butter is placed to melt in the centre into which everyone dips a spoonful of porridge. Egg-size scoops [of porridge] are also dunked into bowls of milk, buttermilk, or scalded milk'.[15]

The two accounts given by la Marquise de la Rochejacquelein and Paul Sébillot provide specific insights into how buckwheat was typically prepared in Breton kitchens. But the *Instruction sur le sarrasin* pamphlet showed remarkable prescience with its mention of 'tasty and nourishing galettes and crêpes'.

Seeds

According to the *Larousse Gastronomique,* the term *galette* is used to refer to any type of round, thin, or flat cake. The entry goes on to explain that *galettes* 'probably date back to the Neolithic period when grain porridges were spread on hot stones to cook'.[16] In Brittany, the common use of *galette* holds traces of the archaic *Larousse* reference as it means a savoury crêpe made by cooking buckwheat batter on a hot, round griddle. (Crêpe is used to denote a wheat flour preparation that usually constitutes a snack or dessert.) The only part of Brittany where a buckwheat crêpe is not called a *galette* is in the Finistère where they are called *crêpes de blé noir*. The distinction reflects the strong Breton language influence in the area: in Breton, buckwheat crêpes are *krampouezh gwinizh du* (*krampouezh* = crêpes, *gwinizh* = wheat, *du* = black). One thing that does not change throughout the areas of Brittany, however, is the basic *galette* batter which, like porridge, calls for just flour, water, and salt.

But oh, what a difference a cooking technique can make. Thin, tender, 'tasty and nourishing' *galettes* also held two practical advantages: they could be made ahead, and they could be – and often were – eaten in place of bread. For a time, porridge and *galettes* were both part of the Breton rural experience. La Mère Denis, a Breton washerwoman whose appearances in washing machine commercials made her a 1970s celebrity, once described how her childhood meals never varied: breakfast was buckwheat porridge,

Figure 2. Drawing of a galette/crêpe maker from the late nineteenth century. Marchande de crêpes à Quimperlé *by Jean-Baptiste-Jules Trayer, Musée de Bretagne archives.*

supper was soup and *galettes*, and Sunday dinner was salt pork with potatoes and *galettes*. By the time she was sharing those reminiscences however, buckwheat porridge had been all but forgotten by everyone except truly poor, rural Bretons.[17]

As *galettes* replaced porridge on Breton tables, they made their way into all aspects of Breton life. Every household, rich or poor, rural or urban, had the utensils needed to make *galettes*: a round, flat cast iron griddle (*galetière* in French/*billig* in Breton), a wooden spoon or rake-like spatula for spreading the batter (*rouable/rozell*), and a long, flat galette-turner for flipping and serving (*tourne-galettes/spanell*). At home, *galettes* were prepared weekly – often on Fridays as a way to adhere to the Catholic Friday Fast. Extras would be stacked under a damp towel to be eaten throughout the rest of the week. Because of the skill and finesse required to prepare *galettes*, a major shift began to occur in Brittany's food culture. Gifted *crêpiers* and *crêpières* figured out that people were willing to pay for good-quality *galettes* (and, by extension, sweet, wheat flour crêpes). A cottage industry developed which would ultimately expand beyond home and hearth (Figure 2) to include cafés, market stands, social events, and an ever-growing number of crêperies. Butter and buttermilk were the traditional accompaniments, though in the early nineteenth century, a *galette* maker in Rennes gained renown for topping his *galettes* with a fried egg for what is perhaps the first filled *galette* on record.[18]

The Near Demise of Breton Buckwheat

It is no exaggeration to say that *galettes* are what saved buckwheat in Brittany. By the end of the nineteenth century, buckwheat cultivation was in sharp decline due to newly introduced root vegetables (potatoes, turnips, and carrots) and nitrogen-fixing feed crops (clover, alfalfa) that had begun to replace buckwheat in field rotation. Innovation, mechanization, and transportation made wheat production easier and more profitable. Between 1890 and 1938, buckwheat production in France dropped from 600,000 hectares to 260,000 hectares.

Ironically, it was during the very time that buckwheat was hurtling toward its nadir that it became the symbol of Brittany that it is today. Once the first railway to Brittany was opened in 1857, the region was discovered by artists and tourists who revelled in the area's rustic authenticity.[19] That outside recognition brought about an increased cultural awareness among Bretons, and the humble, traditional, ubiquitous crop that had saved Brittany from starvation throughout the centuries came to represent all the strength, beauty, resilience, and uniqueness of a region that was just beginning to recognize its heritage.[20]

None of the awareness or recognition increased buckwheat cultivation, though. The worst was to come after World War II when the introduction of nitrogen-based fertilizers facilitated the production of higher-yield grains (wheat, corn). At the same time, the French government embarked on a land re-parcelling initiative that offered economic incentives for incorporating smaller fields – like those in which buckwheat was still being grown – into larger tracts. By the 1960s, buckwheat production had dwindled to just 100,000 hectares in Brittany. Twenty years later, the snowy white fields of buckwheat in flower had all but disappeared from the landscape and buckwheat production plummeted to a mere 200 or so hectares.

But *galettes* were still going strong. '*Galettes* are synonymous with Brittany,' proclaimed Breton food historian Patrick Hervé in 1982.[21] They embodied the heritage of the past while representing a delicious culinary present, especially since fillings (ham, egg, and cheese being the most common and the most popular) had made the fare a lot less monotonous at home and a lot more enticing in crêperies (Figure 3). Thousands of tons of buckwheat flour continued to feed the *galette* habits both in Brittany and throughout France, where crêperies continued to spread. Yet little did most consumers suspect that the buckwheat flour in their Breton *galettes* was being milled from groats that came from Russia, Poland, Canada, Brazil, South Africa, and China.[22]

Figure 3. Galette complète with ham, egg, and cheese, used with permission from the Breizh Café.

Certified 100% Breton Buckwheat

Then, in 1987, a group of farmers decided to bring buckwheat production back to Brittany. It all started with Albert Rolland, an agronomist who wanted to rehabilitate the overgrown plots of land on his farm in central Brittany. After trying various field-clearing methods, Rolland rediscovered what previous generations had long known about buckwheat: that it was particularly, if not uniquely, suited to cultivation in Brittany. Initially planted as a smother crop, his buckwheat experiment exceeded his expectations. Not only did the plants smother out the weeds and replenish the soil, but they yielded a harvest of buckwheat groats – an unexpected bonus that Rolland sold to a Dutch mill because there was no longer a market for locally-grown buckwheat in Brittany. Three years later, Rolland was one of ninety farmers who partnered with local mills to create a Breton buckwheat cooperative.[23] That cooperative would go on to become the Association Blé Noir Tradition Bretagne (ABNTB), a non-profit organization that continues to promote buckwheat cultivation and buckwheat flour production in Brittany. From the outset, the association set high standards and strict guidelines, including banning fertilizers, pesticides, and herbicides and requiring the sole use of a specific strain of buckwheat, *la harpe noire*, developed at the National Agricultural Institute (INRA) in Rennes. In 2010, the ABNTB obtained Protected Geographical Indication (PGI/IGP) EU status for Breton-grown buckwheat. Today, 2100 tons of *Farine de blé noir de Bretagne*® are milled from buckwheat grown on 3300 hectares of land by 400 certified farmers.[24]

Buckwheat Goes Borderless

If the strong associative identity that has defined buckwheat in Brittany is the result of the centuries during which the region was cut off from the rest of France by geography, language, and culture, then its modern-day success story is exactly the opposite. Bygone Bretons may have remained insular in their habits and traditions, but today's population is very much a part of the global community. High-speed trains, high-tech companies, and higher education provide ever-increasing access to the region, which is now deemed the part of France with the highest quality of life.[25] Brittany and all things Breton have become desirable commodities. Pastry aficionados are now fans of *kouign amann*, a rich, flaky, buttery pastry from Brittany – the term means 'butter cake' in Breton – and butter lovers can now find salted butter from Brittany in gourmet shops and high-end groceries around the world.

In this global economic setting, Breton entrepreneurs continue to find innovative and lucrative ways to evangelize their emblematic seed. Perhaps the best known of these is Bertrand Larcher, the founder of the Breizh Café restaurant group. Larcher's Breizh Cafés can be credited with elevating *galettes* to the realm of French gastronomy when he received the special recognition prize from *Le Fooding* restaurant guide in 2010.[26] Since then, the Breizh Café group has become a springboard for Larcher's passion for buckwheat. In 2016, he opened La Maison du Sarrasin, a sleek, modern *épicerie fine* in Saint-Malo that specializes buckwheat products – primarily, but not exclusively, from Brittany. Hubert

Niveleau, a young Breton chef who trained as a professional crêpe-maker, has become another champion of Breton buckwheat at Le Sarra, his restaurant in Paris where he turns *galettes* into tacos and samosas, sprinkles salads with Breton-grown buckwheat groats, and adds Breton buckwheat flour to his desserts. And there are many more acting as ambassadors for the heritage seed who spread the word as they promote and sell their products and services. It's a good time to be in the Breton buckwheat business, too. Buckwheat is *archi-tendance* (ultra-trendy) all over France and has become the darling of foodies, French chefs, nutritionists, and, perhaps most importantly, the media.

As Breton buckwheat expands beyond its regional borders, it is undergoing an identity crisis regarding its name. Both *sarrasin* and *blé noir* have been used interchangeably since the sixteenth century, but *blé noir* has always been the predominant term in Brittany. When the Association Blé Noir Tradition Bretagne had to decide between *sarrasin* or *blé noir* in the name for Breton-grown buckwheat flour for their Protected Geographic Indication (IGP/PGI) application, the group chose *blé noir,* which more closely reflects the seeds' Breton name, *gwinizh du*.[27] Conversely, despite the strong Breton roots of La Maison du Sarrasin and Le Sarra, each has adopted *sarrasin,* the preferred term for buckwheat outside of Brittany. That may seem minor, but linguistically, it denotes a major change in how Breton buckwheat will be marketed and perceived.

In the current culinary landscape, perception is everything. Buckwheat grown in Brittany is already a marketer's dream. It ticks all the boxes: local, sustainable, high-protein, low-glycaemic, gluten-free, heritage, whole grain, good for bees. Add a thrilling name that offers a hint of the exotic (and expunges any misleading reference to wheat), and *le sarrasin breton* could be the next quinoa or freekeh.

All this hype presents both an opportunity and a danger for the future of buckwheat in Brittany. When a food goes posh, its price goes up. Today, a one-kilo bag of Breton buckwheat flour costs three to four times more than a one-kilo bag of wheat flour. Success invites competition: Francine, the largest flour distributor in France, has recently begun marketing its own *farine de sarrasin*. In a fast-changing food world, trendiness can only take you so far, and it can be hard to sustain interest in a market where everyone is forever looking for the next new thing. Finally, while there may be more fields of buckwheat on the Breton landscape, more coverage of Breton buckwheat in the press, and more brands capitalizing on the cachet and quality of Breton buckwheat, there is less buckwheat to be found as an ingredient in Breton cupboards. As a symbol, Breton buckwheat endures. But as a staple, it continues to fade away.

The state of buckwheat in Brittany is just one example of how heritage foods around the world are gaining the much-needed recognition to survive – but losing their essence. To truly preserve these food traditions, we must ask ourselves: what can be done to keep products like Breton buckwheat from being fetishized as specialty ingredients or marginalized as luxury foods? How can we protect them from market fluctuations and an onset of consumer lassitude? How can we ensure that they retain a food staple role, and continue to nourish and sustain generations to come?

Notes

1. Région Bretagne, 'La Bretagne et Son Histoire', <http://www.bretagne.bzh/jcms/TF071112_5063/fr/histoire> [accessed 14 May 2018].
2. Meilang Zhou and others, *Molecular Breeding and Nutritional Aspects of Buckwheat* (London: Academic Press 2016), p. 23 <https://books.google.fr/books?id=YE_pCAAAQBAJ&pg> [accessed 20 May 2018].
3. Em Miège. *Recherches sur les principales espèces de Fagopyrum (Sarrasin)* (Rennes: Imprimerie des Arts et manufactures, 1910), p. 14
4. Association Blé Noir de Bretagne, *Cahier des charges IGP* (PDF), 2009.
5. Jean Bourdichon, illuminator, *Horae ad usum Romanum, dites Grandes Heures d'Anne de Bretagne* (manuscript, 1505-1510), p. 12 V <http://gallica.bnf.fr/ark:/12148/btv1b52500984v/f33.item.zoom> [accessed 20 May 2018].
6. E.S. Oplinger and others, 'Buckwheat', *Alternative Field Crops Manual* (Madison: University of Wisconsin-Extension, 1989) <https://hort.purdue.edu/newcrop/afcm/buckwheat.html> [accessed 3 May 2018].
7. Bleuzen du Pontavice, *Le Blé Noir* (St-Thonan: Coop Breizh, 2005), p. 13.
8. Miège, p. 14.
9. Patrick Hervé, *Fars bretons et kig-ha-farz* (Morlaix: Skol Vreizh, 2014), p. 14.
10. Michel Nassiet, '11 juin 1675, un document inédit sur la révolte des Bonnets Rouges', *Pour une histoire sociale des villes: Mélanges offerts à Jacques Maillard* (Rennes: Presses universitaires de Rennes, 2005) <https://books.google.fr/books?id=oTcUCwAAQBAJ> [accessed 4 May 2018].
11. Hervé, *Fars bretons et kig-ha-farz*, p. 14.
12. Alain Croix, *L'Age d'Or de la Bretagne: 1532-1675* (Rennes: Ouest-France, 1992), p. 138.
13. Commission d'Agriculture et des Arts, 'Instruction sur le sarrasin' (Paris: Imprimerie de la Feuille du Cultivateur, 1795), p. 7.
14. Madame la Marquise de la Rochejaquelein, *Collection des mémoires rélatifs à la Révolution française, Vol. 8* (Paris: Baudouin Frères, 1823), p. 343 <https://books.google.fr/books?id=ZrovAAAAMAAJ&> [accessed 4 May 2018].
15. Louis Le Cunff, *Cuisine et Gastronomie de la Bretagne* (Rennes : Ouest-France, 1976), p. 53.
16. *Larousse Gastronomique*, ed. by Robert J. Courtine (Paris: Librairie Larousse, 1984) p. 471.
17. Patrick Hervé, *Ar Boued: Pratiques alimentaires de Bretagne* (Morlaix: Skol Vreizh, 1982), p. 25.
18. Simone Morand, *Gastronomie bretonne d'hier et d'aujourd'hui* (Paris: Flammarion, 1965), p. 305-306.
19. OT Rennes Bretagne Express <https://www.tourisme-rennes.com/fr/lgv1h25/bretagne-express-lgv> [accessed 4 May 2018].
20. Key word search 'galette', Bibliothèque des Champs-Libres, Rennes.
21. Hervé, *Ar Boued*, p. 25.
22. Patrick Tanguy, 'Le blé noir, richesse des terres pauvres', *Ar Men* no. 45, août 1992, p. 13.
23. Tanguy, p. 3.
24. Blé Noir Tradition de Bretagne, Dossier de Presse 2017-2018 < https://www.blenoir-bretagne.com/images/Actualites/dossierdepresse.pdf> [accessed 14 May 2018].
25. 24matins.fr, 'Qualité de vie en France : La Bretagne arrive en tête, 2016 <https://www.24matins.fr/qualite-de-vie-france-bretagne-arrive-tete-406372> [accessed 15 May 2018].
26. *Le Fooding*, 'Le Palmarès Fooding 2010 est servi' <https://lefooding.com/fr/best-of/le-palmares-fooding-2010-est-servi-tyq6kw> [accessed 17 May 2018].
27. Interview with Christine Larsonneur, director Association Tradition Blé Noir Bretagne, 5 April 2018.

Field Selection in Plant Breeding: Different Ways to Make a Variety

Renata Christen

Farmers and gardeners were the original citizen scientists, discovering novelty in their fields and selecting favoured plants to replicate and steward. They selected and developed cultivars that we know today as our run-of-the-mill vegetables, fruits, and grains. Plant breeding, which began to take off as a formal science in the late nineteenth century, has had forcible implications for Western diets: these plant scientists have wielded enormous power by standardizing the millennia-old practices of food growers around the world in terms of choosing what makes a good variety. If a desired outcome in a formalized breeding program is to develop a potato with the ability to withstand high amounts of frying, there will be a screening process wherein thousands of potatoes are assessed and only a handful chosen for their 'chipping' ability; namely, robustness in becoming a potato chip. Plant breeding has harnessed the vast genetic riches of our collective food heritage and applied it to meet specific needs.

A rote activity of plant breeders is phenotyping, an art of 'seeing'. Plant varieties or crops are reviewed for physical and genetic characteristics, which are often the result of how the plant has been nurtured by its environment.[1] If a crop has struggled after a particularly harsh winter but survived, plant breeders log the observation that this crop is hardy. Other characteristics plant breeders phenotype cover a vast range, from drought tolerance to foliage density. Despite technological advances, plant breeders still depend on growing out plants and recording notes on all they see 'in the field' to determine whether their lab work is on target with pre-established objectives.[2]

Though not an exact science, this formulaic approach to 'making' food has often serviced the needs of an increasingly globalized food system and urbanized citizenry. Plant breeders debating whether to advance or cull a given tomato line in their breeding program have tangible implications for what choice consumers have access to in markets, grocery stores, seed catalogues, and so forth. In this essay, I present several case studies that illustrate how different practices of phenotyping construct new ways of knowing about food, through how seeds are managed and selected, while exploring different ways phenotyping informs whether a given variety is 'good' enough to eventually be made publicly available.[3]

Field Selection in Plant Breeding

Modelling Broccoli Aesthetics

In front of a gaming laptop, the plant breeder, John, clicks through different photos of broccoli. The photos show a lot of crop variation, with his hand in every photo holding a ruler to measure different broccoli heads by width. John had been asked to select for the most ideal form of broccoli, which involves selecting broccoli crowns for their bead uniformity. The crown of a broccoli plant contains thousands of beads or florets. Once John decides on what broccolis in his trial have the 'right' kind of beads, he can broaden his experiment to choose broccolis with other desired characteristics as well, such as broccolis with an appropriate colour at the time of harvest. John works to improve the predictability of performance in heads of broccoli, refining 'varieties with the right combination traits' that won't suffer from problems that affect aesthetics, and that do well in a wide variety and range of environmental conditions.

At John's research station, good uniformity for a head of broccoli is understood as compact and firm. Some broccolis may exhibit what is considered 'really bad uniformity': loose splaying or limp florets. A range of photos have broccoli heads that are yellowing due to heat stress – the effects of which have made their beads degrade prematurely. The way that John assesses broccoli heads and bead uniformity is through a one to five rating. If entire harvests of broccoli heads do not measure up to standard, they will get rejected from grocery stores. John mentions that grocery stores are 'in touch with the pulse of consumer preference', and the breeders at John's research station put faith in grocery stores to translate consumer preference to the breeders as they select for good heads of broccoli. For John, grocery stores set the agenda, because farmers need seeds that will deliver what grocery stores want.

Prior to the experiment, John met with colleagues to collectively agree upon what was a good and bad broccoli bead. It made me wonder how much of their experiment would have turned out differently had there been a different conception of 'best broccoli' – and whether that conception is determined by consumers themselves or by grocery stores based on perceptions of consumer preference? As John explains, it is partly a matter of pulling together as many values as possible in one place to ensure that 'goods' are generalized: 'Our problem was in striving for this idea of "what is cosmic, beautiful broccoli" … it makes you question whether there's one ideotype in the universe that everyone recognizes as ideal broccoli, or is it completely subjective, or are we wasting our time recording these quality scores?'

John reflects on how the interpersonal differences among lab colleagues can be fairly extreme, and how these differences of opinion can affect the outcome of the breeding trial. John and his colleagues advance the best-ranked broccolis, indicating that their conceptions of a 'quality broccoli head' are what eventually get delivered to consumers. John explains the process:

> And it turns out that Stu thought broccoli line ten was the best, and Laura thought broccoli line five was the best, and I thought broccoli line one was the

best. But Laura didn't think broccoli line one was very good. It's still on the higher end, but not her top pick … also from that trial, these are our scores, five to one. So, I gave out a lot more ones than my co-workers did for various traits. It was fascinating to see the variation. Stu thought a lot of the broccoli was a three, which is 'just good enough to sell at the market' like 'average'. This is all a meta-study that I did, and I found out that when we described beautiful broccoli, the two most important things were head uniformity and smoothness, and bead uniformity. And all the different raters that did this trial were able to explain variation in quality in terms of two other more objective traits.

After conducting the field trials, John's colleagues pooled their ratings. Their aim was to produce an all-encompassing representation that captured as many good traits as possible. They collected information on the colour of the broccoli heads, firmness, and width, ranked by a one to five score. For the photos previewed on John's computer, the focus of their study was bead size and uniformity. John thought these are the objective traits, and overall quality is the most subjective trait, 'even though we made our decisions based on overall quality'. He viewed the assessment process as 'too subjective', so he transformed all the one to five rankings into a statistic: 'I was like "that's kinda messed up, 'cause, how do we know we're actually creating good data here?" So, I had this idea to model broccoli quality in terms of all of the other data that we collected using a type of linear regression.'

According to John, it is important to make the most 'professional' recommendations to farmers and retailers on what constitutes the best broccoli possible. Having a linear regression model highlighted all the variables, and attempted to transform a seemingly subjective, process-oriented outcome into something resembling objectivity, implying that technology can help make the subjectivity of scientific practices less personal.[4] As he put it, 'Our first try was to say "overall quality" is what we're aiming for in assigning ranks to these broccoli heads, and that gets philosophical pretty fast. If we look at some pictures of different lines from different populations we developed, there's quite a bit of variation going on here.' The messiness of individual assessment gets reconstructed into a clean graph to communicate professional opinion about seed and crop value. This filtration process highlights how scientists must negotiate with each other regarding which of their recommended selections will advance, while simultaneously meeting client expectations. It demonstrates the constraints involved when making selections, insomuch as John and his colleagues have less freedom to follow the chance encounter if and when novelty presents itself. As we will see, other breeders may still be concerned with satisfying the end user – for farmers, consumers, and businesses – but their methods involve taking a different approach to the selection process.

Winter Wheat in the Field

Clusters of green wheat plants stand vigilant in a sea of exposed hardened soil. With rain clouds passing overhead, we use plastic boot covers to protect our iPad and notebooks. The

Field Selection in Plant Breeding

wheat breeder, Sarah, motions with her rubber boot, 'See this rock? It prevents germination from occurring.' The field is covered with rocks. As we walk through the clusters of different winter wheat varieties, our task is to record the number of plants that survived and how well they're growing – also known as recording the germination of winter kill – and compare these figures to last year's observations. Overall, we assess over fifty different varieties.

Sarah eyeballs each variety to determine their winter kill percentage. We debate several of the stands, some more robust than others. 'It looks like this one group survived, but what qualifies as "good enough" survival?' I ask. 'If it's green and alive,' Sarah replies. Some stands were no longer there, or were shrivelled into brown mush from the encroaching spring thaw. For those stands that appear thriving, I type a note that says 'nice' or 'very good' into the iPad. The heartier plants are vigorous, fully fleshed out and strong looking. It made me wonder how well these capable-looking plants would tolerate insect predation later in the season. Maybe the crops that scored well for winter kill would not be able to handle a drought. Measuring winter kill percentages is just one step in the process of evaluating winter wheat varieties for their overall fitness.

We discuss the possibility of using drones to complete work like winter kill check instead of having to visit the plots ourselves. Sarah explains how drones enable you to look at vastly more plants, thousands and thousands of different varieties that would otherwise be difficult for an individual or crew of technicians to assess. But she explains that we'd then need to be reductionist in how we view the crops. Drones can analyze a lot of data at once, she explains, but at the end of the day, the breeder is still the one who must pore over the drone-captured images and make assessments: 'I think we miss the opportunity that, in the past, the farmer would notice something they weren't even expecting and then have the opportunity to work with the chance encounter.'

Sarah explains how, in the United States today, farmers are farming on larger acreage so fewer eyes are reviewing crops and selecting genotypes per acre. 'Farmers just don't have time to spend observing and looking at a bunch of wheat trials,' she comments. The trade-off with scaling up production has repercussions, insomuch as farmers are growing fewer plants and only working on several commodities during any given season. She says, 'Someone is determining priorities, often scientists are defining whatever priorities should be worked on, and then they make genetic variability [through crossing lines], then they put out a bunch of diversity, select the ones they like best, and then release them to the public. Farmers are only involved in the breeding process as the end user. They're the last tailpiece, they just receive the varieties that are developed.'

While the use of drones could help Sarah spot thriving plants in her experiment more quickly, she explains how it would make the work less precise, and the chance of seeing something unique more fleeting. For Sarah, plant breeding isn't just about selecting based on a predefined outcome, unlike with John's broccoli trials; it's about noticing a winter wheat line that may look stumpy but has incredible resilience in the face of pests and diseases. In her field trials, Sarah also works with small-scale farmers to make selections, which extends the experiments' range of vision; traits that are immediately desirable for the end user get incorporated and co-created at an earlier stage. As farmers are empowered to participate in the breeding process, they can help bridge an ever-increasing divide between people and the source of their food, as farmers are often embedded within the communities they serve.[5]

Nose-to-Tail Winter Squash

Breeders depend on evaluating their crops outside the lab in a 'real life' setting, giving each plant of a given variety a numbered score on the research station farm. Scoring a plant may depend on the trait: for instance, powdery mildew disease, a fungal disease that compromises the appearance and growth of its host, might be scored from zero to one hundred whereas beetle damage is rated on a scale of one to five. The standard protocol of assigning a number or score is part of an assessment guideline. One breeder I spoke with described how his field visits are more about 'deciding which plants will live and which will die' and less about keeping detailed records from the field, highlighting the fact that breeding is a fluid practice.

The squash breeder, Charles, illustrates this point, describing his method as taking 'an older school approach'. If a group of crops fits his predefined criteria, he'll save the seeds and take extensive data on those exclusively while discarding what remains. He tells the following story to illustrate this point: 'We had someone visit our field over the summer, and he was all ready to make selections and take detailed notes on everything and I was like, "Sorry … I know there are some people that do it that way, but I don't." I was like, "Here's a bundle of flags and let's go! Step over the vines, don't trip."'

In the fall, after field selections have been made, the squash Charles liked best are brought in from the field and undergo a curing process in the offices and pole barns of Charles's breeding program, where his technicians work. At different points in the process, field technicians spend weeks chopping up squash in an assembly line, processing the fruit for seeds. The squash whose seed is harvested get tested for soluble sugars known as brix (a refractometer device is used to measure and determine the sweetness of a given crop), dry matter, and colour. Photographs are taken which, altogether, yield a dataset that accompanies merely one packet of seed. This dataset gets evaluated months later. The seeds lie in wait within dust-covered tupperware bins.

Sitting around a computer, one of the field technicians begins clicking through images of squash, 'leading the tour on phenotypic records' while Charles sits with his laptop, following along on a spreadsheet with each squash on display. 'We're looking to see what stores well and retains great colour,' Charles explains. The squash that are being reviewed have cured for six weeks to finish metabolizing: 'they are what someone at a supermarket opens up and sees'.

The desired squash will have a 'really meaty neck without any ribs' and a heavier squash is more interesting, for purée purposes, than a smaller or lighter squash. Loud groans are issued unanimously at images of squash with brown spots on the skin. 'I could tell they were problems,' Charles acknowledges, recalling what he saw in the field. 'I like this but there's no drying information on it.' If data doesn't exist to correspond with a given image, the line in question will get trashed. It quickly becomes evident that Charles likes squash with the colour of a deep orange egg yolk. The stringy, pale yellow fruits are of no interest, nor are the ones with greener rinds. In the current set of seventy-five squash that are previewed, only fifteen make the cut.

Conclusion

> 'Modern methods of statistical design and analysis add precision to all of these decisions and quantitative genetic theory adds rationality to breeding plans, but art and experience – not precision genetics – are the key to successful use of these useful tools.' – *Unnamed plant breeder*[6]

The process of organizing data and reviewing squash at different stages enables Charles to streamline his phenotypic selection. His personalized approach to selection, based on a mix of breeding something he would use at home and simultaneously valued by grocery stores, is how he measures progress during his breeding effort. Charles has built up tacit knowledge from years of experience that guides him to make selections in an expert way.

The context of tidying up data through linear regression models or using drones to shortcut selections may ultimately miss the point about what it means to create something unique – the abbreviations in method posed by technology still only skim the surface of what may or may not be missing from the activity of breeding itself.[7] While a regression model can express the idea of a perfect broccoli in measurable, objective terms, it still remains external to the model itself, as data is ultimately the result of expert opinion. The algorithm is merely a stand-in for the expert's opinion, which solves the problem of efficiency through automation or standardization but retains the value system of the people who created that approach. Whereas food diversity was the result of a slow growth spanning thousands of years, today's breeding appears to value saving time and serving commercial needs in its methods.

Food production is much broader than these isolated stories – it begs the question of what goes missing in the specialization process of breeding for a scientist's or a corporation's version of an 'ideal' crop, and what possibility is latent in field selection that doesn't get the chance to shine. With plant breeding research in universities, the financial constraints are palpable; marketplace constraints are defining the outcome of many breeding efforts.[8] Sarah's winter wheat trials are less constrained than John's research institute broccoli trials insomuch as her audience – the farmers and bread bakers – are equally enthusiastic about overall quality as they are with incorporating novelty, and these end-users are invited to participate in her trials. The example of a perfect broccoli is a fixed idea, namely, arriving at a predefined product that grocery stores can expect farmers to produce: developing a seed that 'performs' as expected. While the squash breeder is also looking for his 'ideotype', his work is constantly re-evaluating itself – a process that is not written down and not fixed, and therefore potentially more explorative.

While these research experiments may be curtailed by limitations on time and resources, they are all innovating toward specific outcomes – prioritizing relationships, professionalism, and utility during their breeding efforts. What is the threshold where novelty is curtailed by necessity or efficiency? Hundreds of varietal lines – seeds – get left behind in breeder storerooms, representing an ocean of untapped potential that is rarely revisited after an initial trial. Such potential reminds me of the citizen-scientist farmers and gardeners who, like our contemporary breeders, selected based on their own ideas about what was a good seed crop. Knowing the multitude of flavours, colours, uses, and more latent in seeds offers much in terms of possibility, particularly when expanding beyond what's currently available in the market. The meaning and significance of a seed varies according to the context in which it is used and the culture in which it is developed.[9] If our current context trends toward selecting seeds by envisioning their commercial potential for instance, then we may be limiting ourselves to only one or two kinds of zucchini in a grocery store versus the hundreds that exist around the world. Such diversity of choice, for seeds and what they become, can only appear through an increased emphasis on collaboration – and, ultimately, a more decentralized food system.

Notes

1. A variety is a crop strain. While cultivar is the proper term for a 'cultivated variety' such as cherry tomatoes or pickling cucumbers, I will henceforth rely on the lay term 'variety' to describe modern cultivated varieties.
2. Use of the phrase 'in the field' throughout this essay is meant to signify trial plots at research stations or on university research farms.
3. The content for this essay comes from several months of participatory observation, in spring 2016, within different plant breeding programs at one university in the United States (names and numbers have been changed to respect the anonymity of the informants). Inspiration for the idea of a 'good' seed comes from F. Heuts and A. Mol, 'What Is a Good Tomato? A Case of Valuing in Practice', *Valuation Studies*, 1.2 (2013), 125-46.
4. See David A. Cleveland, 'Is Plant Breeding Science Objective Truth or Social Construction? The Case of Yield Stability', *Agriculture and Human Values*, 18.3 (September 2001), 251–70.
5. See Salvatore Ceccarelli, 'Efficiency of Plant Breeding', *Crop Science*, 55.1 (2015), 87–97. Ceccarelli shows that 'decentralization and the inclusion of farmers' participation increase the efficiency of a plant breeding program' (p. 88).
6. Callon (p. 265) as reported by D. N. Duvick, 'Genetic Contributions to Advances in Yield of U.S. Maize', *Maydica*, 37 (1992): 69-79.
7. I'm reminded of a quotation from Einstein: 'Supreme purity, clarity, and certainty at the cost of completeness. But what can be the attraction of getting to know such a tiny section of nature thoroughly, while one leaves everything subtler and more complex shyly and timidly alone? Does the product of such a modest effort deserve to be called by the proud name of a theory of the universe?' (qtd. in Ilya Prigogine, Isabelle Stengers, and Alvin Toffler, *Order Out of Chaos* (New York, NY: Bantam, 1984). p. 52-53.
8. We read how grocery stores often take the lead on what an 'ideal broccoli' should look like; however, as Callon offers, 'consumers are the consequence rather than the cause of marketing' (qtd. in Tanja Schneider and Steve Woolgar, 'Technologies of Ironic Revelation: Enacting Consumers in Neuromarkets', *Consumption Markets & Culture*, 15.2 (2012), 183).
9. See B. Latour, S. Woolgar, and J. Salk, *Laboratory Life: The Construction of Scientific Facts*, 2nd edn (Princeton, New Jersey: Princeton University Press, 1986), p. 107.

Preparing Seeds for Palatability: Chickens' Guts and Chefs' Tools

Len Fisher

Introduction

Seed-bearing plants have been around for some 400 million years. In that time, several groups of animals have evolved to be able to digest the seeds. Granivorous rodents have a modified digestive system loaded with fermenting bacteria to do the job.[1] Birds do it by using an even more extensively modified digestive system to break up the seeds and make them palatable. But humans do it with no modification to the digestive system whatsoever. Instead, we use cooking for the same purpose. Here I describe how human cooking not only mimics avian digestion, but improves on it, with examples that include the preparation of corn chowder by a nineteenth-century Boston chef. I argue that human chefs have improved on evolution when it comes to making seeds not only palatable, but also delicious food ingredients.

Seeds evolved to provide protection and food for the growing plant embryo. Often they are protected by an external hard coat, and the food itself comes in the form of starch: crystalline, gritty, and quite indigestible unless it is treated to soften it and break it down.

Birds process the seeds through a modified digestive system in which the seeds make their way progressively through a crop, proventriculus, and gizzard.[2] The crop stores the seeds, passing them gradually to the proventriculus (the upper part of the stomach) where gastric juices soften them, and then to the gizzard (the lower part of the stomach), where they are ground into smaller bits. Sometimes the material is passed back and forth between these two parts of the stomach until it is broken down and softened sufficiently to be passed along to the small intestine, where specialist enzymes break the long starch molecules into their component sugars for easy digestion.

Humans do not possess crops, proventriculi, or gizzards. What we do possess is cooking equipment, recipes, and saliva. The pantry replaces the crop. Knives, mortars, and pestles take the place of the gizzard. Marinades do the work of the proventriculus, and the cooking pot completes the job, bringing the starch to a state where it can finally be broken down by the enzymes in our saliva and intestines.[3]

On Treating Seeds

> 'The surprising discovery: no matter how gritty your whole grain, enough kneading, hydration, and resting will make it smooth.'
>
> Ken Albala (Facebook, 14 January 2018)

The first step in treating seeds is to break open any external covering. Fire often does the job in the Australian bush.[4] Indeed, many seeds will not germinate until they have been through a fire, where smoke may also be a factor.[5]

The chef's equivalent to an Australian bushfire is roasting, which can also introduce new and delicious flavours through heat-driven chemical reactions.[6] If we are happy for the seeds to have a gritty texture when we then eat them (as, for example, with roasted pumpkin seeds), then roasting is enough. But most of the time we want a softer texture and a more easily digestible product. Roasting is then just a start, and not the only one. As Ken Albala implies, grinding will do the job quite adequately if we work at it hard enough.

Birds use their gizzards; chefs can use querns, mortar, and pestle, or even the back of a knife, as in the earliest known recipe for corn chowder (green corn soup) from Mrs Lincoln's *Boston Cookbook* of 1884.[7]

The choice between roasting and grinding – or doing both – can be a matter of opinion when it comes to spice seeds such as cumin, coriander, cardamom, and fenugreek.[8] It depends partly on the flavour effects that we are trying to achieve. What is not controversial is that, if we don't want a gritty texture, then it is necessary for the starch inside to take up water and become hydrated.

When starch does take up water, it can take up quite a lot – up to seventy times the original volume, as I discovered when I heated individual

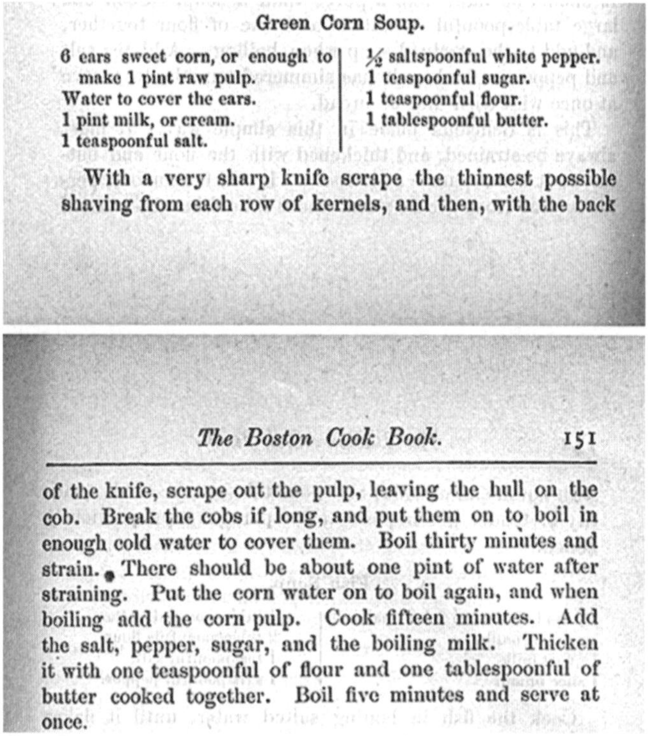

Green Corn Soup.

6 ears sweet corn, or enough to make 1 pint raw pulp.	½ saltspoonful white pepper.
Water to cover the ears.	1 teaspoonful sugar.
1 pint milk, or cream.	1 teaspoonful flour.
1 teaspoonful salt.	1 tablespoonful butter.

With a very sharp knife scrape the thinnest possible shaving from each row of kernels, and then, with the back

The Boston Cook Book. 151

of the knife, scrape out the pulp, leaving the hull on the cob. Break the cobs if long, and put them on to boil in enough cold water to cover them. Boil thirty minutes and strain. There should be about one pint of water after straining. Put the corn water on to boil again, and when boiling add the corn pulp. Cook fifteen minutes. Add the salt, pepper, sugar, and the boiling milk. Thicken it with one teaspoonful of flour and one tablespoonful of butter cooked together. Boil five minutes and serve at once.

Figure 1. Corn soup recipe (Mrs Lincoln's Boston Cook Book *(1884).*

Preparing Seeds for Palatability: Chickens' Guts and Chefs' Tools

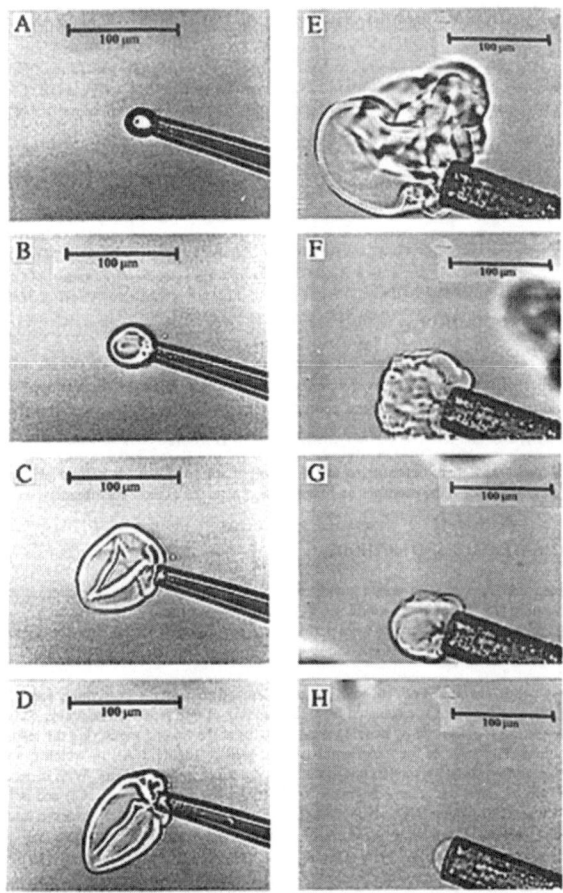

Figure 2: Swelling of individual potato starch granule in water. (A-E) Water temperature increasing from 59°C to 61°C (F-G) Softened granule sucked into capillary tube under hydrostatic pressure. Scale bar = 100μm.

potato starch grains in water under a microscope to make the world's smallest potato pancake.[9]

In taking up water, the starch changes from a granular crystalline substance to a soft, deformable gel, just right for being squeezed and manipulated by our digestive system. It can do so at room temperature (usually under slightly acidic conditions), but the process can take a very long time, which is why we cook. It doesn't require the temperature of boiling water. Potato or corn starch, for example, will hydrate quite satisfactorily at 60°C.

But boiling also creates physical forces to help loosen and separate the starch grains. Birds do this in their intestines, passing the material back and forth between proventriculus and gizzard to break it up, sometimes for hours on end. Luckily, we can produce a similar result by vigorous boiling, which is why the Boston Cookbook recommends boiling corn cobs for thirty minutes.

On Digestion

The long starch molecules that make up the grains are basically chains of different types of small sugar molecules. Once the grains are released and softened, all that is necessary for digestion is to break up the chains to release the individual sugars.

In birds, the enzymes that do this job are located towards the end of the digestive tract, in the small intestines. With us impatient humans, the process starts in the mouth, with the enzyme α-amylase.[10] This enzyme also provides a starting point for the indigenous South American and African beers, such as the Andean corn beer *chicha*, where the corn is chewed and mixed with saliva to start the fermentation process.[11] Bacteria associated with the saliva are also likely to be involved.[12]

But, in general, we must do our digesting inside the body. We can be grateful that, thanks to the activities of cooks and chefs, we do not have to sit on a perch for hours while it happens.

Notes

1. M.R. Perrin and B.A. Curtis, 'Comparative Morphology of the Digestive System of 19 Species of South African Myomorph Rodents in Relation to Diet and Evolution', *South African Journal of Zoology*, 15 (1980), 22-33.
2. Birger Svihus, 'Function of the Digestive System', *Journal of Applied Poultry Research*, 23 (2014), 306-14.
3. See, for example, Charlyne Mattox, *Cooking with Seeds* (Sydney: Da Capo Lifelong Books, 2015).
4. A. Macolm Gill, 'Fire and the Australian Flora: A Review', *Australian Forestry*, 38 (1975), 4-25.
5. Gavin R. Flematti and others, 'A Compound from Smoke That Promotes Seed Germination', *Science*, 305 (2004), 977.
6. Barbara Siegmund and Michael Murkovic, 'Changes in Chemical Composition of Pumpkin Seeds during the Roasting Process for Production of Pumpkin Seed Oil (Part 2: Volatile Compounds)', *Food Chemistry*, 84 (2004), 367-74.
7. D.A. Lincoln, *Boston Cook Book* (Boston: Roberts Brothers, 1884), p. 157.
8. 'Don't Dry Roast Spices', *Azélia's Kitchen*, 2011) <http://www.azeliaskitchen.net/dont-dry-roast-spices/> [accessed 9 March 2019].
9. L.R. Fisher, S.P. Carrington, and J.A. Odell, 'Deformation Mechanics of Individual Swollen Starch Granules', in *Starch: Structure and Functionality*, ed. by P.J. Frazier, P. Richmond, and A.M. Donald (Cambridge: Royal Society of Chemistry, 1997), pp. 105-14.
10. Peter J. Butterworth, Frederick J. Warren, and Peter R. Ellis, 'Human α-amylase and Starch Digestion: An Interesting Marriage', *Starch/Stärke*, 63 (2011), 395-405.
11. T.W. Henkel, 'Parakari, an Indigenous Fermented Beverage using Amylolytic Rhizopus in Guyana', *Mycologia*, 97.1 (2005), 1–11.
12. A.L. Freire and others, 'Bacteria Associated with Human Saliva Are Major Microbial Components of Ecuadorian indigenous Beers (*chicha*)' *Peer J*, 4.e1962 (2016) <10.7717/peerj.1962>.

Fenugreek: Seed of a New History of Modern North Africa

Anny Gaul

On 27 September 1918, a British subject named Muhammad Khalil Bartlett died in Cairo. Surviving him were his Egyptian widow and their four sons and two daughters.[1] The family lived in Sayyida Zaynab, a traditional quarter of Cairo named for its famous shrine of an Islamic woman saint. In the early twentieth century it was also known as a neighbourhood that absorbed many Egyptian families who had recently migrated from villages in Upper Egypt and the Nile Delta, seeking work or education in the city. When he died, Bartlett left behind – among other things – a silver watch and chain, a water buffalo, a quantity of wheat valued at fifty-five pounds, and an unspecified quantity of fenugreek.

Fenugreek's inclusion in Bartlett's probate record is striking because state records do not typically include spices and seasonings: most probates from this era tend to list staple items like grains and draft animals, unless the deceased happens to be an apothecary with a significant inventory of herbs and spices. State records in general offer a great deal of interesting material to scholars of food history, but they are usually along the lines of agricultural policies, schemes for fish hatcheries, or hygiene regulations for food markets: the kinds of things states tend to care about. In my experience, the raw stuff of the colonial archive is useful for understanding the history of the modern kitchen in North Africa, but it doesn't contain much in the way of specific smells, tastes, seasonings, and flavours – and yet fenugreek, time and time again, proved an exception. The mention of fenugreek (*halba*, in Arabic) in Bartlett's will offered a clue about the importance of this pungent seed in Egyptian and Moroccan society over the course of the twentieth century, and particularly the colonial period. As I eventually learned, fenugreek mattered enough to make its way into the colonial archives of both British-occupied Egypt (1882-1952) and France's protectorate in Morocco (1912-1956).

The next twist in the story was not the curious presence of fenugreek in state records, but its puzzling absence from culinary literature: as fenugreek was cropping up in the modern recordkeeping systems of colonial states in Egypt and Morocco, it was being quietly phased out of the culinary styles that were emerging as mainstream national cuisines among both countries' elites and growing middle classes. Starting in the 1930s and 40s, professional chefs, domestic science teachers, and other figures from the newly educated urban middle classes wrote the cookbooks, curricula, and menus that would determine the repertoire of their countries' new 'middling cuisines'.[2] As they did so, common rustic and rural recipes that featured fenugreek were consistently omitted – despite the fact that fenugreek has a centuries-old history in both places and features prominently in culinary landscapes across North Africa: a typical feast dish in rural Morocco, *rafisa*, is a stew of pigeon, lentils, and onions flavoured with fenugreek and served over a bed of shredded buttery flatbreads. And one of the signature breads of Egypt, *bataw*, has fenugreek kneaded into its dough. Indeed, fenugreek was first cultivated in the Eastern Mediterranean and its use likely dates back to ancient Egypt. Why, then, did fenugreek fall so swiftly out of favour among urban elites during the colonial period?

This essay reads fenugreek as the seed of a pungent subplot of North African culinary history that would otherwise remain untold. In part this is a story about the emergence of new notions of urbanity and refinement – in which fenugreek had no place – and how they related to understandings of private space, social mobility, and embodied identity. It is also a story about fenugreek's persistence in an unconventional form of the historical record: in family remedies and herbalists' recipes, spoken language, and the recipes of the countryside that persist largely in gestures and embodied knowledge, not cookbooks. In many ways the history of fenugreek in North Africa touches a nerve that runs deep in food scholarship, a nerve that is at once the connective tissue and the dividing line between rural cultures and agricultures on one hand, and the dictates of urbanity and urban cuisines on the other.

You Are What You Eat (and How You Smell)

One common narrative in modern food history relates to the rise and spread of French cuisine and its refined sauces as a hegemonic culinary style. Egyptian cuisine is a case in point: in the early twentieth century, béchamel arrived in Cairo and Alexandria by way of European chefs and Greek cuisine in particular was initially perceived as a hallmark of elite culture and prestige. Over the next several decades it became a symbol of middle-class refinement, and by the 1960s, béchamel was central to Egyptian national culinary tastes. What people stopped cooking, however, is just as telling as the new recipes they added to their culinary repertoires.

The twentieth century was a period of unprecedented mobility in Egypt and Morocco: rural-to-urban migration swelled the populations of cities, and industrialization spurred economic growth and increased educational opportunities prompted the expansion of the middle classes. Anticolonial nationalist movements arose, bringing with them new questions about how modern Egyptians and Moroccans should define and distinguish themselves. Often we discuss questions of changes in taste in ways that are divorced from the empirical and sensory aspects of the word, but the new nationalist middle classes' rejection of fenugreek has much to do with the visceral aspects of taste and its corollary, smell.

Fenugreek: Seed of a New History of Modern North Africa

Historian Alain Corbin's work details the changing role of smell in determining how people understood themselves as modern, refined, and middle-class in eighteenth- and nineteenth-century France. Ideas about smell, he writes, began to be mapped onto hierarchies of class-linked anxieties in the cities as 'instinct, animality, and organic stench became traits of the masses'.[3] This was linked to new ideas about 'domestication', creating homes that managed smells, whether connected to trash or human waste, in new and specific ways. He describes a process by which, over time, 'abhorrence of smells produces its own form of social power. Foul-smelling rubbish appears to threaten the social order, whereas the reassuring victory of the hygienic and the fragrant promises to buttress its stability'.[4] These new understandings of proper smells, hygiene, and domestic space took root among a certain class in Egypt and Morocco in the early twentieth centuries as well. Corbin focuses on the creation of bathrooms in particular as 'sensually neutral and innocent spaces'; I suggest that parallel to this notion is the creation of the kitchen as a similarly smell-neutral space. Domestic science curricula written for Egyptian and Moroccan schoolgirls emphasized the importance of well-ventilated kitchens, built of slick tile surfaces that made it easy to wash away food waste, and connected, like bathrooms, to modern plumbing and sewage systems. In this context, culinary ingredients like fenugreek – which was not only associated with rural foods, but also perceived as particularly pungent, with odours that lingered on peoples' clothing and bodies – was no longer welcome in the respectable, middle-class urban home kitchen.

This attitude was confirmed by a series of oral history narratives I collected from women who had grown up in the 1940s, 50s, and 60s in the cities of Cairo, Alexandria, Fes, and Rabat. Generally speaking, regardless of their family's regional origin, the more educated my subjects were, the less likely they were to use fenugreek in cooking. Fenugreek-based foods are still common in many parts of Egypt and Morocco today, but they are far more common in rural areas or in families only one generation removed from the countryside.

One Egyptian woman cited her extensive knowledge of several recipes for foods that included fenugreek but rejected the idea of making it herself: 'you can smell it a mile away,' she said by way of explanation.[5] Rejecting fenugreek was a way to imply a class distinction, with foods that featured other kinds of spices, like cinnamon and saffron, proffered as more refined and sophisticated. Frequently an open-ended question about fenugreek prompted emphatic negative responses from oral history subjects. One interview transcript reads, 'no no no no no no: I don't make anything with it…the smell is very strong'.[6] Another woman, Fatima, offered a historical and cultural explanation for why her family refrained from using fenugreek, explaining that as a woman from the city of Fes she would never use fenugreek because it is 'never, ever used in the Fasi kitchen'.[7] Her understanding of the rarefied urban cuisine of Fes, connected, as she explained it, to both the imperial cuisines of the Moroccan court and the city's sophisticated Andalusian cultural heritage, mirror dominant understandings of the role of Fes in Moroccan culture writ large. Indeed, the prestigious dialects, architectural styles, music, and cuisines of Morocco's Andalusian cities (Tetouan, Fes, and Rabat) dominated elite-driven definitions of national culture in the decades leading up to independence, as explained in convincing detail by Eric Calderwood.[8] During our interview, Fatima herself implicitly identified Fasi cuisine with Moroccan cuisine, describing her cooking variously as 'Moroccan', 'Fasi', and 'Andalusian', implying some form of slippage between these terms. 'We wouldn't make something with fenugreek like *those* people do,' she said at one point (emphasis added). For Fatima, and many Fasis proud of their culinary traditions, fenugreek was simply not representative of the best that Moroccan cuisine had to offer.

Despite the documented longstanding traditions of Fasi cuisine and its Andalusian roots, I argue that this identification of the urban and urbane cuisine of Fes with Moroccan national food culture is a relatively modern development. By 'modern' I mean both recent, in the past hundred years or so, and indicative of a specific understanding of the relationship between food choices and social identity that is epitomized by the Brillat-Savarin adage so frequently repeated in food studies circles: 'Tell me what you eat, and I will tell you what you are.' I suggest that fenugreek is one way to historicize and qualify this relationship between food and identity: to point to a specific period during which making the choice to reject fenugreek, to let it drop out of your family's culinary repertoire or to make fun of those who eat it, became newly legible as a way to demonstrate one's social position.

Historicizing this shift requires explaining it as a function of factors that go beyond merely new ideologies of taste, sophistication, national reputation, or class. There were also a number of material and economic factors influencing the position of fenugreek in Egyptian and Moroccan society in concrete ways. In Morocco, one reason fenugreek came to signal a lack of prestige may have related to questions of relative scarcity: namely, because it was locally produced and readily accessible, it was not as attractive to the upwardly mobile or newly urbanized classes interested in distinguishing themselves. Coriander, cumin, and fenugreek, all present in premodern Moroccan cooking styles, were produced during the colonial period in significant enough quantities to have been taxed by the French state and mentioned in news reports alongside commodities like wheat and corn and high-value items like livestock and fruit trees.[9] By contrast, cinnamon and ginger, spices characteristic of the cuisines of cities like Fes and Tetouan, were imported and therefore scarcer, particularly during the two world wars. Food historians have argued that scarcity was one key factor driving the prestige of spices in medieval Europe, and it is possible that the availability of fenugreek and other spices rendered them similarly less desirable in twentieth century Morocco.[10] By the 1930s, in fact, Morocco was producing enough fenugreek to sell it abroad, exporting 188 tons in December 1934 alone, alongside cereal and vegetable crops.[11] And yet by the time the first locally printed cookbook of Moroccan cuisine was published in 1957, written by a French woman who included detailed ethnographic passages amidst her recipes, fenugreek was nowhere to be found in its exhaustive lists of spices.[12] Her book set the tone for other cookbooks of Moroccan cuisine; I have not managed to find a Moroccan cookbook published in Morocco that mentions fenugreek or *rafisa*, the celebratory dish in which it is commonly used, before 1979.

In Egypt, the fates of fenugreek's prestige were more closely tied to changes in bread culture. Among the new middle classes of the early twentieth century, white bread made with refined wheat became a particularly desirable daily comestible.[13] This was not merely a matter of identifying with the cosmopolitan milieu of Egypt's cities at the time, which included French, Italians, British, Greeks, and others who consumed white European-style loaves. It was also a matter of distinguishing oneself from the peasantry and the countryside – a central source of anxiety among new elites, many of whom had little distance from their own rural roots.[14] For many rural Egyptians in the first half of the twentieth century, their staple bread was made from corn flour; fenugreek was added in part because it was a useful binding agent, keeping the corn-based dough together through the baking process.[15] There was a nutritional aspect to the preference for wheat-based bread, too: reliance on a corn-based diet led to high instances of pellagra, a nutritional disease, among the Egyptian peasantry, particularly those who did not have access to a diverse diet.[16] A 1918 report on the epidemiology of pellagra in rural Egypt made clear that when possible, Egyptians mixed wheat flour into their bread. Given the spectre of pellagra, it is possible that this was not merely a matter of social prestige, although it is difficult to know how well the connection was popularly understood.

In any case, as they gained nominally more control over internal Egyptian affairs, Egyptian urban elites began to find ways to prioritize the production of bread that increasingly approximated white European breads.[17] During World War II, which effectively subjected Egypt to a state of siege, the impossibility of importing fertilizers and a number of unfortunate environmental factors meant that wheat and barley, not corn or fenugreek, were the bread ingredients that received priority in terms of acreage and resources.[18] These steps were the start of a complex legacy of wheat and wheat bread subsidies in Egypt, and, although bread made with corn and fenugreek is still eaten, it is nowhere near the staple it once was.[19] One Egyptian scholar estimates that it had ceased to become a principal bread in many Delta villages by the late 1970s.[20] Many Egyptians living in cities who wish to eat it source it from the countryside. I have yet to find an Egyptian cookbook that mentions fenugreek at all; it tends to appear only in non-fiction works about folklore and rural culture.

One such study quoted a middle-class Egyptian civil servant living in a Nile Delta village, who explained that now that the government subsidizes wheat, most people use that as their binding agent in making corn bread, with the fenugreek used 'only for flavour'.[21] But he explained that once people became educated and cultured, they typically stop using fenugreek at all.[22] Looking at fenugreek's decline in popularity, therefore, requires taking into account a complex mix of changing gustatory and olfactory standards, policies, nutritional science, social mobilities, geopolitical events, and even the climate and environmental factors. All of these factors contributed to a new logic according to which making certain choices about food translated into assertions about social position and cultural identity: 'Tell me what you eat, and I will tell you what you are.' For many urban elites, fenugreek ceased to be a part of the way they wished to define who and what they were.

Cultures of Consumption, Pharmacies of Consumption

But there is more to the story, because there is more to fenugreek. Twentieth-century attitudes towards fenugreek make clear that in addition to the advent of new modes of performing and embodying social distinctions, a new division between food and medicine appeared; such a division had not previously existed in North African societies.

As in Europe, earlier understandings of the relationship between food, the body, and identity in North Africa were based on a humours-based system of Galenic medicine, a body of scientific knowledge that had been translated into Arabic, and expanded and developed by scholars in the Islamicate world. According to this system, fenugreek did not signal the peasantry or a desirable or undesirable aroma so much as a substance with specific medical indications based on its drying and warming effects. Within this system food and medicament overlapped significantly; who or what one 'was', in terms of social status or health status, determined whether and when one consumed fenugreek – not the other way around. Part and parcel of the new logic that one's food choices constituted one's social identity, then, was the sidelining of an understanding of food as pharmacy.

And yet this divorce of cultures of consumption from pharmacies of consumption did not obliterate the latter entirely, as much as some modernizing elites might have preferred. Fenugreek offers a thread with which to follow the history of what happened to food as pharmacy in North Africa – and in doing so, counters a teleological narrative of progress in favour of a more labyrinthine story. The fact is that many (though certainly not all) of the women I interviewed had banished fenugreek from their kitchens, but were quick to tell me how it could be put to good medicinal use.

The thirteenth-century Arab scholar Ibn al-Baytar compiled an exhaustive *materia medica* encompassing the body of Greek medical knowledge about thousands of medicinal plants as well as knowledge from the Arab and Persianate worlds. In the entry about fenugreek he cites both Greek and Arab scholars who describe the seed as warming and drying, according to Galenic principles.[23] One Greek authority says that mixing fenugreek with bread offsets its strictly medicinal qualities. These authorities also explain that fenugreek can treat nausea, that eating a little before food prepares the stomach for eating, and that it is beneficial for menstrual pains and for the health of new mothers.

These are remarkably similar to the uses of fenugreek cited by my research subjects, interviewed in 2016 and 2017. One Egyptian woman who never cooked with fenugreek told me to drink a fenugreek concoction for stomach cramps; another explained that foods made with fenugreek would warm the body, open the appetite, and soothe the stomach. Two Moroccan sisters, citing nearly word-for-word the recipe Ibn al-Baytar attributed

Fenugreek: Seed of a New History of Modern North Africa

to Galen himself, told me that fenugreek mixed with honey would benefit the stomach.

In other words, fenugreek may have been written out of cookbooks and banquet menus in Egypt and Morocco, but it has persisted in other ways: in oral knowledge passed from mother to daughter, in learned culinary instincts and the subaltern spaces of the herbalist and the family kitchen and the fields in the countryside. Morocco and Egypt both still export fenugreek today. One anthropologist found that fenugreek-heavy *rafisa* has shown remarkable durability in the face of changing foodways in the area of northern Morocco she studies.[24] In a handful of villages near Damietta, where one of the branches of the Nile meets the Mediterranean, fenugreek is still incorporated into bread dough.[25] Whether we read this as resistance, refusal, or something else, fenugreek offers the seed of a different way of reading – and writing – history. Fenugreek invites us to attend to the pungent unwritten, to stories that persist in the face of teleological national narratives of progress and the often sanitizing values of middle-class respectability.

Fenugreek also underscores the importance of food as a source in history – by which I do not mean merely the subject of food as it is discursively produced and described, but the material seeds, grains, tastes, flavours, and smells that may cease to be 'written' anywhere but in bodies and memories and in the soil – and yet which nonetheless have considerable affective and explanatory power. Perhaps above all, fenugreek drives home the notion that tastes and flavours are not epiphenomenal: they carry real historical weight. Can we understand refinement separately from the significance of refined flour, or urbanity apart from the new kinds of spaces and cultural norms that modern cities produce?

Initially I thought of fenugreek as a spice or a flavouring agent. And yet there is a way in which this kind of approach downplays the seed as inconsequential decoration or ornament. It neglects the fact that an aesthetics (culinary aesthetics included) is also a politics. Tracing fenugreek through the sources brings to light the fact that this seed is far more than a distinctive smell or flavour: it is a substantive legume that can act as a binding agent in a bread flour; it was and is exported by the ton; its pungency wields what Corbin would call 'its own form of social power'. Adding new dimensions to culinary histories frequently narrated in terms of elite tastes and written records, humble seeds like fenugreek can generate new histories that expose the omissions and silences that official or written narratives enfold.

Acknowledgements

This research was funded by grants made through the American Research Center in Egypt, the Social Science Research Council's Mellon International Dissertation Research Fellowship, and the Council of American Overseas Research Centers. The author wishes to acknowledge the assistance of the staff of the British National Archives, the Bury Archives in Bury, England, and the High Institute of Folk Arts in Cairo, Egypt – as well as the many Egyptian and Moroccan women who welcomed me into their kitchens and their memories.

Seeds

Notes

1. British National Archives, London, UK, FO 841/172, Consular Court Records, Probate of Muhammad Khalil Bartlett.
2. Rachel Laudan, *Cuisine and Empire: Cooking in World History* (Berkeley, CA: University of California Press, 2013).
3. Alain Corbin, *The Foul and the Fragrant: Odor and the French Social Imagination* (Cambridge, MA: Harvard University Press, 1986), p. 230.
4. Corbin, p. 5.
5. Interview conducted by author, October 5, 2016.
6. Interview conducted by author, July 13, 2017.
7. Interview conducted by author, August 7, 2017. All names have been changed.
8. Eric Calderwood, *Colonial Al-Andalus: Spain and the Making of Modern Moroccan Culture* (Cambridge, MA: The Belknap Press of Harvard University Press, 2018).
9. Archives du Maroc, Rabat, Morocco, B-45, Tertib (taxation) records, 1915-17; *Tangier Gazette*, 3 March 1923 and 26 May 1923.
10. Maanvi Singh, 'How Snobbery Helped Take the Spice out of European Cooking', *The Salt: What's on Your Plate*, 2015 <https://www.npr.org/sections/thesalt/2015/03/26/394339284/how-snobbery-helped-take-the-spice-out-of-european-cooking> [accessed 22 May 2018].
11. Bury Archives, Bury, UK, BBY/1/3/4/2, British Chamber of Commerce for the French Protectorate of Morocco, Report No. 9-34, 31 December 1934.
12. Zette Guinaudeau, *Fès vu par sa cuisine* (Rabat: J. E. Laurent, 1957).
13. Eric Schewe, 'How War Shaped Egypt's National Bread Loaf', *Comparative Studies of South Asia, Africa and the Middle East*, 37.1 (2017), 49-63.
14. Samah Selim, *The Novel and the Rural Imaginary in Egypt, 1880-1985* (London: RoutledgeCurzon, 2004).
15. Samih ʿAbd al-Ghaffar Shaʿlan, *al-Khubz fī al-maʾthūrāt al-shaʿbiyya, Dirāsa fī al-aṭālis al-fūklūriyya* (Cairo: Ein for Human and Social Studies, 2002), p. 286.
16. British National Archives, London, UK, FD 1/1918, Pellagra reports.
17. Schewe, p. 58.
18. British National Archives, London, UK, FO 922/94, 1943 report on agricultural conditions in Upper Egypt. The report mentions that per government decree, 60% of land had to be devoted to wheat and barley that year, and the fields planted with fenugreek at that point were not 'growing exceptionally well, and a number of them had apparently a very poor crop'.
19. For a succinct overview of the various kinds of breads consumed in Egypt today and which grains are used to make them, see Jessica Barnes, 'Overstating Climate Change in Egypt's Uprising', *Middle East Report* 2018 <https://www.merip.org/mero/mero101118> [accessed 22 May 2018].
20. Shaʿlan, p. 275.
21. Shaʿlan, p. 286.
22. The Egyptian colloquial phrase used to indicate 'cultured' here literally means 'enlightened', indicating less a sense of spiritual awakening than receiving a basic modern education in the Egyptian context; Shaʿlan, pp. 286-87.
23. ʿAbd Allah ibn Ahmad Ibn al-Baytar, *Kitāb al-Jāmiʿ li-mufradāt al-adwiya wa-l-aghdhiya*, 2 vols (Beirut: Dar al-Kutub al-ʿIlmiyya, 1992), I, pp. 280–82.
24. Naʿima al-Madani, *Taḥawwul al-ʿādāt al-ghidhāʾiyya bi-l-Maghrib al-qarawī* (Rabat: Dar al-Aman, 2015), p. 216.
25. Shaʿlan.

A Land of Wheat: In Search of the Lost Grain of Israel/Palestine

B.Z. Goldberg and Ronit Vered

Introduction

This paper explores the story of the lost wheat varieties from one of wheat's 'centres of origin', the area today known as Israel and Palestine. Beginning with domestication and as late as the early twentieth-century, dozens, perhaps even hundreds, of local varieties with agronomic and culinary qualities dating to antiquity informed vital wheat-based foodways. As in much of the world, in the twentieth century traditional wheat landraces from this region were replaced by modern high-yielding cultivars, a change which prompted a narrowing of wheat biodiversity, a loss of foodways and traditions, and a reduction in the spectrum of qualities of this staple. Unlike many regions where conservationists, farmers, and breeders preserved indigenous wheat, due to geopolitical and other issues the local varieties in Israel/Palestine all but disappeared, and today are in danger of extinction. In recent years, a small group of researchers, bakers, and farmers have tracked down some of the region's lost wheat seeds, with the aim to rescue, study, conserve, and restore this historic treasure for breeding programs, fields, and kitchens.[1]

Rusty Olive Tins in a Forgotten Gene Bank Fridge

Summer 2016. Israel's gene bank. Concealed behind a heavy door, a refrigerated room with a temperature close to zero degrees has shelves crammed with metal boxes much like the olive tins one might find in Middle Eastern markets. Inside these tins, many of them rusted and stacked on top of each other, are collections that no one knows anything about. Rummaging around the tins, a few die-hard wheat researchers stumbled onto a collection made by someone named Y. Mattatia: hundreds upon hundreds of tiny envelopes, each with a serial number beginning with the letter M, holding seeds: a few envelopes of tobacco, some with vegetables and pulses, and hundreds with wheat seeds that have been there for almost half a century. Who was Mattatia? Where did he collect this wheat? No one knew. Rumours spoke of a researcher who spent the 1970s at the Volcani institute, Israel's main agricultural research facility, but his name was mysteriously absent from the lists of the institute's retirees, and it was not even clear if he was alive.

The mysterious Mattatia was the last person to exhaustively collect the wheat biodiversity of Israel and the Palestinian territories. But he was hardly the first. Early 'plant explorers' came through the area at the beginning of the twentieth century. Famed Russian botanist Nikolai I. Vavilov travelled the region in 1925 collecting hundreds of samples of local wheat. Vavilov's findings somewhat strengthened his theory that the area now known as Israel/Palestine, Jordan, Lebanon, and Syria sit in or close to one of wheat's 'centres of origin': the general area of the Fertile Crescent where wheat was first domesticated approximately 10,000 years ago.[2]

Landraces and Bottlenecks

For millennia, our ancestors collected wild wheat kernels from spikes that had 'shattered', driven by the evolutionary need to reproduce. For humans to domesticate wheat, a mutation had to appear in which the spikes wouldn't shatter. Humans eventually discovered that it was easier to collect the intact heads rather than the scattered grain, and gradually began sowing and harvesting these non-shattering plants. This process, better known as 'the agricultural revolution', is widely considered to be one of the most significant transformations humanity has undergone. Many argue that human history begins with our transition from hunter-gatherers to a settled agrarian life.

Over the last century a soft consensus has formed placing the locus of wheat domestication in or near the Karacadag Mountains in southeastern Turkey, but there are researchers that claim that the strongest argument of the 'Turkey theory' is that it was published first.[3] Some argue that the site of domestication is actually in Syria (usually Syrian researchers), northern Israel (Israeli researchers), Armenia (Armenians), and so on. Other theories hold that there may have been multiple near-simultaneous loci of domestication.

Once humans chose a mutation which could never survive in nature (wheat heads which don't shatter stand little chance of replicating) and made the first 'selection', wheat biodiversity – which was huge – started diminishing. In professional terms, this is known as a 'bottleneck', but wheat is a wonderfully adaptive plant. During thousands of years of traditional agriculture, wheat spread throughout almost the entire world by modifying itself to diverse terrains and climates. Tens, perhaps hundreds, of thousands of distinct varieties known as 'landraces' developed. These dynamic, heterogeneous populations (in contrast to genetically homogenous modern varieties) evolved varying appearances and agronomic qualities, traits for local adaptation, buffering capacity, and various cooking and baking qualities. Many regions and villages had their own variety, and cultural, culinary, and economic traditions developed around it.

In Israel/Palestine, as early as 500 BC, specific wheat varieties were stipulated by name in the instructions for sourcing wheat for Jewish ritual offerings. The varieties *Mikhmas* and *Mazunikha* were used in preparing the ceremonial 'Presence Bread' (*Lechem Hapanim*) offered in the Holy Temple's inner sanctum.[4] Some scholars have noted that a Jewish text dated to approximately the fifth century AD may allude to 500 distinctly different varieties of wheat in historical Israel: 'A woman from Caesarea took

A Land of Wheat: In Search of the Lost Grain of Israel/Palestine

her son to a baker, and requested, 'teach my son [your] art; [the baker] replied, he will stay with me for five years, and I will teach him [to bake with] five hundred varieties of wheat'.[5]

Some have argued that over the last 2000 years there was relatively little exchange of wheat varieties between this region and the rest of the world. If true, this may be due to Ottoman trade restrictions designed to keep out potential invaders and/or to the agricultural insularity brought on by historical animosity between neighbouring tribes and villages. In 2006 archeobotanists Mordechai Kislev and Yonit Tabak determined that 2000-year-old carbonized wheat kernels and spikes from archeological excavations in Massada were near perfect morphological matches for two landrace varieties grown and collected in the region in the 1920s – 'Hourani' (from the Plain of Horan in Syria) and 'Jaljuli' (apparently from the Palestinian village of Jaljuliah, near modern day Tel Aviv).[6] More recently, examination of DNA from 6000-year-old barley kernels found in the Negev desert showed them to be genetically similar to landrace varieties collected in the early twentieth century in Israel/Palestine (and much less similar to landrace samples collected further afield).[7]

Even in the nineteenth century, when seeds of celebrated wheats made their way from the Ukraine to Bordeaux and from Crimea to Kansas, Palestinian farmers stuck with their dependable varieties.[8] The plant explorer and researcher Aharon Aharonson related in a 1910 USDA bulletin that local villages cultivated unique, often eponymous landraces which were remarkably hyper-locally adapted; attempts by European Jewish immigrants with good intentions and advanced agronomy degrees to grow a certain village's variety in a neighbouring area – even just a few miles away – often failed.[9]

Revolutions

The story of wheat in Israel/Palestine parallels wheat's global narrative. In the late nineteenth century, steel roller milling made refined flour cheap and plentiful. Along with the now well-known nutritional problems that accompanied cheap white flour, the new mills also brought a brand-new biodiversity bottleneck: rigid demand for the particular wheat varieties most suited to the new machines. Traditional varieties less suited to industrial milling began to disappear. In large urban centres in Israel/Palestine, the milling industry began having a profound impact in the 1920s, about twenty to forty years after Europe and North America. In small Palestinian towns and farming communities, however, family-run mills remained the norm until the late twentieth century. In these areas, landraces were cultivated as a subsistence crop till the late 1970s, sometimes on extremely small plots on steep terraced hillsides, areas where no one today would dream of growing wheat. A similar process was driven by industrial bakers with their demand for specific varieties (e.g. wheats which yield flour that absorbs large quantities of water – allowing for higher profit margins). As the industrialization of food spread into the countryside and urbanization processes accelerated, the wide spectrum of local varieties developed over millennia quickly diminished.

Until the 1950s, very little bread wheat was cultivated in Israel/Palestine. Like much of the Mediterranean basin, durum was the main wheat crop which was grown, baked into flatbreads, and used for pasta, bulgur, couscous, etc. It can be argued that Zionist agriculture developed the approach that 'whatever the Arabs do, we'll do the opposite'. The Jewish settlers – familiar with bread wheat from Eastern Europe, and eager to bake lofty European loaves – scorned the traditional agriculture practiced by the *fellahin* (Palestinian traditional subsistence farmers), rejected heritage durum varieties, and imported high-yielding European varieties of bread wheat which were then given Hebrew names. Today the 5/95 ratio of bread to durum wheat common in neighbouring countries has been flipped; in Israel 95% of the wheat grown today is bread wheat, while in Palestine it's probably about 80/20 in favour of bread wheat.

In the 1960s high-yielding, semi-dwarf 'Green Revolution' varieties replaced the tall landraces that had grown in the region for around 10,000 years. The green revolution brought about severe genetic bottlenecks in most of the world, but in Israel/Palestine the effect was even more pronounced. In countries with long histories of wheat cultivation, Dr Norman Borlaug's new lines were cross-pollinated with local varieties to help them adapt to the new terrain and climate. But in Israel – with its prevailing anti-traditionalist approach driven by historical circumstances and political motives – that didn't happen; Israeli breeders shunned local varieties completely and chose to 'cross' Green Revolution varieties with strong wheat strains from North Africa and Australia. As a result, modern wheat in Israel/Palestine today has zero local genetics.

In the early 1970s, Nixon administration policies, designed by Agriculture Secretary Earl Butz to bring down food prices, caused massive overproduction and subsequent drops in the price of wheat, flour, and bread worldwide. In Palestinian farming communities where families had cultivated cherished landraces for generations, it became much cheaper for farmers to walk to the corner store and buy white pitta or refined flour than to go to the expense, effort, and financial risk of growing their own wheat. In early twentieth-century Palestine, there were dozens, perhaps hundreds of local wheat varieties that had adapted over millennia to regional conditions, varieties with hundreds of qualities, perhaps including distinct flavours that informed a vibrant grain-based food culture, but by the end of the 1970s 'local' wheat all but disappeared, and with it much of the wheat-based local food culture.

The Mystery of Local Wheat

Unlike many countries where local varieties were collected, conserved, and utilized as the source of desirable genetic traits in breeding programs, over the last half century in Israel/Palestine, the seeds of the old wheat varieties have completely disappeared – not only from the region's fields and kitchens, but from local gene banks, researcher's freezers, and breeding libraries. Wheat breeders of the 1960s and 70s saw little reason to preserve the region's landrace wheat biodiversity. Retired breeders even relate stories (possibly apocryphal) about massive collections of local wheat landraces that were studied as historical relics, from a taxonomical-morphological perspective, and subsequently, quite literally, trashed.

In 2016 a number of Israeli and Palestinian researchers and a few bakers (among them a co-author of this paper), inspired by the growth of 'local grain economies' in Europe and North America, set out to find out what had happened to the region's traditional wheat varieties. While a handful of local landraces were still being studied and used by breeders, the wide diversity of wheat landraces had virtually disappeared. Palestinian *fellahin* were all growing modern varieties. A quick genetic test for the 'Rht' dwarfing genes present in all Green Revolution wheat determined that most of the few farmers who thought they were cultivating traditional varieties were in fact growing modern wheat. Only a handful of growers were truly cultivating one or two traditional wheat varieties.

Israel's national gene bank listed only ten samples collected before the founding of Israel in 1948; a tiny number of 'lines' (the term for a sample of wheat collected in a particular location at a particular point in time) compared to the vast number of indigenous varieties that once grew in this region, and even these ten lines were nowhere to be found. It appeared as if the traditional wheat of one of wheat's centres of origin had simply disappeared.

Scientific and historical data regarding the history of wheat cultivation in this part of the world suggests that some of the region's landrace wheat varieties contain traits that date to antiquity and that are no longer present in modern wheat. These traits could range from particular flavours and baking qualities, to local adaptability, the capacity to survive in drought or changing climate, and resistance to diseases or pests (whether known or developing in the future.) Because of Israel/Palestine's location in or near the nexus of wheat domestication, and because of the important biodiversity that is associated with wheat from this area, this loss of this wheat, and its potential implications for regional and global food security, are considered to be matters of both local and international concern.

In from the Cold

Einav Mayzlish-Gati, a young researcher who had recently taken over as director of Israel's national gene bank, heard of the dead end the 'wheat detectives' had hit and suggested they try exploring the refrigerated gene bank rooms where uncatalogued collections were kept. In this forgotten room they found hidden treasures – the dozens of rusty olive tins, packed with envelopes of wheat seeds, some of which had not been opened since 1980, inscribed with the name Y. Mattatia.

At the Weitzman institute, renowned geneticist Avi Levy had another surprise in store. In one of the Institute's old buildings, there was a collection of wheat varieties assembled by his mentor, Moshe (Mussik) Feldman, and since Feldman had recently started talking about retiring (at the age of 83) there were thoughts about refreshing his collection. Levi led the wheat-obsessed team to a crumbling corridor containing four domestic freezers. In these freezers – with no power backup, humidity monitor, or precise temperature control – were hundreds of envelopes containing samples of wheat seeds. Most of Feldman's seeds were modern varieties he had received from colleagues all over the world during his long career and breeding material he developed, but in the back of the freezers there were also quite a few heritage varieties he had collected in the 1970s and 1980s as well as varieties he received from Mordechai Kislev at Bar-Ilan University. Feldman – like Mattatia and Kislev – was one of the very few people who understood back then that an entire genetic pool was about to be wiped out. He collected whatever he could, from rare plants he saw growing in a *fellah*'s field to a stalk of wheat that stuck to his son's army boots on his return from a military exercise near the Lebanese border.

Treasure Hunt

Matattia, Kislev, and Feldman collected seeds in the 1970s and 1980s when it was still possible to find the remnants of traditional varieties in Israel. But what about the hundreds of varieties of wheat that grew in the region before the profound changes wheat had undergone in the last century? Searching through gene bank catalogues from around the world yielded a small number of wheat samples, but it soon became apparent that, due to the geopolitical changes that shook this region in the first half of the twentieth century, the origin of the wheat varieties collected here were not necessarily registered in any consistent manner.

In 1929, British botanist A.E. Watkins, then working at Cambridge University, used the official channels of the Board of Trade in London to request samples of local wheat varieties from various officials across the Empire. The director of the breeding department at the first agricultural research station in Palestine complied, and eventually seeds from seven varieties found their way to the gene bank in the J. Innes Centre in Norwich, UK. This letter (shown to us first by Shahal Abo from the Hebrew University) supplied seven variety names and a germplasm request from the Norwich gene bank. With this list of names – Abu Fashi, Jaljouli, Mahmoudi, and so on – came an idea; if the team could put together an exhaustive list of the names of varieties that grew in this region one hundred years ago, perhaps it would be possible to use that list to search gene bank catalogues and figure out where the local wheat had ended up. As it is not possible to know in advance which variety might have a unique trait that can bring about a significant change in how we grow food, the goal was to attempt to reconstruct the region's entire wheat growing culture: every variety the team could get its hands on.

Over approximately one year, the researchers scoured libraries and archives around the world for early twentieth-century agricultural documents. Whenever they came across the name of a traditional variety originating in Israel/historical Palestine they went back to gene bank catalogues, worldwide wheat databases, and collection curators to try and discover where it had ended up. Luigi Guarino, the scientific director of the Crop Trust, became the group's trusted advisor and door opener. They looked for every possible iteration of variety name, location, and collector, every possible combination of longitude and latitude, historical and colonial names of towns and villages. Over about six months the team discovered over one hundred variety names, and identified over twenty gene banks worldwide still holding germplasm collected in the region at the beginning of the twentieth century – sometimes just one or two samples, sometimes dozens.

Germplasm requests were sent out. In some cases, it was necessary to negotiate and find ways around complex regulatory issues, as the question of the ownership of the seeds collected in Greater Syria before present-day political boundaries sparks complex questions. Today, for most gene banks in the world, the transfer of historical wheat seeds is governed by the 2004 International Treaty on Plant Genetic Resources for Food and Agriculture – the treaty created to protect the rights of the world's population to utilize agricultural biodiversity for global food security. Ironically, since Israel is not a signatory to the Treaty – which even North Korea and Syria have signed – it is currently very difficult to return local traditional wheat varieties to the location where they originated and took shape.

From Russia with Love

A number of the wheat samples sent from various gene banks had been originally donated by the Vavilov Research Institute of Plant Industry in St. Petersburg (VIR). Nikolai Ivanovich Vavilov, the Russian botanist and geneticist who researched the origin of plants in the first half of the twentieth century, is considered to have impacted the world of botany and plant science as much as Darwin. He travelled widely in search of places with the meaningful biodiversity of major crops. In 1926 he visited Palestine and sent thousands of samples of seeds he collected to his institute in St. Petersburg. Today, VIR still holds many hundreds of samples collected in this region.

Eager to acquire some of the varieties Vavilov had collected in this region, the wheat project team began negotiations with VIR's curators (assisted by renowned scientists such as Cary Fowler, founder and former director of the Crop Trust and the Svalbard Global Seed Vault in Norway). Eventually VIR proposed an exchange – seventy-seven samples of wheat that Vavilov had collected in the Levant in return for seventy-seven lines from the collection taking shape in Israel.[10]

After about two years of work the project has managed to 'repatriate' close to one thousand lines of wheat, most of which had been collected in the region in the early twentieth century: varieties which had completely disappeared from the region fifty years ago. In gene banks worldwide, it's customary to replenish stored wheat seed every five years. A batch of seeds is germinated and grown out, and the existing seeds are replaced with fresh ones. However, many of the newly found seeds had not been grown out in thirty or forty years. It was not clear how many – if any at all – would germinate and grow into healthy viable plants. It appeared that the region's historical wheat biodiversity was in true danger of extinction, and the project may literally have appeared at the last possible moment.

Seeds

The Land of Wheat

Just before the recent harvest, visitors entering the research greenhouses at the Weizmann Institute in Rehovot and the Volcani Institute in Beit Dagan would have been surprised to see hundreds of unfamiliar wheat varieties. Alongside the short stalks of modern varieties stood plants so tall they touched the greenhouse ceiling from varieties grown from the collection of rare heritage varieties. There is a dizzying variety of colours, heights, and shapes: the biodiversity absent from this region for decades. Approximately 700 different lines germinated and are now growing here. It appears that gene banks around the world (mainly VIR in Russia) hold a few hundred more. If all these can be acquired the project will have gone from having ten lines listed in the gene bank catalogue – all that had disappeared from the freezers – to a thousand lines from Israel/Palestine and another thousand from neighbouring countries.

The Land of Wheat is the name chosen by the partners in this project to bring back traditional wheat varieties. The Israeli Ministry of Agriculture's Chief Scientist recently approved a three-year research grant to evaluate these varieties. The next stage, after adhering to strict import protocols and conserving the old varieties in the national gene bank, is to create a core collection of one hundred varieties, chosen on the basis of diverse traits and genetics, which will form the basis for research and breeding. In the long term, the idea is to merge historical varieties with cutting edge breeding to create the most flavoursome, highly nutritious wheat that can be accessible to a wide population at affordable prices.

At the same time, the project has begun to translate and edit a few recently-discovered historical documents, the only source of information on the agronomic features, culinary qualities, and lost food culture of the region's wheat landraces. Another project is underway to fundraise for ethnographic research focused on the region's aging farmers, bakers, and millers who can provide crucial information and context that will surely be lost in only a few years.

While wheat is the region's largest crop in terms of acreage (in Israel one third of agricultural land is sowed with wheat), like most of the Middle East, Israel/Palestine are far from self-sufficient in wheat consumption today. Between 85% and 95% of annual demand for wheat comes from imports from Eastern Europe, Germany, and North America. Unlike many places in the world where 'local grain economies' are developing, it is almost impossible to find local traditional varieties in Israel or Palestine. (One rare and notable exception is traditional *Nursi* wheat, which originated in the destroyed Palestinian village of Nuris located not far from Jenin, and today is cultivated by a handful of Druze farmers in the Galilee. The *Nursi* wheat is grown exclusively for a dish known as *kubbe niyeh* or raw kubbe, which is prepared from preserved lemons, hot red pepper paste, contraband raw quail, and special bulgur prepared from *Nursi* wheat which village elders swear gives the dish a unique, earthy flavour that cannot be matched by bulgur made from modern durum.)

These days innovative bakers and chefs in the region are eager to work with local varieties, and it appears that the market is ripe. Over the last year, some bakers have made bread with small quantities of local wheat grown in experimental plots, and initial results are promising. The bakers report that working with these varieties is extremely challenging: while getting worthwhile and replicable results will take time and research, the loaves appear to have more depth and flavour than any modern wheat.

Matattia's Collection

Over the past two years, Matattia has become a household name to the researchers and students working on local wheat in labs and greenhouses of local scientific institutions. The researchers have been growing out some the wheat kernels Matattia collected, the last exhaustive collection of varieties that have since vanished from the Israeli-Palestinian eco-geographic region; other researchers are growing tomatoes, eggplants, melons, and lentils from Matattia's seeds. But who exactly was Y. Matattia – the name appearing on the tin boxes? No one knew. Then, in 2017, Naomi Avivi-Ragolsky, a wheat breeder and researcher at the Weizmann Institute, noticed a line in Meir Shalev's *My Wild Garden* about an elementary school teacher who instilled in his students a love for the plant kingdom: 'My fourth-grade teacher, Yaakov Matattia, prepared us for Arbor Day with great seriousness,' Shalev writes, 'he was familiar with all the plants in the area, knew where each of them grew, and took us out to nature to study them.'

'I remember him with great affection,' Meir Shalev recalled when we contacted him to try and obtain more information. 'He was knowledgeable, patient and deeply dedicated, a quality typical of rural teachers at the time.' Shalev added that Matattia's wife's name was Bracha and that the couple was living in a village in the Jerusalem Hills.

The wheat project team has since made contact with Bracha and Dr Yaakov Matattia, and met them in their home. Last January the elderly scholar, 84 at the time, fell and broke his shoulder and hip. The fall also triggered an onset of dementia. Rehabilitation is long and difficult, and his memory – as he frequently mentions during conversations in frustration – is not as sharp as it once was.

He was born in Jerusalem in 1933 but is quick to explain, 'I always felt that I came from Greece, from Ioannina, the home of my ancestors.' The nature-loving, knowledge-thirsty intellectual earned his doctorate in botany at the Hebrew University in Jerusalem. After postdoctoral studies in the USA, he spent six years (1977-1983) as a researcher at the Volcani Institute. His wide-ranging, extraordinary project collecting local heritage varieties was done on his own initiative and in complete contradiction to the spirit that prevailed at the time in the corridors of academe and the Ministry of Agriculture.

Matattia explained that 'the *fellahin* loved the traditional varieties. They said they had the best quality, and over hundreds of years they preserved the same genetic material. I intuited that these were ancient landraces, and I was worried that they would stop growing them because the modern varieties the Ministry of Agriculture was championing had much higher yields'. Over the course of a few years Matattia visited hundreds of Arab villages. His fluency in Arabic facilitated conversation with *fellahin* from the West Bank, the Galilee, the Golan heights, and the Sinai Peninsula, and many grew to trust him and accept him as a member of their families. Matattia mentioned that he always carried notebooks in which he wrote down collection details, and these notebooks turned out to be a kind of Rosetta Stone for the project. The only identifier on the envelopes in the Gene Bank are Matattia's serial numbers. But the notebooks contain the precise coordinates where he collected each variety, its popular name, the name of the farmer, the agronomic or culinary reasons for growing the variety, and stories the farmers told about the relevant food traditions.

In the early 1980s, Matattia's relations with his director at the Volcani Institute had become shaky. No one at the institute understood why he was spending so much time and government resources collecting 'useless' crop varieties. In 1984 he left for a sabbatical and was soon after let go. The institute refused to approve his pension (which he later won back in a labour union dispute). His wife Bracha relates that the bureaucrats ultimately 'broke his spirit, forced him to retire at a young age full of intellectual vitality. He never went back to work'. Matattia, who is now being celebrated as a visionary whose work may one day impact the promise of food security for future generations, explains, 'I put my whole soul into this, but what good will it do now, when I hardly remember a thing?'

Notes

1. The paper's authors are both Israeli, yet very aware of the political contention associated with naming the eco-geographic region addressed in this paper. The terms 'Israel', 'Palestine', 'The Palestinian Territories', 'Historical Palestine', 'British Mandatory Palestine', 'The Land of Israel', etc. are all viewed as the sole valid term depending on one's nationality, political inclination, or simply the point in time from which one is observing. As this paper deals with the historical geographic space itself, and makes no attempt to address questions of political sovereignty or ownership of genetic resources, we have chosen to use the term 'Israel/Palestine', and hope that this will satisfy (or aggravate) all parties fairly equally. Although co-author Goldberg has played somewhat of an active role in some events described herein, for purposes of clarity we describe the events in the third person.
2. Vavilov had postulated that it would be possible to identify the area from which a given domesticated crop originated by looking for the region with the highest biodiversity of that crop and/or its wild relatives.
3. M. Heun and others, 'Site of Einkorn Wheat Domestication Identified by DNA Fingerprinting', *Science*, 278.5341 (14 Nov 1997), 1312-14. Scientists like M. Feldman and M. Kislev have disputed that claim (personal communication, 2016).
4. Mishna, Minhot, 8. There have been some shaky attempts to identify the early twentieth century landraces that match these ancient varieties based on certain baking and keeping properties.
5. Ecclesiastes Raba, Vilnius, Chapter 3. However, it should be noted that the following sentence speaks of a restaurant/inn keeper who states he can teach 500 varieties of eggs, signifying that in all probability the term '500 varieties of wheat' refers to 500 varieties of baked goods, or 500 ways to prepare baked goods. The authors wish to thank Susan Weingarten for kindly pointing this out.
6. In such a contested landscape, one shouldn't assume consensus about the origin of landrace wheat varieties. There are those who claim that Jaljuli refers not to the Palestinian village Jalulia, but to the

Jewish biblical town of Gilgal which is thought to have been located in the vicinity of Jericho.
7   Martin Mascher and others, 'Genomic Analysis of 6,000-Year-Old Cultivated Grain Illuminates the Domestication History of Barley', *Nature Genetics* 48.9 (2016), 1089.
8   The popular 'French' variety Rouge de Bordeaux was originally a selection from an unnamed landrace that arrived from Odessa. Red Fife, highly popular in Canada and the US was originally grown in the Ukraine as Halychanka, and Turkey Wheat was originally brought to Kansas in the 1870s by Mennonite immigrants from Crimea.
9   Aharon Aharonsohn, *Agricultural and Botanical Explorations in Palestine*, Bureau of Plant Industry Bulletins No. 180 (Washington: US Government Printing Office, 1910).
10 It is not completely clear why the exchange involves only seventy-seven lines out of the hundreds Vavilov collected in 1925, or what happened to all the other lines that Vavilov collected. The project participants hope to be able to collaborate with VIR researchers in the near future in order to study the entire collection made in 1925.

Seeds

The Long and Simple History of the Dibble and its Cousins

Peter Hertzmann

'Civilization cannot exist without food-production and that food-production must also be at a pretty efficient level of village-farming before civilization can even begin', Robert Braidword claimed.[1] Food production, or agriculture, is a combination of the growing of crops and the rearing of animals. Growing grains and vegetables requires sowing seeds. At some point in early time, farmers determined that a better yield would result from planting certain seeds below the surface of the soil rather than casting the seeds over their plot of land.

Depending upon how the early farmer tilled the soil, a shallow hole could be dug merely with a finger, hand, or a stick. It is easy to imagine a farmer breaking off a stick from a bush, using it for a while to aid in planting, and then discarding it when finished. Although bone, stone, and iron tools designed for digging have been found around the world, wooden ones from prehistoric times have not.[2]

As obvious as a digging stick may seem to modern minds, this tool was not a standard farming implement in ancient Egypt. The person sowing the seeds walked in front of the oxen pulling the plough and scattered the seed in their path. The oxen tread the seed into the soil as they pulled the plough. If the land was recently flooded, the seed was distributed over the earth, and sheep, goats, or pigs were driven over the ground to tread the seed into the soil.[3]

During the Roman period, Pliny wrote that a dibble was used for making holes and then to cover them for certain sowing and transplanting projects.[4] Although he expended much effort describing when to plant and how to condition the soil, he never gave specific methods of sowing different seeds. I assume that most grains were sown by casting the seed over the prepared land and beans were planted with a dibble.

The casting method was still used well into the early middle ages: 'The sowers held the seed in the lap of their tunics and broadcast it with the right hand'.[5]

Other societies not affected by industrialization incorporated digging sticks into their farming activities. The Dresden Codex illustrates their use by the Mayans.[6] A plate in a German book from 1591 illustrates Native American women sowing beans, maize, or millet with the aid of a 'setting' stick (Figure 1).[7] John Smith's 1626 history of Virginia observes, 'They make a hole in the earth with a stick and into it they put four grains of

The Long and Simple History of the Dibble and its Cousins

Figure 1. Native American men till the earth and women plant seeds. Note the woman using a setting stick in the top-centre of the illustration ('Wie sie ire äcker bauwen und beseen', hand-coloured engraving on paper (Frankfurt am Main: Johann Feyerabend for Theodor de Bry, 1591) pt. 2, plate XXI; Courtesy of the John Carter Brown Library).

wheat and two of beans.'[8] A dictionary of the Navaho language written in 1910 illustrates two separate planting sticks: one straight with a sharpened end and one with a short projecting limb suitable for placing a foot to aid pushing the stick into the ground.[9]

Whether called a planting stick, a digging stick, a setting stick, or just a stick, there's at least one late fifteenth-century English-Latin wordbook that labels the tool a *debylle* or *dibbille*.[10] By the start of the seventeenth century, authors have settled on *dibble* as the proper spelling.[11] At the beginning of the eighteenth century, Boyer, in his French-English Dictionary, defined the dibble as a 'setting tool' and equates it to a *plantoir*, a type of *houlette de jardinier* (a garden tool).[12]

The Oxford English Dictionary Historical Thesaurus lists five synonyms for dibble along with their dates of first usage: 'planting stick' 1552; 'setting-stick' 1553; 'dibber' 1736; 'kippeen' or 'kippin' 1830; and 'dibbler' 1847.[13] Missing from the list is a 'digging stick' and a 'seed drill', often just referred to as a 'drill'. Kippeen and kippin appear to be Gaelic for dibble.[14] These are all synonyms for when dibble is used as a noun; there are additional synonyms for when dibble is used as a verb.

In 1654, Nicholas de Bonnefons used the word *plantoir* many times in his garden

Seeds

Figure 2. Late nineteen-century illustration of typical garden dibbles ('Garden Dibbles', The Country Gentleman's Magazine, September 1871, p. 186; University of California: Public Domain).

guide *Le Jardinier français*. For example, '*Si vous les voulez semer par Trochets, vous ferez des Trous avec le Plantoir, à un bon pied l'un de l'autre*'.[15] When John Evelyn translated the earlier work in 1691, he rendered the previous statement as, 'If you sow them in Heaps, plant them with the Setting-stick, or Dibber, a full foot distance'.[16]

Dibbles and dibbers are such an everyday part of eighteenth-century gardening and farming that authors seemed to assume that their readers knew what one was, and that no explanation was required (Figure 2). Of course, there were exceptions. Mawe and Abercrombie defined a 'dibble or dibber [as] a simple but useful implement of gardening, used for planting out all sorts of young plants, &c'.[17] They go on to say:

> The best sort of Dibble is that made of the tree of an old spade, having the head or top handle entire, and the shank twelve to fifteen inches long, made gradually taper to a point at the lower end, and which to be perfectly complete, should be shod with a thin socket of iron eight or ten inches in length, made also tapering to a point at bottom.

This sort of 'Dibble is proper for planting out almost all sorts of young plants, particularly the fibrous-rooted kinds, and all sorts of cutting, &c'. Mawe and Abercrombie continue:

> For planting potatoes, a particular sort of Dibble is generally appropriated to this occasion: for large quantities, in fields particularly, is long and thick; being commonly two feet and half, or near a yard long, two inches thick at least, bluntith at the lower end, and shod with iron, and with a cross handle at top, to hold with both hands; and generally near the bottom is a sort of shoulder

of iron about six inches from the end, projecting at one or both sides, ranged parallel to the cross handle a the top, and serves as a guide in making the holes all equal depth, and occasionally as a tread for the foot, on thrusting it into the ground [...].

Many authors espoused the use of the dibble for all parts of the kitchen garden.[18] William Nicholson noted that the dibble was also popular for planting sunflowers: 'You may sow broadcast, and afterward thin the plants; but it is better to dibble the seed, placing two in a hole, the holes a foot distant, and the rows two feet asunder'.[19]

An earlier report of the success of dibbling potatoes was promoted in an early nineteenth-century agricultural report from the county east of Edinburgh, where the use of a dibble for oats was reported as superior to the traditional broadcast technique of planting:

> It is asserted in the *Statistical Account of Scotland*, vol. xviii. p. 282. that Mr Robert Graham of Tamrawer, in the parish of Kilsyth and county of Stirling, was the first person in Scotland, who cultivated potatoes in the open field, by dibbling and hand-hoeing. His first essay [...] was in the year 1739, when he planted potatoes by means of the dibble, on about half an acre of croft, or old infield land, at Neilston in that parish; and he continued to carry on the potatoe husbandry, with encreasing ardour and uniform success, for many years, in that neighbourhood, and diffused their cultivation by his example in other districts [...]. One instance of his success is recorded on sufficient evidence, that in 1762, he planted one peck of potatoes with the dibble, and in the October of that year, dug up an increase of 264 pecks.[20]

In addition to pointed and blunt ends, Walter Nicol demonstrates a 'diamond-pointed dibble'. In appearance, the dibble looks to be a triangular piece of metal, maybe four inches on each side, with its base fastened to a six-inch long metal shaft. The shaft is itself attached to a turned wooden cross handle. Nicol goes on to provide detailed instructions of how this dibble may be used to plant seedlings.[21]

J.C. Loudon reinforces the previous authors by describing three dibbles: 'The common garden dibber [a short-handled version made from a broken spade], the potato-dibber [a longer version with a ledge to use a foot for inserting into dense soil], and the forester's or planter's dibber [... with] a wedge-shaped blade'.[22]

An early nineteenth-century dibble, 'invented by Mr. Charles Waistell, of High Holborn', that delivered an acorn into the soil was announced in 1811 and widely reprinted in gardening magazines the following year:

> a represents the handle of the dibble, which dibble is a rod ¾ of an inch in diameter, moveable in the tube of a stave, which stave is externally about two inches diameter. b a tin or metal tube fixed on the exterior part of the stave, and of the same bore or aperture of the tube of the stave: when a hole is made

in the earth by the point of the dibble d, the acorn is dropped down the metal tube, and on drawing up the dibble by its handle to the height of the letter e, the acorn c passes through a large opening into the dibble tube, and from thence falls into the hole made by the point of the dibble in the earth, when by moving backwards and forwards the cross handles g g, fixed on the top of the hollow stave, the soil surrounding the hole in the earth is loosened by the iron wings f f and deposited on the acorn.

Supposing that you wish to plant an acorn in the middle any bush, you are to press the instrument through it into the ground, make a hole in the earth by the point of the dibble rod, then raise the rod above the hole where the two tubes communicate, drop the acorn down the tube b, which falls immediately through it and the lower part of the stave-tube into the hole previously made by the rod, which hole is instantly covered by the soil raised by the wings. The dibble rod may be occasionally passed down the metal tube, to be certain of its being perfectly clear.[23]

The dibble described above could easily be considered the forerunner of the modern 'jab planter' (discussed below). About the same time Waistell was adding a tube for loading the seed into the dibbled hole, a separate version was in use in the New World. An engraving from 1810 purports to show a man in Surinam with a (metre?) long dibble suspended from his waist. He holds a longer tube with a funnel opening and its distal end placed in the dibbled hole.[24] The man takes a seed from the bag suspended from his shoulder and drops it into the tube. This combination of dibble and feed tube may be seen as the forerunner of the modern seed drill.

In an article titled 'On Dibbling Wheat', John Curzon claims that '[i]t is now become very common in the county of Norfolk to dibble their wheat instead of drilling, or sowing it broad-cast'.[25] In France, the opinion of some authors was the

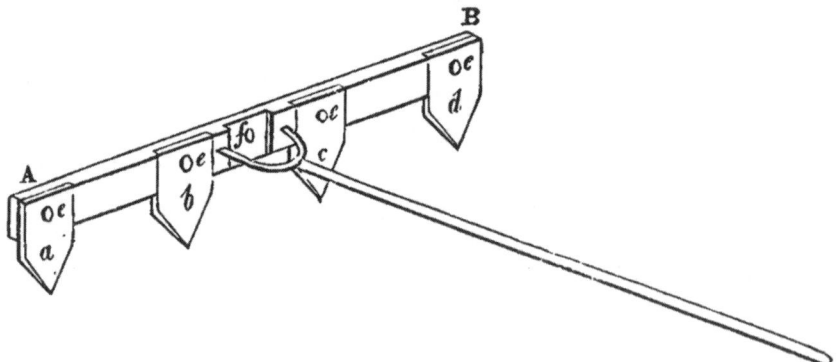

Figure 3. Garden Hand-Drill proposed by A.H. ('Description of a Garden Hand-Drill', The Gardener's Magazine, June 1831, p. 283; University of Massachusetts Amherst Libraries: Public Domain).

same.[26] The argument as to whether dibbling, drilling, or broadcasting is better continued in many forms over the next century, at times becoming further confused because some authors used dibble and drill interchangeably.

In 1758, Thomas Hale discussed a dibble capable of simultaneously making multiple holes:

> The first improvement for the planting of pease was the Suffolk Dibble, so call'd from its place of invention or original use. This is a kind of iron rake with the tines set parallel to the handle. The handle is of the same form as in the garden rake, the cross piece is thicker, and there are four, five, or six large iron spikes let through it. The way of using it is this, a man goes over the field with the dibble, and women follow him with pease in their aprons. He strikes it into the ground, pressing down the tines with his foot upon the back of the cross piece. Thus four, five, or more holes are made, into which the women drop their pease, one into each, and leave them open. This done, the whole field is lightly harrowed over, and all are covered together.

Although Hale describes other planting methods as being more efficient, he claims that '[w]hen the pease are set by the dibble, made according to our directions, the hoer's business is reduced to the one point of cutting up the weeds: and it is easily done, because he is to work in regular spaces'.[27]

In 1831, a certain A.H. proposed a similar rake-like device (Figure 3):

> I herewith send you a drawing of a small hand-drill of my invention, which I find extremely useful for sowing onions, carrots, &c.
>
> A B is a piece of well seasoned wood about 21 in. long, 3 in. wide, and three fourths of an inch thick; a b c d are four pieces of wrought-iron plate about one eighth of an inch thick, and sharpened at the end. The two centre ones (b c) are movable, being retained in their places by two large-headed screws (e e) with nuts on the opposite side. All the plates are let into the wood exactly their thickness.
>
> It is plain that by using the tool as represented in fig. 48. four drills may be drawn at once, 6 in. apart. If the two centre plates be removed, and one of them put into the middle (f), then the tool will make three drills 9 in, apart. Lastly, by using only the two ends, the drills will be 18 in. apart.
>
> The seed may be expeditiously covered by using the tool with the points upwards.[28]

Although dibbles capable of multiple holes seem to be widely reported by the early 1800s, and seed drills capable of automatic planting were well adapted, experiments with traditional dibbles continued well into the century. Hugh Monroe explains:

> I had five men with large dibbles made of hard wood, with which they made holes eight inches apart on the top of the drills, pressing down the dibble with

the foot, each man having a single drill, followed by a woman with a basketful of prepared manure and into each hole made by the dibble she placed a handful of manure. […] After her, followed a girl with a little bag of turnip seed, putting from three to six or more grains on the top of the manure, with her forefinger and thumb, drawing a little earth over it, and in this manner I carried on five drills at a time with fifteen people; viz a man and two women to each drill. I only expended two pounds of turnip seed for each acre.[29]

Although still used for field planting in the nineteenth century, the dibble remained a perpetual part of the toolset for kitchen gardens.[30] Gardening magazines occasionally defined the tool for the uninitiated reader: 'The dibble is a short thick piece of round wood, tapering to a point, and is usually made out of the handle of an old spade; if the point is shod with iron, the tool will last longer and effect its object more readily'.[31] (It was not until the twentieth century that dimensional drawings and instructions were published for dibbles.)[32]

A nineteenth-century article describes how '[a] man will make holes fast enough with the common dibble to keep three sowers employed, and women and children are easily taught the method of dropping the seeds therein'.[33] In another publication from the same period but across the ocean, dibble use is described as an improvement over using a hoe.[34] If the soil is prepared correctly, though, one farmer preferred his finger over a dibble; he claimed he can set 600 onion plants in ten hours.[35]

A search of American patent records yields eleven patents issued for dibbles in some form. One merely updated a universal design.[36] Two attempted to increase the accuracy of the classic dibble with depth gauges.[37] Many combined the seed or seedling delivery with the digging action.[38] Three were just designs that gave the dibbles a pistol shape.[39]

Dibbles are not just an item from the past. A quick search of online shopping pages, such as Amazon or Etsy, produces scores of modern dibbles for sale.

For most of its existence, placement of the dibble was a matter of judgement by the user. In 2017, a patent was granted for a Planting Grid Device designed to optimally space various garden vegetables.[40] The plastic template has a series of evenly spaced apertures for the system's custom dibble to make depressions in the soil.[41] The idea is not new, however: a patent was issued for a similar Planting Spacer for Flats in 1943.[42] Since then, both manual and automated versions with integral seed drills have been used in greenhouses to produce transplantable seedlings.[43]

The jab-planter combines the dibble with both a method to sow a seed or seedling and a method for appropriately compacting the soil. Although described at the beginning of the nineteenth century, the first patent for such a device wasn't issued until the end of the century.[44] A mid-century farming magazine advertised 'The Only Perfectly Reliable Hand Planting Machine': 'With the Jones Improved Hand Corn Planter, one experienced man will plant nearly or quite as much corn in a day as two hands and two horses will with a horse corn planter and it costs less than one-quarter as much. It plants and covers the corn sure every time.'[45]

The Long and Simple History of the Dibble and its Cousins

 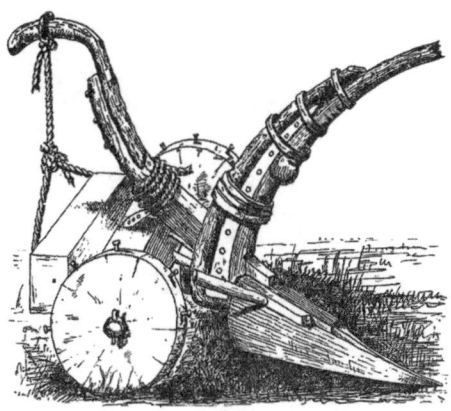

Figure 4. Benjamin Butterworth's The Growth of Industrial Art *includes illustrations of two ploughs with seeding system: 'Primitive Assyrian – B. C. 504' (left) and 'Primitive Italian – A. D. 1605' (right). The text below reads, 'The first seeding machine is said to have been used by the Assyrians, 504 B.C., and was called a drill plow', and continues, 'The Italians claim the honoring of originating, in 1605, the first seeder' ((Washington: Government Printing Office, 1892), p. 6). Butterworth provides no citations. (Smithsonian Libraries: Public Domain)*

Similar looking jab planters are still in use in Africa where they are more efficient than traditional sowing methods, especially in less than ideal soil conditions.[46] Sufficient models are produced that academics compare their usability in various African environments.[47] Jab planters can also be an effective means of single-seed planting in situations where the soil is covered with black plastic film to retard weed growth.[48]

As early as 1664, gardeners referred to the hole prepared for seeds, whether made with a stick or a hoe, as a drill: 'if you sow them of the seed, then you shall make drils by a line with a stick half an inch deep, each drill at a foot asunder'.[49] Drilling could also be the method of planting: 'Drilling is a mode of sowing by which the seed is deposited in regular equidistant rows, at such depth as each kind requires for its most perfect vegetation. It has been practised by gardeners from time immemorial, and from the garden it has gradually extended to the field'.[50]

At the turn of the eighteenth century, Jethro Tull developed a horse-drawn seed drill capable of sowing two side-by-side rows of seeds.[51] The concept of adding a sowing method to a plough was not unknown in the eighteenth century (Figure 4). Tull was arguably the first farmer able to produce a reasonable system. His designs were able to control the three-dimensional placement of seeds, once proper depth was determined:

> Different Sorts of Seeds come up at different Depths; some at six Inches, or more; some at not more than half an Inch: The Way to know for certain the Depth any Sort will come up at is, to make Gauges in this Manner: Saw off 12 Sticks of about 3 Inches Diameter: Bore a Hole in the End of each Stick, and drive into it a taper

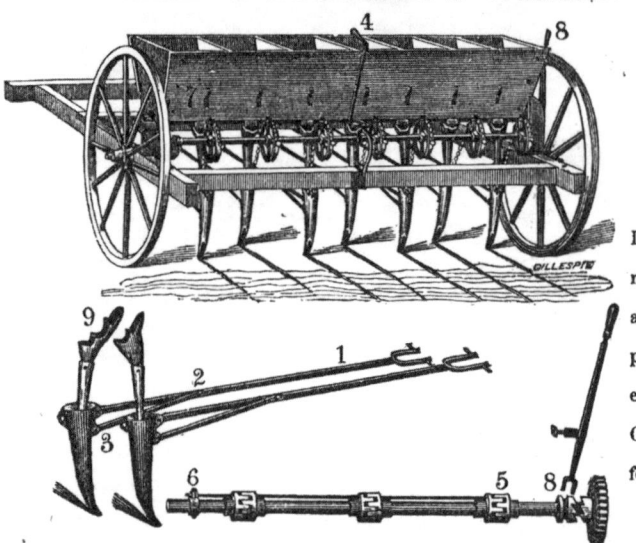

Figure 5. Mid-nineteenth-century horse-drawn seed drill ('Steer & Scooley's Wheat Drill', The American Farmer, 1 October 1859, n.p.). (University of Virginia Library: Public Domain).

> Peg; let the first Peg be half an Inch long, the next an Inch, and so on; every Peg to be half an Inch longer than the former, till the last Peg be six Inches long ; then in that sort of Ground where you intend to plant, make a Row of Twenty Holes with the half-Inch Gauge; put therein Twenty good Seeds; cover them up, and slick the Gauge at the End of that Row; then do the like with all the other Eleven Gauges: This will determine the Depth, at which the most Seeds will come up.

Tull continued:

> But, in Drilling, Seed lies all the same just Depth, none deeper, nor shallower, than the rest; here's no Danger of the Accidents of burying, or being uncover'd, and therefore no Allowance must be made for them; but Allowance must be made for other Accidents, where the Sort of Seed is liable to them; such as Grub, Fly, Worm, Frost, &c.

The elements of the horse-drawn seed drill created by Tull include a means of inserting the drills to a specific depth, a means of delivering a known quantity of seeds at known intervals, and a means of covering the freshly planted seed. If manure or dung was to be used, it was worked into the soil before drilling, although 'Mr. Tull's

The Long and Simple History of the Dibble and its Cousins

Husbandry requires no Manure at all'.[52]

Tull's seed drills were horse-drawn, but smaller systems designed for manpower alone were developed, especially for gardeners. Some were referred to as 'walking dibbles'.[53]

Whereas Tull's seed drills would sow two rows, systems that would plant a wider path were continually being designed. Over 250 patents were issued in the United States before 1900 for either complete seed-drill systems or elemental parts. Advertisements for systems were common in farming magazines throughout the century (Figure 5).

Seed drills were constructed mostly of wood with cast-iron components where required. Following the advent of cheap steel in the middle of the nineteenth century, systems evolved into all-steel construction. Eventually, the horse was replaced by the internal combustion engine-powered tractor, leading to increased efficiency:

> Taking all seed-bed preparation and seeding operations together, the labor requirement for an acre of wheat where the methods and appliances of 1850 were used, was 10.4 man-hours. When the machines available in 1894-1896 were used, the requirement per acre was 1.45 man-hours. A modern tractor-driven disk and drill hook-up [in 1930], operated by one man, has seeded 92.7 acres in one day.[54]

Today, one equipment manufacturer claims that a single person can sow over 38 acres in a single hour.[55] This claim was based on 'an 80-acre field planted with a 16-row planter, a 30-inch row spacing, tendering a 100-bushel seed hopper for 34,000 population, and a 400-gallon liquid fertilizer tank applying 5 gallons per acre'. Headland turning was factored in. These statistics are for a 40-foot wide system. Other seed-drill systems are available that span up to 90 feet.[56]

Modern planting systems take into account moisture level, residual organic material, soil compaction, and nutrient level to automatically make adjustments to the system in real time.[57] With tractor speeds of up to ten miles per hour, it became necessary to develop seed-delivery systems that place the seed without it rolling out of place and systems that compensated for seed spacing on curves.[58]

Today, there's a dibble or one of its cousins available for all sizes of gardens or farms. The farmer or gardener can choose a tool from an old and well-established family tree or maybe a system from one of its newest roots.

Notes

1. Robert J. Braidwood, *Prehistoric Men*, 6th edn (Chicago: Chicago Natural History Museum, 1963), p. 146.
2. Kenneth P. Oakley, *Man the Tool-Maker*, Phoenix edn (Chicago: University of Chicago Press, 1964), p. 29.
3. Jules Janick, 'Ancient Egyptian Agriculture and the Origins of Horticulture', in *Proceedings of the International Symposium on Mediterranean Horticulture Issues and Prospects*, ed. by S. Sansavini and J. Janick (Acta Horticulturae, 582.55-59), p. 28.
4. Pliny (C. Plinius Secundus), *The Natural History of Pliny*, trans. by John Bostock and H.T. Riley, 6 vols (London: Henry G. Bohn, 1855), III (1855), pp. 487, 498; IV (1856), pp. 168, 178, 189.
5. B. H. Slicher van Bath, *The Agrarian History of Western Europe, AD 500-1850*, trans. by Olive Ordish

(New York: St Martin's Press Inc., 1963), p. 70.
6. Walter R.T. Witschey, 'Diet', in *Encyclopedia of the Ancient Maya*, ed. by Walter R.T. Witschey (Lanham [MD]: Rowman & Littlefield, 2016), p. 127.
7. '*Wie sie ire äcker bauuen und beseen*', hand-coloured engraving on paper (Frankfurt am Main: Johann Feyerabend for Theodor de Bry, 1591) pt. 2, plate XXI. <https://jcb.lunaimaging.com/luna/servlet> [accessed 18 April 2018]
8. John Smith, *The Generall Historie of Virginia, New-England, and the Summer Isles*, (London: Michael Sparkes, 1626), p. 28.
9. The Franciscan Fathers, *An Ethnologic Dictionary of the Navaho Language* (Saint Michaels [AZ], 1910), pp. 265-66.
10. *Catholicon Anglicum, an English-Latin Wordbook*, dated 1483, ed. by Sidney J.H. Herrtage (London: N. Turner & Co., 1881), pp. 92, 98.
11. Charles Stevens and John Liebault, *Maison rustique, or The countrey farme*, trans. by Richard Surflet, (Gervase Markham, 1616?), pp. 195, 255-56, 285, 655.
12. Abel Boyer, *Dictionnaire Royal, François-Anglois*, 2 vols (Paris: Adrian Moetjens, 1702), I, n.p.
13. 'dibber: Oxford English Dictionary', *OED Historical Thesaurus Online*, Oxford University Press, March 2018 <http://www.oed.com.ezproxy.sfpl.org/view/th/class/53250> [accessed April 4, 2018].
14. 'kippeen | kippin, n.'. *OED Online*. March 2018. Oxford University Press. <http://www.oed.com/view/Entry/103615?redirectedFrom=kippeen> [accessed 10 April 2018].
15. Nicholas de Bonnefons, *Le Jardinier François* (Amsterdam: Jean Blaeu, 1654), p. 192; see also pp. 138, 149, 185, 192, 201, 209, 212.
16. Nicholas de Bonnefons, *The French Gardiner*, trans. by John Evelin (London: T.B., 1691), p. 168. This use of 'dibber' is forty-five years earlier than recognized by the *Oxford English Dictionary Historical Thesaurus*.
17. Thomas Mawe and John Abercrombie, *The Universal Gardener and Botanist*, 2nd edn (London: G.G. and J. Robinson, 1797), n.p.; Alexander McDonald offers a similar definition (*A Complete Dictionary of Practical Gardening*, 2 vols (London: George Kearsley, 1807), I, n.p.).
18. *The Complete Farmer; or, General Dictionary of Agriculture and Husbandry*, 5th edn, 2 vols (London: R. Baldwin and others, 1807), I, n.p.
19. William Nicholson, 'On the Cultivation of the Sunflower, and its Advantages', *A Journal of Natural Philosophy, Chemistry, and the Arts*, VII (1804), 128.
20. Robert Kerr, *General View of the Agriculture of the County of Berwick* (London: Richard Phillips, 1809), pp. 244, 298.
21. Walter Nicol, *The Planter's Kalendar* (Edinburgh: Archibald Constable and Company, 1812), pp. xx, 351.
22. J.C. Loudon, *An Encyclopædia of Gardening* (London: Longman, Rees, Orme, Brown, Green, and Longman, 1835), p. 518.
23. Charles Waistell, 'Communication and Improvement on an Acorn Dibble', *Transactions of the Society, Instituted at London, for the Encouragement of Arts, Manufactures, and Commerce*, 29 (1811), 60-62.
24. William Marshall Craig, engraving in *Beschreibung einer Reise nach Surinam* (London: G. & W. Nicol, 1810), following p. 100.
25. John Curzon, 'On Dibbling Wheat', *The Agricultural Magazine*, IX, July-December 1803, p. 201.
26. '*Sur la culture de Tournesol, et ses advantages*', *La Décade philosophique, littéraire et politique*, 29 (1803), 507-08.
27. Thomas Hale, *A Compleat Body of Husbandry*, 2nd edn (London: Tho. Osborne, 1758), II, pp. 395, 397.
28. A.H., 'Description of a Garden Hand-Drill', *The Gardener's Magazine*, June 1831, p. 283.
29. Hugh Munro, 'Experiments on the Cultivation of Turnips', *The Magazine of Botany and Gardening*, January 1834, p. 87.
30. 'How You Should Not Make a Garden and How You Should', *The Garden Magazine*, February 1912, p. 9.
31. 'The Useful Arts, No. V: Gardening', *The Saturday Magazine*, 11 July 1835, p. 15.
32. G.W.S. Brewer, *Educational School Gardening and Handwork* (Cambridge: University Press, 1913), pp. 124-28.

33 'On the Cultivation of Autumn Wheat', *Irish Farmer's and Garden Magazine*, November 1835, p. 518.
34 'Account of an Agricultural Excursion into St. John's Berkey', *Farmers Gazette and Cheraw Advertiser*, 5 June 1840, p. 1.
35 T. Greiner, *The New Onion Culture* (New York: Orange Judd Company, 1903), p. 25.
36 US Patent 385,324. 26 June 1888. Thomas Seller, Dibble.
37 US Patent 685,925. 5 November 1901. Jesse G. Moren, Dibble; US Patent 1,900,827. 7 March 1933. William F. Love, Dibble.
38 US Patent 17,260. 12 May 1857. J.H. Bruen, Hand-Seeder; US Patent 1,567,908. 29 December 1925; Walter I. Brigham, Transplanting Trowel; US Patent 1,572,431. 9 February 1926. Holger Hansen, Hollow Dibble; US Patent 4,082,08. 4 April 1978. Erik Hilding Grundström, Göte Einar Grundström, Ivar Waleij, Planting Dibble; US Patent 4,244,308. 13 January 1981. Albert E. Vince, Seed drills.
39 US Patent D22,315. 28 March 1893. Warren E. Warner, Planting Dibble; US Patent 1,503,251. 29 July 1924. William Schoof, Implement Handle; US Patent 7,836,557. 23 November 2010. Bruce Baker, Ergonomic Garden Trowel.
40 US Patent 9,795,075. 24 October 2017. Karl Pratt, Jennifer Pratt, Planting Grid Device.
41 'Seeding Square', <https://www.seedingsquare.com> [accessed 17 April 2018].
42 US Patent 2,382,221. 14 August 1945. Albert T. Groth, Planting Spacer for Flats.
43 US Patent 2001/0203501. 25 August 2011. Craig Mathis, Jim McConnell, Method of Planting Triploid Seedless Watermelon Seeds and Enhanced Watermelon Pollenizer Seeds for Producing Watermelon Transplants.
44 Waistell, pp. 60-62; US Patent 554,669. 18 February 1896. Wallace L. Field, Transplanter.
45 'The Only Perfectly Reliable Hand Planting Machine', *The Prairie Farmer*, 23 February 1867, p. 127.
46 African Conservation Tillage Network, *Jab Planter User Manual* (2010).
47 S.H.M. Aikins, A. Bart-Plange and S. Opoku-Baffour, 'Performance Evaluation of Jab Planters for Maize Planting and Inorganic Fertilizer Application', *ARPN Journal of Agricultural and Biological Science*, 5 (2010), 29-33; P. Osei Bonsu and others, 'Evaluation of Two Jab Planters for Planting Maize in the Forest Zone of Ghana', *International Journal of Innovation and Applied Studies*, 10 (2015), 30-35.
48 SAS Terrateck, *Plantoir PL1: Canne à semer manuelle pour grosses graines* (2013).
49 Stephen Blake, *The Compleat Gardeners Practice, Directing the Exact Way of Gardening* (London: Thomas Pierrepoint, 1664), p. 50.
50 *The Penny Cyclopædia of the Society for the Diffusion of Useful Knowledge* (London: Charles Knight and Co., 1837), IX, p. 148.
51 G.E. Fusell, 'The Agricultural Revolution, 1600-1850', in *Technology in Western Civilization*, ed. by Melvin Kranzberg and Carroll W. Pursell Jr, 2 vols (New York: Oxford University Press, 1967), I, p. 133.
52 Jethro Tull, *Horse-Hoeing Husbandry: or, an Essay on the Principles of Vegetation and tillage*, 4th edn (London: A. Millar, 1762), pp. 58, 60, xvi. This 'very carefully corrected' edition includes an added preface by unknown 'editors'. Tull (1674-1741) originally published his book in 1731.
53 'English Specifications Enrolled During the Week', ed. by J.C. Robertson, *Mechanics' Magazine, Museum, Register, Journal, and Gazette*, 1 November 1851, p. 359.
54 'Mechanization of Agriculture as a Factor in Labor Displacement', *Monthly Labor Review*, October 1931, p. 8.
55 CNH Industrial America LLC (2016). *Early Riser® 2000 Series Planters*, p. 4.
56 CNH Industrial America LLC (2017). *Early Riser® 2160 Large Front Fold Planter*, p. 5.
57 'Precision Seed Spacing & Depth Control | Precision Planting', <http://www.precisionplanting.com/#products/smartfirmer/> [accessed 18 April 2018].
58 Deere & Company (2017). *Planting Equipment: Drawn and integral planters, ExactEmerge^{TM}, MaxEmerge^{TM} 5e, and MaxEmerge^{TM} 5 row units*, p. 2.

'The answers to our ancestors' prayers': Seeding a Movement for Health and Culture

Elizabeth Hoover and Sean Sherman

Prior to European contact, Indigenous horticulturalists in the Western hemisphere developed a vast variety of crops that would go on to feed the world: myriad varieties of corn, beans, squash, potatoes, and chilli peppers, among others. Many of these crops came to form the very foundations of tribal confederacies, like the Haudenosaunee Confederacy whose political power was rooted in their prolific corn production. For these reasons, crops were specifically targeted for destruction by the developing United States government – for example in 1779 General Sullivan and his troops, under orders from George Washington, burned acres of corn fields and millions of bushels of stored Haudenosaunee corn as punishment for Indigenous nations who resisted the new settler government.[1] Over the next 200 years, Indigenous food systems were dismantled through forced relocations, theft of land, forced assimilation, and increasingly through loss of access to traditional seeds. The outcome has been some of the highest rates of diabetes in the world and communities who are struggling to preserve language and culture. In this paper, two Indigenous scholars – a professor and a chef – have teamed up to describe not only the history by which Indigenous seed sovereignty has been threatened, but also current projects through which Indigenous communities are working to bring home heritage seed varieties and reincorporate them into gardens and meals. We conclude with how Native chefs specifically, as illustrated through the work of Chef Sherman, have a role in ensuring that people bring back heirloom seeds not as novelties, but to incorporate into healthy meals.

Seed Sovereignty

Food sovereignty, first defined in 1996 by international peasant and small-scale farmer organization La Via Campesina, and then brought to the world stage at the 2007 Forum for Food Sovereignty in Selingue, Mali, is 'the right of peoples to healthy and culturally appropriate food produced through ecologically sound and sustainable methods, and their right to define their own food and agriculture systems'. The declaration goes on to highlight (1) the importance of putting food producers and consumers, rather than corporations, at the heart of food systems policies; (2) the need to include the next generation in food production, as well as empowering food producers and artisans; (3) the importance of environmental, social, and economic sustainability; and (4) the need for transparent trade, as well as equality between genders, racial groups, and social classes.² Everyone in the food chain is positioned as a potentially powerful actor. When asked to define food sovereignty, several Native American farmers and gardeners highlighted the importance of access to healthy culturally relevant food, land, and information; independence for individuals to make choices on their own consumption and for communities to define their own food systems; the desire to keep food dollars within the community; the importance of tribes having the independence and control to provide the foods they see as appropriate, grown in a manner that is deemed acceptable for their constituents; the importance of education and working with Native youth; and the ability to sustain relationships to the environment, food sources, and other people.³ Native Americans currently suffer the worst rates of diabetes and other metabolic disorders of any ethnic group in the United States, and this is due in large part because of disruptions to traditional food systems and a lack of access to healthy foods.⁴

One of the integral components of food sovereignty for many agriculturally based communities is seed sovereignty, which according to Vandana Shiva 'includes the farmer's rights to save, breed and exchange seeds, to have access to diverse open source seeds which can be saved – and which are not patented, genetically modified, owned or controlled by emerging seed giants. It is based on reclaiming seeds and biodiversity as commons and public good'.⁵ Heritage seeds – most passed down through generations of Indigenous gardeners, with some reacquired from seed banks or ally seed savers – are often discussed as the foundation of the food sovereignty movement for Native communities, not just as living relatives to be protected from patent or modification, but also as tools for education and reclaiming health. As Clayton Brascoupe (Mohawk), director of the Traditional Native American Farmer Association, notes, 'we refer to these as our living relatives [.... I]f you have the ability to interact with your relatives through these seeds, you also have the ability to feed yourself well.'⁶

Mohawk seed keeper Rowen White is one of the founders of the Indigenous Seed Keepers Network (ISKN) as well as the Haudenosaunee Seedkeepers Society; he currently serves as the chair of the board of Seed Savers Exchange. Through these various networks, she works to help Native community members preserve and propagate heritage seed varieties and to make these seeds, and the knowledge that should accompany them, available to a greater number of Native gardeners. When asked, as someone so integral to promoting this movement in Indian Country, to define seed sovereignty, Rowen responds,

> Seed sovereignty is to me when you have an understanding of your inherent right to save seed and pass it on to future generations and that you are exercising it at that same time. It also means that you as a person or as a community are self-informed and dictate your relationship to seed; that says that these are seeds that really do not belong to anyone. They belong to us as a community in the

commons but that we can define our relationship to that seed based upon our own values and not the values of anyone else aside of our community. So, that I think is one aspect, sort of an esoteric way of saying it but I really do think seed sovereignty at the heart is really just taking back the action of saving seed and keeping it again year after year, generation after generation so that we can have the security of knowing that we have seeds that will feed our children and our grandchildren, that we have the means by which to feed our people instead of relying on external sources so that sovereignty is something that we can take care of ourselves, that we can sort of get back to the way it was before colonization, that we can have some sort of control or say of what foods we are able to put on our table and what foods are available for people to have access to in our communities.[7]

Similarly, fellow ISKN member Scott Shoemaker (Miami) defines food sovereignty as 'the ability to seed your own community with cultural appropriate foods'.[8] As a curator of an Indigenous seed collection at the Minnesota Museum of Science, he worked to do that through collaborations with nearly a dozen Indigenous community projects who partnered to form ISKN, which is now growing out seeds from that collection and sharing them with other community members.[9] This project, and others like it that have re-established heritage seeds to Native gardens – and which Chef Sean Sherman has subsequently incorporated into dishes – will be discussed below.

Why Seed Sovereignty Became Diminished in the US

There are myriad reasons, related to the historic and ongoing colonization of the Western Hemisphere, that have contributed to why Indigenous people now need to fight to reclaim food sovereignty. In many cases the disruption of traditional food systems was intentional and included a range of actions, from deliberately destroying food in acts of war to interfering with the transfer of food-related knowledge from one generation to the next.

Scorched-earth battle tactics utilized against Native people in the eighteenth and nineteenth centuries sought to destroy food supplies and the land from which it came in order to make Native people reliant on the American government.[10] Indigenous communities have been pushed to marginalized territories, some relocated to regions with completely different climates from that which they originated, and in many cases the treaty-making system alienated tribes from their land.[11] Land bases were further diminished through the allotment system that apportioned communal land to individuals and families, distributing the 'remaining' land to white settlers to start their own farms.

During this era, many Native youth were also sent to boarding schools, where they were often undernourished.[12] In these schools, youth were encouraged to forget their tribal connections, including traditional methods of farming, and were forced to take on staples of a standard diet that embodied Anglo ideals of food ways.[13] Beginning in the late nineteenth century, the Bureau of Indian Affairs pushed for the elimination of traditional farming by replacing dryland farming in some regions with canal irrigation, ranching, and agribusiness enterprises; substituting individual rights to land for community rights; and replacing the crop genetic diversity present in many traditional seeds by a smaller number of introduced crops and crop varieties, such as alfalfa and hybrid maize.[14]

In recent years, climate change, which has led to unpredictable weather patterns – droughts in some areas while others have suffered unusually wet and cold springs and summers – has made it difficult to grow out seeds adapted to a particular climate. As Potawatomi philosopher Kyle Whyte notes, climate change interrupts the various 'systems of responsibility' that Native communities have with the plant and animal communities that feed them, including heritage seeds, which have been developed to grow in a particular landscape and under particular weather conditions.[15]

In some communities, as tribal populations grow and their reservation land base does not, a continued lack of access to land, as well as to tools and seed, contributes to fewer gardens overall, and fewer places to plant heritage seeds, especially in families who have not maintained this tradition.[16] For urban Indigenous residents, gaining access to land and seeds can be nearly impossible.

Loss of Control over Seeds

In the late nineteenth century, seed breeders and botanists across the Midwest and northern plains began collecting seeds from Native communities, obtaining Indigenous seeds and knowledge of how to breed them from Native Seed Keepers, and in the process building their own profitable businesses. As ethnohistorian Christina Gish Hill notes, 'Like the colonization of land and people, colonization of seeds has involved viewing seeds as a resource that can be appropriated.' She describes how, during this era, Indigenous seeds were classified based on Euro-American categories and removed from their home communities. Genetic material was extracted from the seeds, much in the same way other resources were extracted from Native land. Hill notes that 'based on the assumption that Indigenous seeds, like Indigenous lands or Indigenous children, are not able to reach their full potential in the hands of Indigenous caretakers, seed colonization acts as a parallel form of assimilation. This assumption has justified the colonial control over not only people and land, but their seeds as well'.[17] In this way one can imagine concentric circles of colonization, over land alienated from Native people; over the people themselves; and over the seeds, like children, taken from their home communities to benefit non-Native people.

These seeds gathered from Indigenous people were then stored in private collections, including museums, and marketed in seed catalogues to farmers establishing themselves across the west, farmers who then went on to save and trade the seeds that suited them best, as farmers have for eons. But even these farmers began to gradually lose control over their seed stock. Sociologist Jack Kloppenburg, who has helped to popularize the term 'seed sovereignty', has documented how, since the 1930s, farmers' sovereignty over seeds 'has been continuously and progressively eroded, while the sovereignty of what is now a "life sciences industry" has been correspondingly enlarged'. This erosion began with the marketing and sale of hybrid seeds that needed to be purchased anew every year in order to continue to be productive, creating a profitable seed sector. More recently genetic engineering has been used to develop 'Genetic Use Restriction Technologies' that prevent a seed from germinating unless proprietary chemicals are applied (i.e. 'terminator technologies') in order to prevent farmers from replanting seeds, and even more restrictive intellectual property rights legislation has been passed to expropriate farmers' access to the reproducibility of seed. Over the past two decades, patents have increasingly been applied to crop genetics, and farmers caught planting saved seeds patented by large agro-corporations have faced legal ramifications.[18] Plant breeding has shifted dramatically from community knowledge shared across generations to a privatized system dominated by seed monopolies.[19] Seed sovereignty has now become a global fight – with colonizing forces no longer necessarily nation state based, but rooted in big agri-business.

Indigenous Seed Sovereignty Revival

But there has been a food sovereignty movement sweeping across North America, as tribal communities are fighting and organizing to reclaim their traditional food systems as a means of improving health and promoting culture. Heritage seeds are often discussed as the foundation of this food sovereignty movement, living relatives to be protected, but also tools for education and health. There is a growing network of Indigenous seedkeepers that is coalescing not only to educate tribal people around seed planting and saving, but also to push for the 'rematriation' of Indigenous seeds from institutions that have collected or inherited them, back to their communities of origin. (The term 'rematriation' has been developed in opposition to the more traditionally used 'repatriation' in order to highlight the role of women seedkeepers.)

As part of a broader project titled 'From "Garden Warriors" to "Good Seeds": Indigenizing the Local Food Movement', Elizabeth Hoover travelled to thirty-nine Native community farming and gardening projects around the US and asked participants for their thoughts on how their communities could achieve food and seed sovereignty. One of the questions she asked participants was why they felt it was important to plant and save heritage seeds in their gardens. In addition to wanting to be independent from the commercial commodity agriculture system, respondents' answers focused on needs to maintain cultural connections and to restore health.

Diane Wilson (Dakota), director of Dream of Wild Health in Minnesota, highlighted that planting heritage seeds establishes a cultural connection to planting, and also works to begin healing in her community. She notes that, 'through the loss of land, through the commodity food program, these are the foods that we've lost connection to. And it's a form of cultural recovery to reconnect to those foods in particular'. She pointed to heirloom seeds in particular because they are 'seeds that have their genetic gifts intact. And for us, in particular, what we're trying to do goes beyond simply the genetic integrity of the seed. It also has to do with the history of it, the cultural importance of the seeds and doing that work of cultural recovery with those seeds is important to us as a way of ultimately recovering from the trauma of the past how many hundred years'.

Participants also highlighted the importance of connecting seeds to the land where they originally came from – the land that seeds were developed for and remember. In addition, they described the importance of connecting seeds to the descendants of the ancestors who developed them. For example, Erie Whiteman (Arapaho) who works at Dream of Wild Health relayed to the youth he works with that 'we have our ancient seeds that have been handed down to us, and those, I told the kids, were like our ancestors. That's what we have that our ancestors touched, something that we have in common are those seeds, so they're like our ancestors, and they have spirits'.

In addition, heritage varieties were seen as healthier to consume than conventional varieties. Stephanie Berryhill (Mvskoke Creek) with the Mvskoki Food Sovereignty Initiative in Oklahoma described the Indian Pumpkin, grown by Creek people for thousands of years, as a super nutritious food that should be served every day, not only on special occasions as it currently is. Roberto Nutlouis (Navajo) who runs a farming project in Pinon Arizona for the Black Mesa Water Coalition, described the traditional corns they grow as 'biological and spiritual nourishment' in recognition of the multiple ways these seeds feed his community. For these reasons, the gardeners at these projects are dedicated to accessing and growing out heritage seed varieties.

Collaboration and Rematriation: From Museums to Gardens to the James Beard House

An important aspect of increasing the number of heritage seeds grown out in Native gardens is gaining access to those seeds, and then convincing people to eat them. Chef Sean Sherman (Lakota), from the Pine Ridge Reservation in South Dakota, has spent many years as a chef working to restore and elevate pre-contact Native foods. Much of this work has centred on gaining access to heritage seed varieties, and has been geared towards motivating people to grow these varieties not only to develop connections to their ancestors who also held these seeds, but also to taste the uniquely flavoured dishes that he has created from these seeds – including those described below which have recently been returned to communities. Below we will describe two recent projects to grow out and rematriate seeds back to their communities of origin, and Chef Sherman's work to incorporate these seeds into his menus, as a way of promoting their culinary value to the broader public.

Minnesota Science Museum, Native farms, and the Indigenous Seed Keepers Network

As described above, in the late nineteenth and early twentieth centuries Euro-American botany enthusiasts collected seeds from Native communities, because they recognized the value of these heritage varieties, and because they saw Native people,

Seeds

and their material culture, as imminently disappearing. Wesley Hiller, a dentist and avid amateur anthropologist in Minneapolis, collected seeds from upper mid-west, northern plains, and southwest tribes during the 1930s and 40s. In 1977, the Wesley Hiller Estate donated his entire collection of Native American seeds – including 167 plant specimens (mostly varieties of corn, beans, squash, sunflowers, and tobacco) and ninety food processing objects – to the Minnesota Science Museum.[20] Since 2004, the Ethnobotany project at the museum has been working on stabilizing, revitalizing, and curating the seeds in the museum's permanent collections, each year de-accessioning seeds from the museum's collection and growing them out in an educational garden. The offspring of the de-accessioned seeds are then accessioned into the collections to maintain their viability.[21]

Scott Shoemaker, a citizen of the Miami tribe, joined the museum team as a curator in 2009, and realized that more needed to be done to connect these seeds to the communities from which they were collected, both to benefit those communities and to provide greater opportunity for the seeds to be grown out. Through the Upper Midwest Seedkeepers Alliance (now expanded to become the Indigenous Seedkeepers Network), Scott partnered with growers at the Dream of Wild Health (DOWH), the Shakopee Mdewakanton Wozupi farm, and the White Earth Land Recovery Project to grow out some of the seeds from the museum's collection in their fields. Dakota yellow flour corn was one of these varieties, raised with careful attention to make sure the corn plants didn't cross-pollinate with neighbouring GMO corn. DOWH, run by Dakota director Diane Wilson whose farm is located on traditional Dakota homeland, thought this was an important seed to reunite with their soil. Each summer the program brings urban Native youth from Minneapolis and St Paul up to its farm, where they learn about planting, tending, harvesting, and cooking heritage seed varieties.

While some of the seeds are returned to the museum's collection, this corn continues to be grown out at these farms – and the seeds are then distributed to other Indigenous gardens, and have also been incorporated into events and dishes prepared by Sean Sherman and the Sioux Chef team. For example, the 'Owamni & the Buffalo Sky' event in Minneapolis featured Native American musicians, poets, and a five-course meal which included dehydrated rabbit on a honey hominy cake made from the Dakota flour corn (topped with toasted walnuts and berry jus). Another dinner, 'Moon of the Changing Leaves' hosted in Rapid City, South Dakota, included a smoked elk and Dakota corn cake, topped with pine nuts and corn shoots. In this way the Sioux Chef team is taking an ingredient that had ostensibly disappeared from dinner tables and creating a market for it – and for producers like the Dream of Wild Health farm. At the same time, through hosting community meals specifically intended to connect Native community members with these foods, and through teaching cooking classes to the youth at DOWH, Chef Sherman is getting community members excited about re-incorporating these foods back into their diets as well.

Seeding a Movement for Health and Culture

Mohawk Red Bread Corn and the Hudson Valley Farm Hub

Another example of collaboration between a settler institution and Indigenous communities to increase the availability of heritage seed varieties can be found in the cultivation of Mohawk Red Bread corn on traditional Mohawk territory, on Hudson Valley Farm Hub land, in conjunction with the nonprofit organization Seed Shed.[22] This project began with a collaboration between Mohawk seed keeper Rowen White and Ken Green at the HVFH who wanted to start a Native seed sanctuary on the farm hub's land – as recognition of the original owners of the land and as resistance to a planned pipeline project. Rowen had been given Mohawk Red Bread corn by fellow Mohawk seed keeper Stephen McComber – the variety was nearly lost until he was given the last remaining cob two decades ago and began to grow it out again. Rowen and Ken decided to plant that corn at the HVFH, alongside traditional varieties of beans, squash, and sunflowers, as part of a series of events involving Akwesasne Mohawks, inner city youth, migrant farmers, and staff from the HVFH. Now in its third year, this project has turned that small amount of corn into 900 kilograms, most of which went back to Akwesasne to feed the youth who are taking part in the Ohero:kon rites of passage ceremonies. As part of their education in the rites of passage, youth are taught the importance of heritage seeds, as well as how to prepare and cook them, and the value of eating those seeds.

Figure 1: Chef Sean Sherman and Rowen's daughter Maizie preparing food at the James Beard House. Photo by Elizabeth Hoover, October 27, 2017.

Seeds

This corn also found its way onto the plates of diners at the James Beard House in New York City in October of 2017 when Chef Sherman was invited to prepare a meal. The menu, as for all of Chef Sherman's meals, reflected the fare of local Native people, with seafood sourced from the local Shinnecock tribe and traditional corn, beans, and squash sourced from the Native Seed Sanctuary. The meal began with pumpkin and sunflower seed fritters and continued through a spoon of potato bean spread with smoked sea scallops and dried ramps; raw oysters and quahogs; acorn and Mohawk Red Bread' corn hominy dumplings topped with nasturtium, dried wild onion, and crab apple broth; braised elk leg with a dried cranberry bean cracker, garnished with strawberries, hyssop, and pea shoots; braised rabbit with buffalo creek squash, toasted hickory nut, pawpaw sauce, and dried apple; and for desert maple Mohawk Red Bread Corn pudding with hickory, crispy corn silk, burnt maple sugar, and corn shoots. In a place like New York, where the dominant narrative is that Native people have disappeared, it was a valuable experience for upscale diners to share in foods that local Native people continue to eat, and some of which have only been recently reintroduced.

Importance of Chefs in the Seed Sovereignty Movement

This work to rematriate seeds continues, through organizations like the Seed Savers Exchange – Chef Sherman serves on its board – which are working to grow out Indigenous heritage seed varieties from their collection and send them back to their communities of origin. The University of Michigan is also working with Anishnaabe tribes to grow out seeds in their collections to return them back to their peoples; the project celebrated its first harvest dinner in October 2018. At meeting in Michigan in April 2018, Rowen noted the type of healing that takes place when the colonial institutions that kept and protected Native seeds then return those seeds back to the communities from whence they came, so that they can be incorporated into cultural, health, and healing programs.

But in order to fully incorporate these seeds back into communities, beyond just growing them out, they need to be eaten, reworked into the lives and onto the dinner plates of Native people. To encourage this this, Native chefs like Sean Sherman and the Sioux Chef team are collaborating with Native community programs to grow out and prepare these seeds, getting people excited about eating them so they'll want to grow them, but also helping to create a market for these seeds – creating demand and showcasing historical nutritional cultural value. Native seeds have gone from a target for destruction, to novelties collected by institutions, to now working their way back into Native gardens, kitchens, and homes thanks to the hard work of seed keepers like Rowen White and Indigenous chefs like Sean Sherman.

Chef Sherman's first cookbook *The Sioux Chef's Indigenous Kitchen*, which contains over a hundred recipes of healthy foods, is designed to be an educational tool to give communities ideas about how they can work with the seeds and foods from their own regions.[23] The idea is to encourage them to create and use recipes like the ones featured in the book, using the heirloom horticultural crops and/or the wild foods around them to help improve and maintain their communities' health.

Chef Sherman and his team also just established the non-profit NATIFS, or North American Traditional Indigenous Food Systems, a broader initiative with two main goals: Indigenous culinary education and Indigenous food access. The first step will be opening a culinary hub in Minneapolis, the Indigenous Food Lab, which will be a restaurant and education centre. The restaurant will serve as a live training centre in order to bring in aspiring Native chefs for hands-on learning about how to work with traditional foods in a modern way. The second phase of the project will be to reach out to tribal communities near Minneapolis to help them to develop food businesses in their own communities, offering them a full business model and plan, and giving them the tools they need to create small food businesses by utilizing the main training hub. The third phase of this program will be to replicate this model in other parts of the country, creating food training hubs in large metropolitan areas, where resources and restaurants tend to be more concentrated, and then satellite businesses in surrounding tribal communities, where people tend not to have access to restaurants and other food service resources.

The Indigenous Food Lab and its resulting offshoot businesses and training centres will continue to support local tribal economies, especially seed keepers and small farmers, in order to ensure the sustainability of Native food systems and to encourage the consumption of traditional foods. Only through incorporating traditional foods, and seeds specifically, into the diets of Native people on a more regular basis will people truly become excited about wanting to preserve and grow out heirloom seed varieties. As Chef Sherman expressed in a recent presentation, 'we are the answer to our ancestors' prayers' – prayers for health, continuity, and good food.

Notes

1. Jane Mt. Pleasant, 'The Paradox of Plows and Productivity: An Agronomic Comparison of Cereal Grain Production under Iroquois Hoe Culture and European Plow Culture,' *Agricultural History*, 85.4 (2011), 460-92.
2. 'Declaration of Nyeleni,' February 2, 2007, Selingue, Mali <http://nyeleni.org/spip.php?article290> [accessed 10 March 2019].
3. Elizabeth Hoover, '"You can't say you're sovereign if you can't feed yourself": Defining and Enacting Food Sovereignty in American Indian Community Gardening', *American Indian Culture and Research Journal*, 41.3 (2017), 31-70 <10.17953/aicrj.41.3.hoover>.
4. American Indian/Alaska Native adults (16.1%) are more likely than black adults (12.6%), Hispanic adults (11.8%), Asian adults (8.4%), or white adults (7.1%) to have ever been told they had diabetes. These rates vary by region, from 5.5 percent among Alaska Native adults to 33.5 percent among American Indian adults in southern Arizona (Centers for Disease Control and Prevention, 'National Diabetes Fact Sheet, 2011' <https://www.cdc.gov/diabetes/pubs/pdf/ndfs_2011.pdf> [accessed 10 March 2019].
5. Vandana Shiva, 'The Seed Emergency: The Threat to Food and Democracy', *AlJazeera English*, 6 February 2012 <https://www.aljazeera.com/indepth/opinion/2012/02/201224152439941847.html>

[accessed 10 March 2019].

6 Clayton Brascoupe interview with Elizabeth Hoover, Tesuque Pueblo, NM, 11 June 11 2014.
7 Rowen White interview with Elizabeth Hoover, Nevada City, CA, 16 July 2014.
8 Scott Shoemaker interview with Elizabeth Hoover, Science Museum of Minnesota, St. Paul, 29 August 2014.
9 Shoemaker interview and personal communications with members of the Indigenous Seed Keepers Network 2014-2017, especially at the annual Indigenous Farming Conference hosted by the White Earth Land Recovery Project in Minnesota, which includes panels and sessions by Indigenous Seed Keepers Network members.
10 For example, see the description of Sullivan's campaign against the Haudenosaunee in Mt. Pleasant and, in the nineteenth century, see the stories collected and recorded by the Diné of the Eastern Region of the Navajo Reservation (Title VII bilingual staff, *Oral Histories of the Long Walk = Hwéeldi Baa Hané* (Crown Point, NM: Lake Valley Navajo School, 1990)).
11 Nicholas James Reo and Angela K. Parker, 'Re-thinking Colonialism to Prepare for the Impacts of Rapid Environmental Change', *Climatic Change*, 120 (2013), 671-82.
12 Charlotte Coté, '"Indigenizing" Food Sovereignty: Revitalizing Indigenous Food Practices and Ecological Knowledges in Canada and the United States', *Humanities*, 5.3 (2016): 57 <10.3390/h5030057>.
13 Jennifer Bess, 'More Than a Food Fight: Intellectual Traditions and Cultural Continuity in Cholocco's Indian School Journal 1902-1918', *The American Indian Quarterly*, 37.1-2 (2013), 77-110.
14 David Cleveland, 'Indian Agriculture, United States Agriculture, and Sustainable Agriculture: Science and Advocacy', *American Indian Culture and Research Journal*, 22.3 (1998), 13-29.
15 Kyle Powys Whyte, 'Justice forward: Tribes, Climate Adaptation and Responsibility', *Climatic Change*, 120 (2013), 517-30 <10.1007/s10584-013-0743-2>.
16 For examples of how these struggles to have gardens manifested in the Mohawk community of Akwesasne, see Elizabeth Hoover, *The River Is in Us: Fighting Toxics in a Mohawk Community* (Minneapolis: University of Minnesota Press, 2017).
17 Christina Gish Hill, 'Seeds as Ancestors, Seeds as Archives: Seed Sovereignty and the Politics of Repatriation to Native Peoples', *American Indian Culture and Research Journal*, 41.3 (2017), 93-112 (pp. 102, 103)
18 Jack Kloppenburg, 'Impeding Dispossession, Enabling Repossession: Biological Open Source and the Recovery of Seed Sovereignty', *Journal of Agrarian Change*, 10.3 (July 2010), 367-88 (pp. 371).
19 Sheryl D. Breen, 'Saving Seeds: The Svalbard Global Seed Vault, Native American Seed Savers, and Problems of Property', *Journal of Agriculture, Food Systems, Community Development*, 5.2 (2015), 39-52.
20 'Three Sisters Garden', Science Museum of Minnesota, 2012 <https://vimeo.com/57183594> and Shoemaker interview.
21 'Squash Has a Long Tasty History', *Science Buzz*, Science Museum of Minnesota, 2014 <http://www.sciencebuzz.org/museum/object/2014_05_squash> [accessed 10 March 2019] and Shoemaker interview.
22 Seed Shed <https://seedshed.org/> and 'Native American Seed Sanctuary', *Hudson Valley Farm Hub* <http://hvfarmhub.org/about/seed-sanctuary/> [both accessed 10 March 2019]. See also Rowen White and Elizabeth Hoover, 'Our Living Relatives: Maintaining Resilience and Seed Diversity in Native American Communities', *New Farmers Almanac*, edited and published by the GreenHorns (2019, in press).
23 Sean Sherman and Beth Dooley, *The Sioux Chef's Indigenous Kitchen* (Minneapolis: University of Minnesota Press, 2017).

Fruits of Empowerment in Grazia Deledda's *The Church of Solitude*

Èilis Kierans

At the outset of Grazia Deledda's *The Church of Solitude* (1936), Maria Concezione has recently undergone a mastectomy in order to remove a cancerous breast. Following surgery, she falls into a state of hopeful desperation, and her life is at a crossroad. As she returns to her home located at a fork in the road between valley and mountain, she feels torn between life and death, appetite and asceticism, solitude and marriage. Her fecund garden serves as a middle ground, a sanctuary that nourishes her soul among its abundant fruits, a space of her own in which she feels free from the rigid ideals of her Sardinian society. I would like to explore Concezione's complex relationship with food, which serves as a means through which she seeks to escape patriarchy while society repeatedly attempts to reassign her to it. It is only once her suitors abandon their prey, leaving Concezione alone to live a peaceful existence devoid of male impositions, that she regains her faith in God – as well as a hearty appetite outside of her garden.

The day Concezione returns home from the hospital, an ardent suitor named Aroldo knocks on her door with the expectation of being invited inside for dinner. The prior evening, he had arrived at her home with a little pig intended as a gift. Aroldo expresses his devotion and carnal desire through the pig. However, the presence of the dead animal disturbs Concezione. The narrator describes:

> But returning to the kitchen, Concezione flushed with irritation to see that her mother had taken a dead suckling pig with a red rind out of the cupboard against the wall; its belly was cut open and stuffed with myrtle branches. Her mother looked at it with uncertainty and a bit of disquiet, and seemed to speak to it. 'Poor little beast probably only three days old. Well!' She sighed, resigning herself to the destiny of the tiny victim.[1]

Concezione sees her own transient existence in the dead pig. Etched with the scars of the surgeon's knife on her chest, she empathizes with the recently butchered animal, which is subsequently dismembered and served on a platter. Ultimately she loses her appetite and refuses to consume the meat. Around the table upon which rests the corpse of the suckling pig, Aroldo is at ease, while Concezione impatiently awaits his departure.

Seeds

In many societies, meat is considered a symbol of power. Nick Fiddes analyzes the significance and implications of consuming meats: 'Meat is a venerable symbol of individual and social potency. How we consume it, exchange it, and communicate by using it are all conditioned accordingly, as they may well have since time immemorial.'[2] Aroldo expresses his virility through the pig he gifts to Concezione and consumes at her dinner table. She senses the figurative significance of the meat, and thus she immediately rejects both Aroldo and his offering. In refusing to eat the pig, Concezione attempts to prevent Aroldo from devouring her whole. Numerous theorists have noted that food and sex are intertwined. In Concezione's case, gifts of food likely represent consummation of a sale. In bringing Concezione a freshly killed pig, Aroldo seeks to affirm his masculinity and prowess as a partner. His gift conveys his desire to make Concezione his wife and consummate their marriage – an act that will transform her from an independent woman to a piece of property. Concezione, however, has no need of a husband, as she inherited a large sum of money from her late father and can live securely without the financial support of a spouse.

Concezione evades dominating non-human animals, with whom she identifies, by avoiding cooking or eating meat. Fiddes associates the consumption of animal blood with man's desire to dominate nature:

> Consumption of animal flesh provides a direct and powerful authentication of human superiority over the rest of nature, so for individuals and societies to whom such mastery is an important value, its consumption is typically a central symbol. Killing, cooking, and eating animals is perhaps the ultimate expression of human primacy. Meat stands for the power of humanity – Man's proverbial 'muscle' – in the natural environment.[3]

Concezione refuses all levels of culinary transformation and artifice, also refusing to eat ornate cakes. Claude Lévi-Strauss notes that cooking is a form of culture that transcends nature by transforming the raw into the cooked.[4] Qualifying this famous claim, Sherry B. Ortner maintains that in some instances women serve as a bridge between nature and culture, because they are largely responsible for cooking food in the domestic sphere. However, when it is a matter of high cuisine, in which a more complex level of transformation is required, men outnumber women in the kitchen.[5]

Throughout the book, Concezione accepts many gifts of decadent food from her admirers, but she does not consume them, instead giving them away to the poor. Rather, she eats very little and exhibits behaviour characteristic of one who suffers from anorexia. The reason for her highly ascetic eating habits is manifold. One of the few aspects of her life that she is able to easily control is how she nourishes her body. Carole Counihan explains that '[a]norexic women refuse bodily penetration through food and often sex and voluntarily starve themselves, sometimes to death, in an effort to achieve autonomy, control, and power'.[6] In maternal symbolism, the mouth serves as a surrogate vagina, and the act of eating can be understood as another form of

Fruits of Empowerment

bodily penetration.[7] Numerous theorists have pointed out that women seek to escape objectification through anorexia. As Concezione withers away and ceases to menstruate, she will be rendered incapable of producing fruits from her loin. Although thinness makes some anorectic women feel more feminine, for many others it is thinness that allows them to rebuff femininity.[8] Concezione seeks to defeminize her body and arrest her reproductive capacities. She withholds from eating in an attempt to establish an order of her own making.

Indubitably, Concezione's refusal to marry goes against the traditional gender roles of the time. The local priest Serafino reminds her: 'A woman is made to marry, to create a family for herself, to complete the cycle like our mothers and grandmothers have completed it' (56). Concezione, however, can only imagine a serene existence at her mother's side. As her suitors continue to aggressively pursue her, she pushes them away more decisively. If at first she rejected suitors because she felt inadequate, gradually she spurns them because she senses their desire to possess her. At one point in the plot, the narrator relates: 'Oh, how these bestial men came to hunt her, leaving her like a doe targeted in her lair!' (119). In a passage that follows, a hostile and enamoured suitor desires to 'assault her, kiss her, [and] bite her face' (120). She perceives the connection between male violence against women and animals.

Concezione identifies with the hunted and butchered animal, thus she repudiates both meat and man. Carol J. Adams emphasizes that male power is linked to meat, thus veganism simultaneously rejects patriarchy and meat eating society.[9] Marti Kheel notes that hunting is tied to masculine self-identity. The young boy's first hunt often serves as a rite of passage. During this act of initiation, he learns how to exercise control over others.[10] Perhaps unsurprisingly, hunting is commonly a shared activity among women batterers.[11] Many hunters claim to love the animals they slay. Similarly, the hostile suitor claims to love the woman he seeks to possess through force. Such a relationship is bereft of reciprocal respect and is based on male self-interest. According to Ortner, because men are lacking natural creative functions (such as giving birth), they are constrained to seek creative outlets externally through technology and symbols. She cites warfare and hunting as examples of men's artificial creativity because of the symbolic transcendence (cultural, social) that these activities afford them, which she claims are valued more than the 'perishable' life of a child that a woman bears naturally.[12]

Various theorists have noted that food has been gendered throughout time. In *The Church of Solitude*, Concezione's uncle remarks that 'coffee is for women', and he refuses to drink anything but wine (15). Jackson emphasizes that fruit is typically considered a feminine food associated with gardens, goddesses, and love. Indeed, women were traditionally the gatherers of fruit — the earth's tender offering, 'the most innocently edible substance'.[13] Adams points out that 'women's food' is perceived as passive and inert.[14] Concezione, however, reclaims the fruit of the garden as a means of female growth and agency. She finds peace in a vegan diet that grows freely, devoid of male violence and impositions. Fruits are intended to be plucked and eaten, and if we cease to pick them, they fall to the ground and eventually rise up again in a constant cycle. Fruit will continue to reproduce naturally.

Concezione's faith in her garden and sparse diet becomes inextricably linked to her religious spirituality. Jackson explains that 'to refrain from eating meat has regularly been associated with spiritual commitment, along with that other carnal act, sex, and has also implied a degree of asceticism'.[15] Interestingly, Concezione's asceticism coincides with her waning spiritual commitment. During her convalescence, her relationship with Christ falters. The narrator relates: 'She didn't want to pray anymore; the Hail Mary's came out of her mouth all withered while her thoughts wandered far away. She didn't eat, she grew thin, she wanted to close herself ever more into her circle of death and vanish like the clouds of summer' (91). Seeking solace, she turns to her garden, where she relishes the vegetables her mother grows from the seeds she compassionately cares for with her own hands. Her daily ritual of embracing the flavours of the land represents her desire to exist in a more fulfilling way. She longs to return to a pure life symbolized by a simple pomodoro, in which she sees a reflection of herself. Concezione relishes the scent of the tomatoes, passing her sweetest moments among fresh vegetation. The narrator describes: 'Especially in the evening, after Giustina had watered the little clearing and the row of tomatoes that smelled like tropical plants, a truly religious peace like that of an ancient hermitage reigned around the little church' (111). It is noteworthy that tomatoes are often associated with fertility – a fruit flowing with seeds. Concezione welcomes the fruit of her garden as a substitute for the seed of man.

Why is Concezione so attracted to a garden of ripe vegetables? Bernard Lyman posits that food has a significance that can arouse complex associations composed of various emotions. These associations are both negative and positive. He offers an example of this phenomenon:

> 'We used to raise them in our garden' is a literal statement, but it emerges from a welter of thoughts, images, emotions, and ideas. To the speaker it symbolizes complex mental content containing attitudes towards the 'we' and 'our,' to the garden and to the gardening, encompassing, perhaps, blue skies and summer rains. 'To raise' captures meanings of growth and care, far different from 'to have.'[16]

Lyman maintains that our experiences with food are linked to a series of ideas and attitudes. The nuances of our language often reveal our relationship to food. In *The Church of Solitude*, Deledda uses highly ornate language peppered with religious undertones to describe Concezione's spiritual connection to lush gardens. For example, in one passage she recounts a memory from her childhood: on her way home from school, she climbed a wall to admire a garden of cabbages. From this precise recollection, Concezione communicates that plant life fosters her well-being. Her own garden is a steadfast sanctuary that nurses her back to health. It is a *locus amoenus* that stimulates her appetite and inspires her to take hold of life outside of the male domain. It is a place of healing, where she reflects on her fate and the afterlife tenderly. Concezione even envisions the afterlife as a garden:

> What do we need to live? So little: a breath, a good word, the smell of the garden, the hope for the Kingdom of God that will surely come some day, even with the peace of death, even without asking for it over and over again with careless words. She imagined this kingdom like a garden always fresh, always warm, without mosquitoes; a little bench against the wall illuminated by the moon, her mother's spirit next to hers, for eternity. (112)

Throughout the narrative, Concezione's senses wander to fresh plants. As such, it is understandable that she imagines the 'Kingdom of God' as a garden much like her own. Jackson notes that the primordial paradise is not wild nature, but rather an organized garden, where nature and order unite. It is a place where Concezione has 'learned to tend to [her] own inner garden'.[17]

In choosing to forgo motherhood, Concezione shatters her culturally constructed association with nature. Ortner sheds light on the logic behind 'cultural thinking' that creates the perception that women are inferior beings based on the culture/nature distinction constructed by culture. She posits that women are linked to 'nature', which is devalued in every culture, while men are identified with culture, which seeks to transcend and assert domination over nature. She proposes that it all stems from the woman's body and procreative capacity.[18] Indeed, Concezione rejects her procreative function in favour of free agency to navigate the world as she pleases. This brings her back to nature, a garden with which she interacts on her own terms. Concezione transcends definition within the traditional nature/culture duality. Neither does she want to produce children, nor does she want to enter into the male domain of artifice and capital production. Rather, she enters into a space seemingly suspended between the private domestic sphere of women and the public cultural sphere of men. Ultimately Concezione draws her bridge in an attempt to cut ties with both.

At the close of the book, there is an abrupt turning point in the plot. Just as Concezione's inner garden is replenished, and she has successfully made peace with her suitors, she returns home to find her mother bent over the fire roasting a fat sausage on a spit. In this final scene, Concezione prepares the table without slighting others or overtly refusing the food that has been offered to her. It is noteworthy that the last supper in the storyline echoes the first pig dinner that opens the book; the plot comes full circle. However, Concezione does not perceive the sausages as threatening, but rather they are described as 'harmless serpents' (149). Bunny Crumpacker observes that the most obvious association between food and sex is the shape.[19] Sausage is often considered a masculine food because of its phallic form. It is not explicitly revealed if Concezione relishes the sausage; however, it is suggested that having recently been freed from male predators, that she allows herself to savour her liberation over a triumphant sausage that recalls the penis, often an important source of male pride. In the final lines of the book, Concezione kneels before the Madonna della Solitudine and her eyes '[have] an unquenchable light that [comes] from her soul' (151). Concezione's faith in the church has been restored, and she experiences a resurrection of spirit and appetite.

Notes

1. Grazia Deledda, *The Church of Solitude*, trans. by E. Ann Matter (Albany: State University of New York Press, 2002), p. 3. Subsequent references will be cited parenthetically in the text.
2. Nick Fiddes, *Meat: A Natural Symbol* (London: Routledge, 2015), p. 91.
3. Fiddes, p. 90.
4. Claude Lévi-Strauss, *The Raw and the Cooked*, trans. J. and D. Weightman (New York: Harper and Row, 1969).
5. Sherry B. Ortner, 'Is Female to Male as Nature is to Culture?', in *Woman, Culture, and Society*, ed. by M. Z. Rosaldo and L. Lamphere (Stanford: Stanford University Press, 1974), pp. 68-87.
6. Carole Counihan, *The Anthropology of Food and Body: Gender, Meaning, and Power* (New York: Routledge, 1999), p. 62.
7. Eve Jackson, *Food and Transformation: Imagery and Symbolism of Eating* (Toronto: Inner City Books, 1996), pp. 97-100.
8. Susie Orbach, *Hunger Strike: The Anorectic's Struggle as a Metaphor for our Age* (New York: W.W. Norton & Company, 1986), p. 7.
9. Carol J. Adams, *The Sexual Politics of Meat: A Feminist-Vegetarian Critical Theory* (New York: Bloomsbury, 2016).
10. Marti Kheel, 'Vegetarianism and Ecofeminism: Toppling Patriarchy with a Fork', in *Food for Thought: The Debate Over Eating Meat*, ed. by Steve Sapontzis (New York: Prometheus Books, 2004), pp. 327-43.
11. Carol J. Adams, 'Woman-Battering and Harm to Animals', in *Animals and Women: Feminist Theoretical Explorations*, ed. by Carol J. Adams and Josephine Donovan (Durham: Duke University Press, 1995), pp. 55-84.
12. Ortner, pp. 68-87.
13. Jackson, pp. 47, 37.
14. Adams, *Sexual Politics of Meat*.
15. Jackson, p. 77.
16. Bernard Lyman, *A Psychology of Food: More than a Matter of Taste* (New York: Van Nostrand Reinhold, 1989), p. 157.
17. Jackson, p. 44.
18. Ortner, pp. 68-87.
19. Bunny Crumpacker, *The Sex Life of Food: When Body and Soul Meet to Eat* (New York: Thomas Dunne, 2006), p. 23.

The Seed of Hope: Acorns from Famine Food to Delicacy in European History

Andrea Maraschi

According to scholars, there is little doubt that in the prehistoric stage of human society acorns represented a staple food.[1] They have been a key resource in American history as one of the main foods of Native Americans, and they have been equally important in China; in Korea, the *Dotori muk*, or acorn jelly, was widely consumed in times of war since ancient times, and is still popular nowadays.[2]

However, if the role of acorns is unquestionable for what concerns many areas around the world, their reputation in Europe has been considerably more obscure and controversial.[3] Ancient European intellectuals were aware of the paramount importance of oak nuts in human diet, especially in the past. At the beginning of the first century AD, Strabo noted that acorns were a staple food for Lusitanians in Iberia (specifically, the mountaineers) for two-thirds of the year: they used to dry and crush them, and then grind them in order to make bread with acorn flour.[4] According to Herodotus, the Spartans once went to consult the oracle of Delphi so as to know whether it was advisable to try and conquer the Arcadians. The oracle replied: 'The land of Arcadia you ask; you ask me much: I refuse it. Many there are in Arcadian land, acorn-eaters, who will beat you back.'[5] The oracle meant that the Arcadians were stout men living a harsh life, and were thus hard to conquer: the reference to acorn consumption as a 'primitive' diet is clear, but that sort of 'primitiveness' which is a synonym for fierceness. In fact, tradition wants it that when the 'civilizing hero' Pelasgus founded the kingdom of Arcadia, he invented warm huts and coats, and gave the people a new diet based on 'the acorns of edible oak'.[6] The Arcadians were thought to be the oldest Hellenes, and 'to have lived in the mountains eating acorns even before the moon existed'.[7] In contrast, the namesake mythological land of Arcadia which recurs in many texts represents a past bucolic Golden Age.

Yet, at some point, mankind would benefit from the introduction of a more civilized diet: humans would be taught agriculture by Ceres, and would feed on grain ever since.[8] It was the sign that humans had made a further step along their road to civilization.

For that matter, not all intellectuals agreed whether balanophagy was to be considered a nostalgic characteristic of a utopian past, or rather a peculiarity of a still primitive society. German chemist Friedrich Accum (1769-1838) associated the importance of acorn consumption among archaic societies with the fact that they were spontaneously offered by nature, like berries (and thus required no technological skills whatsoever, unlike bread or wine).[9] Of the same opinion had been the sixteenth-century *scalco* ('steward') of Pope Leo X, Domenico Romoli, who also held that pigs gave tastier meat when they were fed chestnuts rather than acorns.[10] Pliny stated that *glande* constituted the wealth of many peoples still in his days, especially '*per Hispanias*'; but he symptomatically added '*etiam pace gaudentium constant*': 'even when they are enjoying peace'. His clear reference was to a widespread association of acorns with the lack of more desirable foods. And precisely this idea would prevail over others in the following centuries: he himself noted that, 'when there is scarcity of corn', acorns were dried and ground into flour, and the flour was kneaded *in panis usum*.[11] In fact, oak nuts became the replacement food *par excellence* (often in the form of flour). Ceres' gift to men was invaluable, but also an extremely faint one: it required hard work, sacrifice, and the favour of the gods. 'So,' Virgil writes, 'unless you're set to spend the whole day hoeing weeds, and making noise to scare off birds, […] and all your prayers for rain are answered, alas, my friend, […] you'll be raiding oaks for acorns to ease the ache of hunger.'[12]

After Ceres, acorns came to a crossroad: food for pigs, or food for humans in case of emergency. At first sight, it would seem that it was also a matter of identity: as soon as Ulysses' companions were turned into hogs by Circe, she gave them acorns, beech mast, and cornel fruit to eat, 'such as pigs eat': earlier, the sorceress had given them cheese, barley meal, and a brew of honey and Pramnian wine.[13]

Actually, in the vast majority of cases, European historical sources mention acorns primarily in connection with pig feeding, both in a positive and in a negative sense: respectively, they were considered an essential element of the peasant economy, but also – and consequently – an unsuitable food for human consumption. Such a dichotomy summarizes the thorny prestige of acorns. On the one side, they were fundamental in the making of particularly tasty ham since the Visigoths had introduced livestock farming in Spain and paid particular attention to pigs, as suggested by various articles in the *Leges Visigothorum*.[14] This tradition has developed into what is today known as *jamón ibérico de bellota*, a well-known and appreciated ham with a unique flavour. On the other side, they were restricted to this domain only: the domain of animal food.

In the early Middle Ages, forests (which the Romans used to call *saltus*, 'uncultivated lands', culturally irrelevant if compared with *ager*, the cultivated field) would become so important that the chronicler Gregory of Tours (538-594) would even record a kind of famine – 'forest famine' – which Roman historians totally neglected. For instance, Gregory records that, in 591, floods and incessant rain destroyed the hay, and the crops were poor; furthermore, he added, 'acorns grew, but they never ripened.'[15] From this renewed perspective, acorns were a very valuable resource, and the *glandaticum* (a fee for pasturing swine in forests) became an important instrument of power for kings and lords in medieval times.[16] The new 'romano-germanic' Europe of the early Middle Ages was characterized by a marked preference for meat, a proper status-symbol for the elite (large

The Seed of Hope: Acorns from Famine Food to Delicacy

game), and a mainstay for peasants (pork): for this reason, the reputation of *saltus* and acorns greatly improved. The latter in particular, since they were used to feed pigs: it will suffice to note that now forests were not measured on the basis of their actual size any longer, but on the number of swine which could be fattened on its acorns and beechnuts.[17]

In medieval times, acorns were also associated with those who decided to inhabit *saltus*: hermits, for instance.[18] In this specific case, then, oak nuts could become a penance food for those who made the decision of parting ways from the world and of humiliating their bodies. At the same time, the consumption of acorns – alongside that of roots, berries, wild herbs, etc. – also implied a deep knowledge of nature, and of what was edible or noxious. Surviving in the wild is no child's play, as the Middle English translation of the *Romance of William of Palerne* (c. 1340) shows: two lovers, William and Melior, flee to the woods, and the latter tells the former that they can live on their love, but also on bullaces, blackberries, haws, hips, acorns (*hakernes*), and hazelnuts.[19] This was no lover's frenzy: it mirrored folk knowledge, which derived from experience, experiments, failures, and intuition.

However, it might not be surprising that, still in 1644, the Italian agronomist Vincenzo Tanara mentioned acorns simply to state that they '*generano miglior carne*' ('make better meat', with clear reference to pork).[20] Yet, as noted earlier, acorns surface in the sources also as an emergency remedy to situations of famine. Bad harvests, lack of wheat, and hunger required creativity and pragmatism: bread was still made on these occasions, but with inferior grains, with fava beans or, in mountainous regions, chestnuts; in the worst cases, people would make it with acorns, roots, wild grasses.[21] An example of this is Godfrey Malaterra's account of a famine in southern Italy in 1058, so harsh that people had to take acorns from pigs, dry them, and then grind and mix them with millet flour.[22] Clearly, Godfrey shows that acorns were upgraded to 'ordinary' elements in the culinary system and did not alter it whatsoever: eating acorns did not turn men into pigs but, on the contrary, the typical food of pigs was adapted to the cultural act of bread-making (*panes facere*): an act of controlled desperation, of civilized panic.[23]

This was one among many successful experiments made by peasants throughout history to counter the lack of grain – so successful, in fact, that it would be featured in numerous treatises up until the nineteenth century, all of which suggested making bread in the same manner in case of need. Eighteenth-century Italian naturalist Giovanni Targioni Tozzetti, supervisor of the 'Garden of Simples' in Florence, accurately distinguishes among various types of acorns: 'They have served as food for many ancient peoples', he notes, 'and still serve nowadays for some in our Italy'.[24] With 'some', needless to say, he is referring to the '*Povera Gente*', the poor. 'They are hard to digest,' he adds, but then again they were meant for 'robust and hard-working bodies', which were supposed to be fit for such foods. This means two things: acorns may not have been worthy of appearing on middle- or upper-class tables, but the aforementioned, many-a-century-old experiments from the lower tiers of society did reach the polished world of intellectuals. Interestingly, Targioni Tozzetti first notes that, after being dried, shelled, and ground into flour, acorns could be mixed with the flour of chestnuts, buckwheat, or millet in order to make *polente* (porridges) or *necci* (flat bread): they were a rather dynamic replacement food, after all. The use of acorn flour for making bread follows, with careful indications on how to treat them in order to improve their taste and make them as sweet as chestnuts.

In the very same years, the first volume of the monumental collection of works on crafts – published by the Royal Academy of Sciences in Paris – reprised the typical clichés about oak nuts. It noted that acorn bread had been 'the first bread on which certain nations fed on, such as Arcadia', and provided indications on how to make it 'as it was made in Westphalia at the time of the last war'.[25] In other words, a primitive source of nourishment that could still turn out to be useful in times of emergency: in this case, the major concern was taste, which had to be improved by grilling (or boiling) them to remove the bark, by drying them and, finally, by grinding them into flour. 'This preparation softens them by removing a certain sour bitterness' which characterized them otherwise. Not many years later, in the last decade of the century, the *Dizionario universale economico-rustico* remarked the idea that wheat bread was 'the best of breads' (a preference we already find expressed in medieval times), and also listed a series of less tasty breads made with inferior grains. Eventually, it mentioned even more inferior breads such as those made with dates, cassava, tree bark, animal flesh (including that of fish) that had been dried and ground into flour, and acorns, of course. 'In general,' the *Dizionario* reads, 'you can make bread with any kind of food which can be dried and ground into powder. These kinds of bread are not common unless there is lack of wheat and it is necessary to make up for nature's shortcomings by resorting to creativity ['*arte*'].'[26]

In fact, acorns represented this facet of the history of human nutrition: inventiveness which arose from need, if a sort of inventiveness to which not many paid fair homage, though. At the end of the nineteenth century, English author John Cordy Jeaffreson still reiterated the old prejudice according to which, when corn failed, 'hunger gave [… our British forefathers] appetite for acorns – the food of swine, and so bitter a substitute for meat, that the men of these luxurious days can scarcely believe it to have ever been a common article of diet'. This 'nauseous fare' was consumed in recent times of famine as well 'by the poorer folk of England': in the last quarter of the sixteenth century, as recorded in *Holinshed's Chronicles*, they 'ate a bread made partly or altogether of acorns'.[27] Jeaffreson's position was harshly critical, but he was right in highlighting the importance of acorn bread in times of hunger and war: this was true until his times, at least, and it seems that *pan de bellotas* was consumed during the Spanish Civil War of 1936-1939 and in the '*año del Hambre*', that is 1941.[28] Furthermore, *pan'ispeli* ('acorn bread') was consumed in Sardinia until the half of the last century in times of hardship.

Yet, one fundamental passage of the history of acorns has been often overlooked. Theoretically, there could be very little opportunity to know what peasants ate in our past, because for a long time cookbooks were produced by aristocrats and – later – by the new urban upper class as well. Fortunately enough, though, it is quite easy

The Seed of Hope: Acorns from Famine Food to Delicacy

to spot continuities between elite and peasant cooking, starting from late medieval times. Generally, renowned chefs simply added spices to typical peasant food, or used those foods as side dishes to others which peasants could hardly taste (large game, for example).[29] As a result, if one subtracts elite elements from elite recipes, peasant cooking emerges from the mists of oral tradition. In fact, the aristocratic cookbooks which start appearing from the late thirteenth century were heavily based on peasant cooking.

No traces of acorns, however, until 1570, when the famous chef Bartolomeo Scappi, who had served the most important courts of his times in Rome, Milan, Venice, and Bologna, offered a beautiful example of that 'link' between court cooking and 'popular' culture.[30] In his *Opera*, which he dedicated to Pope Pius V (whom he also served), and which remains the most important work on Italian cuisine of the Renaissance, Scappi included an acorn pie as a variation on a *tourte* of fresh or dried chestnuts.[31] In the original recipe, peeled chestnuts are boiled in meat broth or in salted water, ground in a mortar, and passed through a filter; fresh butter and goat's (or cow's) milk are then added, alongside creamy cheese (*cascio grasso*) and grated dry cheese, sugar, ricotta or provatura, cinnamon, pepper, and uncooked egg yolks. All are blended together, and then a *tourte* is made with an upper and a lower shell, and a twist around it; it is put in the oven and then glazed with sugar, cinnamon, and rose water. The recipe, in itself, is a clear example of the juxtaposition of peasant foods (chestnuts) and upper-class elements (cinnamon, sugar): in this way, the former were 'artificially ennobled'.[32]

As earlier observed, this practice allows modern historians to reconstruct peasant cooking by eliminating easily identifiable elite ingredients which would never appear on a peasant's table. Then, Bartolomeo Scappi provides a variation which should be probably considered an even 'poorer' version of the pie: '*se per sorte si volesse far torta di triboli, o di ghiande, si può fare*' ('Should you want to make a *tourte* of blackberries or acorns, that can be done'). The cook was just to make sure that the acorns (preferably those from Turkey oaks, *Quercus cerris*) were clean before parboiling them in broth.

Scappi also suggested to lard jays and stockdoves leaving acorns in their large crops ('*lasciando le ghiande nel gozzo*'), before searing them on the coals.[33] Then, they were sprinkled with salt and fennel flour and put on the spit to be roasted. The identical advice is given by the aforementioned *scalco* of Pope Leo X, Domenico Romoli, writing in the same years: '*così senza votargli ne di ghiande, ne di budella, si coceranno*', he suggests ('cook them [i.e. acorn-eating doves] and remove neither the acorns nor their intestines'). They were to be served with slices of citron.[34]

It is fair to assume that, in this case, culinary trickery was benefiting from traditional peasant cooking, and the result was a continuity of taste which scales down preconceptions regarding the distance which separated the two culinary worlds. Such examples are particularly interesting since, in many earlier and contemporary cookbooks (and in Bartolomeo's *Opera* itself), acorns mostly appear as a size or shape reference for various foods ('as small as an acorn', 'in the shape of an acorn', etc.).

An acorn pie was also featured in another fundamental cookbook of the time, written by the steward of the House of Este, Cristoforo Messisbugo, in 1549. The recipe is rather similar to Bartolomeo Scappi's, but more dynamic: it could be done with either acorns or loquats, quinces, pomes, chestnuts, and more. It suggested boiling the acorns in broth, and then passing them through a filter. Then, the cook was to add grated dry cheese, sugar, cinnamon, pepper, butter, and eggs; after making the pie, it was cooked in the oven, and finally sprinkled with sugar. In line with Scappi, Cristoforo simply specifies that the acorns had to be fresh, and that they were to be boiled in water instead of broth on lean days ('*nei giorni che non serano da carne*'): this would remove the element of meat, which was to be replaced on days of abstinence.[35]

Bartolomeo Scappi and Cristoforo Messisbugo, then, show that the sixteenth century was a little 'Golden Age' for acorns, which were allowed to reach the tables of the elite under the wise supervision of renowned chefs. Domenico Romoli also suggested using acorns to make vinegar, among other numerous alternatives with probable 'poor' origins: little blocks were made by taking unripe acorns and by crushing them along with verjuice, wild cherries, unripe blackberries, and cornelian cherries. Eventually, a little bit of vinegar (the best available) was added. Said blocks were to be sun-dried, and then put in wine when one wanted to obtain vinegar. The fact that Romoli deemed this recipe 'well-known and clear to everybody' says a lot about its plausible non-aristocratic origins.[36]

In the same years, again, acorns surfaced in a popular English handbook of cookery, herbals, and medicine authored by English writer John Partridge.[37] The author gave indications to make acorn conserve, but this time the focus was on medicinal virtues: 'this conserve is good against all sickness of the brain and nerves, and against all diseases of *fleume* [phlegm].'[38] The reference to phlegm is clearly based on Galen's humoral theory, the dominant model until the eighteenth century, and is helpful to highlight a key fact: acorns rarely reappeared in European cookbooks, but would occasionally be mentioned for their medicinal properties.[39] For instance, the extremely popular *Tacuinum sanitatis* – composed by the Arab Christian physician Ibn Buṭlān in the second half of the eleventh century and repeatedly translated and copied in medieval Europe – notes that acorns were healthy when taken fresh and large, and 'help retention' but 'prevent menstruation'. To neutralize the second effect, they were to be eaten 'roasted and with sugar'.[40] As significant as is this mention in such a widespread medical work, it is also a very rare one.

Among other scattered traces, acorns were taken into consideration by English botanist Nicholas Culpeper many years later (1652): 'the thin skin that covers the acorn' is 'most used to stay the spitting of blood, and the bloody-flux'. Furthermore, acorn powder mixed with wine 'provokes urine, and resists the poison of venomous creatures; the decoction of acorns and the bark made in milk and taken, resists the force of poisonous herbs and medicines, as also the virulency of cantharide'.[41] The virtues of acorns were also mentioned in an early eighteenth-century English cookery book written by Mary Kettilby and others 'for the use of all good wives, tender mothers, and

The Seed of Hope: Acorns from Famine Food to Delicacy

careful nurses', and known for having introduced some popular novelties such as orange marmalade. The book suggests drying a large acorn and grinding it into powder, mixing it with an equal amount of Angelica-seed powder. After eating the mixture, the patient was to drink a glass of black cherry water: this would help against a 'stitch in the side'.[42]

In the meantime, as they were struggling to find a stable position on European tables, new exotic products were being imported from all around the world, and acorns continued to play the role they had been accustomed to: that of replacement food. Starting from the beginning of the nineteenth century, indeed, acorn coffee appears to be a valid alternative to its more desirable counterpart. An example is provided by English writer Maria Eliza Rundell (1745-1828), who authored an important cookery book which was clearly intended for a middle-class audience. The recipe of acorn coffee allowed an increasingly important routine in Europe to continue whenever common coffee was not available: 'This receipt,' she notes, 'is recommended by a famous German physician, as a much esteemed, wholesome, nourishing, strengthening nutriment for mankind.'[43]

The mythical land of Arcadia does not seem to be too far away in time and space from this perspective. Yet, it is clear that acorns had taken another step back from their peak of success in the sixteenth century: they became a replacement element for one of the most popular drinks in history, but they were still associated with shortage and hardship. When acorn coffee appears in the pages of American collections of recipes, indeed, it represents an emergency solution in times of war, as in the case of the *Confederate Receipt Book* of 1863: 'Take sound ripe acorns, wash them while in the shell, dry them, and parch until they open, take the shell off, roast with a little bacon fat, and you will have a splendid cup of coffee.'[44] It is a telling note in a text which also features an 'apple pie without apples' and a 'cheap and quick pudding'.

Through war, famine, genius, anxiety, and experiments, the culinary history of acorns in Europe has been troubled, to say the least. They surely – but rarely – acted as a bridge between the poor and the wealthy, the lower and the upper classes. The question is: what has become of them in the globalized world of the twenty-first century?

Silently, acorns have been benefiting from the growing prestige of local traditional cooking in Europe, as it has happened with the use of lesser cereals in bread-making. The current trend seems to be that the food of the past is healthier, just because it was eaten in the past: this implies the acknowledgement of that genius which stemmed from emergency and fear. Francesco Rizzuti, in Potenza in southern Italy, has been one among an increasing number of chefs who have been rediscovering acorns and elevating them to the status of delicacy; Paolo Perella, in his Sardinian restaurant of Villasalto, proposes a gateau made with acorn flour and honey, and *frittelle* ('fritters') similarly made with acorn flour. Furthermore, five years ago, the popular Italian TV cooking show *La prova del cuoco* dedicated one episode, on national television, to acorn coffee.

Maybe, oak nuts were bound to be accepted on our tables only when history and tradition would make them more desirable: as Claude Lévi-Strauss observed, food must not only be good to eat, but also 'good to think'.[45]

Seeds

Notes

1. David A. Bainbridge, *Acorns as Food: History, Use, Recipes, and Bibliography* (Scotts Valley, CA: Sierra Nature Prints, 2006); Shawn Overstreet and others, 'Acorn Production and Utilization in the Republic of Korea', in *Proceedings of the 7th California Oak Symposium: Managing Oak Woodlands in a Dynamic World, 3-6 November 2014, Visalia, CA*, ed. by R.B. Standiford and K. Purcell (Washington, DC: USDA Forest Service Gen. Tech. Rep. PSW-GTR-XX, 2015), pp. 265-71; Slavomil Vencl, 'Acorns as Food: Again', *Památky archeologické*, 87 (1996), 95-111; Tereza Šálková and others, 'Acorns as a Food Resource: An Experiment with Acorn Preparation and Taste', *IANSA*, II, 2 (2011), 139-47; Olivier Aurenche, 'Balanophagie: Mythe ou réalité?', *Paléorient*, 23 (1997), 75-85; Sarah L.R. Mason, 'Acornutopia? Determining the Role of Acorns in Past Subsistence', in *Food in Antiquity*, ed. by J. Wilkins, D. Harvey, and M. Dobson (Exeter: University of Exeter Press, 1995), pp. 12-24.
2. Sarah L.R. Mason, *Acorns in Human Subsistence* (unpublished Ph.D. thesis, University College London, 1992); see, for instance, Sun-young Chang, *A Korean Mother's Cooking Notes* (Seoul: Ewha Womans University Press, 2009), p. 202.
3. William Bryant Logan, *Oak: The Frame of Civilization* (New York: Norton, 2005).
4. Strabo, *Geography*, ed. and trans. by H.L. Jones, 8 vols. (Cambridge, MA: Harvard University Press, 1917-1932), II (book 3), p. 75.
5. Erodoto, *Storie*, ed. by Luigi Annibaletto, 2 vols. (Cles: Mondadori, 2000; 1st ed. 1956), I, 66, p. 75 (translation mine).
6. Pausanias, *Description of Greece*, trans. by W.H.S. Jones and H.A. Ormerod, 5 vols. (New York: G. P. Putnam's Sons, 1918-1935), III, 8.1.6.
7. Apollonius of Rhodes, *Argonautica*, trans. by William H. Race (Cambridge, MA: Harvard University Press, 2008), IV, p. 349.
8. Virgil, *Georgics*, trans. by Peter Fallon (Oxford: Oxford University Press, 2006), I, pp. 6, 10.
9. Friedrich C. Accum, *Culinary Chemistry: Exhibiting the Scientific Principles of Cookery* (London: R. Ackermann, 1821), p. 49.
10. Domenico Romoli (Panunto), *La singolare dottrina* (Venice: Michele Tramezzino, 1560), VI, 4, p. 205.
11. Pliny, *Natural History*, ed. by H. Rackham, 10 vols. (London: Heinemann, 1960), vol. 4, xvi, 6, pp. 396-97.
12. Virgil, I, p. 11.
13. Omero, *Odissea* (Torino: Utet, 2001), X, 241-243, p. 375 (translation mine).
14. *Leges Visigothorum*, ed. by K. Zeumer, MGH, LL, LLNG, 1 (Hannover and Leipzig: Hahn, 1902), p. 345.
15. Gregory of Tours, *Historiae Francorum libri decem*, ed. by B. Krusch, MGH, SSRM, I (Hannover: Hahn, 1937), X, 30, p. 525: '[...] *quercorum fructus ostensi effectum non obtinuerunt*'; see also Massimo Montanari, *Gusti del Medioevo. I prodotti, la cucina, la tavola* (Roma-Bari: Laterza, 2012), p. 45.
16. Renato Bordone and Giuseppe Sergi, *Dieci secoli di Medioevo* (Torino: Einaudi, 2009), p. 150.
17. Massimo Montanari, *Alimentazione e cultura nel medioevo* (Roma-Bari: Laterza, 1988), p. 38.
18. Andrew Jotischky, *A Hermit's Cookbook: Monks, Food and Fasting in the Middle Ages* (London: Continuum, 2011), p. 93.
19. *The Romance of William of Palerne*, trans. by Humphrey de Bohun, ed. by Walter W. Skeat (London: P. Kegan, 1890), v. 1811, p. 64.
20. Vincenzo Tanara, *L'economia del cittadino in villa* (Bologna: Eredi Dozza, 1651; 1st ed. 1644), pp. 517-18.
21. Massimo Montanari, *Food Is Culture*, trans. by Albert Sonnenfeld (New York: Columbia University Press, 2006; 1st ed. 2004), p. 105.
22. Godfrey Malaterra, *De rebus gestis Rogerii Calabriae et Siciliae Comitis et Roberti Guiscardi Ducis fratris eius*, ed. by Giosuè Carducci and others, Rerum Italicarum Scriptores, V, 1 (Bologna: Zanichelli, 1900), xxvii, p. 21: '[...] *et quercinis sive ilicinis nucibus, quas glandes diciumus, porcis substratis, et mola post exsiccationem tritis, panes facere, modico milii admixto, tentabant*'.
23. Montanari, *Food Is Culture*, p. 107.
24. Giovanni Targioni Tozzetti, *Breve istruzione circ'ai modi di accrescere il pane col mescuglio d'alcune*

The Seed of Hope: Acorns from Famine Food to Delicacy

sostanze vegetabili alla quale si sono aggiunte certe nuove e più sicure regole, per ben scegliere i semi del grano da seminarsi nel corrente autunno del 1766, s.i., (unknown publisher and place of publication, 1766 or 1767), xvi, pp. vii-viii.

25 *Descriptions des Arts et Métiers, faites ou approuvées par messieurs de l'Académie Royale des Sciences*, ed. by Jean Elie Bertrand, 19 vols. (Neuchâtel: Société typographique, 1771-1783), I, pp. 286-87.

26 *Dizionario universale economico-rustico*, ed. by G. Fontana and V. Pini, 24 vols. (Roma: M. Puccinelli, 1793-97), xvi, pp. 35-36.

27 John Cordy Jeaffreson, *A Book About the Table*, 2 vols. (London: Hurst and Blackett, 1875), I, p. 25.

28 Łukasz Łuczaj and Andrea Pieroni, 'Nutritional Ethnobotany in Europe: From Emergency Foods to Healthy Folk Cuisines and Contemporary Foraging Trends', in *Mediterranean Wild Edible Plants. Ethnobotany and Food Composition Tables*, ed. by María de Cortes Sánchez-Mata and Javier Tardío (New York: Springer, 2016), pp. 33-56 (p. 35); Enrique García Gómez and others, 'Historia, elaboración y consumo de pan de bellota en España', *Pastry Revolution*, 3 (2013), 84-97 (p. 94).

29 Montanari, *Gusti del Medioevo*, p. 191.

30 Montanari, *Gusti del Medioevo*, p. 184.

31 Bartolomeo Scappi, *Opera dell'arte del cucinare* (Venezia: Tramezzino, 1570), V, cxxx, p. 365.

32 Montanari, *Gusti del Medioevo*, p. 191. See also Alberto Capatti and Massimo Montanari, *Italian Cuisine: A Cultural History*, trans. by Aine O'Healy (New York: Columbia University Press, 2003; 1st ed. 1999), p. 61.

33 Scappi, II, cxxxi, p. 55. The choice of leaving the acorns in the birds' crops might have depended on a typical attitude of late-medieval and Renaissance chefs, who often liked to serve game and birds as if they were alive. See Andrea Maraschi, 'Parlare attraverso il cibo. Banchetti e artifici gastronomici per le nozze Bentivoglio-d'Este (Bologna 1487)', *Proposte e Ricerche*, 74 (2015), 179-86.

34 Romoli, V, 50, pp. 148-149.

35 Cristoforo Messisbugo, *Banchetti, composizioni di vivande et apparecchio generale* (Ferrara: G. de Buglhat and A. Hucher, 1549), ch. 22.

36 Romoli, XII, 156, p. 330.

37 *The Treasury of Hidden Secrets*, ed. by S. R. Holman (Cambridge, MA: Rhwymbooks, 2002), pp. 1-9.

38 John Partridge, *The Treasurie of Commodious Conceits, & Hidden Secrets, and may be called, The huswiues closet, of healthfull prouision* (London: R. Iones, 1573), ch. xxvii.

39 Melitta Weiss Adamson, *Food in Medieval Times* (London: Greenwood, 2004), pp. 205-07.

40 Luisa Cogliati Arano, *The Medieval Health Handbook. Tacuinum Sanitatis* (New York: G. Braziller, 1976), pp. 43-45, and plate xv; early fifteenth century, Bibliothèque municipale, Rouen, MS 3054.

41 Nicholas Culpeper, *The Complete Herbal* (London: T. Kelly, 1850), p. 129.

42 Mary Kettilby et al., *A Collection of Receipts in Cookery, Physick and Surgery* (London: R. Wilkin, 1714), p. 207.

43 Maria Eliza Rundell, *The New Family Receipt-Book, Containing Seven Hundred Truly Valuable Receipts in Various Branches of Domestic Economy* (London: Squire and Warwick, 1810), pp. 84-85. Rundell also wrote that acorns were appreciated for their medicinal qualities as they 'have been found to cure the slimy obstructions in the viscera, and to remove nervous complaints when other medicines have failed'.

44 *Confederate Receipt Book. A Compilation of Over One Hundred Receipts, Adapted to the Times*, ed. by E. Merton Coulter (Athens: University of Georgia Press, 1960), p. 26.

45 Claude Lévi-Strauss, *Totemism*, trans. by R. Needham (London: Merlin Press, 1964), p. 89.

Seeds

Sacralized Grains in the Americas: The Culinary Preparations of Maize and its Symbolic Use in Religious Rituals

Myriam Melchior, Marcella Sulis, and Carolina Sulis

Introduction

Originating from the Americas, maize was revered by Pre-Columbian civilizations. According to Sophie Coe, many archaeological findings of Mayan culture unveiled vessels and sculptures used in rituals with and for maize. Utensils made for sacred offerings contained maize grains, which represented fertility, that were offered to the underworld gods.[1]

In Brazil, maize was also important in sacred practices.[2] As Rafaela Basso states, maize was of notorious significance in the 'Tupi-Guarani peoples' war practices and rituals'. According to Basso, 'so remarkable was the importance of this product within these peoples' everyday lives, that many of their myths held it as the protagonist of their story'.[3]

Notwithstanding its prestige among the autochthonous people, the importance of the sacralization of maize in Brazil has been difficult to recognize in the absence of a civilizational nucleus like those in Mesoamerica, where monuments testify to its contribution to history and tradition. In the absence of such testimony, understanding how maize helped diffuse Brazilian culinary practices seems more difficult, especially after European colonization. From that epoch on, maize was represented less as sacrament and more as subsistence food for European colonizers and enslaved peoples.

Within this change we find two parallel phenomena: on one hand, the colonizer's world vision does not associate maize with religious symbolism, because that specific status was held by wheat; on the other, we find maize assimilated as a means of subsistence and its appropriation as a sacred food for the enslaved peoples. As Cláudia Lima notes, in African and Afro-Brazilian religious cults, where 'eating is contacting and establishing fundamental links with life existence, of *axé* (strength), of religious and ancestral principles', maize is among the primary foods.[4]

Although maize did not originate from Africa, in Brazil the descendants of enslaved Africans assimilated it as a basic food. *Angu* (a special porridge) of maize and *fubá* (maize flour) became foods of resistance – supplying nutritional and subsistence needs – especially from the seventeenth century on, when freed slaves sold food on the streets and maize was of great significance.

Sacralized Grains in the Americas

Maize connects the foodways of native Amerindian and Afro-descendant peoples in Brazil. Myriam Pimentel and Laila Melchior explain:

> An attentive look towards some of the famous Brazilian regional dishes, which became part of the national traditional cookery – as, for example, the *angu*: from the Tupi *angau*; the *pamonha*: from the Tupi *pamundá*, meaning maize thick mush – points towards the importance of an interchange still not much explored among the habits and the knowledge of the native Amerindian and Afro-descendent people around the maize culture.[5]

Fundamental to this interchange were the folkloric and religious uses of maize in sacred Afro-indigenous practices that helped transmit maize's gastronomic and cultural value across the centuries. However, these aspects are often invisible, hidden by the construction of bias against Afro-indigenous cults and maize itself. Through narratives about maize and its uses, preparation, and consumption, this text seeks to point out the negative modes of reception against this grain. In this analysis we start from the assumption that, as explained by sociologist Jean-Pierre Poulain, 'the symbolic qualities of the food emerge within the classification systems that give it meaning and are specific to each culture'.[6]

We consider that this investigation may unveil the importance of maize as a food of resistance associated with a sacredness barely visible in the official historiography. In respect to this subject, the work also seeks to recall to social memory the ways this grain is fundamental to Brazil's culture, sense of identity, and foodways.

Maize in Food History

During the colonial occupation, maize that had been part of the daily life of the indigenous peoples was given a new role by European settlers. In their view, maize became a food for slaves and animals, and its cultivation and cookery helped support the colonial enterprise. It was thanks to maize that European settlers could launch the exploration and settlement of the colony.[7]

Nevertheless, indigenous and enslaved peoples found in maize more than mere food. As Melchior states, 'maize employed in works linked to magic and purification rituals (indigenous and Afro-Brazilian cults), denote correlated modes, which are established between humans and plants, of little relevance to societies shaped by ideologies of efficacy, calculation, exploitation and profit'.[8] In this sense, notions about the relation between nature and culture occur in ways distinct from and even opposed to those of the West. Indigenous and African cosmologies held that humanity was shared in between animals, plants, and humans. By this idea, it would be more appropriate to speak of multi-naturalism than multiculturalism, since in the first perspective there is no assumption of human superiority over nature, animals, plants, and things, unlike in the Western worldview.[9]

These ontological differences marked, since the Great Navigations, the way in which maize came to be represented according to the European hegemonic mentality. In researching maize references in the alimentary culture of the Americas, we noticed a similar attitude in European food history sources, where the field of food studies and its 'history' had its origin. There, emphasis on the actual importance of maize to the American elite or population is either absent or held in contempt. Given the influence of that literature, at least for academic study in the field of gastronomy and related areas in Brazil – studies which have emerged in greater numbers after the acceleration of globalization in the 1990s – it seems relevant to point out this problem.[10]

We believe that discourses and mentalities based on a belief in historical and technological progress, in different times and contexts, have rendered invisible the importance of maize and dismissed Afro-indigenous religious cults as 'primitive' practices. Likewise, historiographic and scientific narratives devaluing maize helped to degrade memories and retarded the very construction of an Afro-indigenous and Brazilian gastronomic identity through claims of pretended logic and rationality.

This is the case in studies of food history. For example, in her research about the school of Annales, in France, Rafaela Basso mentions the work of historians Lucien Febvre and Fernand Braudel, portraying them as 'chiefly responsible for the formation of a historiographical tradition'. The first generation, with Lucien Febvre as its main exponent, attempted to understand the crisis of subsistence from economic structures of production, an approach that attracted many historians to the study of food. In the second generation, Fernand Braudel, who headed the Annales in 1961, was guided by this first tradition, directing his interests in the study of material life; his research involved studies of 'agricultural productivity, technological inadequacies, hunger, price, consumption in terms of quantity and calories'.[11] For Basso, however, a change of focus in food studies was undertaken only by the third generation of scholars, represented by Jean-Louis Flandrin.

We will focus on Flandrin's work in regards to his classification of the negative aspects of maize. Basso draws attention to Flandrin's gaze, which changed food studies by 'shift[ing] the focus from studies of supply issues to the symbolic and social analysis of food'.[12] However, in his *Food: A Culinary History*, which he produced with the Italian historian Massimo Montanari, when Flandrin refers to maize, we note, on the contrary, an approach that fits into the old focus on supply oriented around an emphasis on technological and historical progress.

In this work, maize stands in an eccentrically exogenous place. Unlike other American foods, such as potatoes and tomatoes, which obtained a permanent place in European food culture, maize was perceived as an evil that had to be resisted, maintained by a substantial negative representation from the historian's point of view.

This mentality shows in the first pages of chapter 'The Early Modern Period':

> The most striking historical fact of the early modern period (1400-1800) – namely, the European conquest of the Seven Seas and the subsequent integration of the

Sacralized Grains in the Americas

other continents into Europe's commercial network – had an impact on the European diet that has continued to the present day. Not until the nineteenth and twentieth centuries did the tomato, potato, corn (maize), and other American crops transform European agriculture and cooking. Nevertheless, while it took three centuries for these new crops to be fully assimilated (and then only as a result of a gradual deterioration in the popular diet), other exotic crops entered the European diet much more quickly.

In analyzing this 'deterioration' of food, the authors discuss the demographic growth of a Europe in the process of becoming industrialized; in highlighting that the increase in cereal cultivation 'came at the expense of land reserved for grazing, hunting, and gathering', they lament 'a higher proportion of grains in the public diet'.[13]

Now, the evolutionary and quantitative treatment of data that was the hallmark of the second generation of Annales is quite evident. The authors even refer to 'a very persuasive mathematical argument' by Fernand Braudel: 'given the technology available at the time, one hectare (2.471 acres) planted with wheat yielded five quintals (one quintal equals 100 kilograms equals 220.5 pounds) of grain, or 1,500,000 calories, whereas one hectare used for grazing yielded at best one and a half quintals of beef, or just 340,000 calories'. They conclude that 'to sustain the rapid rate of demographic growth, pasture had to be sacrificed to grain fields, and bread largely replaced meat in the popular diet'. It is within this context that these historians consider the assimilation of maize into the European diet, namely, in a time of 'low technological progress', serving initially as fodder for animals and in peasants' gardens (whose practices were already decadent).[14]

In this narrative we see the constant symbolic and cultural linkage of maize to poverty and a lack of technical progress. Accepted as a substitute food during crisis, the implication is that maize should be replaced by a superior one as soon as possible. In this they insist that during the eighteenth century:

> In Pannonia, [maize] yields ran as high as eighty to one, compared with six for rye and even less for wheat. Impressed by these results, landlords cleared large fields for planting corn and compelled peasants to eat greater and greater quantities of this relatively inexpensive food. Only then did resistance to its spread develop, especially since the crop was [...] resented by some as a less palatable substitute for wheat.[15]

It is worth noting that these historians do not take into more consideration the productive advantage of maize.

Notwithstanding the economic reasons which should explain a temporary adoption of maize, the authors added a still more derogatory argument from nutrition: pellagra, a disease caused by an exclusively maize-based diet. They argued that 'resistance' to maize, this degraded food 'proved justified', because 'as barley cakes and millet gave way to polenta and cornbread, epidemics of pellagra broke out'. They explain that '[t]his disease, a consequence of niacin deficiency, can cause skin eruptions, nervous disorders, and even death'.[16]

Then, as if that claim was not enough, the historians charge maize for the delay in adopting potatoes in Europe.

These arguments give us important evidence about the establishment of social control over the food universe. Such controls, as Jean-Pierre Poulain asserts, are rooted in biological need: 'To take the example of the need for food – considered generally the most fundamental and hence the least subject to cultural elaboration – the [distinction between edible and inedible creates a] hierarchy that transcends individual subjective tastes and asserts itself as the cultural value shared by the group as a whole.'[17] In this manner, maize, with its vegetal potency within the edibles, was transformed into a dangerous, almost abominable, food.

It is worth explaining that *pellagra* (from the Italian *pele* (skin) and *agra* (rough)) is indeed a serious disease. It was also known as 'Spring Harm of Solstice', since after a severe winter the disease would appear in people whose diet was exclusively based on maize. The Europeans, who knew the plant through the Columbian Exchange, did not realize that indigenous American peoples had created a process, nixtamalization, to prevent pellagra. Soaking maize or maize flour in a solution of calcium hydroxide, quicklime, generates niacin, vitamin B3, that is insufficient in maize. This alkaline solution was also obtained by mixing wood ash into cooking water use to cook or soak corn.[18] Fermenting maize beverages, like those used in the Amerindian ritualistic practices, had the same effect.[19]

However, it was difficult to recognize such sophisticated practices 'in the light of the philosophic-theological and juridical discussions during the sixteenth century'.[20] If, as Patrick Menget puts it, indigenous peoples were considered 'savages and people without history', it is easy to draw similar conclusions about their foods, cooking techniques, and medicinal knowledge.[21]

Flandrin and Montanari seem similarly misguided in alleging that maize was rejected on the European continent. As Éric Birlouez argues, during the Renaissance a reversal took place as the dominant classes in France, 'interested in adopting Italian customs', turned to vegetables and greens that until then 'were considered inappropriate to their social status'. Birlouez writes:

> The Italian historian Allen Grieco, who remarked the influence of the Vatican curia in this movement: their dignitaries not being allowed to eat meat (the successive councils compelled abstinence), sought to diversify their vegetable foods, and were passionate about new methods of having them prepared and cooked. Anxious to imitate their transalpine neighbours, the French ruling classes started to look favourably upon vegetables, which all of a sudden had their status reversed: from despised became a potent trend.

Figure 1. Rudolf II som Vertumnus. By Guiseppe Arcimboldo (1590). Skokloster Castle (Wikicommons).

This tendency, Birlouez notes, helps explain 'the allegoric portraits of the painter Arcimboldo', who portrayed his main protector, Rudolf II, king of Hungary, Croatia, and Bohemia, with flowers, fruits, and vegetables: maize replaces his ear (Figure 1).[22] Rudolf reigned in regions of the old Pannonia, where, according to Flandrin and Montanari, maize was 'decadent' during the eighteenth century. However, the painting allows us to contemplate another version: we see a vanguard that assimilated tendencies in fashion, as the French did.

If Flandrin and Montanari's characterizations of maize were correct, it could not have become a tradition, at least in Romania, Hungary, and Italy. Certainly, *polenta*, *mamaliga*, and *puliska* are not sacred preparations, but these dishes are gastronomically important to the identity of these regions.

Sacred Maize: Prejudices and Classifications in Brazil

Attempting to show why maize is categorized as 'feast food', the anthropologist Hugo Menezes Neto comments in his text that the 'history of maize associates it with the traditional cooking and the popular classes, therefore it grants it a lower status as food for poor people'.[23]

Examining Neto's classification, where maize is symbolically associated with the lower classes, we intend to briefly point the roots of this prejudice and to suggest the poetical and political paths to escape such classification. In analyzing how Neto justifies his classification, we found that he refers to the conclusions of authors whose work does not reflect his summaries. For example, he writes:

> According to Cláudia Lima and Câmara Cascudo, long before the arrival of the Europeans, maize was already a traditional food of the American people: 'after manioc, the ethnographic complex of maize is wider and comprises a larger folkloric prominence in the traditional cuisine [...]'. The authors maintain that in Brazil maize flour was the food of slaves and *Bandeirantes* [pioneers].

Consequently, being linked to indigenous people, slaves, and pioneers makes it difficult for maize to be considered part of 'fine cuisine'.[24]

Seeking to contextualize those justifications, we note how prejudiced values and judgments came to be established that associate indigenous and Afro-Brazilian people with rural practices and, in that context, to maize. Briefly: (1) attempts to integrate indigenous people in Brazil were abandoned during the nineteenth-century influence of social whitening, when indigenous and Afro-Brazilians were pushed out of cultural, social, and economic systems; (2) misguided twentieth-century policies reduced investments in rural areas, concentrating them instead in industries and *latifundia*, leaving indigenous and Afro-Brazilian communities extremely vulnerable; still, (3) as urbanization accelerated, eating preferences bifurcated, favouring the extremes of gourmet food, with its emphasis on French culinary art, or North American fast-food, which push cheap, popular foods like maize out of common food practices. Bourgeois eating habits have an obvious tendency towards Western hegemonic models, a set of attitudes and practices that have displaced maize.

Neto's analysis reflects this bourgeois worldview, and this approach leads to a limited understanding of maize's incorporation in Brazilian cooking culture. Neto's interest in differentiating maize from festive food leads to tensions in the resulting view of maize as a segmented object within the consumer society.

The feast with which Neto concerns himself is our June Festival, the greatest collective Brazilian celebration after Carnival. During this festival, as stated by Neto, maize becomes the 'food for everyone', and this status hides 'tensions between social classes and restrictions that are most evident in other classifications. Theoretically, influenced by this party mood, all will eat the same food'.[25] It is as if by being transformed into a food of celebration maize happened to be accepted by all social classes, thus escaping other classifications.

In this context, which would be those classifications? According to Neto, they include: 'food for animals' (this applies to maize as a feed grain); 'regional food', when meals based on maize are offered in gastronomic spaces (either regarding its gastronomic or touristic importance); 'typical food', when offered in hotels (and/or tourist venues); 'popular food', referring to cheap food preparations; 'strong food', when speaking of 'symptoms of any disease known by popular medicine and/or it is indicated as medicine'; 'rural food', designating the collective symbology of maize served in June Festivals; and, at last, as 'saint's food'.

In this last designation, Neto sees an exception to all other classifications, and thus he states: 'this classification reveals that food also possesses religious values, may be involved with spirituality and the supernatural. I stress that not everyone knows (these are the secrets of religion), or can consume *saint's food* […].'[26] It should be clarified that the so-called 'saint's food' is offered to the deities in Afro-indigenous religious rituals. In Brazil, African religions retain traces of native indigenous religions, revealing common characteristics: often, for example, 'deifying nature through the intermediary of a shaman figure through [...] the use of magical instruments, ritual adornments made of bird feathers or done through bodypainting, and ritual feeding'.[27] Vagner Silva, scholar of Brazilian religions, points out that the Catholicism popular during the colonial period – though monotheistic and thus different in its structure from indigenous and African religions – relied on a mystic cult of saints that proved quite favourable for religious syncretism.

African and indigenous natives, forcibly converted to the religion of the Portuguese colonizers, added to their own religious beliefs and practices to their new faith in a disguised manner, giving rise to the Afro-indigenous cults. Similar adaptations are evident in the celebrations of the Catholic saints, including the June Festival, which starts with the maize sowing on 19 March, the feast day of the Catholic Saint Joseph.

June festivals celebrated in Europe have their origins in pagan celebrations of natural cycles, cycles that became linked to cults to the gods. The Portuguese brought these practices to Brazil, linking the Catholic saints to the sowing and harvesting cycles. Instead of wheat, maize was the symbolic food.

To Saint Joseph, Saint John, Saint Anthony, and Saint Peter, the patrons of the festivity, Africans descendants designated an *Orixá* (in African religions, the forces of nature that care for the energetic equilibrium of their sons). The aim was not to correspond, through syncretism, the history of the saints or their characteristics with those of the *Orixás*, but rather, through syncretism, to allow the oppressed enslaved populations to venerate their saints. The so-called 'sons of *Orixás*' made their votive offering on those days, based on Brazilian foods: corn grain and popcorn have always had an important place in these rituals.

An example is the *Sabajé* ceremony, consecrated to *Orixás Obaluiê* and *Omolu*:

> *Obaluiê* and *Omolu* are considered the *Orixás* of contagious and skin diseases, maize, the native cereal, acts symbolically in the ritual with its potencies of strength, peace and healing. Consequently, maize reveals that having hardness as its essence, making it difficult to be consumed, when submitted to fire it becomes a soft popcorn, similar to a flower. And *flor de santo* [flower of a Saint] is the popcorn prepared for *Omolu* and *Obaluiê*.[28]

It would be ironic to note that maize, disqualified by the mistaken allegation that it causes diseases and skin wounds, be the very food chosen to symbolize the healing of skin diseases in these Brazilian cults. Such an association is metaphorically enlightening about the importance of maize as a protective food for black and indigenous bodies deprived by the hegemonic perspective. As Pimentel and Melchior write, 'maize and its popular character broadly associated with regional festivities and religions that developed in Brazil, reappears in some artistic manifestation that nowadays claim traces of union between indigenous, Afro-descendants and the Brazilian identity.'[29]

For example, maize figures centrally in this way in the case of *Bori Performance Art*

 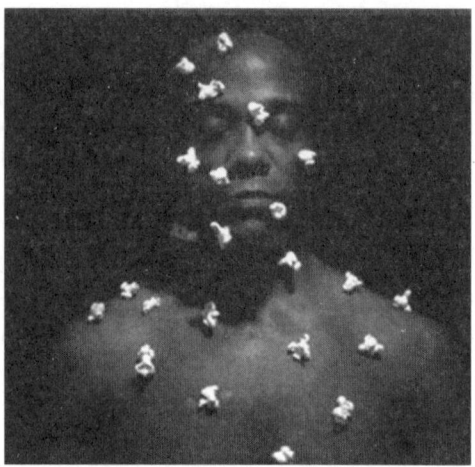

Figure 2. Bori Performance Art, *by Ayrson Heráclito (2009).* <http://ayrsonheraclitoart.blogspot.com.br/2009/03/bori-performance-art.html>.

Figure 3. Buruburu, *by Ayrson Heráclito (2010).* <http://site.videobrasil.org.br/acervo/obras/obra/1349363>.

(Figure 2) and *Buruburu* (Figure 3), works by Brazilian artist Ayrson Heráclito.

In the first work of art, Heráclito 'rehearses vocative and iconographic representations of the *Candomblé's Orixás*', using the corn-cob and grain, which are offered to *Orixás*, around his head. The *Bori* is a ritual of the traditional *yorùbá* religion of the African *Keto* nation. In this ritual, the communion between physical and spiritual bodies is sought. Thus, the artist also draws attention to food as a way to evoke protection of the mind and body. Pimentel and Melchior note:

> If all of Heráclito's works revolve around the question of the black body, its myths and legends in front of a history meant to make it invisible, *Buruburu* seems to be the one that gives more space to the spiritual practices, highlighting the immaterial aspect that makes up a culture through the ritual of purification. A downpour of popcorn – in its lightness and beauty – speaks of traditional practices that, despite its visual gracefulness, only generate an invisibility process in the shade of the colonizer's culture legitimacy. It is by means of the awareness with regard to this invisibility that the popcorn shower acquires strength and vigor in the image. It is a mode of resistance that, being on the scene in *Buruburu*, is a result of an agile alliance: almost always invisible and deprecated in the field of history.[30]

These works of art suggest a re-enchantment of food, especially of maize, as valued in its organic, cultural, gastronomical, and historical simplicity, beyond the logic of its merchandising or possible gourmetization.

However, considered as food for all, perhaps maize can only spring up in such quality by juxtaposing its senses and significations otherwise fragmented by the consumer society. Very far from such multi-naturalistic cosmic visions, we post-modern subjects hardly understand foods without their representations and classifications. However, we can consider it from other perspectives: for example, as a curative food seen in its sacredness, when maize becomes potent protection for mind and body, as opposed to today's perpetrated violence, in which transnational entities produce mere commodity maize and banish vulnerable populations, infect soils, and poison nature.

To resist this logic is to poetically evoke a sacred maize through its symbolism as a deified food – in thankfulness to the earth, to the collective work of sowing, to rainfall and natural chemical synthesis, and, at last, to its immense harvest that imbues every festivity as a symbol of fertility and life.

Notes

1 Sophie Coe, *America's First Cuisines* (Austin: University of Texas Press, 1984).
2 Maize has archaeological records pointing out its presence in Brazil back to, approximately, 10,000 years ago (Thereza L. de A. Camargo, 'O Milho e a Mandioca: nas Cozinhas Brasileiras, Segundo Contam Suas Histórias', in *Cadernos de Folclore* (São José dos Campos, SP: Centro de Estudos da Cultura Popular, Fundação Cultural Cassiano Ricardo, 2008), XVIII, p. 24).
3 Rafaela Basso, 'Avati na Mesa e no Sertão: Um Pouco da História do Milho na Colonização da América Portuguesa', in *Gastronomia, Cultura e Memória: Por Uma Cultura Brasileira do Milho*, ed. by Myriam Melchior (Rio de Janeiro: Fólio Digital, 2017), pp. 57-70 (p. 57).
4 Cláudia Lima, *Tachos e Panelas: Historiografia da Alimentação Brasileira* (Recife: Raízes Brasileiras, 2009), p. 79.
5 Myriam Melchior Pimentel and Laila Melchior, '*Reencantamentos e Novas Apropriações: Alimento Como Vivência e Memória na Arte Brasileira*', in *Revista Esferas* (Brasília: UCB/UNB/UFG, 2015), p. 148.
6 Jean-Pierre Poulain, *Sociologias da Alimentação: Os Comedores e O Espaço Social Alimentar* (Florianópolis: Editora UFSC, 2013), p. 233.
7 Rafaela Basso, *A Cultura Alimentar Paulista: Uma Civilização do Milho? (1650-1750)* (São Paulo: Alameda, 2014).
8 Myriam Melchior, 'Memória e Resistência: Argumentos para a Valorização de Uma Cultura do Milho Particularmente Brasileira', in *Gastronomia, Cultura e Memória: por uma cultura brasileira do milho*, ed. by Myriam Melchior (Rio de Janeiro: Fólio Digital, 2017), p. 71.
9 Eduardo Viveiros De Castro, *A Inconstância da Alma Selvagem* (São Paulo: Cosac &Naify, 2002).
10 An example is *Gastronomia no Brasil e no Mundo* (Rio de Janeiro: Senac, 2012) by Dolores Freixa and Guta Chaves. This manual is an integral part of the academic syllabus of the technological and baccalaureate gastronomy courses in Brazil. In its glossary there is no mention of maize, but millet (which is not even Brazilian or American) does appear.
11 Rafaela Basso, 'O Lugar da Alimentação nos Estudos históricos da escola dos Annales' in: *Revista Helikon*, v.2, n.3 (Curitiba: Revista Helikon, 2015), pp. 50-63, 55, 56.
12 Basso, 'O Lugar', p. 56.
13 Jean-Louis Flandrin and Massimo Montanari, *Food: A Culinary History from Antiquity to the Present*, ed. by Albert Sonnenfeld, trans. by Clarissa Botsford and others (New York: Columbia University Press, 1999), pp. 349, 350.
14 Flandrin and Montanari, p. 351.
15 Flandrin and Montanari, p. 356.
16 Flandrin and Montanari, p. 356.

17 Jean-Pierre Poulain, qtd. in Mondher Kilani, *Introduction à l'anthropologie* (Lausane: Payot, 1992), p. 157.
18 Luiz Mors, '*O Milho e suas Potências envolvendo os Aminoácidos*', in *O Etnobotânico*, 31 July 2014 <https://oetnobotanico.wordpress.com/2014/07/31/o-milho-e-suas-polemicas-envolvendo-aminoacidos/> [accessed, 20 April 2018].
19 The *Avatikyky* ceremony occurs when maize is harvested. In general, the preparation starts many weeks before with the manufacture of *Chica* or *Cauim*, which is an alcoholic fermentation prepared by women and consumed during the whole ritual; see Egon Schaden, *Aspectos Fundamentais da Cultura Guarani*, 3rd edn. (São Paulo: EPU/EDUSP, 1974).
20 *Religiões e Religiosidades no Rio Grande do Sul – Manifestações da Religiosidade Indígena*, ed. by Eliane Cristina Deckmann Fleck (São Paulo: ANPUH, 2014), III, p. 12.
21 Patrick Menget, '*Entre Memória e História*', in *A outra margem do Ocidente*, ed. by Adauto Novaes (São Paulo: Companhia das Letras, 1999), p.154.
22 Éric Birlouez, *Festins Princiers et Repas Paysans à la Renaissance* (France: Editions Ouest-France, 2014), pp. 26, 26-27, 120.
23 Hugo Menezes Neto, '*Que Cheirinho Bom! O Milho para Além do Comer*', in *Dimensões Socioculturais da Alimentação: Diálogos Latino-Americanos*, ed. by Renata Menasche, Marcelo Alvarez, and Janine Colaço (Rio Grande do Sul: Editora UFRGS, 2012), pp. 122, 120.
24 Neto, p. 120.
25 Neto, p. 122.
26 Neto, p. 122.
27 Vagner Gonçalves da Silva, '*Formação e dinâmica das religiões afro-brasileiras*', in *Religião e Sociedade na América Latina* (São Bernardo do Campo: Universidade Metodista de São Paulo, 2010), pp. 93-100 (p. 94).
28 Julyane Alves and Luana Costa Pierre de Messias, '*Pipocando: a Pipoca nos Rituais Religiosos Afro-indígenas*', in *Anais do IX Simpósio Linguagens e Identidades da/na Amazônia Sul-Ocidental: línguas e literaturas indígenas*, Universidade Federal do Acre (Rio Branco: Nepan Editora, 2015), pp. 350-70.
29 Pimentel and Melchior, p. 150.
30 Pimentel and Melchior, p. 150.

Bittersweet Coffee and the Seeds of Hope: European Immigrants' Memories of Vegetable Gardens in Early Twentieth-Century São Paulo, Brazil

Sandra Mian

Introduction

'*I va in Merica*', an 1897 poem by the Veronese Berto Barbarini, explains the most important reasons for the mass immigration of Italians and other Europeans to the Americas: the poverty and lack of opportunities that was the norm for European peasants.[1] At the same time, a seed was changing the face of the State of São Paulo and by consequence, the whole country of Brazil: coffee. 'Without coffee,' wrote A.E. Taunay, 'Brazil would be only a little more than Angola.'[2] At the end of the nineteenth century Brazil was on the verge of ending slavery. A group of 'progressive' plantation owners in São Paulo decided to replace this free labour with European immigrants, mainly Italians.[3] The equation was done.

In this paper I will retrace the daily lives of those immigrants through the stories told by their descendants. Through in-depth ethnographic interviews, information was recollected about their eating patterns, the rhythms of daily routines and special occasions, and the relationship of food, gender, economics, and power. Through the eyes of seven descendants of those immigrants I was able to understand many aspects of their foodways and especially how tending vegetable gardens, mainly women's work, helped them survive and even thrive economically. The harsh conditions those people lived in were forever associated with coffee; in their own words, 'coffee was sometimes sweet, sometimes very bitter'.

Using Oral History to Reconstruct the Past

Using oral history to reconstruct what immigrants ate in the coffee plantations is subject to many criticisms. Traditionalists would agree with Eric Hobsbawn's dismissal: 'most oral history today is personal memory which is a remarkably slippery medium for preserving facts.'[4] Others, though, side with Penny Summerfield, agreeing that even the written sources have their flaws.[5] I follow this later view: oral history can indeed be a powerful tool to understand a subject like the one treated in this article.

Much has been written about the Great Migration of Europeans to Brazil, but almost nothing has been told about the foodways of those immigrants and their descendants:

their sources of food, the adaptations those women had to undergo to feed their families and make some pocket money in their new homeland. Their daily lives were considered too humble a subject to merit serious investigations. But when one takes care to listen to their stories, it is possible to find not only the diamond but also the rough.

As beautifully explored in the works of Arlene Avakian, Meredith E. Abarca, and Karina Moyer-Nocchi, food is like a canvas on which participants can paint their personal memories and emotions.[6] Food was the trigger for a much deeper understanding of their lives and their relationship with power, gender, class; the creation or recreation of their own identities; the creation of bonds within the group; and, also, the striking social inequalities of Paulista society at that time.

The Methodology

Narrating the past is a process of interpretation, of making sense of people's lives and presenting their own selves to another. Interviewees are not only narrating what happened in their view, but also integrating elements and discourses generated *a posteriori*.[7] Because of that, the selection of the interviewees was crucial: they had to be part of a community so the memories of one would complement the memories of the others in time and space. It was also extremely important for the interviewer to be fluent in the language of the participants and their jargons as well as having a good understanding of their points of references, of the food they were talking about, and of their values.[8]

The data used in this article was collected using in-depth ethnographic interviews, conducted in September 2017 in the District of Sousas, Campinas, São Paulo State, Brazil. There were seven participants, recruited through the snowball method. The list of potential participants was greater than that, but those seven interviews reached the saturation point, so no more interviews were done.[9] The data was analysed using Grounded Theory.[10] The interviews were recorded and can be consulted on request. Only three participants gave permission to disclose their identities.

The Participants

Participant A: female, 88 years old. Spanish descendant. B's mother was the godmother of her sister.
Participant B: male, 83 years old. Married to C. Spanish and Italian descendant.
Participant C: female, 80 years old. Italian descendant.
Participant D: female, 90 years old. Portuguese descendant. Godmother of the daughters of A and B.
Participant E: female, 82 years old. Italian descendant. Sister-in-law of F.
Participant F: female, 90 years old. Italian descendant.
Participant G: female, 65 years old. Daughter of F.

Who They Were and What They Ate in Italy

Eleven million Europeans immigrated from Europe to Latin America between 1830 and

1930, of which 38% were Italians, 28% Spanish, 11% Portuguese, and 3% French and German.[11]

The first wave of immigrants were Italians from the region of Veneto. Later on, in the beginning of the twentieth century, they started to come from the centre and especially from the south of Italy (61.2%).[12] The second largest group of immigrants to São Paulo were Spanish, who from 1827 to 1936 represented 13.33% of the total number of foreigners that entered in São Paulo.[13]

The participants gave some clues about the foods their parents and grandparents liked or that made them remember the homeland. A noted, 'My father liked olives and olive oil, he used to tell us about an olive tree he could see from the window of his home back in Spain.' C explained that '*Nonna Pina* [her mother] told us that her mother told her that in Italy they ate bread and wine but here in Brazil they didn't have [wine] and they missed it a lot'.

The immigrants from Veneto were used to eating polenta with almost nothing. They loved bread, but wheat flour was too expensive for them, so they had to eat polenta every day.[14] Theirs was one of the poorest diets in Italy. These immigrants introduced polenta to Brazil, which has a cult following to this day.

To understand what the southern Italians were eating before they came to Brazil we only need to read *I Malavogli*. In his magistral work, Verga synthesizes in one family and in one village all the struggles of all the *contadini* and shows the poverty and monotony of their diet.[15] It was a diet of hunger, based on bread, onions, beans and other legumes, some salted fish, chestnuts, and wine.[16] Italians of the lower classes were used to this diet of hunger: bread was something to be cherished to the last bite.[17] The idyllic image we have today of Italian foodways was created in recent times and has been highly exploited by the tourism industry. Tables laden with food, al fresco dining, endless meals – all that is something that only quite recently Italians other than the Monsù have been able to experience. The ancestors of our participants must have been much alike *Il Mangiafagioli*, the famous painting by Annibale Carracci.

Mérica, Mérica! The Difficult Sea Crossing

The conditions of the Atlantic crossing of those immigrants were sometimes quite frightening.[18] E shares, 'My father-in-law got sick during the trip and he had no family on the ship. My mother-in-law took care of him, otherwise they would have thrown him on the sea, they did that to people very sick with no family to care for them. She took care if him and he married her […] in Brazil.'

Life in the New Country

Italian immigration to São Paulo was subsidized by the plantation owners. Through a company called *Sociedade Promotora da Imigração*, these owners created a network for recruiting and promoting the immigration of Italians to Brazil. The company paid for the sea journey from the port of Genova to Santos, and then for the train trip from Santos to São Paulo. In São Paulo the newcomers were received at *Hospedaria do Imigrante*, a temporary shelter. There the process of hiring the immigrants as workers in the plantations started, usually with a contract called *contrato de colonato*. In general, the farmers preferred large families with a *pater familia* that acted as father, brother, spouse, and especially, as the boss of the group. They also tried to group families from the same village or region in one farm as it helped the group to adapt more easily and also could create a support network.[19] As A remembers, 'Everyone knew everyone, we were all kind of family of everybody.'

This system was also a clever way to reduce costs, as children as young as six or seven and women, almost all the time pregnant (D, E, F), were payed as 'half hoe'. Adult men were considered 'one hoe', but many women and even children worked as much as men.[20] F insists, 'I was like a machine. I did a bet with [a man from the same working team] and he lost for fifty trees' – in other words, she harvested coffee from fifty trees faster than he could. G remembers starting work very young: 'At the age of 10 I started to milk all the cows.'

Besides the hard work, these Italian immigrant women had to cope with the figure of the *pater familia*, usually the oldest man of the family, or the 'chosen one', not necessarily the oldest son but the one the *pater familia* found suitable to be the chief of the group. When our participants talk about those father figures one can almost hear Padron 'Ntoni, the head of the Malavoglia family: '*Gli uomini son fatti come le dita della mano: il dito grosso deve far da dito grosso, e il dito piccolo deve far da dito piccolo.*'[21] E recalled that 'we feared him and our husbands were all against us', and G remembered that 'the grandchildren feared him'. E pointed out that this figure often enforced gender norms: 'My father-in-law, let's say that one of the husbands would come help the women to do something, my father-in-law would say: You are a man and a man does not help women.' F explained how these norms included reserving some food for the men: 'The work was not the problem; the problem was the family. He bought that bread from the bakery, they said it was easier to digest, but it was only for my father-in-law and for my brother-in-law Lindo. I asked my mother-in-law to give a little piece to my [daughter].' Interestingly, when the male figure was not present, some women assumed the role of the *pater familia*, as happened with participant C, whose mother took this role when she became a widow.

The Seeds of Hope: Vegetable Gardens and Orchards

'For us to see the garden, the vegetable beds so beautiful, it was happiness.' (E)

In one way or another, meals were based on the products of the vegetable gardens. There were basically two ways of producing food: to plant vegetables among the rows of coffee or to have a plot of land near the house. Almost everyone grew vegetables like onions, garlic, kale, cabbage, and lettuce and other greens, like the wild chicory that they foraged among the coffee trees. They also grew herbs like parsley. Other vegetables participants recalled included potatoes, zucchini, chayote, carrots, and tomatoes. Participant D also mentioned okra and turnips. This produce constituted the bulk of their diet, as E explained: 'In the vegetable garden we had everything. We only bought sugar, salt and wheat flour.'

Maintaining the garden was women's work. In homes where the mother had too much to do and no children to help her with the garden, families had to do with fewer vegetables. B explained that his grandmother who stayed home to take care of him didn't have 'a vegetable garden [.... W]e had orange trees, mangoes and bananas, but vegetable garden no because there was no one else at home to help her, I was very young. But there was always a family that had a garden and they sold or exchanged [the vegetables] for something they didn't have.' As B mentioned, some families had bigger gardens that produced enough food not just for their own use but also for selling or exchanging for other goods. The vegetable garden thus had a double duty: food for the family and animals and also some extra money or goods. F recalled, 'Vegetable gardens I had two. One for us and another for selling the vegetables.'

All participants mentioned that corn, rice, and beans were staples, but those were planted apart from the vegetable garden. Rice was planted in boggy areas. Sometimes the plantation owner let the settlers plant corn and beans between the coffee rows, and in this manner the family could take care of the plants while working in the coffee rows. When they could, they also planted sweet potatoes, peanuts, and winter squash among the rows.

Winter squash mixed into a paste made with sugar was – and still is – a prized sweet in Brazil. This sweet was sometimes made in larger amounts to be sold, as B explained: 'There was a time when she did winter squash sweets, she let them dry well and uncle Mingo would sell them at the *bocha* games.' Besides being widely used as food, winter squash was also used as fodder for the pigs, which B remembers: 'They took some big buckets, twenty litres, then cut the squash in big pieces and when salt was available, they sprinkled some salt over it, and gave it to the pigs.'

Corn and beans were planted together, in the same way ancient Mexicans did in their *milpas*: the corn stalk served as a support for the beans, and beans added nutrients into the soil, fixating nitrogen. Another widely mentioned legume was peanut.

Corn was one of the most important plants for the immigrants. Corn represented the daily food in the form of polenta and was also used to feed poultry and pigs. Without corn, then, there was no meat or eggs. Corn was also transformed into a kind of flaked flour, consumed with milk like the morning cereals we have today, or mixed with beans and other saucy dishes.

Seeds were carefully selected, cleaned, and dried to be kept until the next year. Extra care was taken in this process as it was the guarantee of good crops in the future. D emphasized how much care was involved:

The first fruit, it was sacred. The first watermelon, the first cucumber, the first squash, we didn't eat them, my father kept them until completely ripened to save the seeds. [...] For the corn we used only the seeds from the middle, the tips of the cob were not good to keep for seed. [...] My father applied a product on them in order not to have worms and then he kept the seeds in small paper bags, each one with its name: seed of this, seed of that.

Sometimes seeds were bought in the nearby city or exchanged with other settlers.

The vegetable garden had another function: it contained the plants used not just as seasoning but also as medicine. Besides the ubiquitous parsley and green onions, the garden had herbs like mint, pennyroyal, *macela* (*Achyrocline satureioides*), rue, anise, and elderflower, each one being used to treat some kind of illness or even, like rue, used to keep away the evil eye.

Fruits most mentioned were oranges, bananas, papayas, and mangos. Guava, prunes, watermelon, *jabuticaba*, and sugar cane were also mentioned but were less common. These were eaten *in natura* or used to make sweet pastes, a kind of dessert that still is much loved in Brazil.

The Rhythm of the Day: Breakfast, Lunch, and Diner

Things on the coffee plantations moved as slowly as religious time, or, as the historians of l'École des Annales put it, as *La Longue Durée*. The participants described almost the same patterns and foods eaten for each weekdays' meals. As B put it, 'everything was more or less the same on the farm, things changed very little. [...] On the farm it was more or less the same for all those families, the old ones.'

The day started at 5:00 a.m. or earlier with what Brazilians still call '*café da manhã*', the morning coffee. Breakfast was simple and eaten at home: black coffee and bread or polenta. The better-off families had milk in this first meal, with polenta, bread, or even with corn flaked flour. Others had to wait to the next meal to have milk, and the poorer immigrants had no milk at all as they were not able to keep cows, as C remembers: 'Cow we didn't have, milk we only drank when the owner gave us some.'

Later in the morning, around 8:00 or 9:00 a.m., there was another meal called *almoço* (lunch), composed of rice and beans and some *mistura*, the accompaniment for the bulk of the meal. Most common were vegetables – potatoes, sweet potatoes, chicory (wild and cultivated), kale, zucchini, cabbage – prepared in many ways. Better-off families that could afford to keep cows had some cheese, usually fried. Sausages were often mentioned. Eggs were used in the form of omelettes and frittatas for the Italians and tortillas with onions and potatoes for the Spanish. But in general eggs were jealously kept by the mothers to be sold. Eggs were a common way women had to get some pocket money, money they used to buy clothes for the family and also to buy the trousseau for the daughters. As D recalled, 'Eggs she kept for my father only, he ate an egg every day. The rest she kept to sell to buy fabric for our clothes.'

Sometimes a kind of snack was eaten in the middle of the afternoon: fruits, if they were available, roasted peanuts, or again polenta and coffee or sweet potato with coffee.

When there was no more sunlight, they came back home and ate dinner. Again, the same foods appeared on the table: vegetable soups, rice, beans, polenta, stewed or cooked vegetables, and, with luck, eggs or a piece of sausage or pork meat.

Weekends and Special Occasions – Red Meat as a Status Symbol

Food varied a little on Sundays, when there was pasta with tomato sauce on most tables. Even non-Italians often ate pasta on Sundays. The better-off families might roast a chicken or two but never the laying hens for the obvious reason that eggs were too precious to those women. Bread was baked once a week, and on some special occasions women added eggs, butter, and sugar to the dough to make a treat for the family.

As almost everyone was Catholic, the real change in eating patterns occurred around religious periods or special events: Carnival, Lent, Easter, Christmas, New Year's Eve, weddings, and baptisms. Many remember those times with pleasure. For example, C exclaimed, 'Feast days were wonderful! She cooked eggs that we almost never ate [...] and said they were Easter eggs, [...] she roasted chickens', and she went on to explain that 'on Carnival there were *crustoli*, [her mother] said her mother told her it was a tradition in Italy to prepare *crustoli* for Carnival'.

On Lent they ate only vegetables, cheese or milk when available and salted or tinned fish. Sardines and cod were the norm. Not a drop of blood was permitted, as F insisted: 'Neither eggs we could eat, as they could have a drop of blood.'

When the participants talked about meat, they meant red meat, beef. Beef was so rare and expensive that all mentioned its consumption only three times a year – Easter, Christmas, and New Year – or, sometimes, during a wedding feast. D said, 'We ate so little of it that my mother didn't know how to cook it.'

Being so rare, beef became a sign of social distinction, as A explained: 'The owner of the farm was very rich, from São Paulo, a director of a bank. They ate different things, they ate meat.' A also recalled that beef was sometimes given as a gift: 'The wife of the owner asked me and my sister to make a list of all children under twelve. For each child she gave one kilo of meat as a Christmas' gift.'

On those special days, families that could slaughter a bigger animal would roast a suckling pig. On New Year's Eve, groups of men singing and playing accordion would go from house to house, asking for something to drink and to eat. Not all families opened the doors, but the ones who did often offered them fried pastries covered in sugar and anisette, homemade anise seed liquor.

The (Even More) Difficult Times

If life was hard in normal times, it was even worse in periods of crisis. These participants remembered three struggles in particular: the Great Depression of 1929, the Constitutional Revolution of 1932 (a revolutionary movement that occurred in the São Paulo State), and World War II.

Seeds

The whole economy of São Paulo – and consequently of Brazil – was based on coffee for the export market. With the global crisis of 1929 coffee lost its value, and everyone involved in coffee production was affected. Some plantation owners burned piles of coffee in a failed attempt to raise prices.[22] As E recounted, 'I don't know what happened but father-in-law had bought the Santa Maria farm and he wanted to give the farm back to the original owner. He said "how can I pay for it if I have no money?", he was counting on the money he'd make with the coffee. [...] My father-in-law didn't burn the coffee but there were places where they burnt it, it was only loss.' C remembered families living on the edge of starvation: 'They say the Romano family during the coffee crisis had nothing more to eat than polenta and wild chicory.' For immigrants who had saved some money, however, the crisis was an opportunity: they could buy land at very low prices. Many started their own plantations during those hard times.

During the 1932 Revolution, soldiers and rebels arrived on the farms demanding food and animals to feed the troops. Women feared being raped – D remembered that 'my mother hid the children under the table, she had fear' – and food was scarce. C recalled, 'Nonna told us that there was no [wheat] flour so they had to buy dried pasta and put it in water in order to make bread', and F said simply, 'We lacked everything during those times.'

During World War II many goods were exported, like sugar, or were scarce, like salt. Salt was fundamental for those settlers, because the main source of protein was the meat and lard from pigs and there was no refrigeration. B remembered that 'there was a time when the pigs were so fat that they could not walk but we could not kill them. There was a crisis and there was no salt. [...] Then my mother when she used that salted lard, she scraped it very well to use it'. C noted that 'there was no sugar either'.

Creating and Maintaining Bonds with Food

The colonies were like a clan, and the bonds among the members were through blood or the christening of each other's children. Food was used to strengthen these bonds. For instance, there was a tacit agreement that pigs would be slaughtered in different times and the meat shared, so that everyone could have some protein. A remembered, 'My mother, when the pig was killed, started putting aside pieces of meat for this or that *compadre*. [...] When she baked bread, she did some smaller ones and we, the girls, would carry them to this or that godfather or godmother.'

Food and Identity

It is well known that food is one the most important things human groups use to maintain or create their own identity. For the Italian immigrants it seemed very important to preserve their foodways as much as they could.[23] The Italian influence was so extensive in the plantations that eventually almost everyone ate like the Italians. Polenta became a staple for everyone, regardless of background.

On special occasions, though, or through the use of special ingredients the ethnicity of each family would appear. The Spanish and their descendants used a little olive oil to season salads and special dishes. They prepared dishes like *escabeche* and Spanish tortillas in place of the Italian *fritatte*; they preserved pork loins by making confit.

But it was in pastry making for special occasions that non-Italians showed they were from another food culture: instead of *crustoli*, the Spanish and their descendants made *mantecaos*, and Portuguese descendants baked manioc-starch biscuits.

The Last Cup: 'Brava Gente' and Bittersweet Coffee

I conclude by letting the participants themselves recall why life on the coffee plantations was a bittersweet experience:

> 'As father says, those women will all go to heaven.' (C)
> 'The Germans when they came to the south [of Brazil] the government gave them land. Italians and Spanish had to eat the bread that the devil kneaded, working like slaves for [the plantation owners].' (B)
> 'On the farm it was a lot of suffering, we had to steal coffee to drink.' (C)
> 'Life was very hard […] but we had friends.' (A)
> 'That life was very suffered but we were used to it. But it was good because there was no wickedness.' (D)
> 'We had good times but also very bad times.' (E)
> 'Our life was more bitter than sweet.' (E)
> 'They were always crying while stirring that huge pot of polenta.' (G)
> 'Life is better now but we almost miss those times. Nobody had envy of nobody because we were all equal. We all were poor.' (C)
> 'Almost all of them won. But look, doing that [working really hard] but they won.' (C)

Notes

1. Barbarani, B. '*I va in Mérica*', *I pitochi*, 1897 <http://www.sitoveneto.org/i_va_in_merica.htm> [accessed 28 March 2019].
2. A. D'E Taunay, *A propagação da cultura cafeeira* (São Paulo: Edição do Departamento Nacional do Café, 1934), p. I.
3. K.C. Petri, '"*Braços para a lavoura*": a subvenção paulista para imigração (1886-1896)', *Cordis: Revista Eletrônica de História Social da Cidade*, 3-4 (2009/2010) <https://revistas.pucsp.br/index.php/cordis/article/view/9549> [accessed 28 March 2019].
4. E. Hobsbawn, *On History* (London: Weidenfeld and Nicolson, 1997), p. 206.
5. P. Summerfield, 'Culture and Composure: Creating Narratives of the Gendered Self in Oral History Interviews', *Cultural and Social History*, 1 (2004), 65-93.
6. *Through the Kitchen Window – Women Explore the Intimate Meaning of Food and Cooking*, ed. by A. Voski Avakian (Oxford: Berg, 2005); M. Abarca, *Voices in the Kitchen* (Corpus Christi: Texas A&M University Press, 2006); K. Moyer-Nocchi, *Chewing the Fat: An Oral History of Italian Foodways from Fascism to Dolce Vita* (Perrysburg, OH: Medea, 2015).
7. S. Aguilar-Rodriguez, 'Cooking Modernity: Food, Gender and Class in 1940s and 1950s Mexico City

and Guanajuato' (unpublished doctoral thesis, University of Manchester, 2008), p. 28.
8   Moyer-Nocchi, loc. 144 of 6452.
9   R.S. Weiss, *Learning from Strangers* (New York: Free Press, 1995); D.L. Jorgensen, *Participant Observation: A Methodology for Human Studies* (Newbury Park, CA: Sage, 1989)
10 J. Corbin and A. Strauss, *Basics of Qualitative Research: Techniques and Procedures for Developing Grounded Theory* (Newberry Park, CA: Sage, 2008); D. Silverman, *Interpreting Qualitative Data* (Newberry Park, CA: Sage, 2015).
11 F.A. Novaes and N. Sevcenko, *História da Vida Privada no Brasil* (São Paulo: Companhia das Letras, 2006), III, pp. 216-87.
12 R. de A. Calsani, '*O Imigrante Italiano nos Corredores dos Cafezais: cotidiano econômico na Alta Mogiana (1887-1914)*' (unpublished masters thesis, Universidade Estadual Paulista Júlio de Mesquita Filho, 2010), pp. 17-18.
13 O. Da Cruz Paiva, *Histórias da (I)migração :Imigrantes e Migrantes em São Paulo entre o final do século XIX e o início do século XXI* (São Paulo: Arquivo Público do Estado, 2013), p. 63.
14 Novaes and Sevcenko, pp. 216-87.
15 G. Verga, *I Malavoglia* (Milano: Fratelli Treves Editori, 1907).
16 M.I. Tanga, *I Malavoglia alla Tavola – Giovanni Verga y la cucina dei contadini siciliani* (Torino: Edizione Il Leone Verde, 2008).
17 P. Camporesi, *Bread of Dream. Food and Fantasy in Early Modern Europe* (Chicago: University of Chicago Press, 1989).
18 N. Marcone, *Gli Italiani al Brasile* (Roma: Tipografia Romana, 1877).
19 K.C. Petri, '*Terras e Imigração em São Paulo: Política Fundiária e Trabalho*', *Revista Histórica: Arquivo Público do Estado de São Paulo*, 2 June 2005.
20 M. Del Priore, *História das mulheres no Brasil* (São Paulo: Contexto, 2004), p. 557.
21 Verga, p. 2.
22 C. Furtado, *Formação econômica do Brasil* (São Paulo: Companhia Editora Nacional, 2005), pp. 185-202.
23 F. La Cecla, *La pasta e la pizza.L'identità Italiana* (Bologna: Società Editrice El Mulino, 2011).

The Impact of Seed Laws on Agricultural Biodiversity

Katharina Mojescik

Throughout history farmers and laypersons alike experimented with seeds to cultivate and grow vegetables, crops, and berries. Through artificial selection and crossbreeding, they promoted the development of certain traits, resulting in a multitude of novel varieties. Jack R. Harlan (1975) assumes that the main sources of our present nutrition come from plants that were already domesticated by mankind in the Stone Age. As early as 300 BC, many different wheat varieties were described by Theophrastus in *Enquiry into Plants*, which were distinguishable by 'color, size, form, and individual character' (Fowler and Mooney 1990: 26). Therefore, the agricultural diversity of vegetables, fruits, and crops can be regarded as a result of cultural processes of social exchange and transfer of prevailing knowledge throughout generations and regions. This form of exchange is not an ancient practice, but still persists among farmers worldwide. According to Almekinders and Louwaars (2002), it is still the most significant form of seed production. Scientific terms categorize such practice into traditional, local, informal, or farmer's seed markets (Cromwell and others 1992; Almekinders, Louwaars, and de Brujin 1994; Almekinders and Louwaars 1999). Despite the slightly different focus, they all emphasize the farmer's significant role in seed production, dissemination, and accessibility on a local level. Hence the non-profit exchange of seeds within their social network (e.g. family, friends, neighbours): seeds can also be considered as a common good of public interest. Furthermore, the reciprocal exchange of seeds among farmers is commonly regarded as a basis for the development and conservation of agricultural diversity. The courgette, for example, is a pure cultivated plant as a variety of garden pumpkin. At the same time, however, the disadvantage of this unregulated and unstandardized exchange of seeds in the informal seed market may be the resulting inconsistent seed quality in terms of variety purity and harvest volume (Almekinders, Louwaars, and de Brujin 1994: 214). As McAndrew states, the 'conclusion of the studies on informal seed diffusion is that the speed and effectiveness of the system depends largely on: the quality of the variety to be diffused; kinship relationships; the existence of a culture of local agricultural experimentation; and the economic stability of the farming enterprise' (2001: 198).

Agricultural biodiversity and thus food security through seeds is closely linked to social factors and practices. It is often argued that the increasing demand for food by an increasing world population can only be met by applying standardized processes to global seed production (Wattnem 2016). To ensure a more stable and reliable quality of seeds, most European countries created laws which led to a formal seed market in the twentieth century. The formal seed market is 'characterised by a vertically organised production and distribution of tested seeds and approved varieties, using strict quality control' (Almekinders, Louwaars, and de Brujin 1994: 207). In order to achieve this, it is codified by legal administration in two ways: the introduction of 'intellectual property rights' on the one hand, and the mandatory 'certification seed laws' on the other. While the first gives right holders – often supra-national companies – the opportunity to privatize seed varieties, the mandatory certification seed laws follow the guiding principles of maintaining purity and producing the optimal physical, physiological, and sanitary quality (Louwaars 1994). Their (potential) influence on agricultural diversity is primarily discussed for the Global South (for example in Tanzania (Mkindi 2013)), as these laws have not yet entered into force here. However, in many EU countries, mandatory certification laws were passed at the beginning of the twentieth century. In this paper, I want to enrich the discussion on the agricultural diversity of seeds and resulting potential threats by focusing on national legislation in the context of the mandatory certification seed laws. Therefore, I will discuss the current situation of the German seed market, with a special emphasis on regulation by the 'Saatgutverkehrsverordnung' (SaatG).

Firstly, I will provide a brief overview of the historical background and the circumstances that led to the regulation by law. Secondly, I will explain the procedures of licencing seeds using standardized criteria. As will be shown, the legislation provides certain exceptions for conservation and amateur varieties. Thirdly, based on an analysis of data provided by the Federal Plant Variety Office, I will show the distribution of these conservation and amateur varieties. To conclude, I will discuss the national legislative regulation in a broader context by referring to the actual debate on the power of supra-national companies and existing seed monopoles.

Formal Seed Market and Legislation in Germany

The origin of the regulation of the seed market and the institutionalization of a formal seed market in Germany dates as far back as the nineteenth century. Due to the proceeding industrialization and a rapid population growth from 41 million in 1871 to 62 million in 1925 (Federal Office of Statistics 2011), the informal seed market that had dominated in Germany until then was regarded as insufficient for maintaining food security. Farming on a large scale should provide reliable food (re)sources to meet the increasing demand for food and prevent hunger periods. Therefore, seeds needed to provide and ensure high yields in order to feed as many people as possible. As early as 1869 the German chemist Friedrich Nobbe, internationally regarded as the founder of seed testing, established the first seed control station in Germany. In field experiments, Nobbe was able to prove that some of the samples contained only 30% true seeds (Steiner 2007: 12). His goal was to improve the – at that time predominantly inconstant

– seed quality by means of systematic controls.

The 'Deutsche Landwirtschafts-Gesellschaft' (German Agricultural Society) introduced the first variety register in 1905, a 'centralized database that would prevent the duplication of cultivar names and rebuild trust in the industry' (Wattnem 2016:7).[1] Germany was one of the first European countries to pass national laws for the registration for plant varieties in order to 'ensure seed quality, to protect seed users from false specifications and to promote the use of high yielding varieties that would produce enough food for all […] citizens' (IFOAM 2013: 4). The first state-run regulations were passed in 1934 and are still the basis of the SaatG. After World War II, the 'Bundessortenamt' (Federal Plant Variety Office, or FPVO) was founded in 1949 as the executive authority to monitor and transpose the legal regulations on seeds. The FPVO describes its purview as '(1) responsibility for granting of Plant Breeders' Rights (PBR), (2) the registration of varieties in the National Listing (NL) of varieties, and (3) responsibility for variety and seed affairs' (FPVO 2017).

Two types of legislation have shaped the formal seed market in Germany: the Plant Breeders' Rights (PBR) as a private property right, and the German Seed Law (SaatG) as a public law. Based on PBR, breeders can protect their 'intellectual property of a clearly defined plant variety […] comparable to a patent for technical inventions' (FPVO 2016: 10). Breeders thus have the exclusive right to produce and distribute propagating material of these varieties.[2] However, trading seeds officially in Germany requires the prior approval of these varieties and the licensing and distribution of seeds and planting material according to SaatG and the associated ordinances, which are based on EC Seed Guidelines.[3] While the PBR concentrate on the protection of breeding activities and breeders' intellectual property, the National List, according to the FPVO,

> serves to protect the consumer and ensures the provision of high quality seed and planting stock material of resistant and high performance varieties for farmers and horticulturists. Therefore, varieties of agricultural species are tested for characteristics of value, they are tested for yield, quality, health, and cultivation qualities. This regulates the addition of only high-value varieties to the National List and protects the interests of farmers and other seed consumers (2017).

The registration of seeds is therefore supposed to protect consumers by providing and testing standardized criteria. On a national and EU level, the test guidelines are based on the DUS-criteria (distinctness, uniformity, and stability).[4] To meet the criteria of distinctiveness, applicants need to prove that the seed variety can be clearly distinguished in at least one morphological feature from other already listed seed varieties in the 'National Listing' of the FPVO. In order to prove uniformity, the distinctive morphological feature must be uniform and variation of the essential characteristics must be minimal, regardless the particular propagation methods. Stability is tested through several propagation cycles: if the essential morphological features of the variety remain the same throughout propagation, it is considered stable.

The test guidelines follow the recommendations of the Union for the Protection of New Plant Varieties (UPOV) for the conduct of tests regarding DUS criteria.

Although a detailed description of the single test parameters defined by UPOV is beyond the scope of this paper, it is important to note that of the forty-three characteristics tested in total (e.g. for an eggplant), none is aimed at nutritional value. While uniform appearance is crucial, consistent nutritional value and/or palatable taste of a variety is irrelevant. This seems particularly surprising when one takes into account that the legislation was passed to maintain food security through high quality standards for seed. However, the strong concentration on the formal seed market leads to unintended side effects: seeds of old – unapproved and therefore unlisted – varieties are not available for sale and are increasingly disappearing. Because of SaatG and the associated EU directives, only approved seeds in the National Listing can be traded; trading unlicensed seeds is illegal. Old seed varieties were unable to meet these strict guidelines. Not only does the uniformity criterion pose a particular challenge, but the fees for approval and extensive trials by the FPVO are often an insuperable obstacle for farmers and small-scale breeders. However, the sale of plants or vegetables grown from unlicensed seeds is not affected by this prohibition. Farmers who obtain their harvests from unlicensed seeds may thus offer these agricultural products (e.g. cereals or vegetables) for sale, but they may not sell the seeds themselves. Informal exchange among farmers, not based on financial interests, remains permitted. Since taking effect, these regulations have caused a substantial decrease of unlicensed seeds in the market, affecting old plant varieties in particular, which could not meet the criteria and thus did not represent a profitable business for commercial seed producers. To counter this effect, the EU introduced a different procedure in certain cases.

Conservation and Amateur Varieties

Since the disappearance of old varieties was increasingly perceived as a threat to biodiversity, the EU passed a directive to provide certain derogation 'for acceptance of agricultural landraces and varieties which are naturally adapted to the local and regional conditions and threatened by genetic erosion and for marketing of seed and seed potatoes of those landraces and varieties' (CD 2008/62/EC). Conservation varieties do not have to meet the general requirements: the trials of the FPVO are not required as long as the applicant can prove that the variety has a value for the conservation of genetic resources. Directive 2009/145 EC extends the scope to 'vegetable varieties with no intrinsic value for commercial crop production but developed for growing under particular conditions and for marketing of seed of those landraces and varieties'.

In Germany, this directive is implemented in the 'Ordinance on the Approval of Conservation Varieties and the Marketing of Seeds and Seedlings of Conservation Varieties' (Erhaltungssortenverordnung (ErhaltV)). ErhaltV differentiates between conservation varieties and amateur varieties. An agricultural variety or vegetable variety can be registered as a conservation variety if it (1) is traditionally bred in a certain predefined area (region of origin) and (2) has a significance for the conservation of plant genetic resources. The determination of the variety's adaptation to prevailing natural conditions is required to prove its significance. For the national listing of conservation types, the VCU test by the FPVO is not required; unofficial test results and breeder's information on practical experience in cultivation are sufficient. While varieties listed under SaatG can be traded without constraints, the distribution and marketing of conservation varieties are subject to narrow conditions. Seeds must be produced in their regions of origin, which is defined in the application. In addition, trading is subject to legal limits: it may not exceed 10% of the annual demand for conventional seeds.

In contrast, amateur varieties are defined as varieties of vegetables bred for cultivation under special conditions without value for commercial purposes. Their origin is not subject to regional restrictions in seed production and distribution. However, packaging size for amateur varieties is regulated for resale. They may only be sold in packaging units aimed at private individuals.

Procedures for National Listing and Plant Breeders' Rights				
National Listing (SaatG)		**National Listing of Conservation Varieties /Amateur Varieties (ErhaltV)**		**Plant Breeders' Rights (SortG)**
Application at the BSA		Application at the BSA		Application at the BSA
DUS testing: Distinctness, Uniformity, Stability, Variety Denomination	VCU testing (agricultural species): National Cultural Value for Cultivation and Use (resistance, yield, quality)	Requested information: Variety Denomination, Applicant's Knowledge based on practical Experience, Results of unofficial tests	VCU testing (only for Conservation Varieties): Value determined by Importance for Conservation of plant genetic resources	DUS testing: Distinctness, Uniformity Stability Variety Denomination, Novelty[5]
Trials at BSA and other stations, in Germany and abroad		No Trials needed		Trials at BSA and other stations, in Germany and abroad
Examination report and decision				
Admission to the National List and to the Common Variety Catalogue		Admission to the National List and to the Common Variety Catalogue as a 'conservation Variety'		Granting Plant Breeder's Rights
Listed variety maintanance				Protected variety maintanance

Table 1: An overview of the different procedures for National Listing and Plant Breeders' Rights.

ErhaltV simplifies the requirements for breeders of conservation and amateur varieties for National Listing. While the procedure according to SaatG usually requires an examination based on the DUS criteria, trails by the FPVO are not mandatory in the case of conservation and amateur varieties. However, applicants must either provide evidence of their own documented test procedures or send seed samples to the FPVO for cultivation in field trials. Fees are also lower: the cost of registration as an amateur or conservation variety ranges from 60 to 200 euros, depending on the procedure, while the cost of national listing according to SaatG can vary from 1410 to 3080 euros depending on the species. In addition, an annual fee of 30 euros is due for amateur and conservation varieties, but for national listing it ranges between 60 and 1040 euros depending on the year and species. The advantages attributed to old varieties, such as special adaptation to the conditions prevailing in the region of origin, are thus equated with those of DUS-certified varieties. This was intended to reintroduce seeds that were illegal at that time onto the seed market. In this way, old varieties should be preserved. ErhaltV stresses the essential role of old seed varieties in terms of the conservation of biological diversity. For this reason, it can be seen as an interface between the formal and informal seed markets.

The Role of Conservation and Amateur Varieties in the Formal German Seed Market

In order to show the influence of ErhaltV on the German seed market, I will compare conservation and amateur varieties in accordance to ErhaltV with those approved in the National Listing. The database is composed of data sets available on the FPVO website.

To date, the FPVO has approved forty-two seed varieties as conservation seeds. In 2018, six more applications have been submitted. The average application period takes one year, with a standard deviation of two hundred and seventy-one days and total durations reaching from 101 to 1108 days. In contrast, according to the 'Bundesverband Deutscher Pflanzenzüchter' (German Plant Breeders Association), approval under SaatG takes on average two years.[6] The same reference indicates a period of two to three years for the approval of PBR. No official figures are provided by the FPVO for the period between application and approval. So far, thirteen different types of agricultural plants have been accepted as conservation varieties. Winter wheat (*Triticum aestivum*) has been approved most frequently (thirteen varieties), followed by winter spelt (*Triticum spelta*), winter rye (*Secale*), summer barley (*Hordeum vulgare L. sensu lato*) and potato (*Solanum tuberosum*) (four varieties each). From the nineteen applicants in total, only two are (biological) seed producers. The remaining applicants are primarily associations (seven), followed by scientific institutions (three), private individuals (three), organic farms (two), and companies (two). Notably, none of the applicants is a member of the German Plant Breeders Association (German Plant Breeders Association 2016). Marketing conservation varieties therefore does not seem to offer any (financial) incentive to large seed companies.

Compared with the total amount of registered varieties, conservation varieties make up a negligibly small proportion of 1.57%. However, it should not be forgotten that listing as a conservation variety is a result of the EU Directive of 2009, whereas the

SaatG came into force as early as 1954. Therefore, the proportion must be considered in relation to the period.

In contrast to conservation varieties, amateur varieties mostly consist of vegetables. A total of ninety-nine amateur varieties have already been listed, and twenty-three further applications have been submitted in 2018. These amateur varieties cover thirty different vegetables. Tomatoes are listed the most (twenty-one varieties), followed by courgette (nine varieties) and giant pumpkin (seven varieties). The first listing is the garlic variety 'Barettas Sunshine' submitted by a private individual in 2012. On average, the period between application and listing is one hundred ninety days, whereby the standard deviation is forty-nine days.

As with conservation varieties, there are no members of the German Plant Breeders Association among the applicants. At the same time, there is no overlap between applicants of conservation and amateur varieties. Beyond that, though, there are parallels in the comparison to conservation varieties: most of the amateur varieties have been applied for by four associations (total of forty-five amateur varieties), followed by companies (thirty-seven), private individuals (five), and scientific institutions (one). All but one applicant have submitted applications for a large number of different vegetable varieties.

Amateur varieties represent 18.17% of all listed vegetable varieties. Like conservation varieties, they can be listed due to the EU Directive in 2009. It is therefore surprising why they were able to assert themselves proportionately, especially in comparison to the low percentage of conservation varieties. At first glance, it seems as if ErhaltV – and mainly the listing as amateur varieties – would actually offer an opportunity to preserve seeds of old varieties and counteract the loss of seed diversity on a small scale.

Although procedures are meant to simplify registration, the documentation of trials made by the applicant are still bureaucratic and represent a major obstacle for farmers and private breeders. Further documentation requirements (e.g. quantity of produced and distributed seeds) and the restriction on the amount of seeds to be sold (regulated by packaging size) are disproportionate to potential profit, and in any case amateur varieties may not yet be sold for commercial use. In these small quantities, seeds can only be sold to self-suppliers and private individuals, but not to farmers who resell their products to customers.

As discussed earlier, historically these laws date back to the beginning of the twentieth century, when seeds were often contaminated and of poor(er) quality. Controls and the approval according to SaatG (1954) were established to benefit farmers, consumers, and seed producers alike. The standardized procedures aimed to increase food security and prevent crop failures and periods of hunger. In the light of social and global transformations, it seems doubtful that legislation continues to serve the purpose of food security today. Climate change is already causing crop losses due to persistent and recurring periods of drought and flooding. As a result, conserving the biological diversity of seeds and thus valuable genetic resources is increasingly becoming the focus of public attention. Old varieties with diverse genetic material are considered so valuable that they are already collected by scientists worldwide and stored in seed banks under optimal conditions and the highest safety precautions far away from human civilization. But seed should also be accessible to people in order to spread.

Adapting and simplifying testing procedures through the legislation of ErhaltV was a step in the right direction, but it is clear that hitherto only marginal use has been made of this option – especially with regard to conservation varieties, which are already defined in law as an important genetic resource for a particular geographic region. However, the application process remains a significant barrier, and, even after successful approval, the seed in question may only be cultivated in a defined geographical region and may not exceed certain (well defined) maximum quantities. Seed varieties adapted to particular climatic conditions are therefore limited to a narrow area or origin, although they might certainly be suitable for other regions with similar growing conditions.

In addition to listing as a conservation seed, ErhaltV enables listings of amateur seed without geographical restrictions. In return, these seeds may only be distributed in very small quantities without any commercial purpose. To date, a total of 141 amateur and conservation varieties have been listed in Germany, with amateur varieties making up almost 70% of the applications. ErhaltV can thus on one hand be seen as a way to legalize seed breeding, which had been banned under SaatG. On the other hand, the legislation hereby offers at best only a niche, which imposes bureaucratic barriers – due to quantity restrictions and documentation requirements – especially on private breeders. Due to these factors and the small proportion of conservation varieties and amateur varieties in overall comparison to SaatG, the influence of ErhaltV on the conservation of agricultural diversity can only be described as marginal.

This legislation will not reduce dependence on seed companies, which are often regarded as a major threat to biodiversity. Howard examines the consolidation in the global seed industry and concludes that an 'increasing monopoly/oligopoly power for a decreasing number of transnational corporations, is fundamentally incompatible with renewable agricultural practices that are barriers to large-scale capital accumulation, such as saving and replanting seed' (2009: 1282).

Developments in industrial agriculture also indicate the increasing power of seed companies. The DUS criteria are designed to meet the requirements of industrialized agriculture, which demands standardized plants (e.g. concerning growth and ripening time) for the flawless use of agricultural machinery. The number of small-scale farms is continually declining, while the number of large farms is increasing (Federal Statistical Office, 2014). With increasing levels of industrialization, the demand for high-performance seeds, which are above all homogeneous, will likely continue to rise. At the same time, the disappearance of small-scale farms and farmers means that the proportion of those who still breed their own seeds is also reduced. Farmers in heavily industrialized Germany, however, still produce more than 50% of their own seed from their own harvest (Banzhaf, 2016: 101). Current legislation, with its restrictive requirements, is hardly capable of preserving old varieties and therefore agricultural biodiversity.

Notes

1. The German Agricultural Society was founded in 1885 and is to this day one of the leading lobbying organizations in the agricultural and food sector in Germany.
2. Since numerous publications are already devoted to the problem of PBR and the resulting consequences, this article only addresses them where necessary for understanding. For further reading, see Ragonnaus (2013), Mammana (2014), and Kloppenburg (2014).
3. In particular see Council Directive 70/457/EEC on the common catalogue of varieties of species of agricultural plants.
4. The DUS criteria are also relevant for the examination within the context of PBR, whereby the criteria of novelty of a variety is also included here.
5. The criteria of novelty is met when 'plants or parts thereof have not been marketed for a period of more than one year within Germany and not more than four years outside of Germany' before application (FPVO 2016: 17).
6. The German Plant Breeders Association is a lobbing association of the German seed industry. It has 130 members, including supranational companies such as Monsanto and BASF. In addition to representing its interests in politics, its tasks also include promoting new breeding technologies and protecting intellectual property in seeds.

References

Almekinders, Conny J.M., and Niels P. Louwaars. 1999. *Farmers' Seed Production: New Approaches and Practices* (London: IT Publications).

—— 2002. 'The Importance of the Farmers' Seed Systems in a Functional National Seed Sector', *Journal of New Seeds*, 4.1-2: 15-33 <10.1300/J153v04n01_02>.

Almekinders, Conny J.M., Niels P. Louwaars, and Nicolaas G. de Bruijn. 1994. 'Local Seed Systems and Their Importance for an Improved Seed Supply in Developing Countries', *Euphytica*, 78: 207-16.

Banzhaf, Anja. 2016. *Saatgut. Wer die Saat hat, hat das Sagen*. (Munich: Oekom).

Cromwell, Elizabeth, Esbern Friis Hansen, and Michael Turner. 1992. 'The Seed Sector in Developing Countries: A Framework for Performance Analysis', *Working Paper 65* (London: ODI).

Federal Office of Statistics. 2011. *Federal Statistical Yearbook 2011. For the Federal Republic of Germany including »International tables«* (Wiesbaden).

Federal Plant Variety Office (FPVO). 2017. 'About Us' <http://www.bundessortenamt.de/internet30/index.php?id=12&L=1> [accessed 10 November 2018].

—— 2017. *Bundessortenamt* <https://www.bundessortenamt.de/internet30/index.php?id=3&L=1> [accessed 10 November 2018].

—— 2106. *Plant Breeders' Rights and National Listing* (Wiesbaden).

Fowler, Cary and Pat Mooney. 1990. *Shattering: Food, Politics, and the Loss of Genetic Diversity* (Tucson: University of Arizona Press).

IFOAM EU Group. 2013. *Towards More Crop Diversity: Adapting Market Rules for Future Food Security, Biodiversity and Food Culture* <http://www.ifoam-eu.org/sites/default/files/page/files/ifoameu_policy_seed_position20130530_0.pdf> [accessed 10 November 2018].

German Plant Breeders Association. 2016. 'Bundesverband Deutscher Pflanzenzüchter' <www.bdp-online.de> [accessed 10 November 2018].

Harlan, Jack R. 1975. 'Our Vanishing Genetic Resources', *Science*, 188.4188: 618-21.

Howard, Philip. 2009. 'Visualizing Consolidation in the Global Seed Industry. 1996–2008', *Sustainability*, 1.4: 1266-87 <10.3390/su1041266>.

Kloppenburg, Jack. 2014. 'Re-Purposing the Master's Tools: The Open Source Seed Initiative and the Struggle for Seed Sovereignty', *Journal of Peasant Studies*, 41.6: 1225-46.

Louwaars, Niels. 1994. *Seed Supply Systems in the Tropics: International Course on Seed Production and Seed Technology* (Wageningen: International Agriculture Centre).

Mammana, Ivan. 2014. *Concentration of Market Power in the EU Seed Market* <https://www.greens-efa.eu/en/article/concentration-of-market-power-in-the-eu-seed-market/> [accessed 10 November 2018]

McAndrew, Neville. 2001. 'Coordinating Regional Mechanisms for Facilitating Collaboration and Exchange of Expertise Among Stakeholders Dealing with Seed Production in Latin America and the Caribbean', in *Seed Policy and Programmes in the Latin America and the Caribbean: FAO Plant Production and Protection Paper 164* (Rome: FAO), pp. 171-83.

Mkindi, Abdallah R. 2003. *Farmers' Seed Sovereignty Is Under Threat: The Example of Tanzania: No Reliable Access for the Farmer-Managed Agricultural Sector to Quality Seed* (Berlin: Rosa Luxemburg Stiftung).

Ragonnaus, Guillaume. 2013. *The EU Seed and Plant Reproductive Material Market in Perspective: A Focus on Companies and Market Shares* (Brussels: European Parliament) <http://www.europarl.europa.eu/RegData/etudes/note/join/2013/513994/IPOL-AGRI_NT(2013)513994_EN.pdf> [accessed 10 November 2018].

Steiner, Adolf M. and Michael Kruse. 2007. 'Nobbe's "Statute Concerning the Testing of Agricultural Seeds" of August 1869', *Seed Testing International*, 134: 11-13.

Wattnem, Tamara. 2016. 'Seed Laws, Certification and Standardization: Outlawing Informal Seed Systems in the Global South', *The Journal of Peasant Studies*, 43.4: 850-67 <10.1080/03066150.2015.1130702>.

Growing and Eating God: The Mental Image of Wheat in Traditional Romanian Communities

Raluca Parfentie

Looking long enough at one of Ad Reinhardt's seemingly monochrome paintings reveals a cruciform composition. After spending many years in their monochromatic yellow wheat fields, Romanians have found a similar phenomenon, seeing in wheat the signs of divinity. Gradually, these grains turned from seeds into concepts. For Romanians, wheat and bread became synonymous with a complete and essential food; for example, in Romanian folk literature having wheat bread often means having everything you need.[1] This connection passed down through generations both in the form of linguistic expressions and through oral literature and religious texts.

Of all foods, bread was the only product requested daily through prayer. And there was no fiercer curse for Romanians than one invoking the disappearance of bread. Romanians used bread to feed their folktale heroes, to defeat their enemies, to represent their bountifulness. And their hospitality is based around sharing bread and salt with guests, with bread symbolizing the desire to contribute to the material well-being of the guests and salt – the sign of permanence and wisdom – symbolizing the desire for the guests to maintain their hosts' traditions.[2]

The question is why wheat acquired greater significance than other cereals. To answer, we have to go back to the roots; we must descend to the wheat seed. In the Romanian imagination, the wheat seed has come to have divine characteristics from a close connection with God.

A Short History of the Romanians from an Anthropogeographic Perspective

Socio-economic changes favouring the settlement of the Romanians, originally a nomadic nation, contributed to the emergence of intensive agriculture, a key marker of the 'civilization process', centred around the construction of the traditional oven and the cultivation of bread grains.

From the very beginning, wheat was considered valuable, and its importance was seen as both material and spiritual. During the Dacian period, wheat bread was seen as a sign of distinction.[3] Because for a long time wheat was the most expensive cereal, peasants often cultivated wheat just to sell it or to pay *dijmă* (taxes) to their feudal masters. Due to this high value, peasants seldom used wheat in their cuisine, commonly saving it for religious feasts. In such circumstances, wheat became associated with central events in Christian life. But its spiritual value was sustained much earlier, during the formation of agrarian societies.

Fertile land transformed Romania into a predominantly agricultural country, which became known as 'Europe's granary', intensely cultivating and exporting wheat (both for the development of the internal economy and for payments of tributes to the Ottomans). At the same time, this agricultural orientation generated a new vision of the world, which resulted from working with seeds in general and from the cultivation of wheat in particular.

Agrarian Life: Bringing Seeds Closer to God

In his studies, historian of religions Mircea Eliade suggested that one effect of cultivating the earth was the theory that man has developed while being involved in the agricultural process: 'What he saw, what he learned while getting in touch with the seed [...] has become a lesson [...]. The most important mental syntheses emerged from this revelation: rhythmic life, death regarded as regress, etc.'[4]

These 'mental syntheses' included the concepts of religion: it is worth recalling that the very concept of Paradise 'translates into Latin by *hortus*, which means garden'.[5] The symbolic connection between God, vegetation, and happiness suggests the need for humans to get involved in agriculture to rebuild the lost Paradise.

Indeed, God has been considered one with the earth/nature. From such beliefs come practices like the Romanian desire to treat the earth as if it was alive and to equate the sleep of divinity with the sleep of nature (signified by the non-germination of seeds). In the Romanian imagination, the earth rests – hence man does not plant at night – and the earth also eats: the first furrow cut by the plough is considered to be the earth's mouth. This idea can be found in Romanian stories and also in carols, where God appears as a seed that is asked not to sleep in order to germinate. Curiously, the request takes place through a song with magical connotations, sung in winter, the season in which the future harvest is planned.

From the multitude of seeds people eat, however, Romanians chose to cultivate the idea that wheat embodies divinity, most likely relying on pagan beliefs and Christian doctrine communicated through oral literature and linguistic meanings.

Wheat Grains: Cultivating an Edible God

Humans are inclined to seek order and patterns in the natural world because order indicates God's presence. Therefore, as Michel Foucault said, knowledge is to be found not only in demonstrations but also 'in fiction, reflexion, narrative accounts'.[6]

Since pre-Christian times, wheat had sacred connotations and, as a result, so did its ears, its sheaves, and the bread that could be made from it. These beliefs must have served as a source of inspiration for the Christian ideas and legends that spread to what became Romania, and shaped assumptions about wheat. For example, the first three (or nine) ears of wheat, placed near icons, or left untouched on fields, were called *Barba lui Dumnezeu* (God's beard).

In the Greek Eleusinian Mysteries, the ear of wheat was seen as a 'son', born after the mystical reunion between the sky and earth. The Romans believed that bread had divine origins 'because the term *panis* was derived from Pan, the god of the wild, the first who baked it and whose image could be seen on it'.[7]

In the Christian tradition, during the Annunciation God let His word sprout on earth and embody Christ. In the Romanians' view, the fruit of the divine word was wheat: 'as we are made of clay, so the body of Christ is made of wheat'.[8] Romanian iconography sometimes depicted the Virgin Mary wearing clothes made from wheat sheaves – in the Romanian imagination, wheat has a mother, like Christ.

In Romanian folk tales, wheat appears both as a divine gift and as a predestined food. According to local legends, when Adam and Eve were banished from Paradise, God did not let them go empty-handed. He gave a digging tool (the spade) to the man to practice agriculture, and a *cociorvă* (a kitchen tool) to the woman to remove bread from the oven.[9] Legend also holds that He came down on Earth to teach people how to cook bread.

Moreover, in Romanian Christian communities, as in pagan ones, wheat carried on its surface the image of Divinity, with the slight difference that this time it represented the face of Christ.[10] Therefore, wheat was invested with similar qualities to those given to *acheiropoieta* images, icons which are said to have come into existence miraculously. Like the icons, wheat started to be seen as holy and to be treated like a supreme authority, that could even serve as a witness when legalizing vows. In ballads like 'The Master Builder Manole', the builders swear on bread, promising to keep the secret that would allow the construction of the Cathedral of Curtea de Argeș.

Because an icon 'is a true opening to the otherworld' – through it man can participate in heavenly things – wheat has also turned into a connection between Romanians and the afterlife, a connection that may have started in the practice of baking bread and offering it as *pomană* (alms).[11] Likewise, wheat flour was considered indispensable for the deceased.[12]

The connection between Christ and wheat could be also justified by the plant's destiny. Once buried, the grains resurrected, just like the Saviour.[13] Similarly, wheat's fate was reminiscent of Christ's. The seeds were sent to the world where they had to suffer, by becoming flour and then dough. Making dough, usually involving actions like forcefully hitting or kneading it, was later associated by Romanian media with the persecution of Jesus.[14] This association again revealed the human desire 'to turn nature into a mirror that reflects all the trials through which Christ has passed'.[15]

Curiously, just as Christ had a moment of doubt, a sense of abandonment, when crucified, the wheat in Romanian folktales questions the divine justice of its own treatment. The anthropomorphic wheat addresses God as a victim of unfairness: 'My Lord, humans are cutting me, bringing me to the mill where they tear and torture me.'

At the end, wheat receives an encouraging response: 'It's ok. This is the way you can multiply and grow.'[16] Wheat thus served as an example of patience and faith.

There also seems to be a direct linguistic relationship between bread and Jesus. Jewish scholars have shown that sacrifice is referred to in the Torah as 'the bread of God'.[17] In Romanian usage, 'the bread of God' designates a noble person, someone ready to sacrifice for the good of others.

While wheat gained more and more religious connotations, the other cereals often became associated with the devil. In legends, millet is the favourite food of the devil. Maize, from which Romanian peasants prepared the traditional dish *mămăliga*, has become associated with negative meanings, denoting sin, stupidity, or laziness. Even in dreams it was believed that, with the exception of wheat, most cereals predict bad things.

In addition, cereals such as maize, barley, rye, and oats were used to produce a type of alcohol described in all Romanian legends as a diabolical creation, as testified by the very name *rachiu*. According to a story mentioned by the folklorist Ion G. Shiera, initially the devils wanted to call it '*drachie*' from their name: *drac* (devil). But fearing that people, knowing its bad origins, might refuse to drink it, the devils changed the name, calling it *rachie* or *rachiu* (brandy).[18]

In such context, we can understand the importance given by the Romanians to wheat and the need to cultivate this plant. Thus, wheat-God became omnipresent in all the crucial moments in the lives of Romanians, followers of the idea *Nihil sine Deo*, the motto of the Kingdom of Romania from 1878 to 1947.

Eating Concepts: Symbolic Cannibalism

In the Bible, during the Last Supper, Christ stated that he is 'the bread of life', establishing a direct connection with bread, a connection that was officially recognized at the thirteenth meeting of the Council of Trent in the sixteenth century. Long before then, however, the followers of Christianity treated this statement as authentic, as reflected in innumerable artistic representations of the Last Supper that have circulated since Paleochristian times, as well as in oral literature.

In a civilization fed for so long with wheat bread, we can see what symbolic resonance would be found in the statement: This is my body.[19] Romanians believed it. Therefore, various superstitions and bans appeared, such as the belief that bread can bleed, that it must be buried, that it is a sin to throw or trample bread, etc. (Burying bread crumbs recalls the Jewish custom of burying the *genizah*.) The belief that eating bread is eating God led to a pious attitude toward wheat products. Romanians used to keep wheat bread only in clean places, on white towels, near icons. They chewed it carefully and took care not to drop the crumbs.[20]

The recognition of wheat's divine identity also manifested in the special attention paid to the 'preparation of God' (as food), a process accompanied (just like the wheat planting), by a ritual of cleansing (cleaning the body/clothes, providing a quiet environment, the use of prayers, etc.), a ritual meant to overthrow the human condition and to bring man closer to the sacred.

'The consumption of God', sometimes in impressive amounts – as much as five to nine loaves per person each week – was not only due to wheat's ability to appease hunger.[21] Romanians believed that both wheat and bread, as incarnations of God, could be useful in countless cases, such as saving them from calamities, helping them to fight diseases, and obtaining love or wealth.[22] Wheat bread was also seen as a way to acquire divine qualities such as kindness or wisdom.

Therefore, even though civilization eliminated human sacrifice, a subtle form of 'cannibalism' continued to exist, as a reminiscence of the belief that consuming someone is a way to show affection or to assimilate virtues.[23] So, the consumption of wheat could have actually meant the assimilation of divinity, the public recognition of God's existence/presence and a form of community integration (love is believed to be able to project humans inside those they love).[24]

Wheat started to serve as a basic ingredient in a 'spiritual cookbook', acquiring different tastes. After all, the soft interior of the bread (gr. *psycha*/ψίχα) reminds us of *psyche* (soul).

The Tastes of Hierophany: How and When to Cook God

God was supposed to be present not just in people's thoughts, but also in their flesh and bones, just as He appeared in Romanian folk tales. That's why He was invoked during the most important moments of life, often with the help of wheat.

Immediately after birth, humans became familiar with wheat. In some Romanian villages, there is still a habit of striking the newborn over the mouth with a loaf. In this way it is considered that the baby will take over bread's qualities. In the Romanian language, and in other languages as well, kindness became equated with bread, used to designate persons with irreproachable behaviour: '*bun ca pâinea caldă*' ('as good as bread', or compare '*e buono come pezzo di pane*').

Wheat bread was baked immediately after a child's birth to serve as food for the *Ursitoare*, the three mythological sisters who were supposed to determine a newborn's course of life. It was believed that they will wish for a good future only on a full stomach.[25]

Subsequently, while being baptized, children received the body of the Lord in the form of the Eucharistic bread, which guaranteed their entry into the Christian community. In the Romanian tradition, there was a belief that when a child is born, he or she takes on seven of the mother's sins, in this way rewarding her for all the pain she has gone through. This idea reiterates the old principle of the potlatch.

At marriage, wheat bread appeared again, as a decorative element and as a ritual object: for example, the godparents broke bread above the bride's head, both as a blessing and to ensure fertility. The presence of bread during weddings might be closely tied to the ideas that were spread through different legends, in which wheat bread (*jemne*) saved the groom's life from the forces of evil, or the wedding rings, which were passed through wheat to guarantee the success and strength of the newlyweds.

Each of the two great Christian feasts, the birth and Resurrection of the Lord, were also marked by wheat. On Christmas Eve, in memory of Christ's birth and in remembrance of the women who brought Him swaddling clothes, Romanian housewives prepared a cake called *Pelincile Domnului* (Jesus's swaddling bands). This dish consists of thin sheets of wheat dough, baked on the tray or hearth, sprinkled with crushed almonds, sugar, and orange flower water, or, in poorer environments, with *julfă* (hemp seeds and other grains, crushed and boiled together).

The importance of wheat for traditional Romanian communities can also be noticed in folk poems often recited on winter holidays. Just mentioning the word 'wheat' in a house was considered to have enough power to bring it peace and wealth. Similarly, Romanians began their Christmas meal with wheat products and also threw wheat grains upwards, believing that, in such a way, wheat will yield more fruits.[26]

At Easter, Romanian housewives baked a sweet cream cheese cake, *Pasca*. All the ingredients were symbolic: 'The added spices represented the mixture of myrrh and aloes brought by Nicodemus, while cloves – the true nails with which Christ was fastened on the cross. Everything in this dish has had to remind people of Jesus and his goodness'.[27] In Bukovina, *Pasca* is also called *nafură*, a similar name to the one given to the Eucharistic bread, *anafură*, thus linguistically giving the traditional Easter cake thaumaturgical powers.

At death, wheat was offered again, by the deceased's relatives in the form of flour, bread, or *colivă*, to ensure that the deceased has an easy journey without suffering from hunger. *Colivă*, a dish based on boiled wheat, was believed to forgive the sins of the deceased: the number of wheat grains people swallowed, by eating it, represented the number of sins taken away from the deceased.

Rituals involving wheat preparations for the dead continued even after burial, thus transforming wheat, as the Romanian ethnographer Artur Gorovei (1864-1951) noted, into a real and imaginary instrument of payment. There were special baked goods intended for the souls not yet departed (up to forty days after death), for the souls departed but not yet integrated in the otherworld (up to seven years), and for the departed and integrated souls (*uitații* – the forgotten ones).[28] By giving such products, the living reflected the idea that the main beneficiary of the gift remains the giver.

It is worth mentioning that, for the most part, Romanians used wheat products with a circular shape (*colac*), considered the bearers of good things. The circle also symbolizes eternal life, as well as being a magical form of protection and the simplified form that God acquired in archaic communities. *Colac* is among the few words that turned from a noun designating a type of food, into a verb designating an action. The verb '*a colăci*' signifies improving someone or attracting good things to someone's side. Simultaneously, the thunder which foretold rain and thus rich harvests were visualized in Romanians' imagination a God walking with *colaci* in his hands.

Birth, baptism, marriage, great feasts, and even death were considered by Romanians to be perfect moments to bring God closer through various foods. However, with the modernization of society, wheat grains fell on infertile soil. 'God' was consumed less often.

Demystifying Society: Profaning Wheat

Making the sign of the cross in front of the oven, bringing offerings to it, or going through a ritual of purification before baking bread have become unnecessary at a time when science, mass production, and historicism have primacy. As the cleric Filippo Picinelli suggested, the difficult preparation of bread played an important role in transforming it into a divine symbol that could strengthen one's spirit and ensure man's entrance into the sacred.[29] Romanians had once seen the oven as holding a protective spirit for the house – which had to be fed – but bread lost its aura, especially in urban environments full of bakeries and shops.

In the Romanian interwar media, the loss of bread's sacredness was frequently described as a horrible phenomenon. The media often reported on negligent practices and poor conditions in bread factories. This coverage in newspapers and other media came to associate wheat/bread with notions opposed to divinity: dirt, politics, corporeality.[30] Once considered an icon, wheat and bread have become subjects for caricature.

Around the same time, the idea that bread makes you gain weight has led to the gradual removal of 'God' from the menu. Although nutritionists have claimed that 'whole-wheat flour contains all the necessary substances for the organism' – a statement that can be read as an affirmation that God is everything humans need – advertising and media coverage seem to have disproved this point of view, equating fat with ugliness and animality.[31]

Nevertheless, wheat has preserved some of its magical powers, even though many of its capabilities have acquired scientific explanations. Wheat could ensure people's health (thanks to vitamins); it was invoked as a means of reducing drunkenness, therefore the evil in the world; and it could still embody God through special Christmas or Easter dishes. In these ways, bread has remained, for Romanians, the shortest way to reach heaven, a place promised to the poor, with whom bread was often associated.

Conclusions

Once planted in the ground, wheat started to sprout in the imagination of the Romanian people too, embodying God and His Word and generating superstitions and prohibitions concerning how humans should behave.[32] In such a context, wheat became both a constant presence at the most important events in the lives of humans, and a central subject in magical actions, such as distinguishing Good from Evil, healing diseases or attracting wealth.

Modern society has grafted new ideas onto the old idea of wheat, giving this grain an ambiguous status. Except at religious feasts, when people still follow the rituals of wheat preparation, bread is usually prepared in factories, in profane spaces, often under improper conditions. Thus, bread has become merely one product among others, good for the greedy stomach but less so for the ethics of the soul.

Today, wheat still seems to have some power. According to surveys, the smell of bread is one of the most appreciated aromas worldwide: that same scented steam that, in Romanian legends, ascended into heaven, in order to talk with God.[33]

Notes

1. Elena Niculiță-Voronca, *Datinile și credințele poporului Român* (Cernăuți: Tipografia Isidor Wiegler, 1903), p. 254.
2. Ivan Evseev, *Dicționar de magie, demonologie și mitologie românească* (Timișoara: Editura Amarcord, 1998), p. 359.
3. Ioan Claudian, *Alimentația poporului român* (București: Fundația pentru literatură și artă «Regele Carol II», 1939), p. 71.
4. Mircea Eliade, *Tratat de istorie a religiilor* (București: Humanitas, 2013), pp. 366-67. According to Pierre Bourdieu, seeds have also contributed to a 'gender vision' of the world. The activity of sowing/harvesting was attributed to males, and production/germination, to women. Such attribution was possible because seeds are subjected to a natural process of transformation, similar to that taking place in the uterus, thus, to the reproductive cycle (*Dominația masculină* (Art: București, 2017), pp. 28-29). Psychoanalyst Eve Jackson suggests a similar theory: 'The very word «culture» means [...] agriculture, from the Latin *ager*, a field and *colere*, to till, which comes from [...] *kwel* meaning to move around. So, culture is moving things (originally the earth) around as opposed to leaving them in their natural state; it is rearranging nature' (*Food and Transformation: Imagery and Symbolism of Eating* (Canada: Inner City Books, 1996), p. 67.).
5. Umberto Eco, *Istoria tărâmurilor și locurilor legendare* (București: RAO, 2014), p. 168.
6. Michel Foucault, *The Archeology of Knowledge* (London: Routledge, 2002), p. 202.
7. Silvia Malaguzzi, *Mâncarea și ritualul mesei* (București: Monitorul Oficial, 2012), p. 120.
8. Niculiță-Voronca, p. 132. In the old Romanian riddles, a seed signifies the word of God (M. Gaster, *Literatura populară română* (București: Ig. Haimann, 1888), p. 233). In local legends, until the birth of the Saviour, the earth was small; after His birth, it started to grow, and wheat appeared wherever Christ went.
9. Niculiță-Voronca, p. 221. In the same context, *cociorva* appears as a protecting charm, which drives away the fear of those who hold it in their hands. It is also believed that a baby can be left unattended as long as there is a *cociorva* in the room. The spade points again to the connection between divinity and agriculture, since the ancient goddesses, like God, were usually represented as vegetarians.
10. According to archaic beliefs, those who looked closely at wheat could see 'the face of Christ imprinted on grains' (Romulus Vulcănescu, *Mitologie românească* (București: Editura Academiei Republicii Socialiste România, 1987), p. 558).
11. Paul Evdochimov, *Arta icoanei, o teologie a frumuseții* (București: Meridiane, 1993), p. 193.
12. Similarly wheat bread was indispensable for folktale heroes who wanted to travel in the otherworld (Andrei Oișteanu, *Ordine și Haos. Mit și magie în cultura tradițională românească* (Iași: Polirom, 2013), p. 160).
13. In many mythologies, wheat is the symbol of food that ensures immortality (Evseev, p. 166).
14. N. Kirițescu, '*Cozonacii*', *Universul*, 31.12 (1928), p. 3.
15. Jacques Gélis, *Corpul, Biserica și Sacrul, Istoria corpului. De la Renaștere la Secolul Luminilor*, 2 vols, (București: Art, 2008), I, p. 26.
16. Niculiță-Voronca, p. 181.

17 George Steiner, *Gramaticile creației* (București: Humanitas, 2015), p. 72.
18 Ion G. Sbiera, *Povești și poezii populare românești* (București: Minerva, 1971), p. 398.
19 It seems worth recalling how things are influenced and defined by culture. In regions where, for socio-geographical reasons, other plants were grown more than wheat, 'God' gained a different form and taste. For example, in Salmon Rushdie's novel *The Enchantress of Florence* (New York: Random House, 2008), the Indians' God is made from turnips and maize.
20 There was the belief that if someone was eating bread and the crumbs fell down, this was a sign of misfortune, because the bread one has touched represented one's fate, strength, and luck (Artur Gorovei and Gh.F. Ciaușanu, *Credințe și superstiții românești* (București: Humanitas, 2012), pp. 359-60).
21 Zoltán Rostás, *Alți București interbelici. Studii și cronici gustiene* (București: Vremea, 2014), p. 56.
22 Romanian women believed that if they eat the corner of the loaf, they would win the love of others. Invoked in spells, bread could have served to buy a remedy. Many Romanian magic spells end with the phrase '*Leac și babei colac*' (a round bread) to obtain a cure.
23 According to the German anthropologist H.P. Duerr, only the closeness to savageness favours initiation (qtd. in Ioan Petru Culianu, *Jocurile minții. Istoria ideilor, teoria culturii, epistemologie* (Iași: Polirom, 2002), p. 172).
24 Claude Lévi-Strauss has hypothesized that cannibalism might be seen as an act of love and civilization: 'Jean Jacques-Rousseau saw the origin of social life in the sentiment that impels us to identify with others. And after all, the simplest means to identify others with oneself is to eat them', which means to assimilate the other for who he is, in the way he is (*We Are All Cannibals* (New York: Columbia University Press, 2016), p. 88.
25 Adrian Fochi, *Datini și eresuri populare de la sfârșitul secolului al XIX-lea. Răspunsurile la chestionarele lui Nicolae Densușianu* (București: Minerva, 1976), p. 351.
26 Maria Berijan, '*Credințe și obiceiuri de Crăciun*', *Universul*, 25.12 (1935), pp. 1-2.
27 Ana Iorga and Filip-Lucian Iorga, *Mesele de odinioară. De la Palatul Regal la Târgul Moșilor* (București: Corint Books, 2015), pp. 19-20.
28 Ofelia Văduva, *Steps toward the Sacred. From the Ethnology of Romanian Food Habits* (Bucharest: Romanian Cultural Foundation Publishing House/The Encyclopaedic Publishing House, 1999), p. 67.
29 Qtd. in Malaguzzi, p. 120.
30 Bread was used as support for electoral messages (B.C., '*Lupta electorală și pâinea*', *Universul*, 26.04 (1926), p. 1).
31 Adrian Maniu, '*Pâine*', *Universul*, 20.10 (1934), p. 7.
32 Before wheat, the place of God was held by buds used instead of the Eucharistic bread by Romanian shepherds (Traian Herseni, *Forme străvechi de cultură poporană românească. Studiu de paleoetnografie a cetelor de feciori din Țara Oltului* (Cluj-Napoca: Editura Dacia, 1977), p. 185).
33 Romulus Antonescu, *Dicționar de simboluri și credințe tradiționale românești* (Iași: Tipo Moldova, 2016), p. 518.

In a Sense, Imperfect: Seedlessness and the American Quest for Convenience in Fruit

Jeffrey Rubel

'Maybe it ran on the obituary page and I just missed it,' wrote David Margolick in a 2003 *New York Times* op-ed. 'But a notable death has occurred and has thus far gone unrecorded.' The death of the seeded watermelon.[1]

And the death of the seeded grape. And the seeded lime. And the seeded clementine. The seeded fruit is dead, or – at the very least – under attack. There's a seedless revolution underway.

This revolution undermines the exact purpose of a fruit: in Aristotle's words 'a "seedless fruit" is in a sense imperfect'.[2] A fruit is a vessel for seed distribution. Fruits attract animals that then help distribute the plant's seeds.

But these seeds can ruin our enjoyment of a perfectly good bowl of cherries, or of a juicy slice of watermelon. So, we've developed methods to remove seeds from fruits – ways to make our consumption more convenient, more enjoyable, more efficient. Because, as Margolick wrote, 'Americans love not only to eat a lot, but to eat easily.'[3]

Thus, through technological innovation and human ingenuity, seeds have disappeared from fruits. In the nineteenth and twentieth centuries, American inventors developed devices to remove pits from fruits, increasing efficiency and saving time. The Industrial Revolution led to the proliferation of these labour-saving devices. The goal was to cut down on cooking time, to free up the housewife, and to make fruit-eating easier. So cherry pitters and grape seeders flooded the market, each claiming to be the perfect time-saving solution to fruit consumption.

While some inventors turned to mechanical technology, others turned toward genetics – their goal, the same: improving convenience and efficiency. It is so much easier to eat a grape or a watermelon without seeds. The American consumer wanted convenience, so the industry developed fruits that removed one of the main hassles of consumption: the seed.

We want our food ready-to-eat. We want to cook quickly and efficiently. Therefore, we want our fruit without seeds. Inventors, scientists, and marketing executives responded to these demands – ease and speed – by creating new fruits and new devices to remove seeds from the vessels designed to carry them.

In a Sense, Imperfect: Seedlessness and the American Quest

The Apple Bee

Before the Industrial Revolution, removing seeds from fruit was a hassle. If you wanted to make a cherry pie, you needed to remove cherry pits with a pointed stick. If you wanted to make cider or apple pie, you needed to core and peel each apple, one by one.[4] Colonial American convenience was – by our modern standards – anything but convenient.

The Puritan settlers believed water was unsafe to drink, so they turned to hard cider as their drink of choice, given the ubiquity of apple trees in colonial America. The fruit was easy to dry and store in barrels, so it became a year-round staple in the New World diet.[5]

Peeling and coring these apples for cider, pie, and storage, took hours on end. In early America, this task fell either to slaves or – in many communities – the town as a whole. After the harvest, farming communities held 'apple bees' where people circulated among the farms, paring and coring the newly harvested apples.[6]

Often, at these gatherings, there would be apple-paring contests 'to see who can peel an entire apple without breaking the paring'.[7] And young unmarried women would squint at these peel scraps in search of their future husbands' initials.[8] As Arthur Cecil Perry wrote in his 1873 *American History* book, 'the men as well as the women take part in these [bees], and great jollity prevails.'[9]

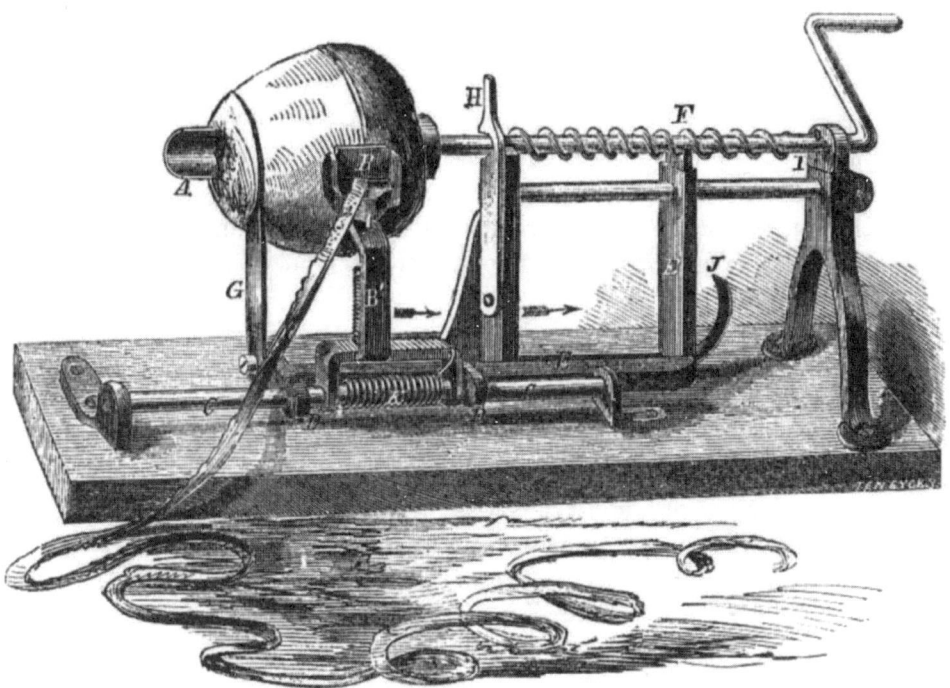

Figure 1. 'Apple Parer, Corer, Slicer' *new invention notification from the May 10th, 1856 issue of* Scientific American.

Thus, coring apples led to the development of elaborate social gatherings and an opportunity to enliven life in early America. Before the Industrial Revolution, the labour fell on the people.[10] It was a time-consuming task, so a culture arose around the practice. But this culture died with the introduction of time-saving technological devices.

Early apple parers, made with leather straps to spin the apples and wooden planks to hold the device steady, were shared among neighbours at apple bees, increasing paring efficiency and decreasing the need for apple bees (see Figure 1 for an early apple parer-corer from the nineteenth century).[11] As apple parers spread, apple bees disappeared – there was no need for the party now that the task could be completed faster, and with fewer hands.

The Cherry Pitter

In a 1998 *Christian Science Monitor* article, Regis McKenna – a Silicon Valley marketing pioneer – said, 'Time is a measurement. It's not time itself. We've given it borders, and the more finite we make it, the faster it goes.' The goal of most technology, from a phone to a cherry pitter, is to make life easier and to save time. These technological advancements have framed time as a distinct measurement that can be shortened to increase efficiency. 'Technology's mission,' wrote Paul van Slambrouck in that same article, 'is to speed things up by packing more functions into smaller increments. The result is a world in which technology is collapsing time and space.'[12]

This technological drive fuelled the invention of labour-saving devices at the turn of the twentieth century. Maria Parloa, in her 1880 *Miss Parloa's New Cook Book*, wrote, 'The homemaker will find there is continually something new to be bought.' Parloa even included a two-page list of ninety-three kitchen utensils essential for a well-furnished home.[13] Kitchen utensils proliferated in the nineteenth century, and these new tools allowed even an inept cook to prepare meals more easily. One of these tools was the cherry pitter.

To cook with a cherry, you need to remove the pit. Eliza Leslie, in her 1839 cookbook *Complete Cookery*, notes that 'drying cherries with the stones in (to save trouble) renders them so inconvenient to eat, that they are of little use'.[14] Prior to the invention of the cherry pitter, cooks needed to remove pits one by one, often using a stick they would poke into each cherry.

While some twentieth century cookbooks assumed the cook knew to pit cherries before cooking, other books specified this step. On one hand, *Aunt Babette's Cook Book* from 1889 calls for cooks to 'fill [the pie] with cherries' in the 'Cherry Pie' recipe, specifying nothing about how to prepare the cherries.[15] On the other hand, in the 1919 *The International Jewish Cook Book*, Florence Greenbaum's 'Cherry Pie, No. 2' recipe calls for cooks to 'seed [the cherries]' (though 'Cherry Pie, No. 1' does not mention pitting.)[16] Often, in the nineteenth century and onward, this laborious task of pitting fell to a simple tool – the cherry pitter.

In a Sense, Imperfect: Seedlessness and the American Quest

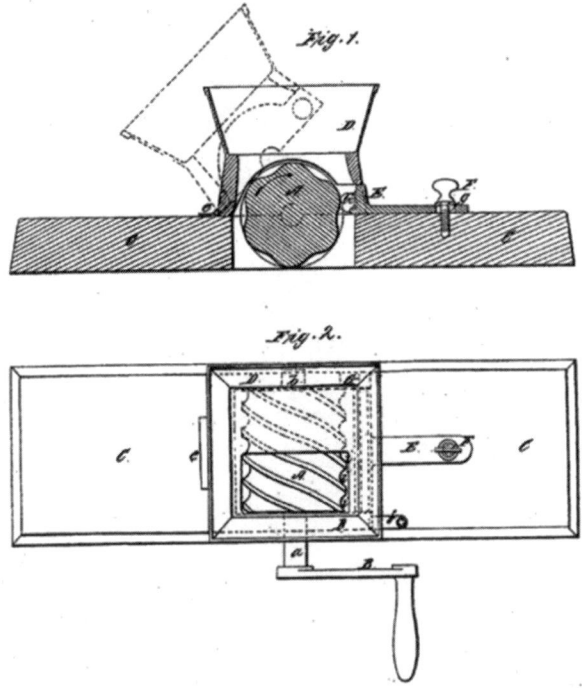

Figure 2. Diagrams for the 'Machine for Stoning Cherries' by Edwin C. Custer.

Around the turn of the twentieth century, there was a proliferation of patents for cherry pitters: from 1865 to 1940, sixty-two patents were filed, according to Google Patents (with no pitter patents filed prior to 1860).[17] The possibility for making cherry-eating easier was ripe for reinvention at the beginning of the twentieth century.

Bee Wilson, in a 2012 *Guardian* article, wrote: 'For most of history, there were no labour-saving devices. Because there was little incentive to save labour when the labour in question was not your own – when meals were prepared by wives and servants.' But, with the Industrial Revolution, labour patterns were shifting, and servants were no longer found in middle-class households. Now, middle-class homeowners were cooking, not hired help – so they wanted to make their own life easier.[18] Thus, the proliferation of the cherry pitter.

The first cherry stoner patent in the United States was filed in 1859 by Edwin C. Custer for 'Machine for Stoning Cherries' (Figure 2).[19] Unlike subsequent patents, Custer's design ran the cherries through a turning spiral wheel that removed the pit by smashing the fruit into a chunky mush. While efficient, the output resembled a pile of bloody innards – hence the failure of the design. Three years later, Theophilus van Kannel patented a more modern pitter.[20] Using a spring-loaded plate

Seeds

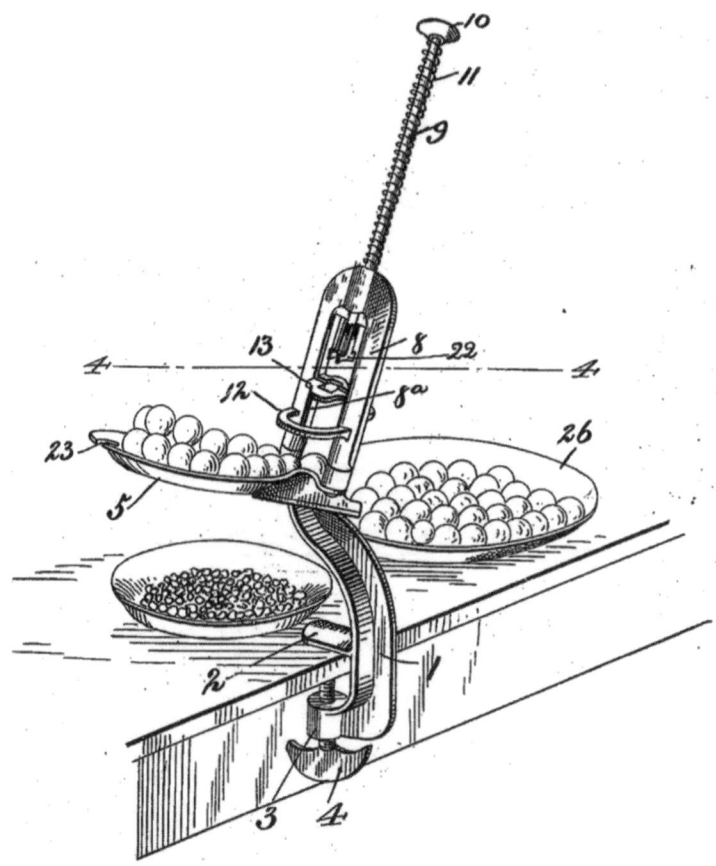

Figure 3. Diagram for the 'Cherry Stoning Machine' by Michael Rollman.

and a prong, it would stone a cherry one by one, and then the user would use a 'finger-piece' to remove the cherry after each use.

Following these early patents, there was a proliferation of pitters. Each claimed to be the perfect solution to removing the pit from the cherry. Each claimed to be more efficient than the last. Each claimed to save the user more time or improve the output of the pitted cherry.

While all pitters strove to increase efficiency, designs often varied in the quantity of cherries they could process. Van Kannel's pitters could only pit one cherry at a time. Similar devices, such as Michael Rollman's 1901 'Cherry Stoning Machine' (Figure 3), clamped onto a table and fed cherries one by one through a plunger that needed to be continuously pressed and released, increasing efficiency over Van Kannel's device but still requiring constant reloading.[21]

However, some designs evolved to pit many cherries at once. For instance, in Oscar L. Robinson's 1867 'Cherry Stoner', a horizontal plate holds a couple dozen cherries which are then all pitted at once when a second plate – with prongs – is pushed down on top of the cherries.[22] Or, there are the pitters that used a spinning blade to chop the cherries, separating flesh from pit. These rotary pitters were clamped onto tables, and the user would spin a crank, turning the rotary, which would pull in and slice up cherries, depositing the flesh below and spitting the pits out of a nozzle.[23] A patent notice in *Scientific American*'s May 14, 1870 issue for an 'Improved Cherry Stoner' by Geer, Stewart and Brother, using this rotary design, claimed: 'Thus, the pits may be removed almost as fast as a child can turn the crank, and the operation is so rapid that the juice does not escape.'[24] In a constant movement toward time-saving, these pitters each claimed to be easier and more efficient than the last.

Time was a pitter's measurement of success. A 1956 *The Science News-Letter* notice for a cherry pitter claimed the device 'will pit a quart of cherries in one minute'.[25] Albert Weinhardt's 1908 'Cherry-Pitter' was designed to 'provide means whereby the pits may be expeditiously removed from the cherries'.[26] Designing a pitter was a balancing act between increasing efficiency and preserving the form of the cherry, though it was the former that drove the invention: technology was about saving time, and every inventor believed they had the best solution.

While pitter patents are still aplenty, many iterations fail to make it to market, leaving only a few iterations – the most successful – still in production. As Bee Wilson wrote in *Consider the Fork*, 'The birth of a new gadget often gives rise to zealous overuse, until the novelty wears off.'[27] This is exactly what happened with the invention of the cherry pitter: the novelty of the invention led to a proliferation of designs – but the poor designs fell victim to the passage of time, and today, the pitter market is dominated by the handheld single-plunger design.[28] As the technological era wore on, attention turned away from invention and toward reinvention. Reinvention of the fruit itself.

The Thompson Grape

The search for the most efficient way to eat fruit drove the transition from technological invention to genetic manipulation. Around the turn of the twentieth century, scientists learned, through some tweaking of a plant's genome, they could breed fruits with no seeds inside. Thus, arose the age of genetic modification – and the seedless grape.

In her 1796 cookbook *American Cookery*, Amelia Simmons noted that grapes 'grow spontaneously in every state in the union' and that 'trifling attention only is necessary for their ample growth'. Consequently, grapes and raisins were essential to many colonial dishes – such as mincemeat pie and plum puddings. However, to cook with raisins, one first needed to remove the seeds. Many recipes would instruct the cook to 'stone' the raisins, which often involved soaking them, a time- and labour-intensive process.[29] Until the raisin seeder.

Technology's desire to save the user time – and to compress time into the smallest units possible – drove the invention of raisin seeders. The popular Enterprise raisin seeder

Figure 4. Advertisement for the Enterprise Raisin Seeder.

(patented 1895) claimed it could 'seed a pound in five minutes,' while another seeder – the Everett (patented 1889) – claimed it could seed 'one pound of raisins in less than ten minutes'.[30] The Enterprise design fed raisins through a rubber gear and toothed cylinder, separating the seeds from the fruit (Figure 4), while the Everett was a roller to run over moistened raisins.[31] For both of these seeders, their efficiency – 'a pound in five minutes' or 'one pound […] in less than ten minutes' – was their selling point. These were devices designed to make life easier by accelerating the laborious task of raisin seeding. Because, as marketer Regis McKenna said in 1998, technology's mission is to speed things up and decrease 'the distance between what you want and where you are'.[32] Efficiency was the raisin seeder's sole purpose, especially as they would leave the raisins in a mutilated pile after use.

But raisin seeders were short-lived. Just years before these patents were filed, William Thompson engineered the seedless grape, rendering raisin seeders obsolete.[33] This loss was an inevitable consequence of an endless search for convenience – a seedless raisin saves even more time than the raisin seeder. When grapes lost their seeds, the world lost the seeders.

Scientists and philosophers were musing over the idea of a seedless fruit centuries before Thompson created his grape. Ancient Greek philosophers such as Hippocrates and Platon prized seedless fruits as an 'infertility' marvel.[34] Similarly, Francis Bacon (born 1651) wrote, 'The making of fruits without core or stone is likewise a curiosity.' Bacon, Platon, and Hippocrates were fascinated by seedless fruits as bizarre natural phenomena, but it wasn't until the late nineteenth century that science caught up with imagination and led to more intentional breeding efforts. As E. Lewis Sturtevant wrote in his 1890 Torrey Botanical Society article, 'Unless correlated with a development or increase of other means of propagation […] seedlessness must eventually bring about the destruction of the variety which its advent marks.'[35] Sturtevant's view aligns with that of Aristotle's: 'A "seedless" fruit is in a sense imperfect'.[36] The prevalence of seedlessness can only be a human invention because its presence in a fruit undermines the fruit's fundamental job of facilitating reproduction.

Therefore, the rise of the Thompson seedless ushered in a new age of removing seeds from fruit, one in which human ingenuity dominated over natural tendencies.

To make his seedless grape, Thompson grafted three cuttings onto an existing root.[37] While the cherry relies on its pit for reproduction, grape vines reproduce through vegetative propagation, where new grape vines are grown from cut sections of older vines. Therefore, the lack of seeds in seedless grapes does not pose a problem for reproduction.

Presented at the 1915 Panama Pacific International Exposition in San Francisco, Thompson's grape caught the attention of consumers and producers.[38] It was efficiency at its finest. You could cook directly with the raisins you bought, or immediately eat the grapes from the market. There was no preparation time. It epitomized convenience and time-saving. And consumers were hooked.

By the 1930s, the seedless Thompson grape was the American grape. Today, nearly all raisins in the supermarket are from a Thompson variety. The efficiency of the seedless grape spurred a reinvention in the fruit world. Scientists and marketing experts saw new potential to grow fruit consumption, capture new markets, and make life easier for consumers. The seedless fruit was the way of the future.

The Seedless Watermelon

'The watermelon industry was facing a real dilemma in the mid-to-late 1980s,' David

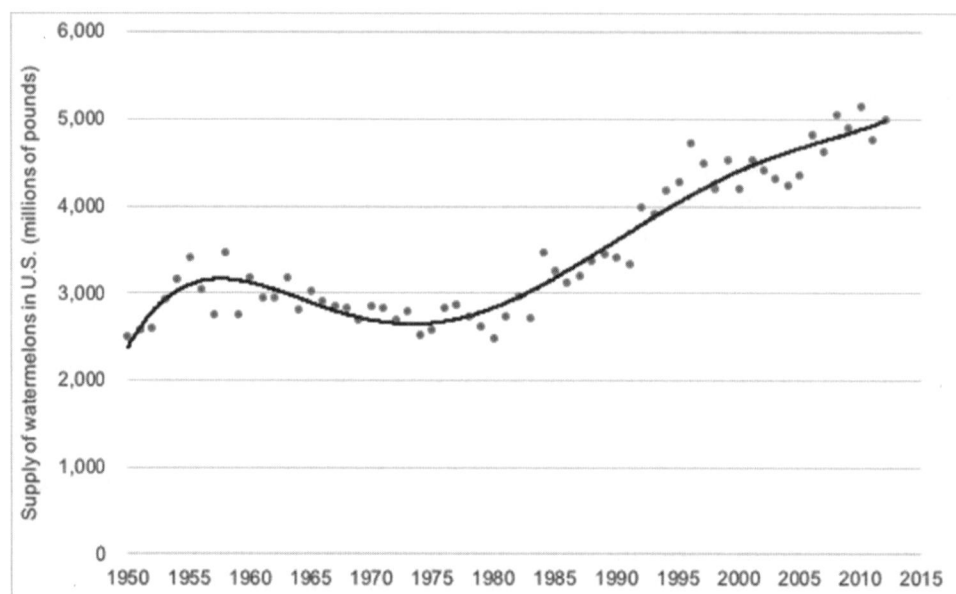

Figure 5. From 1955 to 1975, the total supply of watermelons in the United States (in millions of pounds) decreased, due to the declining popularity of the large, seeded watermelon, but following the introduction of the seedless watermelon in the 1980s, the total supply increased steadily. Data from the USDA's National Agriculture Statistics Service.

Marguleas, senior vice president at Sun World International, said in an interview with the *San Francisco Chronicle* in 1996. 'Other fruits were on the rise, but the one exception was watermelon. Our own research found people considered it to be an inconvenient fruit because of two things – the size, and the seeds.'[39]

Smaller family sizes and greater competition from snack foods drove the decline in watermelon consumption. In 1960, Americans ate seventeen pounds of watermelon a year, but by 1980 this number was down to ten pounds.[40] So began the movement to resurrect the watermelon.

The goal was to create a more convenient fruit, and the first step was removing the seeds. As William Watson, executive director of the National Watermelon Promotion Board, said in a 1994 *Chicago Tribune* article, 'Families today are more interested in convenience. With both parents working, time off is more valuable, so they want items that are quick, easy and efficient. They don't want to buy the watermelon for the seeds.'[41]

In the 1940s, a plant geneticist named Orie 'O.J.' Eigsti, from Goshen, Indiana, developed the first seedless watermelon – a fruit that was infertile, producing no viable seeds.[42] (The white seeds you find inside of seedless watermelons are immature – if planted, they would not grow.[43])

The process of creating a seedless watermelon, developed by Eigsti, requires a bit of clever chemistry and some plant breeding know-how. It starts with colchicine – a

In a Sense, Imperfect: Seedlessness and the American Quest

chemical derived from the crocus and developed, first, to treat and prevent gout (since ancient Egyptian times).[44] Colchicine also affects the development of chromosomes – the DNA holders – within plants. The chemical allows the chromosomes to duplicate, but when they would normally split into two cells, they don't. Because of the colchicine, you get cells that contain four, rather than the normal two, chromosomes – though these four-chromosome watermelons still contain normal seeds.[45]

All seedless watermelons are triploid – their cells contain three chromosomes. So, to get these triploid watermelon, breeders cross a normal two-chromosome watermelon with a colchicine-treated four-chromosome watermelon. They are crossing a regular watermelon with a mutated one to produce an infertile one. When this triploid watermelon matures, it contains thirty-three chromosomes (rather than the normal twenty-two), preventing the black seed coat from forming.[46]

While this process was first discovered in the 1940s, the seedless watermelon did not become popular until the 1980s when fruit company Sun World International partnered with Eigsti to market his creation. Sun World, founded by Howard Marguleas, led an intensive marketing campaign to facilitate the widespread acceptance of the seedless watermelon in the United States.[47]

However, despite the current popularity of the seedless watermelon (today, over 90% of US watermelons is seedless), there was initially pushback.[48] The price of the seedless watermelon was higher than the price of regular seeded watermelon: the seeds for the seedless watermelon cost $500-$1,000 per pound, compared to only $30 for the seeded variety, affecting the list price at supermarkets. In a 1988 *New York Times* op-ed, Michael Hostovich wrote, 'The melons are 49 cents a pound in Pathmark supermarkets in the New York area, about twice the price of regular watermelons. And seedless watermelons aren't much fun at a picnic.'[49]

This latter point led most of the watermelon's criticism. 'A seedless melon? It sounds like an insidious Yankee invention,' said Walter Edgar, director of the Institute for Southern Studies at the University of South Carolina. 'What would Southerners – black, white, male and female – do if they couldn't spit watermelon seeds at each other? It's part of growing up in the South. I guess it must be designed for the Yuppie market.'[50] Seen as an attack on Southern culture, the seedless watermelon undermined the very reason to eat watermelons in the South: to spit out the seeds. The fruit was embroiled as a symbol of Yankee dominance in America and as something designed for the Northern consumer, not the 'real' Southern eater. 'What is summer without spitting out watermelon seeds, either on a plate or on the ground?' asked David Margolick in his 2003 *New York Times* op-ed.[51]

Southerners, unsurprisingly, were slow to accept the seedless watermelons, while West Coast and Northeastern residents were early adopters of the new fruit.[52] A USDA-Cornell survey from 1988 found that 12.2 and 14.8% of watermelon consumers in the Northeastern and Western United States, respectively, were consuming seedless watermelon, compared to 7.9% in the Southern United States.[53] 'We had to overcome a lot of stubbornness,' said David Marguleas in a 1999 *Chicago Tribune* article. But, in a few years, the seedless watermelon took over. 'It's becoming pretty clear that people like the convenience of no seeds,' said Tim Hartz, a watermelon expert at the University of California Davis, in a 1996 *San Francisco Chronicle* article. Convenience and time saving – the same factors that drove the proliferation of cherry, apple, and raisin pitters – led to the popularity of the seedless watermelon. 'Small kids don't choke on the seeds or make a mess all over the place,' said Bill Weinheimer of Swank Farms in the same *Chronicle* article. 'And the seedless are a lot easier to make into fruit salad.'[54]

The seedless watermelon was driving category growth (Figure 5). It was the saviour of the watermelon industry – because of its ease and convenience. In 1995, the average American ate nearly sixteen pounds of watermelon, the most since 1963 and up nearly three pounds since 1991 – because it was so much easier to cook and eat with the seedless variety.[55]

The era of genetic reinvention in fruit is far from over. If anything, it's just beginning. The seedless grape and watermelon exemplify how successful genetic manipulation is in increasing consumption of fruits. If you don't need to seed your raisins when making oatmeal raisin cookies or seed your watermelons when making a summer salad, you'll buy more raisins and melons. The fruit is ready to go, and the convenience is now something American consumers expect.

Scientists are turning their attention towards more and more fruit, armed with new tools to further modify genomes. A December 2017 article from National Public Radio discussed the 'latest in avocado innovation'. A seedless avocado. The result of un-pollinated avocado blossoms developing into seedless fruit.[56] Articles abound on attempts at seedless apples, and seedless pears, and seedless lemons. The desire to remove seeds from fruit before they reach the consumer is growing, and if the seedless watermelon is any indication, it doesn't take long for a successful variety to find its way to dominance.

•

We are in search of the easy way to eat and cook. We want to find the way to save the most time, to be the most efficient, to have the most convenient snack or dinner. This relentless drive toward efficiency has removed seeds from fruit. While fruits are, by their very nature, vessels for seeds, we cannot make a cherry pie with pits, or a summertime fruit salad with watermelon seeds.

American approaches to seed removal have shifted with new technology and changes in mindset. The Industrial Revolution brought an explosion of inventors, each designing new devices to remove seeds from fruit – countless cherry pitter patents flooded the US Patent Office, even though only a few varieties are still in production today. As our understanding of genetics sharpened, our attention turned inside the fruit, a quest to remove the seed before the fruit developed. And now seedless watermelons and grapes dominate supermarket shelves.

However, with the rise of pitters and seedless fruits came the disappearance of a culture. Gone are the apple bees and community gatherings built around the task of removing seeds from fruit. In their place? Efficiency and convenience. But with this ease comes isolation. We do not need the help of others to make our cherry pie or our watermelon salad.

Aristotle wrote, 'A 'seedless' fruit is in a sense imperfect.' In nature, perhaps he is right, where a seedless fruit serves no use. But, for us, as consumers, Aristotle is wrong. Because the seedless fruit contains exactly we want and avoids what we don't. The seedless fruit is a combination of natural evolution and human ingenuity. It's the efficiency of a perfect cherry pitter and the convenience of a bag of seedless grapes.

It is, in a sense, perfect.

Acknowledgements

Thank you to Darra Goldstein, Sara Hetherington, and Anya Sheldon for their feedback on the proposal and idea for this paper. And thank you to Melissa Rubel and Grace Flaherty for editing drafts of the full paper.

Notes

1. David Margolick, 'The Seeds of a Summer Revolt', *The New York Times*, 25 Aug 2003, p. A15.
2. *Metaphysics*, 1023a, qtd in Michael Marder, *The Philosopher's Plant: An Intellectual Herbarium* (New York City: Columbia University Press, 2014), p. 31.
3. Margolick.
4. Andrew Smith, *The Oxford Companion to American Food and Drink* (Oxford: Oxford University Press, 2009), pp. 20-21.
5. Smith, pp. 20-21.
6. Don Thorton, 'Apple Parers: A Slice of American History', *Gastronomica*, 2.1 (Winter 2002), pp. 58-61.
7. Mary Eliza Moxcey, *Good Times for Girls* (New York: The Methodist Book Concern, 1920), p. 56.
8. Sarah Lohman, 'Kitchen Histories: Easy-as-Pie Apple Peeler', *Etsy Journal*, 14 November 2013 <https://blog.etsy.com/en/kitchen-histories-easy-as-pie-apple-peeler/> [accessed 6 April 2019].
9. Arthur Cecil Perry, *American History* (New York: American Book Company, 1873), p. 52.
10. Lohman.
11. Kelly Stewart, 'Peeling Back History with the Gadgets that Processed Apples of Yesteryear', *Edible Manhattan*, 14 (November/December 2010) <https://www.ediblemanhattan.com/departments/notable-edibles/peeling-back-history/> [accessed 6 April 2019].
12. Paul Van Slambrouck, 'A Culture Obsessed with Time', *Christian Science Monitor*, 5 March 1998 <https://www.csmonitor.com/1998/0305/030598.us.us.3.html> [accessed 6 April 2019].
13. Maria Parloa, *Miss Parloa's New Cook Book: A Guide to Marketing and Cooking* (Boston: Estes and Lauriat, 1881), pp. 66, 64.
14. Joanna Church, 'Cherry Stoner, circa 1870', *Montgomery County Historical Society*, 12 October 2011.
15. Aunt Babette, *Aunt Babette's Cook Book* (Cincinnati: Block Pub. and Print Co., c. 1889), p. 204.
16. Florence Kreisler Greenbaum, *The International Jewish Cook Book* (New York: Bloch Publishing Company, 1919), p. 276.
17. Google Patents database (<https://patents.google.com>).

18 Bee Wilson, 'Kitchen Gadgets: Innovations Old and New', *The Guardian*, 24 October 2012.
19 Edwin C. Custer, 'Machine for Stoning Cherries (Patent 24856)' (The United States of America, 1859).
20 Theophilus Van Kannel, 'Improved Machine for Stoning Cherries (Patent 36683)' (The United States of America, 1862).
21 Michael Rollman, 'Cherry-Stoning Machine (Patent 44166)' (The United States of America, 1901).
22 Oscar L. Robinson, 'Improved Cherry-Stoner (Patent 66889)' (The United States of America, 1867).
23 Paul Schaffner, 'A Quick Survey of Cherry Stoners', *University of Michigan* (n.b.).
24 'Improved Cherry Stoner', *Scientific American,* 22.20 (14 May 1870).
25 'New Machines and Gadgets', *The Science News-Letter,* 70.1 (7 July 1956).
26 Albert G. Weinhardt, 'Cherry Pitter (Patent 886906)' (The United States of America, 1908).
27 Bee Wilson, *Consider the Fork: A History of How We Cook and Eat* (New York City: Basic Books, 2013), p. 173.
28 A search for 'cherry pitter' on Amazon.com highlights the ubiquity of the handheld single plunger design. While other pitter designs are on Amazon, they are few and far between – and aren't the 'best sellers' or 'high rated' products.
29 Sandra Louise Oliver, *Food in Colonial and Federal America* (Westport, CT: Greenwood Publishing Group, 2005), p. 69.
30 'The Everett Raisin Seeder', Everett Specialty Co.
31 'Enterprise Raisin Seeder', The Enterprise Manufacturing Company of Pennsylvania.
32 Van Slambrouck.
33 Randal Oulton, 'Thompson Seedless Grapes', CooksInfo.com (15 April 2004), <https://www.cooksinfo.com/thompson-seedless-grapes> [accessed 6 April 2019].
34 Fabrice Varoquaux and others, 'Less Is Better: New Approaches for Seedless Fruit Production', *Trends in Biotechnology*, 18 (June 2000).
35 E. Lewis Sturtevant, 'Seedless Fruits', *Members of Torrey Botanical Club*, 1.4 (30 May 1890), pp. 141-85.
36 Marder, p. 31.
37 Anna Palecek, *Sun-Maid Raisins and Dried Fruits* (London: DK, 2011), pp. 46-47.
38 George Slate, John Watson, and John Einset, *Grape Varieties Introduced by the New York State Agricultural Experiment Station 1928-1961* (Ithaca, NY: Cornell University, 1962), p. 35.
39 Carl Hall, 'A Kinder, Gentler Watermelon / Seedless Variety is on a Roll', *SF Gate*, 2 September 1996.
40 Knight-Ridder/Tribune, 'Nothing to Spit At: Seedless Watermelon', *The Chicago Tribune*, 26 June 1994 <https://www.chicagotribune.com/news/ct-xpm-1994-06-26-9406260256-story.html> [accessed 6 April 2019].
41 Knight-Ridder/Tribune.
42 'A Short History of the Seedless Watermelon', *The Garden Spotter*, 29 August 2016.
43 Stephanie Barlow, 'Where Does Seedless Watermelon Come From?' *American Farm Bureau Foundation for Agriculture*, 18 July 2017 <https://www.agfoundation.org/news/where-does-seedless-watermelon-come-from> [accessed 6 April 2019].
44 April Fulton, 'Where Did All the Watermelon Seeds Go?' *NPR's The Salt*, 26 July 2012 <https://www.npr.org/sections/thesalt/2012/07/26/157427994/where-did-all-the-watermelon-seeds-go> [accessed 6 April 2019].
45 Julia Davis, 'Where Did All the Seedless Watermelons Come From?' *Mental Floss*, 16 July 2012 <http://mentalfloss.com/article/31211/where-do-seedless-watermelons-come> [accessed 6 April 2019].
46 Barlow.
47 'Seedless Melons Imperil Spitting', *News OK*, 9 August 1987 <https://newsok.com/article/2194963/seedless-melons-imperil-spitting> [accessed 6 April 2019].
48 Barlow.
49 Michael Hostovich, 'And Now, the Seedless Watermelon', *The New York Times*, 22 June 1988, p. C7.
50 Knight-Ridder/Tribune.
51 Margolick.

52 Eric Zorn, 'Seedless Watermelon Took the Oblong Way to Success', *The Chicago Tribune*, 31 August 1999 <https://www.chicagotribune.com/news/ct-xpm-1999-08-31-9908310083-story.html> [accessed 6 April 2019].
53 USDA and Cornell University, 'The Packer' survey, 1988.
54 Hall.
55 Hall.
56 Maanvi Singh, 'Avocado Hand Injuries Are Real. Is a Seedless Fruit the Answer?', *NPR's The Salt*, 15 December 2017 <https://www.npr.org/sections/thesalt/2017/12/15/570822807/avocado-hand-injuries-are-real-is-a-seedless-fruit-the-answer> [accessed 6 April 2019].

Chocolate and Vanilla: Seeds of Taste

Kathryn E. Sampeck

Seeds of Opposition

Chocolate and vanilla are metaphorical opposites today, a vivid and relatively rare example for food. Do strawberries, cheese, nutmeg, or peanuts have culinary opposites? The closest examples that come to mind are oil and water, salt and pepper, and fire and ice. These others are examples of contrasting materials as well as tastes – to mistake one for the other could lead to culinary disaster. Chocolate and vanilla, however, both derive from seeds and can be used together or even as parallel alternatives within certain classes of recipes such as cakes, puddings, sauces, etc.[1] Questioning when and where the gastronomic and symbolic contrast of chocolate and vanilla arose involves examining the earliest evidence of their use and semantic associations. Recipes from pre-Columbian as well as sixteenth- through nineteenth-century texts provide examples of preparations that included cacao and/or vanilla. This essay compares this evidence in two ways, through flavour summaries, which give a sense of the predominant tastes by region, and through systematic comparisons of ingredients in recipes.

Divorcing the ecologically symbiotic pair of cacao and vanilla in agriculture parallels their distinction in culinary use, heightened flavour contrasts among regions, and their increasing divergence in social meaning. This analysis is thus an exploration of the antecedents of what Michaela DeSoucey has phrased 'gastronationalism'.[2] DeSoucey and other culinary scholars focus on contemporary culinary geopolitics.[3] However, cuisine in pre-Columbian and early modern and early modern periods provided necessary antecedents for contemporary gastronationalism.[4]

The Shared Origins of Chocolate and Vanilla

Both cacao and vanilla were cultivars in pre-Columbian Mexico and Central America (Mesoamerica) with potent symbolic meanings. Mesoamericans equated cacao with the highest echelons of morality: Central Mexican Nahua authors of the *Florentine Codex* advised '*itlan xaquj in metlatl, in atl, in venchioaliztli*' (be diligent with the grinding stone, the chocolate, the making of offerings), and K'iché Maya authors of the *Pop Wuj* personified cacao as a female guardian of sustenance, Lady of the Day Toj. Even though Mesoamericans did not deify vanilla, they associated vanilla and cacao with each other, fertility, and potency.[5]

Chocolate is made from the seeds of trees of the genus Theobroma. There are

Chocolate and Vanilla: Seeds of Taste

more than thirty different Theobroma species, all edible, and people use many of them today. *Theobroma cacao* is the species used today to make industrial, mass-produced chocolate as well as fine chocolate. Vanilla is made from the pod of an orchid, genus Vanilla, which has three different species. *Vanilla planifolia* is 97% of today's market.

Mesoamericans may have linked cacao with vanilla because they are ecologically symbiotic.[6] Cacao and vanilla grow in tropical environments and are intolerant of cold and dry weather. They are both forest understory plants, so they need just the right amount of shade to grow well. They both also need the right amount of water and rich soils.[7]

They share even more needs. Neither vanilla nor cacao is self-pollinating. The intricate, tiny flowers of both require miniscule insects to pollinate them. The pistil of the vanilla flower is protected by a membrane that prevents pollination unless something, such as an insect, tears it open.[8] Because pollination for both plants depends upon wild rainforest insects, microenvironments that encourage insects such as midge flies to thrive are crucial. Bits and pieces of partially eaten cacao fruit dropped by foraging monkeys help disperse uneaten seeds as well as attract midges to both cacao tree and vanilla orchid flowers. In fact, until the nineteenth century, vanilla was not grown in large quantities outside of Mexico because the right kinds of insects did not live in other places.

Both vanilla and cacao are long-term investments. It takes a good five years (or more for cacao) for a new plants to begin producing pods.[9] Vanilla's odourless, pale yellow flower, unless pollinated, dies within a few hours. Vanilla pods are green at first, then gradually yellow as they ripen. The fully mature pod is a deep brown.[10] The seed pods, like human children, take nine months to develop. Vanilla pods contain a multitude of minute, black seeds imbedded in an aromatic pulp.[11] Cacao fruit has a tough rind covering a layer of fleshy, sweet pulp. In the centre of the fruit are thirty to forty slightly plump yet flat seeds completely enrobed in a mucilaginous coating. Cacao and vanilla thus contrast in the size of their seeds: cacao's are large, while vanilla's are miniscule.

Cacao and vanilla have equal needs for careful handling and processing. Cacao pods have to be removed from the tree so that the trunk is not damaged, as that is where the next set of blossoms form. To extract the seeds from their mucilaginous coating requires fermentation for several days, which also serves to kill germination and develop flavour. The fermented seeds have to be dried slowly so as not to promote bitter, acid flavours, but also completely, or mould will form. The fermented, dried seeds have to be cracked and winnowed to remove the less tasty shell from the nibs. After this, cacao nibs must be ground, heated, and cooled repeatedly to form chocolate.

The string-bean-like pods of vanilla become very dark brown and fragrant only after a curing process that takes several months.[12] The pods are 'wrapped in clothes and stored in boxes for hours to days, massaged, manipulated, laid in the sun to dry each morning and brought in to rest each evening'.[13] An 1878 account related that the pods are wrapped in woollen cloths to 'sweat'.[14] Pomet's 1737 *Compleat History of Druggs* gives the most detailed account of vanilla processing, saying harvesters 'gather them, and hang them up by one end in the shade to dry; and when they are dry enough to keep, they rub them with oil to hinder them from drying too much, and prevent their breaking, and then put them up in little bags'. Pomet also described a low-grade form of vanilla harvesting that produced a black balsam that was a vanilla culinary divide – Spaniards consumed it, but other Europeans did not.[15]

Given the demands of all of these factors, Spanish colonial policy initially left production and processing in indigenous hands. The pluriculture of cacao and vanilla show up in early colonial historical accounts in different regions of Mexico and Central America.[16] The timelines for the move away from production under indigenous control to enslaved African labour are quite different for cacao and vanilla. By the end of the nineteenth century, they end up in the same place: Africa. The ecological, semantic, and task-intensive twins of vanilla and cacao appear to divorce at about the time of the shift to cacao production with enslaved labour. The values of pluriculture so evident in the sixteenth century were lost.

While cacao production expanded, vanilla agriculture eventually contracted. By the end of the seventeenth century, production relied upon careful cropping of known vanilla stands and a frantic search for new producing regions, including Venezuela and western Panama.[17] The Mexican Gulf coast held a near monopoly in vanilla, which did not change until 1841, when Edmond Albius, an enslaved twelve-year-old, discovered a technique of hand pollination for the orchid that is still used today. After this discovery, the French developed large vanilla plantations on Reunion. An 1874 article in the *New York Times* documents the meteoric rise in price and productivity in just over twenty years with the technological and geographic shift in the vanilla industry (Figure 1).[18] The dramatic expansion of both the cacao and vanilla markets happened in concert with geographic relocation of primary centres of production. By the nineteenth century, cacao agriculture moved to western Africa and vanilla to Madagascar.

Year	Weight (kg)	Price (francs)
1851	30	50
1861	15,779	119
1872	11,000	160

Figure 1. Increase in the production on Reunion and the market price of vanilla in the second half of the nineteenth century.

Divergent Culinary Paths?

What had been symbiotically joined became distinct, and that splitting involved new people making all of the decisions that so strongly affect quality and taste. Both subtle and more obvious flavours of the products undoubtedly changed. For consumers, access to cacao expanded, while vanilla contracted until the nineteenth century. These transformations beg the question of how the timing of these production shifts compares to culinary uses of cacao and vanilla.

Chocolate and Vanilla: Seeds of Taste

Vanilla and Desire

Chocolate and vanilla both in the Americas and abroad shared associations with desire and fertility. Medieval people took the idea seriously that the food they consumed could influence their sex lives, as food and drink could solve sexual problems, including impotence and infertility.[19] Vanilla and chocolate became part of early modern culinary pharmacopeia, with both increasingly identified over time with sexual desire, but in strikingly different ways. By 1571, Europeans renamed the Mesoamerican *tlilxochitl* to *vaina* or *vainillo*, 'small sheath', a word that evoked sexual mimesis: the long slender pods of the orchid were like a sheath, which in the early modern mind described a penis, but also is the same root as 'vagina'.[20] In contrast, cacao and chocolat both are from Mesoamerican languages; Europeans adopted these names, leaving them virtually unchanged.

This rebranding of vanilla undoubtedly helped it become known as an erotic stimulant in Europe and fuelled its popularity among the European elite. In 1602, Hugh Morgan, apothecary to an aging Queen Elizabeth I, suggested that she use vanilla as a flavouring; she indulged regularly in vanilla-infused pastries. In 1684, Stephano Bachot described vanilla as the most important ingredient in chocolate after cacao and could indeed be a substitute for cacao in terms of its pharmaceutical and sensory value, saying that vanilla was a 'delicacy for kings and nobles that gave their hearts strength and joy'. Slightly, later, Madame de Pompadour, Louis XV's mistress, subsisted on an aphrodisiac diet of vanilla, truffles, and celery.[21]

The medical use of vanilla persisted well into the nineteenth century. An 1874 example in *The Lancet* mentions vanilla as a flavouring as part of the treatment of a nine-year-old boy with pleuritic effusion. He was being treated with supplements of iron, quinine, and cod-liver oil, a mix 'readily taken by ladies and children'.[22]

Chocolate Cravings

In contrast to vanilla, chocolate became controversial as a food and flavour – banned, even! While both were associated with sexuality, chocolate became strongly linked with nefarious love-magic.[23] Special substances made into powders were mixed and ground with solid or powder chocolate. Many medical treatments involved mixing substances in liquids such as wine; mixing love powders in chocolate had the potential to double the aphrodisiacal effect.

Methodology

This analysis employs two ways of comparing recipe ingredients: flavour summaries (in a table), to give an overview of flavours, and a dendrogram, to compare individual recipes. Both compare simple calculations of percentages. Previous analyses produced the first dendrogram of chocolate recipes and flavour wheels for pre-Columbian Maya and colonial cacao preparations.[24] The flavour wheels and flavour summaries are two ways to present similar data. The results presented here are of a greatly expanded recipe database and the addition of vanilla-only recipe information.[25]

Seeds

Flavour Summaries
In this analysis, recipes that include cacao, chocolate, and/or vanilla are grouped by region. The percentages show how many times a particular item appears in all of the recipes of the region, providing a way to understand the prevalence of particular spices, sweeteners, and other ingredients.

Recipe Family Tree
The second kind of analysis compares the degree of relatedness of individual recipes to each other. The comparison of individual recipes lets us evaluate the degree to which taste is anchored by place.[26] The main groupings are largely geographic, with a few branches due to the presence of vanilla.

Results

Pre-Columbian Maya Flavour Summary
The recipes in this part of the analysis are in fact Maya hieroglyphic texts about foods and drinks painted on bespoke Classic Period (400-850 ACE) vessels. None of the terms deciphered so far, however, are a word for vanilla. So, this analysis starts with a deep view of cacao, but no glimpse of vanilla. This comparison of Maya inscriptions shows that recipes and flavours of pre-Columbian cacao preparations were not standardized, varying a great deal from one region to the next.[27] Overall, the suite of flavours named in these texts show two strong preferences: fruity and starchy. Popular terms were fruity *yutal*, and maize-related *nal* and *ul*, a triad that may be a common language of Maya cacao taste preferences (Figure 2). The overall terrain of ancient Maya preferences in cacao taste, scent, and appearance is a diverse culinary landscape.

Early Modern Flavour Summaries
Maya people use some of the same names of cacao preparations today. This does not mean, however, that the cuisine of indigenous people in Mexico and Central America was unchanging. A survey of cookbooks and other early modern works gives a view of just what flavours dominated in different locations in the Americas and Europe. The prevalence of the number and kinds of ingredients for each region gives an overview of the importance of vanilla compared to cacao or chocolate and the other sorts of flavourings that people combined with them. The principal distinction between American and European recipes is the lack of corn and abundance of pungent floral, citrus, and nuts in European recipes. This continental divide is evocative enough; a more detailed view of regional tastes shows that adjacent areas in Europe and the Americas had highly different chocolate- and vanilla-related flavour profiles.

Britain/Early Anglo-America. The major flavour categories for recipes from British or British colonial sources have a limited occurrence of vanilla and cacao together,

Chocolate and Vanilla: Seeds of Taste

Description category	Maya word	English translation	% of total (n=307)
Cacao variety/ preparation	b'alam	pataxte	0.3
	k'uhul	divine	0.3
	ach'	fresh, new, green	0.3
	tzihil	Fresh, unadulterated, pure	5.2
	k'an	ripe	1.3
	k'in	Sun, day, hot	0.3
	to b'o	finished	0.3
	kal	drunk/inebriating	0.3
	koxoom mul	crested guan cup	0.3
	nal /nal te'el)	young maize tree	34.5
Maize/starch	ixim te'el/iximte'	maize tree, wild cacao	3.3
	sa', sa'al	Atole gruel	1.3
	sak ha'	Cold maize drink	1.6
	ul	Cold drink with maize	3.3
	ich	chile	14.0
Ingredients	ta' ibil	lima bean	0.3
	tzah	sweet	2.0
Sweetness	ho'kab	honey	1.0
	kaab'il/ chaab'il	honey	1.0
	yutal	fruity	27.4
	suutz	cherry	1.3
Location	witik	place	0.3

Figure 2. List of pre-Columbian Maya cacao terms, their translations, and frequency of appearance.

although the general category of floral tastes is one of the most prominent flavour notes (Figure 3). Botanical flavours are only slightly less common than floral elements and more common than sweet. The most prominent category is spice.

An 1875 chemistry journal article claimed that, 'as a flavor, vanilla undoubtedly occupies the first rank, and here is at its best when used pure and simple' in creams, ices, or sauces; the form he recommended was vanilla extract. This source also noted that some 'foreign writers' note that vanilla extract 'is frequently adulterated with a mixture of tonka essence. The flavor of the latter somewhat resembles that of vanilla, but is much inferior in every respect'.[28]

The flavour summaries for other European recipes show that they have fewer flavour notes than British ones.

Seeds

Flavour category	Ingredient	% of total (n=58)
	cacao	14%
	milk	3%
	sack	2%
	egg	3%
Sweet	sugar	9%
Floral	orejuela	2%
	vanilla	3%
	mecaxochitl	3%
	orange blossom	2%
	rose water	2%
	anise	3%
Spicy	chile	2%
	long pepper	2%
	Jamaica Pepper	2%
	cinnamon	9%
	cardamom	2%
	nutmeg	3%
	clove	2%
Botanic/herbal	achiote	3%
	saunders	2%
	rhubarb	2%
	sarsa[parilla]	2%
	china	2%
citrus	citron	2%
	lemon peel	2%
umami	musk	3%
	ambergris	3%
	odoriferous aromatic oil	2%
starch-nut	almond	5%
	pistachios	2%
	hazelnut	2%
other	steel	2%

Figure 3. Flavour summary for British and British American recipes.

Chocolate and Vanilla: Seeds of Taste

Flavour category	Ingredient	% of total (n=131)	Vanilla only
chocolate	cacao	11%	
	chocolate	2%	
	water	4%	
creamy	milk	1%	
	cream	1%	
	egg	7%	
sweet	sugar	12%	present
fruit	fruta	1%	
floral	orejuela	3%	
	vanilla	7%	
	Tlatlalayotic	1%	
	Yoloxochitl	1%	
	Mecaxochitl	4%	
	Izquixochitl	1%	
	orange blossom	3%	present
	anise	3%	
	rose water	1%	
spicy	Tabasco/Chilpatagua pepper	2%	
	chile	4%	
	long pepper	1%	
	Mexican pepper	1%	
	cinnamon	4%	
	cardamom	1%	
	nutmeg	1%	
	clove	2%	
umami	achiote	4%	
	olli (rubber)	1%	
	musk	2%	
	ambergris	1%	
	essence d'ambre	1%	
starch-nut	almond	4%	
	filberts	1%	
	pistachios	1%	
	hazelnut	1%	
	zapote seeds	1%	

Figure 4. Flavour summary of French recipes.

France. In 1745, Louis Limery, Physician to the French King, described how the French emphasis on cacao quality as well as preferred ingredients to make chocolate resulted in a vast improvement over chocolate from other empires.[29] The preferred ingredients included vanilla, which was nearly twice as common in French recipes compared to British ones (Figure 4). The late seventeenth-century work *Le Bon Usage du Chocolat degraissé* mentions vanilla quite often. The author claims that it is the most preferable of all possible additions to chocolate, especially if dealing with a case of the vapours.[30] In the last case, vanilla is reported to be less strong than musk or essence of amber. Spicy flavours were second in frequency to the dominant category of floral, but significantly less, about 16% of all ingredients. French recipes, unlike British ones, mentioned water.

The fourth column in Figure 4 shows the overlap in flavours between vanilla only and chocolate bearing recipes. Ingredients that appear only with vanilla and not cacao or chocolate are lemon balm, tea, coffee, and coffee milk. It is a surprise that the 1812 imprint of Menon's *Professed Cook*, despite having recipes for chocolate creams, tortes, toasts, pastille pastes, conserves, mousses, drams or cordials, has not a single listing of vanilla, even as a secondary flavouring. This is despite the same kinds of recipes with fruit, saffron, coffee, and other flavours. Nor do other kinds of recipes appear for other, non-chocolate preparations that include vanilla.[31]

Italy. Italian use of vanilla is unusual because with chocolate, the vanilla flower was used, while vanilla-only recipes relied on the vanilla bean (Figure 5). Although the main European flavour categories appear, creaminess is very common, and spicy and umami flavours are not, nor do they include American substances.

The 1910 *Manuale di Cucina* lists vanilla in aromatic spices, and advised that artificial vanilla is not as delicate as the original. The same work lists a vanilla sauce (which can use lemon instead) as well as another sweet sauce that can be vanilla or cinnamon flavoured. Lemon also appears as an alternative to vanilla in the recipe for *fritte de pasta*. A chestnut soup and a chestnut *ripeini* also have vanilla as a flavouring.[32]

In all, most of the flavourings were from Eurasia.[33] Later recipes specified prepared chocolate and made use of egg and salt. No starchy element such as nuts or seeds were part of Italian recipes for chocolate.

Flavour category	Ingredient	% of total (n=31)
chocolate	cacao	10%
	chocolate	13%
	water	19%
creamy	milk	16%
	cream	3%
	egg	10%
sweet	sugar	13%
salt	salt	3%
floral	vanilla flowers	3%
	jasmine petals	3%
spicy	cinnamon	3%
umami	ambergris	3%

Table 5. Flavour summary of Italian recipes.

Chocolate and Vanilla: Seeds of Taste

Flavour category	Ingredient	% of total (n=42)
chocolate	cacao	14%
	water	2%
sweet	sugar	7%
floral	orejuela	2%
	vanilla	2%
	mecaxochitl	2%
	anise	2%
	powder of Alexandria	5%
spicy	Tabasco/Chilpatagua pepper	5%
	black pepper	2%
	cinnamon	7%
	nutmeg	2%
	clove	7%
	ginger	2%
botanic	logwood/Campeche tree	2%
	Doradilla herb	2%
	Valencia	2%
starch-nut	almond	5%
	hazelnut	5%
	toasted nuts	2%
	melon seed	2%
	squash seed	2%
	zapote seeds	2%
starch-maize	maize	2%
	massa	2%
umami	achiote	5%

Table 6. Flavour summary of Spanish recipes.

Spain. Spanish recipes are distinct because the starchy elements are almost as common as spicy ones (Figure 6). Spanish recipes stand out from other European examples because of their use of maize, which is a significant part of the starchiness. Vanilla is a small part of all floral notes, which are about twice as common as botanical flavours.

Guatemala. How do these examples compare to chocolate in its birthplace? One quarter of all flavours are floral, including vanilla (Figure 7).[34] A couple ingredients may have to do with colour: smoky, deep red achiote, the lone umami flavour, and botanical, dark logwood. Starchiness, spiciness, and floral qualities balance each other. Cacao pods and almond milk as ingredients also make Guatemalan chocolate unique.

Flavour category	Ingredient	% of total (n=53)
chocolate	cacao	11%
	cacao pod	2%
	Pataxte	2%
	water	9%
creamy	almond milk	2%
sweet	sugar	8%
floral	orejuela	8%
	vanilla	2%
	mecaxochitl	2%
	xochipatli	2%
	orange blossom	2%
	anise	6%
	powder of Alexandria	4%
spicy	Tabasco/Chilpatagua pepper	6%
	chile	2%
	cinnamon	6%
	clove	6%
botanical	logwood/Campeche tree	2%
starch-maize	atole	6%
starch-nut	almond	4%
	hazelnut	2%
	toasted nuts	2%
umami	achiote	8%

Figure 7. Flavour summary for Guatemalan recipes.

Mexico. Mexican recipes are about as sweet as Guatemalan ones, but explicitly named honey (Figure 8). Likewise, floral, spicy, and starchy ingredients balance each other, but include sesame and hazelnut. The range of umami ingredients reaches beyond achiote. Vanilla is not the most common floral flavouring, but is relatively prominent compared to the wide array of Mexican flavourings.

Chocolate and Vanilla: Seeds of Taste

Flavour category	Ingredient	% of total (n=166)
chocolate	cacao	16%
	water	9%
sweet	sugar	6%
	honey	3%
fruit	fruta	1%
floral	cacahuapatli	1%
	orejuela	6%
	vanilla	5%
	Tlatlalayotic	1%
	Yoloxochitl	1%
	Mecaxochitl	5%
	Izquixochitl	1%
	orange blossom	1%
	mahax	1%
spicy	Tabasco/Chilpatagua pepper	5%
	chile	5%
	anise	3%
	cinnamon	3%
	acahar seco (Achaar Ka Masala)	1%
	clove	2%
	logwood/Campeche tree	1%
umami	achiote	7%
	olli (rubber)	1%
	musk	1%
	essence d'ambre	1%
starch-maize	maize	5%
	atole	5%
starch-nut	almond	1%
	hazelnut	1%
	toasted nuts	1%
	zapote seeds	2%
	sesame	1%

Figure 8. Flavour summary for Mexican recipes.

Peru. Peruvian recipes in the recipes in this survey did not include vanilla (Figure 9). In fact, umami and chocolate are the only flavours. These examples show that sweet was not always a part of chocolate flavour.

Flavour category	Ingredient	% of total (n=13)
chocolate	cacao	23%
	egg	8%
umami	acahar seco (Achaar Ka Masala)	23%
	musk	23%
	essence d'ambre	23%

Figure 9. Flavour summary for Peruvian recipes.

Recipe Family Tree

The summaries give an overall sense of preferences by region, and the evidence is that this distinction was significant with chocolate and vanilla recipes. The summary, however, does not say how similar or different individual recipes might be. For this, the best comparison is a calculation of the percentage of shared ingredients, here displayed as a dendrogram (Figure 10). Jonathan Thayn expanded and updated the dendrogram he created for our 2017 analysis. This new analysis including vanilla offers the insight that vanilla was a prominent way to distinguish different branches of the recipe family tree.

The dendrogram shows two principal branches, which means that all of the recipes on the left branch are much more like each other than the branch to the right. The branch on the left contains almost all of the Guatemalan recipes. The two 'daughter' branches within the left side includes the farthest left cluster, which are recipes that include vanilla. The right main branch of the dendrogram also sorts highly consistently in terms of time period and region. Overall, the degree of overlap in flavour profiles is low from one region to another and from early modern to later periods. To move from one place to the next meant experiencing chocolate and vanilla in very different ways.

Discussion

This inquiry reveals the complex interplay of geographic, cultural, and culinary boundaries, the seeds of which were sown, quite literally, by shifts in where and how cacao and vanilla were produced. Pre-Columbian interrelationships of geography, politics, and taste were distinctions that transformed with the global spread of cacao and vanilla consumption during the early modern period. This spread was uneven and offered opportunities to place chocolate and vanilla in opposition, despite their shared ecologies, agriculture, and meanings. Chocolate and vanilla were a way both to form connections through a shared experience of preparing and consuming, but also craft

Chocolate and Vanilla: Seeds of Taste

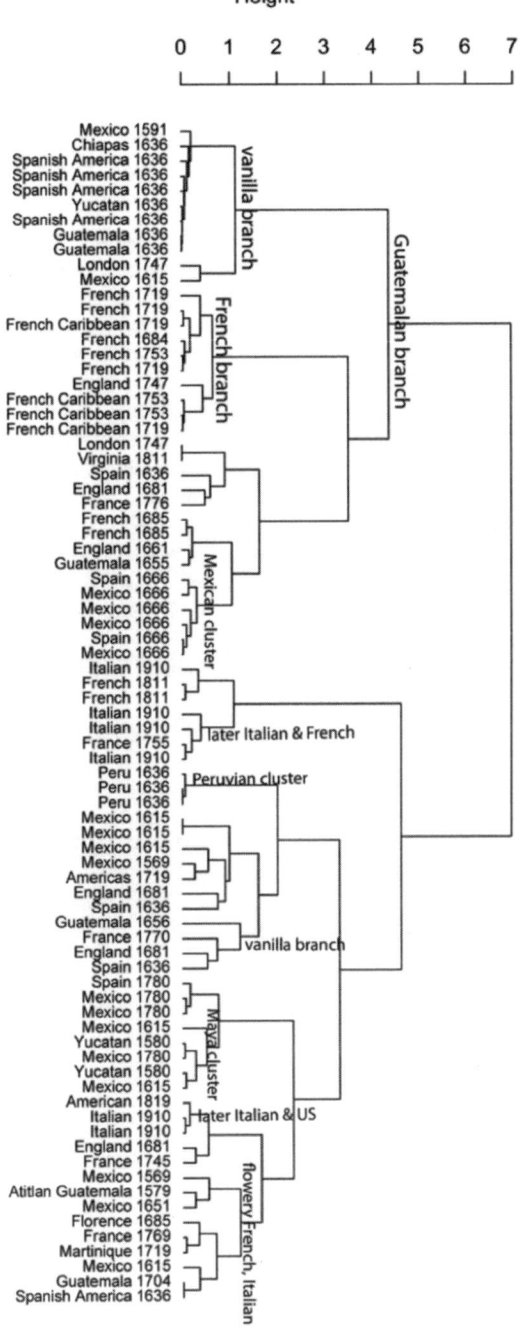

Figure 10. Family tree of relationships of all recipes considered in this study.

difference through taste. Summaries of regional flavour preferences and a systematic comparison of individual recipes both show that vanilla and chocolate links taste and place earlier than is typically considered in culinary history. It takes time to transform twins into a Manichean duality.

Notes

1. Natasha Macaller, *Vanilla Table: The Essence of Exquisite Cooking from the World's Best Chefs* (London: Jacqui Small, 2013); Maricel E. Presilla, *The New Taste of Chocolate, Revised: A Cultural & Natural History of Cacao with Recipes* (Emeryville, CA: Ten Speed Press, 2009).
2. Michaela DeSoucey, 'Gastronationalism: Food Traditions and Authenticity Politics in the European Union', *American Sociological Review*, 75.3 (2010), 432-55; Stephen Mennell, *All Manners of Food: Eating and Taste in England and France from the Middle Ages to the Present* (New York: Basil Blackwell, 1985); Priscilla Parkhurst Ferguson, 'A Cultural Field in the Making: Gastronomy in 19th-Century France', *American Journal of Sociology*, 104.3 (1998), 597-641; Priscilla Parkhurst Ferguson, *Accounting for Taste: The Triumph of French Cuisine* (Chicago: University of Chicago Press, 2006); Donna R. Gabaccia, *We Are What We Eat: Ethnic Food and the Making of Americans* (Cambridge, MA: Harvard University Press, 1998).
3. *Consuming Geographies: We Are Where We Eat*, ed. by David Bell and Gill Valentine (London: Routledge, Taylor & Francis Group, 1997); Christy Shields-Argeles, 'Imagining the Self and the Other: Food and Identity in France and the United States', *Food, Culture & Society* 7 (2004), 14-28.
4. Rachel Laudan, *Cuisine and Empire: Cooking in World History* (Berkeley: University of California Press, 2013).
5. *Bocabulario de Maya Than*, ed. By René Acuña (México: Instituto de Investigaciones Filológicas, Universidad Nacional Autónoma de México, 1993).
6. Allen M. Young, *The Chocolate Tree: A Natural History of Cacao*, rev ed. (Gainesville: University Press of Florida, 2007).
7. 'Vanilla', *New York Times*, 29 August 1874, p. 6.
8. 'Vanilla', *New York Times*, p. 6.
9. 'Vanilla: Madagascar', *Africa Research Bulletin*, 16 May-15 June 2016, p. 21295.
10. 'Vanilla', *New York Times*, p. 6.
11. JHS, 'Vanilla: Vanilla Extract', *Boston Journal of Chemistry*, 12.7 (1867-1880) [1 January 1878], 74.
12. Henry Bruman, 'The Culture History of Mexican Vanilla', *The Hispanic American Historical Review*, 28.3 (1948), 360-76 (p. 361).
13. Laura Caso Barrera and Mario Aliphat Fernández, 'Cacao, Vanilla and Annatto: Three Production and Exchange Systems in the Southern Maya Lowlands, XVI-XVII Centuries', *Journal of Latin American Geography*, 5.2 (2006), 29-52; 'Mejores son huertos de cacao y achiote que minas de oro y plata: huertos especializados de los Choles del Manche y de los K'ekchi'es', *Latin American Antiquity*, 23.3 (2012), 282-99.
14. JHS, p. 74
15. P Pierre Pomet, *A Compleat History of Druggs* (London: printed for J. and J. Bonwicke, R. Wilkin, S. Birt, T. Ward and E. Wicksteed, 1737), p. 132.
16. Francisco Antonio de Fuentes y Guzmán, *Recordación Florida* (Guatemala: Sociedad de Geografía e Historia de Guatemala, 1933), vol. 2, book 2, chapter 7, p. 100; AGI, Guatemala 151 bis, f. 134v, cited in Caso Barrera and Aliphat Hernández, p. 46.
17. Bruman, p. 368.
18. 'Vanilla', *New York Times*, p. 6.
19. Jennifer Evans, *Aphrodisiacs, Fertility and Medicine in Early Modern England* (Woodbridge, Suffolk, UK: Royal Historical Society, The Boydell Press, 2014).

20 Alonso de Molina, *Vocabulario en lengua castellana y mexicana* (Mexico City: En casa de Antonio de Spinosa, 1571), p. 148; *Le Bon Usage*, p. 36; Pomet, p. 131; Bruman, p. 366.
21 Miriam Hospodar, 'Aphrodisiac Foods: Bringing Heaven to Earth', *Gastronomica*, 4.4 (2004), 82-93 (p. 89).
22 'Birmingham', *The Lancet*, 18 April 1874, p. 569.
23 Joan Bristol and Matthew Restall, 'Potions and Perils: Love-Magic in Seventeenth-Century Afro-Mexico and Afro-Yucatan', in *Black Mexico: Race and Society from Colonial to Modern Times*, ed. by Ben Vinson and Matthew Restall (Albuquerque: University of New Mexico Press, 2009), p. 66.
24 Kathryn Sampeck and Jonathan Thayn, 'Translating Tastes: A Cartography of Chocolate Colonialism', in *Substance & Seduction: Ingested Commodities in Early Modern Mesoamerica*, ed. by Stacey Schwartzkopf and Kathryn Sampeck (Austin: University of Texas Press, 2017), pp. 72-101; Kathryn Sampeck, 'Chocolate, Place, and Space: Cacao Terroir and Pre-Columbian to Early Modern Political Geographies', in *Foodscapes: Food, Space, and Place in a Global Society*, ed. by Carlnita Greene (New York: Peter Lang, 2018), pp. 73-100.
25 The sources considered in this analysis (not cited elsewhere) also include *Vocabulario copioso de las lenguas cakchikel, y jiche,* manuscript in the John Carter Brown Library, Providence, RI, 17th or 18th century; *Relaciones geográficas del siglo XVI: Guatemala*, ed. by René Acuña (Mexico City: Instituto de Investigaciones Antropológicas Universidad Nacional Autónoma de México, 1982[1591]); Juan de Cárdenas, *Problemas y secretos maravillosos de las Indias* (Mexico City: Pedro Ocharte, 1591); *Storia Antica del Messico*, trans. by Francisco Javier Clavijero and Gregorio Biasinim (Cesena: Gregorio Biasini All' Insegna Di Pallade, 1780); Antonio Colmenero de Ledesma, *Della cioccolata : discorso diuiso in quattro parti* (Rome: R[everendissima] C[amerata] A[postolica], 1667); *Thesaurus verborum* […], ed. by Thomás de Coto and René Acuña (Mexico City: Universidad Autónoma de México, 1983[1656]); *Encyclopédie, ou dictionnaire raisonné des sciences, des arts et des métiers* […], ed. by Denis Diderot Jean le Rond d'Alembert (University of Chicago: ARTFL Encyclopédie Project (Autumn 2017 Edition [1753]), ed. by Robert Morrissey and Glenn Roe) <http://encyclopedie.uchicago.edu/> [accessed 29 March 2019]; Philippe Sylvestre Dufour, Antonio Colmenero de Ledesma, and John Chamberlayne, *The Manner of Making of Coffee, Tea, and Chocolate: As It Is Used in Most Parts of Europe, Asia, Africa, and America, with Their Vertues* (London: Printed for William Crook […], 1685); Agustín Farfán, *Tratado brebe de medicina y de todas las enfermedades* (Mexico: Pedro Ochoorta, 1592); Thomas Gage, *A New Survey of the West-India's, Or, The English American,* […], 2nd Ed. (London: E. Cotes, 1655); Hannah Glasse, *The Art of Cookery Made Plain and Easy* (Alexandria: Cottom and Stewart, 1812); Pantaleón de Guzmán, *Compendio de nombres en lengua cakchiquel*, manuscript in the John Carter Brown Library, Providence, RI, 1705; Francisco Hernández, *Qvatro Libros*, manuscript in the John Carter Brown Library, Providence, RI, [1615]; Augustín León Pinelo, *Question moral, si el chocolate quebranta el ayuno eclesiastico* (Madrid: la viuda de Juan González, 1636); François Massialot, *Le Confiturier Royal*[…], 5th ed. (Paris: [veuve Savoye, Le Clerc and others],1776); François Menon, *La Cuisiniere Bourgeoisie* (Paris: Chez Guillyn, 1769); Denis Quélus, *Histoire Naturelle du Cacao et du Sucre* […] (Paris: Chez Laurent d'Houry, 1719); *Carta del Padre Pedro de Morales*, ed. by B. Mariscal Haz (Mexico City: Colección Biblioteca Novohispana, V. Centro de Estudios Lingüísticos y Literarios, El Colegio de México, 2000 [1579]); Francesco Redi, *Bacco in Toscana* (Florence: Piero Matini, 1685); Maria Eliza Ketelby Rundell, *American Domestic Cookery, Formed on Principles of Economy, For the Use of Private Families* (Boston: W. Andrews, 1807); Bernardino de Sahagún, *Historia general de las cosas de nueva España*. Manuscript in the Medicea Laurenziana Library, Florence, 1577 <https://www.wdl.org/en/item/10619/view/1/53/> [accessed 29 March 2019]; Henry Stubbe, *The Indian nectar, or, A discourse concerning CHOCOLATA* (London: J.C. for Andrew Crook, 1662). The results are a synthesis of identifications found in David Mora-Marin, 'The Primary Standard Sequence: Database Compilation, Grammatical Analysis, and Primary Documentation', Report filed with FAMSI, 2004; Dmitri Beliaev, Albert Davletshin, and Alexandre Tokovinine, 'Sweet Cacao and Sour Atole: Mixed Drinks on Classic Maya Ceramic Vases', in Pre-Columbian Foodways: Interdisciplinary Approaches to Food, Culture, and Markets in Ancient

Mesoamerica, ed. by John E. Staller and Michael D. Carrasco (New York: Springer Press, 2010), pp. 257-72; Stephen Houston, David Stuart, and Karl Taube, 'Folk Classification of Classic Maya Pottery', American Anthropologist, 91 (1989), 720-26; David Stuart, 'The Rio Azul Cacao Pot: Epigraphic Observations on the Function of a Maya Ceramic Vessel', American Antiquity, 62.1 (1988), 153-57; David Stuart, 'Hieroglyphs on Maya Vases', in The Maya Vase Book: A Corpus of Rollout Photos of Maya Vases, ed. by Justin Kerr (New York: Kerr Associates, 1989), I, pp. 149-60; David Stuart and others, 'Glyphs on Pots: Decoding Classic Maya Ceramics', in *Sourcebook for the 29th Maya Meetings at Texas*, ed. by David Stuart (Austin: University of Texas at Austin, 2005), pp. 110-97; David Stuart, 'Chili Vessels', Maya Decipherment, 24March 2016 <https://decipherment.wordpress.com/2016/03/24/chili-vessels/> [accessed 29 March 2019]. For the translation of *koxoom mul* in Figure 2, see Kerry Hull, 'An Epigraphic Analysis of Classic-Period Maya Foodstuffs', in *Pre-columbian Foodways: Interdisciplinary Approaches to Food, Culture, and Markets in Ancient Mesoamerica*, ed. by John E. Staller and Michael D. Carrasco (New York: Springer Press, 2010), pp. 235-56.

26 A detailed description of the methodology is available in Sampeck and Thayn.
27 For a map of flavor wheels, see Sampeck.
28 JHS, p. 74.
29 Louis Limery, *A Treatise of All Sorts of Foods, Both Animal and Vegetable* […], (London: T. Osborne in Gray's Inn, 1745).
30 [Nicolas de Blégny], *Le bon usage du chocolat dégraissé*, ed. by Léonard Biet (Paris: les artistes du laboratoire royal du College des quatre nations, between 1687 and 1700), pp. 5, 21, 29.
31 B. Clermont and François Menon, *The Professed Cook; or, The Modern Art of Cookery, Pastry, & Confectionary, Made Plain and Easy* […] (London: C. Richards, 1812).
32 [Lucia Gius], *Manuale di cucina, pasticceria e credenza per l'uso di famiglia;* […] (Venice: tipografia-libreria Emiliana, 1910), pp. 50, 210, 146, 185.
33 Paul Freedman, *Out of the East: Spices and the Medieval Imagination* (New Haven: Yale University Press, 2008).
34 '*Bocabulario de Maya Than*'; Motul II, a Spanish-Mayan Dictionary, photocopy from a Gates reproduction at Tozzer Library, Cambridge, MA (original at the John Carter Brown Library at Brown University, Providence, RI, n.d.); *Solana Dictionary*, Hispanic Society manuscript number b2005, microfilm provided by the Hispanic Society of America, New York, NY, n.d.; Oscar Michelon, *Diccionario de San Francisco* (Graz: Akademische Druck und Verlagsanstalt, 1976).

Replenishing the Seeds that Made Southern Cookery

David S. Shields

Two major projects of systematic seed repatriation have taken place in the United States in the past three decades: the Native Seeds/Search collection, based in Tucson Arizona, and the Carolina Gold Rice Foundation's rebooting of the crop systems of the Southeastern Lowcountry. Dr Gary Nabham and Mahina Drees inaugurated the consolidation of the horticultural legacies of the Tohono O'odham Nation in 1983; their successors have banked 2000 varieties of arid lands-adapted seeds for use of the Native peoples of the American Southwest.[1] I have been involved in the second effort, which began roughly a decade later, to restore the landrace grains, heirloom field crops, and traditional provision crops of the coastal Southeast.[2] This restoration of regional ingredients has fuelled the revival of southern cooking in the past dozen years.[3] The potency of that revival is vividly evidenced in 2018's James Beard Awards, in which Birmingham, Alabama's Highlands Bar and Grill took the prize of national restaurant of the year, and Seattle's one southern restaurant, Junebaby, was named America's best new restaurant.[4] Both chef Frank Stitt and chef Eduard Jordan depend extensively on ingredients that the Carolina Gold Rice Foundation brought back into production.

I highlight the role of culinary professionals here because the restoration was undertaken in response to pleas from chefs such as Donald Barickman and Frank Lee in 1993 about the lack of flavour in the commodity grains and vegetables available in Georgia and the Carolinas.[5] This region's cherished recipes were not producing the flavour kept in the memory of the oldest generation of residents. In 1998 Glenn Roberts formed Anson Mills, a business intent upon providing chefs with the best quality milled heirloom cereals.[6] He and Dr Merle Shepard, head of Clemson University's Coastal Research and Education Centre in Charleston, decided to bring back Carolina Gold Rice, the staple cereal of the Lowcountry, and a grain that had ceased commercial production in Carolina on the eve of World War I.[7] This project formed in 2002. In 2003 I hosted a conference in Charleston on the cuisines of the Lowcountry and the Caribbean.[8] It was unusual in bringing together scholars, chefs, and producers (farmers, fishermen, orchardists). At the end of the conference Glenn Roberts approached me and said, 'I wish it were a cuisine; it was at one time. Cuisines are expressions of growing systems. The only things in the fields growing now that's the same as when the food of this place became famous are okra and collards. All the rest is gone. So much of it is gone we don't even know what was here.' It was then that Roberts made his overture: 'You do research. You could help us know what was here – the rotation crops, provision crops, co-crops – and help us bring them back.'

Bringing back the elements of a degenerate cuisine is a fundamentally different project than collecting the biotic heritage of an indigenous community. Here is what is distinctive about the project undertaken in the American Southeast. We thoroughly researched to determine what had to be brought back before we began searching for plants and seed. In effect we had the histories/stories of every significant plant in the growing system, before we had the first plant.

In much of modern seed saving there is an element of ethnobotanical serendipity. Someone secures seed from an old-timer. Often there is no history or story.[9] The plant doesn't correspond to anything that was known or particularly significant as a historical commercial variety. It has great flavour. It becomes a hit – like the Cherokee Purple Tomato – or not – like over 700 of the 800 bean varieties from Appalachia collected by John Coykendahl of Blackberry Farm, Tennessee.[10]

We proceeded differently. We organized into a foundation. The membership of its board included geneticists, crop scientists, entomologists, millers, historians, and growers. Since our goal was to secure seed and stabilize it in sufficient quantity to make the restored ingredients commercially available to the culinary profession and the public, we only sought the plants that had shaped the cuisine to begin with. Instead of total inclusiveness in one's collecting protocol, we had to know the essential, enduring plants that made the farm, the market, and the culinary culture of the region work.

Since southern cuisine was formed during the agricultural age of experiment in America – that period from 1810 to 1880 responding to the soil crisis occasioned by over-exploiting land with successive plantings of cash crops – one had to filter out the multitude of crops grown experimentally to determine whether they built soil or could supply an alternative to cotton, that most taxing of crops on southern fields.[11] Quinoa, coffee, chocolate, jujube, arrowroot, dasheen, and tea were tried in coastal Carolina and Georgia.

The research – drawn from plantation records, nineteenth-century agricultural journals, seed catalogues, newspaper stories, and experimental station reports of the late nineteenth century – took three years to complete, from 2003 to 2006. We've published the findings in several venues: the garden vegetables (their varieties, dates of introduction, seed suppliers) in my monograph *Southern Provisions* (2015), and the fruit in my website 'Old Southern Orchards' hosted at the University of South Carolina.[12] Here are the landrace cereals that constituted the grain system of the southeastern coast of the United States.

Replenishing the Seeds that Made Southern Cookery

THE GRAIN CROP SYSTEM OF THE LOWCOUNTRY

RICE
Madagascar White-introduced 1690 to 1788
Carolina Gold Rice-introduce 1786 and commercially-produced until 1919
Carolina White Rice – the white husk mutation of Carolina Gold.
Carolina Long Gold Rice 1845 to 1861
Red Bearded Upland rice from Africa, 1789 to *c.* 1900

CORN
Sea Island White Flint Corn pre-contact to present
Guinea Flint Corn 1830 to present
Jimmy Red dent Corn 1850 to present
Stowell's Evergreen Sweet Corn 1850 to 1960
Cocke's Prolific/Marlboro Prolific White Dent Field Corn 1860s to 1930s
Hickory King White Dent Corn 1880 to present

RYE
Seashore Blackseed Rye from 1800 until present
Mountain white rye from 1800 to 1930 in Piedmont Carolina and GA [not yet found]
Abruzzi Rye, since 1904, in inland and northern portions of SC and GA

WHEAT
Madeira durum wheat 1710s until 1790s [projected 2019]
Sicilian durum wheat 1750s to 1861. Introduced by Salzbergers in Ebenezer, Georgia
White May wheat in upland South Carolina 1700 to 1830
Purple Straw Wheat, from 1790s until 1970s

OATS
Brunswick/English black oats 1710s to 1880s
White Barley (potato) oat, 1780s to 1880
White Tartarian oat, 1850 to present
Virginia Gray Winter oats (livestock) 1800 to 1900
Rustless Red Oats (1848 to 1930)

BARLEY
Bere barley 1730 to 1850

PSEUDO CEREALS:

GUINEA CORN
African White Sorghum 1700 to 1920

SWEET SORGHUM
Amber 1855 to present

Seeds

Honey Drip 1870 to present

BUCKWHEAT
White 1730s to present
Black Japanese 1870 to present

All of the grains on this list, except Carolina Long Gold rice and Stowell's Evergreen corn, were landraces – plants improved to a distinct configuration by seed selection by farmers over many plant generations.[13] Flavour was a primary selection criterion for these varieties. Grain flavour was judged on the basis of a simple grain porridge made from the cereals by the grower/breeders.[14] The quality that was sought was wholesomeness.

Wholesomeness is a curious category of flavour. It is different from taste sensations of bitter, sour, salty, or sweet; it is more like umami – or perhaps the whole-body registration of heat from capsicum. It is as much about the body's reaction of satiety as the immediate pulse of flavour. So it is an experience of longer duration, including the beginning of the body's registration of the absorption of carbohydrates. It is both a quality recognized in myriad languages and a gestalt triggered by retronasal smelling tasting of certain chemicals found in food.

I will make a polemic interjection at this point. Wes Jackson and a number of the adherents of permaculture farming have lauded the benefits of perennial grains – particularly kernza.[15] Perrenializing grain forfeits the benefits of annual improvement of cereals in terms of flavour and nutrition that went on for millennia until the agronomic breeding of grains in the late nineteenth century. Let's recall the primordiality of the good flavour/nutrition connection. Every animal from the paramecium to the primate identifies what is edible and nutritious in its environment by chemical signatures registered by its taste buds.[16] The signatures of edibility are hard-wired into the nervous systems and brains of animals. Human beings are one of the few creatures that manipulate their environment to make it more tasty and more nutritious – indeed the telos of agriculture, beyond food security, has been nutriment improvement, a process judged by the taste of plant varieties registered over thousands of growing seasons.

The improvement of landraces with an eye toward flavour would be supplanted in the nineteenth century with the expansion in scale of cereal agriculture. Then other needs framed breeding: the need for disease and pest resistance, heat or cold tolerance, productivity per acre, millability, absence of awns. The landraces remained in the fields, but they were shaped toward different ends, including livestock feed.

Landraces possess both stability of form and adaptability to growing conditions, but at the price of productivity when compared to modern cultivars. Their intrinsic diversity enables them to perform in changeable circumstances – droughts, wet seasons, cold snaps, heat spells. When long cultivated in a particular region, they maintain great fixity in their phenotypic configuration unless seed selected for change; these are called autochthonous landraces. But with the rise of the grain seed market in the nineteenth century, landraces became spread across the continent. Colonial South Carolina bought its black oat seed from New Brunswick, its oats from Virginia and Pennsylvania. These allochthonous landraces had a penchant for changing in response to new growing conditions – and changing quite rapidly. From the 1830s on, regional agricultural societies policed the varieties and formulated ideals for production and configuration. For instance, the Winyah Society in the Pee Dee Region of South Carolina annually took a random wineglass full of rice seed to count the number of red weed rice seeds in different members' crops. The one with the fewest became the chief seedsman for the Society for the year.

The deviation in form and quality among allochthonous landraces, the move away from taste as a breeding criteria, the move toward hybridization with agronomic aims, and the supplanting of old strains with new more productive varieties, all led to a situation early in this century where the surviving plant material had lost much of its focus. Even strains preserved in the United States Department of Agriculture's Germplasm Resources Information Network (GRIN) had been grown out on three-year cycles to maintain viability; there had been no systematic effort to improve the landrace. So when we brought back the grains, we found that we had to focus the genetics somewhat – enough for consistency of form and taste for a variety to have market identity. Dr Anna McClung of the USDA took the surviving strains of Carolina Gold and bred Carolina Gold select, the current variety grown and marketed in the South.[17] It was an F_5 improved landrace, still possessing some genetic diversity to assist in adapting to climate and *terroir*. F_6 (the current ideal for open pollinated grains and vegetables in commercial production) is too narrowly bottlenecked in its genetics in our opinion. We concur with the approach pioneered by Dr Steve Jones of Washington State University.[18]

What ideals did Dr McClung maintain in her efforts to conform Carolina Gold? Fortunately a substantial agricultural literature survives from the 1820s through 1860s describing its habit and form. There was also ample literary testimony concerning the signature starch bloom that this variety possesses when put into the mouth – that texture and taste that conveys wholesomeness and permits the marrying of other flavours onto its matrix.

The amount of seed one needs to generate in order to make a grain commercially viable even as a niche crop is substantial. Numbers of the cereals we revived had survived in minuscule batches of seed: one cob of Jimmy Red Corn, a small sample of sea island white flint corn. Increasing seed rapidly in a few generations does strange things to the seeds, particularly when grown in a locale different from where it survived. The sea island white flint corn lost much of its flavour, and had to be mass selected for five years before enough of its original taste and fragrance had returned to make it marketable. Dr Brian Ward, of Clemson University's Coastal Research and Education Centre south of Charleston, has done the initial grow outs of many of the grains – purple straw wheat, white may wheat, Jimmy Red Corn.[19] In other instances, experienced and talented farmers who specialize in landrace varieties – Glen Roberts, Eufren Ninancaro, Ben

Dubard – do the early grow outs. We do scientific analysis of our results – chemistry, productivity, disease vulnerability, and palatability.

The importance of sensory analysis cannot be overstated. Because we undertook this crop restoration to supply culinary professionals with heritage ingredients possessing classic flavours, we must be sure that the flavour is there. So we test all of our crops repeatedly. While the genetics of the plant are greatly important in the expression of that flavour, they are not wholly determinative. The quality of the water, the condition of the soil, the co-crops and rotation crops, the fertilizers and pest inhibiters all bear on the way a grain tastes. During the initial research into the varieties we undertook from 2003 to 2006, we studied old growing schemes as well, trying to understand how challenges were met in the era before chemical herbicides and pesticides, and before gene editing. We were particularly interested in the way green manures (ploughed in rotation crops such as cowpeas, sorghum, or buckwheat) built tilth. The more robust the microbial population, the more earthworms in a field, the more organic matter that thrives, the more mycological interaction taking place with roots, then one can count on the more uptake of nutrition from the soil. Landraces have greatly extensive and complex roots – significantly more so than green revolution cereals bred for commodity production.[20] Those extensive root systems only operate optimally when the soil in which a grain is planted (a) has not been sterilized, and (b) does not have the entirety of its nutritive matter injected into the soil in the form of petroleum derived chemical supplements. Landrace roots evolved to interact with living soil.

Risks attend growing landraces using the methods of conventional agriculture. The fertilizer packages trigger excessive growth. Landrace corn can grow fifteen feet tall and blow down (lodge) with the first wind storm. Rye becomes leafy instead of heady. These varieties were shaped at a time when water and fertilizer were scare, when bugs were ubiquitous, and when weed pressure was greatly competitive and not well managed by people. One has to cultivate these varieties in a way that recognizes these propensities: not simply organic farming, but a generally careful way of handling growth. One of the things the Carolina Gold Rice Foundation has done has been to assist farmers in learning how these old crops behave.

Whenever I inform twenty-first-century grain breeders of our project, they are quick to criticize: these plants have no inbred resistance to fusarium, or anthracnose, or downy mildew, or a host of pests. They are surprised to learn how clean the grains have been in trial grow outs. But they shouldn't, for they have all been schooled about the 'Red Queen effect'.[21] That is, pathogens co-evolve to interact with the latest forms of grain dominating the fields of America. Because of the rapidity of their evolution, new grains with new resistances have to be released at an ever quickening schedule. This further spurs the pathogen's evolution. Alterations happened quickly and substantially in a rather short span of time. And this leads to an odd circumstance. The oldest forms of certain plants are so different genetically from the current commercial field cultivars that the pathogens that afflict today's cereal are no longer key to features of the landrace.

Thus the antique features of the plant grant it an immunity.

With pests the matter is different. Most pests (nematodes are an exception) that characteristically devil a plant family will infest the oldest enduring forms of that family. How does a grower evade the pestilence? First, one does not monocrop the landrace; one does not attempt to cover vast swaths of the landscape with it, for such concentration is a beacon to birds, deer, and bugs. One thing we've done is seek out growing plots in counties where no one else grows a plant in the same family. We avoided the onslaught of the sugar cane aphid last year when the plots growing revived purple ribbon sugar cane were all planted in areas where cane culture lapsed decades ago. Avoidance has minimized insect damage; birds, however, remain a perpetual problem.

Since farmers who embrace one of these renovated cereals will be growing a grain producing fewer bushels per acre than a twenty-first-century commodity cereal, and since they will be planting fewer acres, the grain itself has to command a higher price at the market than standard varieties. Fortunately, better taste and a rich history warrant charging a higher price. The Carolina Gold Rice Foundation believes that obtaining a premium price for landrace product is necessary to attract growers to it. This approach opposes the view of Dr Steve Jones, who seeks to make improved landraces as cheap as commodity varieties, believing that cheapness to the consumer is the greatest good. There is no way, however, that small scale organic grain farmers can compete with mega-farmed cereal producers at the same low price point. Glenn Roberts's Anson Mills, founded in the 1990s, supplies the model for high-price, high-quality landrace grain.

Roberts underwrites the grow out of sixty tons of Carolina Gold Rice seed each year. Because of crop losses due to hurricanes, flooding, and drought in both the Texas rice belt and the Lowcountry in the past three years, Roberts now keeps four years of seed in reserve: a costly but necessary decision, given the loss of two years of seed in 2017. Carolina Gold of all the revived landrace grains is that grown most extensively (nine plantations in South Carolina). Jimmy Red Corn and Seashore black seed rye are the next most extensively grown crops. Because seed of Jimmy Red Corn is given to growers, and growers keep and manage their seed, saving a portion for planting in the following year, the sort of improvement each grower seeks in seed selection is individual. Some are less rigorous in their selection, and one can see a vagrancy in the plants' form and colouration. Since most of this corn goes into the manufacture of bourbon, it may be that growers are exploiting the genetic diversity of the plant, seeking a special character in the strain under their controls. In contrast, the Carolina Gold Rice seed is rigorously policed and assessed several times a growing system by scientists and Glenn Roberts.

Because the market for grain seed is markedly different from that for heirloom vegetables, there is no central seed broker for landrace cereals in the United States. Because landrace grains are in the public domain, no company can claim a proprietary right over the seed or any of the landrace's characteristics. Since the landraces are open-pollinated field crops that lend themselves to seed saving, they do not suit the desire of agribusiness to exercise a monopoly on the cultivar and compel, by hybridizing plant types, a farmer to annually purchase seed (hence the fascination of seed companies with asexual propagation and plant triploids that don't breed true).

At the present time there is no commercial entity that has stepped forward to be a commercial brokerage for landrace seed. Yet I don't think that this absence will continue much longer. One circumstance has arisen recently, incidental to the Carolina Gold Rice Foundation's operation, that is creating interest in landrace grains: the turn in craft distilling to superb tasting corn, wheat, and rye. The success of High Wire distillery's Jimmy Red Corn Bourbon, in particular, has made distillers across the South look to heirloom grains. I have recently consulted with distillers in Kentucky, Tennessee, South Carolina, and Virginia about the historic grains most closely connected with the spirits of their regions. Because the demand is large, intense, and quite specific for certain landrace varieties (Purple Straw Wheat, Seashore black seed rye, Jimmy Red Corn, Leaming Yellow Corn, Hickory King Corn, Webb Improved Watson Corn, Cocke's Prolific, and Bloody Butcher Corn), the money that would permit a major expansion of landrace corn planting is now changing hands. Having a reliable source of supply for seed corn and landrace wheat and rye would make the distillers secure in a knowledge that the flavour of their releases would remain superlative into the future. Bob Perry of the University of Kentucky is currently organizing a guild of craft distillers as a venue where growers can debate the merits of various methods and ingredients in the mash. This will be, I suspect, a threshold event, instilling in the field of southern landrace cultivation an expanded sense of scale of cultivation. Distillers, being better monetized than bakers and most chefs, will pay more for good tasting corn, wheat, or rye. Bakers and cooks will benefit from this move by the distilling industry.

In the absence of commercial seed houses for landrace grains, one sees another set of institutions step in to insure that the horticulture legacies of many ancient cultures are not relegated to the ice vault or agribusiness breeding collection. Certain universities have taken an interest in keeping the world's most historically resonant flavours alive. Foundations, too, have undertaken some of the work of growing out and distributing seed. Growers' guilds, such as the Grand Prairie Grain Guild, also insure that the ideal of crop improvement remains vital in the consciousness of grain cultivators. A select group of small heirloom seed companies have embraced a few signal grain projects: I think particularly of John Scher Seeds and Dancing Star Farm Seeds. But we stand at a transitional moment. Will the six agribusinesses who control the seed market swoop in once they see that heirloom seed generates profit, despite their inability to assert proprietary control over the varieties? Will the universities generate a network of seed suppliers for landraces? There is a point that we are fast approaching where the Carolina Gold Rice Foundation will not be able financially or logistically to distribute landrace seed gratis to all who wish it. And it is not at all certain that distributing starter seed to farmers to do their own bulk up and improvement will prevent strains from declining given the absence of grower organizations and guilds to monitor seed purity. Still, considering the state of affairs in 2018 with that in 2000, one can only feel gratified that all but one of the original landrace cereals for our region have been found and are now in the ground ready for use and improvement.

Notes

1. 'Our Story', *Native Seed/SEARCH* <https://www.nativeseeds.org/pages/history-mission> [accessed 29 March 2019]; Gary Paul Nabham, *Enduring Seeds: Native American Agriculture and Wild Plant Conservation* (Tucson: University of Arizona Press, 2002).
2. 'Home', *Carolina Gold Rice Foundation* <http://www.thecarolinagoldricefoundation.org> [accessed 29 March 2019]; David S. Shields, 'Introduction', *The Golden Seed: Writings on the Culture of Carolina Gold Rice*, ed. by David S. Shields (Charleston: Carolina Gold Rice Foundation, 2007), pp. iii-xi.
3. Burkhard Bilger, 'True Grits: In Charleston, a Quest to Revive Authentic Southern Cooking', *New Yorker*, 31 October 2011, pp. 40-53.
4. 'The 2018 James Beard Award Winners', *James Beard Foundation* <https://www.jamesbeard.org/blog/the-2018-james-beard-award-winners> [accessed 29 March 2019].
5. Donald Barikman was chef of Magnolias Restaurant in Charleston in the 1990s; Frank Lee was chef at The Colony House where he sought the aid in forming the menu from another important voice descrying the loss of original ingredients in the region's cuisine, John Martin Taylor. *Taylor's Hoppin' John's Lowcountry Cooking* (New York: Bantam Books, 1992) was the first publication to alert the public to the problem of ingredient loss on the quality of the region's cooking. Chef Elizabeth Terry in Savannah was the first in that city to voice concerns.
6. 'Glenn Roberts', *Anson Mills* <http://ansonmills.com/biographies> [accessed 29 March 2019]; Chris Chamberlin, 'Anson Mills Boss Glenn Roberts Is the Guy to Know for Heirloom Grains in America', *Food Republic*, 6 April 2015 <http://www.foodrepublic.com/2015/04/06/anson-mills-boss-glenn-roberts-is-the-guy-to-know-for-heirloom-grains-in-america/> [accessed 29 March 2019].
7. Dr Merle Shepard speaks of the origins of the revival of Carolina Gold and his initiative to create an aromatic version of the non-aromatic Carolina Gold to be named Charleston Gold <https://www.youtube.com/watch?v=EkV12zr3J0A>.
8. Co-sponsored by the College of Charleston's Program in the Carolina Lowcountry and Atlantic World and Johnson & Wales University of Charleston. Dr Jeffrey M. Pilcher was program chair of the conference; I was director of the program hosting the event.
9. North America's major sponsor of seed saving is the Seed Saver's Exchange in Decorah Iowa. As this public appeal to seek out seed stories for the 80% of the SSE collection (20,000 varieties) that lack histories indicates, the modern norm of seed saving is retaining material whose value and historical importance is largely unknown <https://www.seedsavers.org/how-to-share-seed-stories> [accessed 29 March 2019].
10. The story of the discovery of the Cherokee Purple Tomato is one of the classic seed saving narratives of the past quarter century in the United States: the variety corresponds to nothing in seed catalogues (Eliza Barclay, 'Cherokee Purple: The Story Behind One of Our Favorite Tomatoes', *The Salt*, NPR, 18 August 2015 <https://www.npr.org/sections/thesalt/2015/08/18/432771713/cherokee-purple-the-story-behind-one-of-our-favorite-tomatoes> [accessed 29 March 2019]). John Coykendall and Bill Best (of Berea, Kentucky) are the two most important bean collectors of the mountain South. Both are totalizers, seeking every bean to register the extent of biological diversity in this indigenous family of pulses (Rose Kennedy, 'Knoxville's Seed-Saver to the World, John Coykendall', *Knoxville Mercury*, 15 April 2015 <http://www.knoxmercury.com/2015/04/15/john-coykendall-knoxvilles-seed-savior-to-the-world/> [accessed 29 March 2019].
11. Shields, 'Introduction, Special Issue: American Food in the Age of Experiment', *Common-Place*, 11.3 (April 2011) <http://www.common-place-archives.org/vol-11/no-03/intro/> [accessed 29 March 2019].
12. Shields, *Southern Provisions: The Creation and Revival of a Cuisine* (Chicago: University of Chicago

Press, 2015), pp. 41-49; 'Orchard', Old Southern Orchards <http://www.digitalussouth.org/oldsouthernorchards/index.php> [accessed 29 March 2019].

13 A term in use in biology since 1908, the current understanding of landrace is summarized in Francesc Casañas and others, 'Toward an Evolved Concept of Landrace', *Frontiers of Plant Science,* 8.145 (February 6, 2017) <https://www.ncbi.nlm.nih.gov/pmc/articles/PMC5296298/> [accessed 29 March 2019].

14 Jill Neimark, 'Porridge, the Food that Built Empires, Stages a Savory Comeback', *The Salt, NPR,* 27 October 2016 <https://www.npr.org/sections/thesalt/2016/10/27/499358436/porridge-the-food-that-built-empires-stages-a-savory-comeback> [accessed 29 March 2019].

15 I made this point in a debate with Wes Jackson that took place at Slow Food Nations, Denver, July 2017.

16 John McQuaid, *Tasty: The Art and Science of What We Eat* (New York: Scribner, 2016), pp. 17-23.

17 Alfredo Flores, 'ARS Scientists Aid Revival of Historic American Rice', *USDA Agricultural Research Service News,* 18 August 2005 <https://www.ars.usda.gov/news-events/news/research-news/2005/ars-scientists-aid-revival-of-historic-american-rice/> [accessed 29 March 2019].

18 Steven S. Jones, 'Kicking the Commodity Habit: On Being Grown Out of Place', *Gastronomica,* 12 (2012), 74-77.

19 Scott Miller, 'Clemson Research Feeds Restaurants and Farms with a Long Lost Crop', *The Newsstand,* 24 February 2016) <http://newsstand.clemson.edu/mediarelations/clemson-researcher-feeds-restaurants-farms-with-long-lost-crop/> [accessed 29 March 2019].

20 J. G. Waines and B. Ehdale, 'Domestication and Crop Physiology: Roots of Green-Revolution Wheat', *Annals of Botany,* (2007), 991-98.

21 Leigh Van Valen, 'A New Evolutionary Law', *Evolutionary Theory,* 1 (1973), 1-30.

Traditional Crops: The Case of Bambara Groundnut

Hanna Simonsen

The Tanzanian region of Kagera is situated in the north of the country, bordering Rwanda to the west, Lake Victoria to the east, and Uganda to the north. Bambara groundnut, a legume, is cultivated by the small-scale farmers there. In the rainy season the headman of a village selects a plot of the village's communal grassland, which will only be cultivated for one season as the next year a new plot will be selected. The headman performs a ceremony to inaugurate the land, and subsequently the women of the village divide the land between them. Each woman is assigned a plot that corresponds to the size of her family; she will be the one tending the bean. Further south in Tanzania, in Dodoma, bambara groundnut is also cultivated. But here it is cultivated on one of the farmers' fields, in rotation with other crops, tended by both men and women.

Bambara groundnut is cultivated and consumed all over sub-Saharan Africa. It is described as delicious and as a food that 'feeds well'. Its original Latin name was *Voandzeia subterranean*, and it is argued that it originates from the Malagasy term '*Voanjo*' which consists of two parts: '*voa*' meaning 'seed' and '*anjo*' being 'the one which satisfies well' (Doku and Karikari 1969). Its current Latin name is *Vigna Subterranea* (L.) Verdc, but here it will be referred to by its common name, bambara groundnut, which comes from the tribe Bambara, mainly living in Mali (Hepper 1963).

Customarily it is a woman's crop, meaning that only women cultivate it, and it is also custom to cultivate it on plots of land furthest away from the homestead – much as in Kagera where grassland is used. There are ceremonies and taboos linked to this bean, many having something to do with gender. While many crops presently cultivated on the African continent, such as maize, were introduced by Europeans, bambara groundnut is a traditional crop with a long history in African agriculture (Linnemann and Azam-Ali, 1993, Adzawla and others 2015). Due to its traditional role and delicious taste, it is well known and consumed well outside its growing areas, such as in the mountain regions where it is too cold for its cultivation (Ntundu 1995).

The cultivation of bambara groundnut has a long history. Arabs described what is presumed to be bambara groundnut, '*gerti*', in 1380. It spread to the Americas through the slave trade; there are reports of bambara groundnut roasted in the streets of Rio de Janeiro and traded among the black population (Doku and Karikari 1971). At the

African-American History Museum in Detroit, bambara groundnut is displayed as one of the crops that slaves brought with them from their homelands and cultivated in what became the United States. As with many other traditional crops, bambara groundnut was replaced when the crops of the colonial powers were introduced. The groundnut most of us know now has a higher oil content than bambara groundnut, and thus has the greater economic potential of producing plant oil. Consequently bambara groundnut was considered the poor man's crop and not given much attention by colonial powers (Azam-Ali and others 2001).

Production volumes are hard to establish, but it is reported to be the third most consumed legume in sub-Saharan Africa (Mkandawire 2007, Hillocks and others 2011). It rarely reaches markets, in part due to its status as a food security crop which smallhold farmers are unwilling to sell (Hillocks and others 2011, Ntundu 1995). Moreover, bambara groundnut consists of low yielding, genetically diverse landraces, without well-established best agronomic practices; thus its cultivation is not considered a priority as cropping systems change (Linnemann and Azam-Ali 1993, Ntundu 1995). As a result, bambara groundnut risks being pushed out of cultivation (Ntundu 1995) even though it has a number of attributes which make it attractive, especially its high nutritional value (Azam-Ali and others 2001, Amartefio and others 2006, Onimawo and others 1998, Yao and others 2015), its resistance to abiotic stresses such as poor soils (Azam-Ali and others 2001, Toungos and others 2009) and drought (Linnemann and Azam-Ali 1993, Karikari and Tabona 2004, Mwale and others 2005, Berchie and others 2012), and its cultural importance (Goli and others 1995, Ntundu 2002, Anchirinah and others 2001).

An Orphaned Crop

This threat to bambara groundnut makes it an orphaned crop (Azam-Ali and others 2001). 'Orphaned' crops or cultivars are those considered neglected, underutilized, or minor (IPGRI 2002). These crops generally have nutritional or agronomical importance or potential, especially for poorer farmers (IPGRI 2002). In addition, they often have attributes that formally bred varieties lack, especially drought tolerance and yield stability under changing climatic conditions – attributes frequently lost when common crops have been bred to produce higher yields (Cleveland and others 1994, Padulosi and others 2011, Mayes and others 2011). Yet, orphaned crops are falling into disuse as they cannot compete with formally bred varieties on parameters such as yield, support by extension services, or other cultural, economic, and agronomic issues (Padulosi, S. and Hoeschle-Zeledon, I. 2004). This trend is accelerated as local knowledge of cultivation practices and crop use is lost through rural exodus and urbanization (Nass and others 2009).

Bambara Groundnut in Two Regions in Tanzania

Bambara groundnut is therefore simultaneously an important source of protein for many families in Tanzania and an orphaned crop. An interview study has been carried out to get some insight into what factors might compensate for the comparably low

Traditional Crops: The Case of Bambara Groundnut

yield. When possible, the interviews were complemented with informal talks. Key criteria considered included the crop's cultural importance, ability to grow on poor soils, and better drought tolerance than other legumes.

A total of fifty-eight interviews were carried out in several villages in the regions of Dodoma and Kagera. In each region a local extension officer was contacted who selected the villages and invited bambara groundnut farmers to participate. The contacted farmers were asked to spread the message in the village, and finally all gathered in the selected interview location. The interviewees each represented a household.

In both regions agriculture is the predominant activity. However, Dodoma is drier and, as the region of the capital, better-connected through infrastructure than Kagera. When the study was carried out, Kagera was not connected with a paved road to the capital.

In the discussion below, when something is described as equal or not equal, that judgement is based on a fisher test for categorical data (data recorded as characteristics not numbers) and a t-test for continuous data (data recorded as a measurement of a number).

Cultural Importance

In this study, farmers in Kagera and Dodoma equally describe bambara groundnut as a crop to which cultural beliefs are associated, according to roughly a third of the interviewees in each region. However, when those that had associated cultural beliefs with the crop were asked to identify those beliefs, the character of the answers differed between the regions. In Dodoma, the crop was frequently associated with the supernatural, unlike in Kagera. In Dodoma, farmers believed that cultivating bambara groundnut in the same field for two consecutive seasons would result in severe yield loss and/or cause death in the family. Furthermore it was reported that women outside the family or having their period were not allowed to enter the fields, as this was believed to cause the pods to rot or to cause death in the family. The farmers explained that while bambara groundnut was only cultivated by women in the past, this practice has changed. In Kagera, farmers mentioned that men were not traditionally allowed to cultivate, harvest, or prepare bambara groundnut. But crop-related beliefs with a supernatural component were also mentioned: two women explained that bambara groundnut is not supposed to be cultivated across the slope as this would affect the fertility of the men. Additionally they mentioned that it is important for the women to give the first harvest to their parents-in-law, and women believed they have to cultivate bambara groundnut to 'keep their men strong and happy'.

A Woman's Responsibility

In Kagera only women cultivate bambara groundnut; it was emphasized that this was tradition. A woman's children are allowed to help her in the bambara groundnut field, although the male children are only allowed to help until they get married. When there was money and need, hired labour was used, and in this case men were allowed to work the crop. In Dodoma, the interviews revealed that bambara groundnut had previously been a crop cultivated only by women, but the situation had changed: now the most common scenario was that the whole family participated in cultivation. The farmers explained that with the whole family participating they could finish the tasks faster. Still, a little more than half of the farmers in Dodoma considered shelling the crop to be something that should be carried out by women. The reason given was that men and boys would not do the job as thoroughly as women or girls. When it came to selling the crop, some families thought it was better to send a woman to the market because 'they are better than men at manipulating the price'. Others explained that the lack of a market in the village, the nearest one being in the capital Dodoma, made it a task for men.

For Consumption and Subsistence

In Kagera, 35% of farmers considered bambara groundnut solely as a subsistence crop, while in Dodoma almost everyone considered it to be both a subsistence and cash crop. However, there was no difference between the regions in regards to the proportion of the harvest that was consumed or sold.

When not in season, the large majority of people in Kagera did not consume bambara groundnut, while it was common in Dodoma to consume it every week. However, during the harvesting season bambara groundnut was consumed daily by most people in Kagera; in Dodoma, most ate it about four times a week. Most farmers in Kagera sought to sell the share they wanted to trade as soon as possible after harvest, while farmers in Dodoma usually waited a little to get a higher price.

In Kagera, bambara groundnut was consumed fresh, boiled, or roasted. In Dodoma, it was also milled into flour or prepared as a paste. In Dodoma, the red-seeded landrace was often mentioned as the one to use for the local dish '*kande*', a bean and maize mixture, while the white-seeded landrace was perceived as better for '*ugali*', a kind of polenta. In Kagera some farmers considered the more popular red-seeded type suitable to cook with bananas. A common way to prepare bambara groundnut would be to boil it with sweet potato and cassava.

Apart from serving as food six (of thirty-three) respondents in Dodoma used the crop as a medicinal plant. Four respondents reported it to be good for constipation, especially when cooked with papaya. The two other respondents reported that the red- and the black-seeded types both had medicinal value.

As a Cash Crop

None of the villages had their own market: most farmers sold their bambara groundnut from their homes, or combined that practice with either using a middleman or going to a market. In Kagera it was more common for the farmers to take their crop to a market themselves, whereas in Dodoma a middleman was more frequently employed.

The regions differed in how they considered the price. A fifth of the farmers in

Traditional Crops: The Case of Bambara Groundnut

Kagera considered it to be high, whereas no one in Dodoma considered the price to be high – indeed the majority considered it to be low.

In Kagera farmers were more positive about the marketability of the crop, compared to other legumes, as they considered it somewhat easier to sell (some considered it very easy to sell).

Tolerance to Poor Soils

In Dodoma, bambara groundnut cultivation varied between fallow land and continuously cultivated land. The farmers choosing fallow land all reported that they did so because of soil fertility reasons. Of the ones who only used continuously cultivated land, all but one did so because they did not have enough land to practice fallowing.

In Kagera, where the crop is cultivated on grassland, further from the homestead, one of the women explained that 'the crop does not like normal cropland'; she had been trying to cultivate bambara groundnut close to her house, as she does with her other legumes, but she said that because the crop 'does not like shade it did not grow well there'. A farmer in Dodoma made a similar statement. In one of the villages in Kagera, all of the women intercropped bambara groundnut with cassava. They reported that the crop did worse when intercropped, but, because an increase in weevil damage was reducing the harvest of bambara groundnut, they were supplementing that harvest with another crop.

Neither region commonly used any kind of fertilizer. The most common comment in both Kagera and Dodoma was that it is not needed. In Dodoma there was awareness about the crop's ability to fix nitrogen. In both regions, concern was raised about increased levels of pests and diseases as a consequence of fertilizer use. Only in Kagera did the farmers mention access and cost as the reason why they did not consider fertilizer use.

Drought Tolerance

A majority of the farmers did not consider bambara groundnut drought tolerant in comparison to other legumes. However 39% (thirteen) of respondents in Dodoma did think it needed less water than other crops. Additionally, a large majority of the farmers in Dodoma considered excessive rain to be a bigger problem than drought.

Bambara Groundnut's Continued Place in the Farming System

A few factors indicated that the Kagera farmers were in a harder economic situation than those in Dodoma. The interviews revealed that they owned less land and had, in general, bigger families. These factors may account for why they sold their harvest earlier rather than waiting for a better price.

In both regions there continued emphasis on this crop's cultural role, but only in Kagera was it still a women's crop. That used to be the case in Dodoma too, and it could be speculated that this change in attitude might be due to the lack of land for fallowing in Dodoma and also to the relative proximity to the coast, Dar es Salaam, and tourism. An extension officer claimed that people in Kagera are more shy and traditional than in Dodoma. Even though the attitude towards the crop in Dodoma had shifted towards the less traditional involvement of men, they also more often mentioned superstitions, though perhaps because of that aforementioned openness.

Whereas cultural reasons to keep growing this crop in Dodoma seem to be diminishing, there was a higher awareness there, compared to Kagera, of the benefits it could have as a nitrogen-fixing legume. In Dodoma, there were also more farmers who considered it to be somewhat drought resistant than in Kagera. So, while cultural reasons may still be very important to its continued cultivation in Kagera, more practical agricultural concerns may be significant in Dodoma.

References

Adzawla, W., and others. 2015. 'Technical Efficiency in Bambara Groundnut Production in Northern Ghana', *UDS International Journal of Development*, 2.2: 37-49.

Amartefio, J.O., O. Tibe, and R.M. Njogu. 2006. 'The Mineral Composition of Bambara Groundnut (*Vigna subterranea* (L.)) Verdc Grown in Southern Africa', *African Journal of Biotechnology*, 5: 2408-11.

Azam-Ali, S., and others. 2001. 'Assessing the Potential of an Underutilized Crop: A Case Study using Bambara Groundnut', *Experimental Agriculture*, 37: 433-72.

Berchie, J.N., and others. 2012. 'Evaluation of Five Bambara Groundnut (*Vigna subterranea* (L.) Verdc.) Landraces to Heat and Drought Stress at Tono-Navrongo, Upper East Region of Ghana', *African Journal of Agricultural Research*, 7.2: 250-56.

Cleveland, A., S. Daniela, and S.E. Smith. 1994. 'Do Folk Crop Varieties Have a Role in Sustainable Agriculture?', *Bioscience*, 44: 740-51.

Doku, E.V., and S.K. Karikari. 1971. 'Bambara Groundnut', *Economic Botany*, 25: 255-62.

Ezesika, O.C., and others. 2012. 'Factors Influencing Agbiotech Adoption and Development in Sub-Saharan Africa', *Nature Biotechnology*, 30.1: 38-40.

Hepper, F.N., 1963. 'Plants of the 1957-58 West Africa Expedition: The Bambara Groundnut (*Voandzeia subterranea*) and Kersting's Groundnut (*Kerstingiella geocarpa*) Wild in West Africa', *Kew Bulletin*, 16: 395-407.

Hillocks, R.J., C. Bennett, and O.M. Mponda. 2011. 'Bambara Nut: A Review of Utilization, Market Potential and Crop Improvement', *African Crop Science Journal*, 20.1: 1-16.

IPGRI. 2002. *Neglected and Underutilized Plant Species: Strategic Action Plan of the International Plant Genetic Resources Institute* (Rome: International Plant Genetic Resources Institute).

Karikari, S.K., and T.T. Tabona. 2004. 'Constitutive Traits and Selective Indices of Bambara Groundnut (*Vigna subterranea* (L) Verdc) Landraces for Drought Tolerance under Botswana Conditions', *Physics and Chemistry of the Earth*, 29: 1029-34.

Linnemann, A.R., and S. Azam-Ali. 1993. 'Bambara Groundnut (*Vigna subterranea*)', in *Pulses and Vegetables*, ed. by J.T. Williams (London: Chapman and Hall, London), pp. 13-58.

Mayes, S., and others. 2011. 'The Potential for Underutilized Crops to Improve Security of Food Production', *Journal of Experimental Botany*, 63.3: 1075-79 <10.1093/jxb/err396>.

Mkandawire, C.H. 2007. 'Review of Bambara Groundnut (*Vigna subterranea* (L.) Verdc.) Production in Sub-Saharan Africa', *Agricultural Journal*, 2.4: 464-70.

Mwale, S.S., S.N. Azam-Ali, and F.J. Massawe. 2005. 'Growth and Development of Bambara Groundnut (*Vigna subterranean*) in Response to Soil Moisture 1. Dry Matter and Yield', *European Journal of Agronomy*, 26: 345-53.

Ntundu, W. H., 1995. 'Tanzania Country Report', in *Bambara Groundnut (Vigna subterranea (L.) Verdc.): Promoting the Conservation and Use of Underutilized and Neglected Crops, Proceedings of the Workshop on Conservation and Improvement of Bambara Groundnut (Vigna subterranea (L.) Verdc.), 14-16 November 1995, Harare, Zimbabwe*, ed. by J. Heller, F. Begemann, and J. Mushonga (Rome: Institute of Plant Genetics and Crop Plant Research, Gatersleben/Department of Research and Specialist Services, Harare/International Plant Genetic Resources Institute), pp. 53-58.

Onimawo, I.A, A.H. Momoh, and A. Usman. 1998. 'Proximate Composition and Functional Properties of Four Cultivars of Bambara Groundnut', *Plant Foods for Human Nutrition*, 53: 153-58.

Padulosi, S. and I. Hoeschle-Zeledon. 2004. 'Underutilized Plant Species: What Are They?', *LEISA Magazine*, 20.1: 5-6.

Padulosi, S., and others. 2011. 'Underutilized Species and Climate Change: Current Status and Outlook', *Crop Adaptation to Climate Change*, ed. by S.S. Yadav and others (New York: Wiley), pp. 507-21.

Toungus, M.D., A.A. Sajo, and D.T. Gungula. 2009. 'Recommended Fertilizer Levels on Bambara Groundnut (*Vigna Subterranea* (L) Verde) in Yola Adamawa State, Nigeria', *Agricultural Journal*, 4: 14-21.

Yao, D.N., and others. 2015. 'Nutritive Evaluation of the Bambara Groundnut C_{i12} Landrace [*Vigna subterranea* (L.) Verc. (*Fabaceae*)] Produced in Côte d'Ivoire', *International Journal of Molecular Sciences*, 16: 21428-41.

Seeds

Zoochory

Raymond Sokolov

> The civets [...] are among the most important seed-dispersers in the forests of Asia and Africa. They are nocturnal animals possessing a great skill in climbing trees in the jungle. They live on small birds, but more largely on fruits, which they probably find by scent. The common Musang or Palm Civet of Malaya (*Viverra malacensis*) was very abundant in Singapore, often living in the roofs of houses. It leaves its abode at dusk and wanders about in search of food most of the night. Some living in my house returned regularly at 9 o'clock to the nest, and went out later, returning again at sunrise. It is very destructive to cultivated fruits, and I have seen in the excreta the seeds of coffee, [as well as] *Gnetum sylvestre* [...]. In the days of Coffee cultivation this and other civets fed largely on the Coffee berries, and when the Coffee estates extended round the Baru caves in Selangor, I often saw in distant dark parts of the caves small groups of white etiolated seedlings of Coffee which had sprung up from the excreta of these animals, which retire to these dark shady spots in the day-time. The civets have the habit of voiding their excreta on bare spots, such as jungle paths or open patches in the forests, places highly suitable for the seedlings, as giving them more light and a better chance of developing. Coffee seeds so voided in open spots on the estate were at one time much valued by the planters, and boys were employed to collect them. They were known as Monkey Coffee or Green Coffee, and fetched a higher price in the market, as the animals, civets and monkeys, always selected the finest fruit to eat.
>
> H.N. Ridley, *The Dispersal of Plants Throughout the World*, 1930[1]

In our era of mass agriculture, where the seeds of edible plants are mechanically distributed in ploughed furrows or drilled into the ground at intervals favourable for germination, we easily overlook the myriad primordial ways that the vast majority of all flowering plants (angiosperms, plants with enclosed seeds, the phylum whose members overwhelmingly outnumber all other plants) once and still also colonize the world with no help at all from *H. sapiens*.

Human agency is only one factor, and a relatively recent one, in the Darwinian survival of plant species. Wind also carries seeds to their destiny. Seeds by the millions float downstream or wash ashore on ocean waves. And they hitch rides with birds and

Zoochory

bats, rats and tigers. Sometimes, a burred seed will cling to the fur of a passing creature and travel with that squirrel or buffalo for miles. Sometimes, animals will eat the fleshy outer part of the fruit and cast the seed off in the distance. In still other cases, and these are the ones I will be considering primarily here, animals will eat an attractive fruit, seed and all, digesting the delicious fleshy outer portion of a peach or other drupe and then excrete the inedible stone in its dung, far from the plant that grew it. Or the animal may consume the soft desirable pith and regurgitate the unassimilable seed after moving it to new ground. Often their sojourn in the stomachs of beasts changes seeds and improves their chances of growth.

So, shitting and spitting are two major ways that animals have assisted the spread of the angiosperm billions around the planet from prehistoric times to our day.

The technical word for this mechanism is zoochory, one of dozens of similar botanical terms for the multiple varieties of seed dispersal. Botanists have formed them from pairs of ancient Greek words. The first half denotes the force or creature involved in seed transportation, which in turn is expressed by -chory, derived from the verb χωρέω, *choréo*, meaning, among many other things, 'spread abroad', as in a reputation.

There are a score of these -ochory words: for example, anemochory (wind), myrmecochory (ants), chiropterochory (bats). The -ochory lexicon includes various special cases of zoochory: epizoochory (seeds attached to the exterior of an animal), endozoochory (seeds consumed by an animal), and diploendozoochory (in which an animal ingests a seed and is then itself ingested by another animal while still with seed – perhaps this should be called turduckenochory).

This hilariously pedantic vocabulary originated in the restless mind of a giant of nineteenth-century biology, the German polymath Ernst Haeckel (1834-1919). Among his many achievements, Haeckel was a prodigious coiner of words, including phylum, stem cell, and, in 1914, 'first world war'. Long before that, in 1866, the year he met with Darwin and the pioneering geologist Charles Lyell at Darwin's home in England, he invented the word 'ecology', a concept of lasting power, and paired it with 'chorology', a general term for plant dispersal that, shall we say, never caught on.[2]

But chorology's spawn still swarm in the special botanical literature that focuses on seed dispersal. Meanwhile, without its proper name, zoochory reaches the general public in accounts of invasive species carried to new habitats in the droppings of roving animals and in the symbiotic exploitation of natural zoochory by human beings. Anthropozoochory.

For the most part, however, zoochory proceeds unnoticed by mass media, as it always has, a silent collusion between animals and plants. The most comprehensive source for zoochory as well as the entire planetary phenomenon of chorology is *The Dispersal of Plants Throughout the World* by Henry Nicholas Ridley, Director of Botanic Gardens, Straits Settlements (1855-1955). Ridley spent much of his life in Singapore, immersing himself in the exotic plant world there and in the rest of the surrounding British colony known as the Straits Settlements. He promoted the local rubber industry with such passion that he was nicknamed Mad Ridley. With his walrus moustache and long colonial bachelorhood, he was a sort of Maugham character, imperturbably advancing the imperial mission in the tropics. He was also so eminent that in the botanical literature, a reference to Ridl. needed no further explanation. He married at 83 and died just short of 101. But, to judge from his masterwork on seed dispersal, he was much more than a stereotyped Briton or a taxonomic pedant. Although the 744 pages of *Dispersal* contain much dry listing of plants with their scientific names, Ridley frequently digresses into vivid vignettes of the drama to be found in the movement of seeds, as he himself had experienced it directly or through prodigious reading.

For example, in the course of a panoramic discussion of the zoochoric role of monkeys, he notes that these arboreal creatures generally make a mess of the fruits they attack, breaking branches, dropping as many as they eat in their haste to carry them to a safe place before consuming them in earnest:

> It has been pointed out to me, that *Willughbeia* seed requires to be thrown at the base of, or near, a large tree in order that the climber may have a support to climb on, and this is brought about in the following way: A monkey seizes a fine fruit to eat it, and his companions immediately rush at him to take it away. He scrambles off to the nearest big tree and, getting into the fork or behind a bough, devours it hurriedly for fear of being robbed, throwing the seeds to the comparatively bare ground close up at the foot of the tree, up which the young plant can eventually climb. The seedlings, on developing, by climbing up the bushes and low trees surrounding the bigger one, and, climbing ever higher, reach the top of the bigger trees, where they obtain full sunlight, and eventually form immense masses of foliage, flowering and fruiting plentifully.[3]

This adaptation of *Willughbeia* and monkeys is effective in its messy, antic way at spreading the plant species. It illustrates the basic mammalian zoochoric mechanism – the smell of the sweet fruit flesh attracts the monkey, monkey eats this pith, exposing the seed and improving its chances for germination, which are further enhanced when the monkey throws the seed onto clear ground under the tree where he has taken the fruit: attraction, removal from the mother plant to a better location, consumption of pith, casting of seed to earth.

Fruit bats take this one step further with far greater efficiency and, one might say, elegance, as Ridley witnessed countless times in the forests near his base in Singapore and when they came to mate in droves every ten years in the jungle of his Botanic Gardens.[4] Instead of carrying fruit and dropping it a short distance from the parent plant, they swallow it whole with the seed, digest it in under twenty minutes while in flight, and then, in dark clouds of thousands, expel what is left of their carpal booty miles away in a hail of scat known as seed rain.

Their cargo in other places include fruits of significant size: *Sapotaceae* (sapote, mamey sapote, shea, and argan) and *Mangifera* (mangoes), among others. In the wild,

Zoochory

bats can be their salvation. 'Most of these fruits,' Ridley continues, 'have no method of inland dispersal except by rolling or bounding when fallen from a high tree, and dispersal by mammals, such as bats, or, when they are fallen, by rats, or, in islands, by land-crabs.'[5]

Having reached ground level, Ridley at last turns his attention to the *Carnivora*, beginning with the big cats, or as he would say, *Felidae*. In addition to devouring smaller quadrupeds and straying farm tots, '[t]he tiger is reputed in the Malay Peninsula to be very partial to Durians, and has been known to attack natives carrying baskets of them, and to carry off the fruit'.[6] Avocados also attract a wide range of *Felidae*, including jaguars, as reported by one naturalist who stumbled upon a quartet lolling under a tree, contentedly gnawing on fallen fruit.

Through the Ridley lens, we see jackals wolfing down melons, but *Mustelidae* – that diverse clan of weasels, badgers, mink and wolverines, although the largest family among the carnivores – are a disappointment, zoochorically speaking. Ridley sniffs:

> [...] they do very little in seed dispersal. However, St. John (in *Wild Sports and Natural History of the Highlands*) states that the Marten-Cat (*Mustela martes*) eats wild raspberries and blackberries.
>
> The Skunk (*Mephitis*) lives mainly on animal food, like the badgers, but Dr. Avery reports finding the seed of a Persimmon (*Diospyros*) in the rectum of a skunk in North America.[7]

Ridley has his limitations. He neglects the most important vectors of seed dispersal, which are both the result of human intervention, agriculture and the role of domesticated animals. And when he does focus on *H. sapiens,* we are treated like any other mammal, as inadvertent vectors of seed movement, carriers of seeds caught on our clothing or carried along in mud on our shoes, and, in a passage redolent of the unconscious racism of the past, he retails reports of 'savages' consuming fruit seeds and all, rambutan and durian, and a dubious anecdote about a 'Chinaman' who died from an intestine blocked by 'a vast amount of the seeds of the Mangosteen (*Garcinia mangostana*) he had been in the habit of swallowing with the pulp'.[8]

There is a middle ground, between this narrow view of our species as yet another chorologic organism mindlessly transporting seeds in its gut and on its feet and as a deliberate controller of seeds in ecologically destructive, pesticidal agronomy. I will offer two examples of human collaboration with Ridleian zoochory. Both combine spontaneous or feral fruit consumption by domesticated animals with human exploitation of seeds in excreta resulting from the unplanned feeding.

The more famous case involves Moroccan goats climbing argan trees (*Argania spinosa*) to eat their nuts. Argan oil, highly valued as a food and in cosmetics, is hand-pressed (or was, but is increasingly extracted by machine) from these nuts, which grow in the semi-desert of southwest Morocco near Essaouira. The traditional argan harvest begins with goats, which climb the thorny branches and consume the fruit as well as the leaves. Eventually, after the goats have metabolized the pithy pericarp, they excrete the digestively cleaned nuts in their poop. Local Berbers pick out the nuts by hand and press the oil.

Argan oil is available today at major retail outlets such as Walmart, for shampoo, for a 'toe-smoothing' ointment, and for 'hair butter'. The pure edible oil, almost odourless with a nutty flavour resembling popcorn, is currently advertised at roughly £12 a litre. Profits from the argan boom have benefited the Berber women who dominate the industry. They in turn have invested in goats, a traditional form of wealth, whose greater numbers threaten the survival of the fruit- and leaf-stripped argan forests, despite their designation as a UNESCO biosphere reserve.[9]

At least as picturesque, and more economically important, is the story of the modern domestication of the guava (*Psidium guajava*) by Spanish settlers in what is now Colombia in the mid-sixteenth century.[10]

The guava is a small tree of the myrtle family (*Myrtaceae*) widespread throughout tropical America from prehistoric times. Its name may derive from the language of the indigenous Tainos of Hispaniola. The fruit is round, ovoid or pear-shaped, on the scale of the apple, with a green or yellow rind and flesh ranging in colour from white to pink, filled with many small black seeds and rich in pectin, which makes it gel easily. British children of my generation, including Jane Grigson, learned to loathe it during World War II, when guava jelly replaced more beloved traditional jams made scarce by the hostilities.

Spanish colonial settlers in Colombia faced a different sort of deprivation. They had left behind a traditional conserve made from quince (*Cydonia oblonga*). *Carne de membrillo*, a flat solid cake sold in tins and often served with manchego cheese, is an omnipresent and beloved dessert in Spain, but quince was not adaptable to American tropical conditions.

Spaniards were able to transport cattle (*Bos taurus* AKA Bossy) from the Motherland to plough their sugar cane fields, and those beasts provided the ideal condition for aggressive guavas to establish themselves in unexpected numbers. The cattle disturbed the ground with furrows and, when off duty, they consumed the fruit of nearby wild guavas, depositing the seeds in the cowpies they dropped in the furrows and elsewhere. Before long, fields filled with guava trees, hardy and laborious to extirpate. Soon they had become guava plantations, *guayabales,* and their fruit offered a miraculously convenient substitute for the unobtainable quince.

Colombians soon were producing guava paste with an enthusiasm and pride that survive today. The centre of the industry is in the mountainous department of Santander, deep in the interior, and has been chronicled with verve by Klaus J. Meyer-Arendt.[11]

Capitalizing on the two colours of guava flesh, producers in the village of Velez, a regional centre in indigenous Chibcha country, invented the *bocadillo* (snack), a bicolored quince paste sandwich, with a centre layer of pink paste surrounded by layers of white, wrapped traditionally in the leaf of the bijao (Calathea lutea), which protected the *bocadillo* and imparted its own bouquet, according to Meyer-Arendt.

In Velez and everywhere else at the present moment as it always has, zoochory impinges on human life and the environment. And *H. sapiens* continues to turn this fundamental life force to its own advantage.

Because zoochory, in its estimated ninety-million-year history, has occurred primarily in tropical forests rich in fleshy fruit, the current attempts by scientists and conservationists to harness it or limit its effects usually take place in the same sorts of steamy arboreal locales that dominate Ridley's magisterial survey.[12]

To prevent wild pigs from infiltrating invasive species to the already challenged nesting habitat of a small grey-and-white insectivorous bird in the remote Alakai forest of Kauai, the US Fish and Wildlife Service has put up an eight-foot-high, five-mile-long pig-proof fence. It is also preventing threats to other native species in the same area.[13]

Across the Pacific in southern Mexico, a team of biologists recently began experimenting with fruit bats to see if they could attract them to burnt-out parts of the El Ocote Forest Biosphere Reserve in the State of Chiapas, an old Mayan area that borders Guatemala.[14]

The experimenters baited the sites with halved and peeled mangoes and bananas purchased at local markets, which lured gaggles of fruit bats, which consumed the fruit and later returned to deposit the seeds of other nearby species they had feasted on, species suitable as reforestation pioneers. The experimenters separated these seeds from the bat feces and planted them. Some of them germinated and raised the prospect that a similar scheme on a larger scale could cheaply and efficiently jump start the reforestation of El Ocote's forest-fire-damaged clearings.

*

In the early stages of my research for this article, I had considered appending a recipe for fruit bat soup from Palau in Micronesia. Whatever enthusiasm I may then have had for testing this delicacy has now flown off.[15]

Notes

1. Henry N. Ridley, *The Dispersal of Plants throughout the World* (Ashford, Kent: L. Reeve, 1930), pp. 352-53. *Gnetum sylvestre* are known as *melinjo* in Indonesia, where it figures commonly in local cuisines.
2. Ernst Haeckel, *Generelle Morphologie* (Berlin: Druck und Verlag Georg Reimer, 1866), II, chapter 11.
3. Ridley, pp. 342-43. *Willughbeia* are various members of a genus named after the British 18th-century naturalist Francis Willughby (sic, although other members of his family spelled it Willoughby), whose fruits resemble grapefruits, are edible, sweet and have been compared in taste to mango, pineapple and soursop. They are common across southeast Asia and India.
4. Ridley, pp. 347-50.
5. Ridley, pp. 347-48.
6. Ridley, p. 350.

7   Ridley, p. 354.
8   Ridley, pp. 340-41.
9   A video of the goats and Berbers in action is available on YouTube at <https://www.youtube.com/watch?v=z2YKwGtcMY8>.
10 For a fuller account, see my *Why We Eat What We Eat* (New York: Summit, 1991), pp. 68-71.
11 Klaus J. Meyer-Arendt, 'The Guava in the Upper Suárez Basin of Southern Santander and Adjacent Boyacá, Colombia' (unpublished master's thesis, Louisiana State University, 1979).
12 T.H. Fleming and W.J. Kress, 'A Brief History of Fruits and Frugivores', *Acta Oecologica*, 37 (2011), 521-30.
13 Jennifer Kahn, 'Life Support', *The New York Times Magazine*, 18 March 2018, p. 34.
14 Odette Preciado-Benítez and others, 'The Use of Commercial Fruits as Attraction Agents May Increase the Seed Dispersal by Bats to Degraded Areas in Southern Mexico', *Mongabay.com Open Access Journal: Tropical Conservation Science*, 8.2 (2015), p. 301-17.
15 I would like to dedicate this article to the memory of Ilka Sokolov. While still a puppy, she devoured a platter of *vitello tonnato* left unattended in the kitchen. Soon after, during a walk in Riverside Park, she left behind the residue of her meal, which included several tiny olive pits. Unfortunately, the climate in Manhattan in the late fall was not conducive to their germination.

Revisiting the Acorn-Eater: The Case of the Arkadians in Greek Antiquity

Corey Straub

The Acorn-Eaters

Acorns have been utilized as a source of food in human diets for millennia. Throughout the Jōmon period, it formed, along with horse chestnuts, the staple of peoples' diets in Japan.[1] Acorns continued to be consumed through the Kōchi prefecture and in the region of Hida, where they were turned into flour that was used to make dumplings. Although acorn consumption fell out of practice by the World War II, prior to that families living in these regions sometimes consumed 'upwards of ten large bales of acorn a year'.[2] The same is true among the indigenous peoples of California, where acorns were the main staple of most groups at contact. These indigenous peoples also turned the acorn into a flour; however they used it to make mashes, gruels, soups, and breads rather than dumplings.[3] Yet flour is not the only way to prepare the acorn. Again, in the Kōchi prefecture in Japan, the community of Aki is still noted for making a tofu from acorns.[4] As well, in Korea, acorns are still enjoyed in a jelly form known as *dotori-muk*.[5] Finally, the oil of the acorn can be used in preparing foods, as seen among the indigenous peoples of the American Southeast.[6] As such, the acorn is a diverse foodstuff, capable of being transformed into a variety of products, so long as one has the technology and ingenuity to do so.

In the ancient context, the Arkadians were famous for their *balanophagy*, or acorn eating. Indeed, according to Herodotus, the oracle at Delphi called the Arkadians 'eaters of acorns'.[7] The same story is picked up and repeated in Plutarch.[8] Pausanias's account differs slightly, wherein the Arkadians are the ones who approach the Pythia and are named acorn-eaters.[9] Apollonius of Rhodes describes the Arkadians as a people who lived before the moon and ate acorns.[10] Some scholars have understood this epithet to be derogatory, a gesture to Arkadia's presumed agricultural poverty and alleged primitivism.[11] For most Greek people, a characteristic of civilization is the ability to work and transform the land, particularly through Demeter's gift of grain.[12] Yet it might be unwise for contemporary scholars to apply such ideas to the ancient Greeks more generally, as these are Athenian and Ionian centric and, as this paper will explore, may not reflect the Arkadian point of view.[13]

Seeds

Civilizing Grains

As Jessica Romney has recently pointed out, there is a civilized-uncivilized binary when it comes to ancient food technologies.[14] Most prominently, this construction of civility is centred around bread and the technology to produce it. In Hesiod, a similar division is made between the pre-civilized Golden Age and the civilized contemporary age. In the Golden Age, the earth produced food spontaneously, thereby inhibiting the development of agriculture. The civilized age, however, has developed agriculture and the technology to produce *sitos*, bread or cooked grains. This is true for all ages of man until the Heroic and Iron ages. For example, in speaking of the third age of man, Hesiod says 'they ate no bread', whereas when he refers to men of the Heroic age or of his own age, the Iron Age, as men who eat bread, signifying that he is referring to an age of civilization.[15] As such, bread made from cultivated grain became a signifier of civilization. Meanwhile, the acorn is for animals. As Boethius reminds his reader, once Odysseus's men had been transformed into swine, they exchanged Demeter's food, grains, for the acorn, associating it with food for livestock.[16] Moreover, multiple authors speak of acorns as the first food of man. Horace tells his reader that when men first came upon the earth 'mute and dirty' they fought one another over acorns and caves.[17] Pliny the Elder adds to this by telling his reader that man traded acorn for Demeter's grain, which she then taught them how to grind and turn it into bread; it was at this time that Demeter also established laws.[18] In sum, whereas grain is the food of civility, capable of being transformed and, in the last case, even associated with the introduction of laws, acorns were the first foods, now more fit for swine or the mute and dirty than for the civilized. Whereas the civilized have the ability to cultivate grain, only animals, like the first men, consume the acorns the earth gives to them. The Arkadians' association with this epithet thus associates, implicitly, with concepts of primitivism and pre-civilization.[19]

It is certainly true that Arkadia was not as plentiful as Boeotia; it was an extremely mountainous landscape, much of which was beyond cultivation.[20] That is not to say, however, that it could not be utilized, as it is in fact still used today, for pasture or as a source for game animals and wood products like timber or fuel; moreover, grains were known to have been cultivated in Arkadia, even though its basins and plains were high enough to be mountain land.[21] Xenophon mentions that Mantinea had an abundant supply of grain, and Hekataios includes barley-cakes in his description of the Arkadian meal.[22] The Arkadians also cultivated grapes: we learn from Aristotle of an Arkadian wine so thick that it had to be scraped out of the wineskin.[23] It is clear from these sources that the Arkadians possessed the proper food technologies to turn grains into bread and grapes into wine. As such, they could not be equated to Herodotus's man-eating *Anthropophagoi*, or the long-lived Ethiopians with the Table of the Sun providing them with the boiled meat of every animal. And yet, while they may have laboured for some or most of their food, their epithet suggests that agriculture did not account for their entire diet. This is because the earth provided them with acorns, which they did not need agriculture to obtain. With this viewpoint, the diet of the Arkadians is a mix

Revisiting the Acorn-Eater: The Case of the Arkadians

of civilized and pre-civilized, placing these consumers in a state of quasi civilized status, nearly civilized, but due to the acorn, not fully.

Acorn-Eaters Revisited

Despite the negative connotations of acorn consumption, it appears the Arkadians did not attempt to disabuse themselves of the baggage that acorns or acorn-eating carried. In fact, there is numismatic evidence of acorn iconography from Mantinea which seems to show, at least in the Mantinean case, a sort of pride toward their association with the acorn.[24] This suggests that, from the Arkadian perspective, the acorn may not have held the same negative connotations as it did elsewhere. Moreover, the idea of Arkadians eating acorns is not outrageous. The landscape of Arkadia was well known for its abundant oak trees. Pausanias makes special note of the oak forests between Mantinea and Tegea; their abundance suggests it would be foolish for the Arkadians to abstain from this food source.[25]

As mentioned above, civilization and food technology go hand in hand. It is the ability to cultivate the land and then transform the grain that makes people civilized. Yet, contrary to ancient stereotypes, acorns were not consumed raw and unprocessed. While the Arkadians may not have had to cultivate the land, the processing of acorns to render them edible requires a sophisticated degree of food technology: one must learn how to grind and leach the acorns in order to remove their bitter tannins. Once this is done, acorn flour could be transformed into all the same 'civilized' foods produced from grains. Flour made of grains was turned into mashes, gruels, and breads. Ground acorns, as seen above from the Californian case, could also be turned into mashes, gruels, and breads. Moreover, closer to Greece, Strabo tells of the Lusitani, another *balanophagious* group in Spain, who grind their acorns and turn the flour into bread.[26] It only makes sense then that those with plenty of access to acorns, such as the Arkadians, would supplement their grain supply with acorn meal, which could be utilized in the same preparations as grains. Moreover, if one considers that acorns can be stored for a period of four years under the right conditions, as opposed to the two years of other grains, then acorns, abundant and with long-term storage abilities, would be a sensible supplement to the diet of the everyday Arkadians.[27]

The Mythic Acorn

Even if acorns were part of the diet, why use acorn iconography on coins if, as many ancient authors insist, to do so associated the Arkadians with a primitive trope? The answer may lie in the fact that this primitive trope comes from Athenian and Ionic sources. The Arkadians may not have seen it this way at all. According to their foundational myths, relayed by Pausanias, the Arkadians claimed that Pelasgus introduced them to the acorn:

> Pelasgus on becoming king invented huts that humans should not shiver, or be soaked by rain, or oppressed by heat. Moreover, he it was who first thought of coats of sheep-skins, such as poor folk still wear in Euboea and Phocis. He too

it was who checked the habit of eating green leaves, grasses, and roots always inedible and sometimes poisonous. But he introduced as food the nuts of trees, not those of all trees but only the acorns of the edible oak.[28]

As such, the Arkadians may have wanted to associate themselves with their progenitor. Like the Athenians, this myth privileged the Arkadians by giving them an autochthonous genealogy. Unlike the other Greek peoples, only the Athenians and Arkadians could claim to be indigenous to the land they inhabited. While civilization (as defined above) would not be introduced until Arkas, the eponymous king of Arkadia who introduced the people to agriculture and baking bread, Pelasgus took the first step. It was Pelasgus who first elevated the Arkadians from their primitive living conditions, and it would make sense that some would choose to remember this by continuing to associate with the acorn. Moreover, if the acorn recalled a time of elevation beyond the primitive, this could also mean that the Arkadians did not make the same associations as the Athenians and Ionians. The acorn first elevated them beyond primitivism, and so it would make no sense to associate it with primitive living. Moreover, how could they dismiss the food of their autochthon: if they dismissed this food they would also be dismissing the very claim to the land that made them exceptional.

Unfortunately, there are no surviving sources from Arkadia to allow contemporary scholars to truly discern what the acorn meant to Arkadians. Was it a tie to their mythic origins? A reflection of the lived diet of the peoples? Or something else altogether? However, one thing that can be certain is that the trope of the primitive acorn-eater is not Arkadian but comes out of an Athenian- and Ionian-centric point of view. It is up to scholars to continue to try and piece together a more balanced image of Arkadia by surveying extant material evidence and utilizing the writings of the ancient authors to help supplement our understanding, rather than allowing these sources to be the foundation upon which we build our understanding. Attempting to reconstruct an authentic Arkadia from these sources is methodologically problematic, the equivalent of adducing an authentic Egypt from the writings of Herodotus, who does not appear to have ever visited the region about which he wrote.

Notes

1. Takamune Kawashima, 'Food Processing and Consumption in the Jōmon', *Quaternary International*, 404 (2016), 16.
2. Eric Rath, *Japanese Cuisine: Food, Place and Identity* (London: Reaktion Books, 2016), pp. 200, 211.
3. Shannon Tushingham and Robert Bettinger, 'Why Foragers Choose Acorns before Salmon: Storage, Mobility, and Risk in Aboriginal California', *Journal of Anthropological Archaeology*, 32 (2013), 530; Thomas Jackson, 'Pounding Acorns: Women's Production as Social and Economic Focus', in *Engendering Archaeology*, ed. by Joan Gero and Margaret Conkey (Oxford: Basil Blackwell, 1991), pp. 301-28 (p. 305).
4. Rath, *Japanese Cuisine*, p. 200 n. 100.
5. Korean Tourism Organization, <http://english.visitkorea.or.kr/enu/ATR/SI_EN_3_1_1_1.jsp?cid=1917319> [accessed 16 November 2018].

6   Roger Owen, James Deetz, and Anthony Fisher, *The North American Indians: A Sourcebook* (New York: MacMillan, 1967), p. 406.
7   Herodotus, *The Histories*, 1.66.
8   Plutarch, *Caius Marius Coriolanus*, 3.
9   Pausanias, *Descriptions of Greece*, 8.42.6.
10 Apollonius of Rhodes, *Argonautica*, 4.237-66.
11 Philippe Borgeaud, *The Cult of Pan in Ancient Greece* (Chicago: University of Chicago Press, 1988), p. 15.
12 This idea comes out of our earliest sources. As John Wilkins and Shaun Hill note, throughout Odysseus' Mediterranean travels in the Odyssey, the uncivilized are those who 'do not eat the grain and olives and drink the wine that he does' (*Food in the Ancient World* (Oxford: Blackwell, 2006), p. 5). Here they mean people who do not have agriculture and therefore cannot grow grains to make bread, or grapes to drink wine.
13 One example of such an author is Galen of Pergamum, who said that only once the pigs had been slaughtered in desperate winters would one resort to eating from the pigs' storage pits and eat acorns (6.620).
14 Jessica Romney, *Bekos: Food and Notions of Civilisation in Ancient Greek Literature*, YouTube, 10 November 2016, <https://www.youtube.com/watch?v=yUn2zRTOvo8&t=1040s> [accessed 16 November 2018].
15 See Hesiod, *Works and Days* 145-150; 80-83.
16 Boethius, *Consolatie Philosophiae*, 4.M3.
17 Horace, *Satires*, 1.3.
18 Pliny the Elder, *The Natural History*, 7.57.
19 This is certainly not the only time Arkadians have fallen into the cliché of primitivism. As James Roy has noted, the cliché of rural mountain dwellers and civilized plains dwellers is nothing new ('The Economies of Arkadia', in *Defining Ancient Arkadia*, ed. by Thomas Nielsen and James Roy (Copenhagen: Kongelige Danske Videnskabernes, 2000), pp. 320-81 (p. 323)). Another Greek people, the Macedonians, were civilized by Philip by bringing them down from the mountains (Roy, p. 324). Alternatively, returning to Japan, the Kōchi, due to their distance from the capital and their mountainous dwelling, where also considered backwards. Plus, as mentioned above, the Kōchi also consumed acorns, contributing to their rural status.
20 In fact, Thucydides makes it clear to his reader that the Arkadians were agriculturally poor when describing the most fertile areas of Greece. He says that the most fertile lands in Greece were Thessaly, Boeotia and the Peloponnese, but taking care to explicitly say this is except Arkadia (*History of the Peloponnesian War*, 1.2).
21 Roy, pp. 323, 326.
22 Xenophon, *Hellenica* 5.2.4; Hekataios fragment 9 qtd. in Athenaeus, *Deipnosophists*, 4.148f.
23 Aristotle. *Meteorology*, 388b.
24 Churchill Babington and W.A. Wright, *Catalogue of a Selection from Colonel Leake's Greek Coins, Exhibited in The Fitzwilliam Museum* (Cambridge: Clay, 1867), p. 32. Unfortunately no literary sources survive to us from Arkadia; instead the Arkadian narrative has been crafted by outside sources, particularly from Athens and Ionia.
25 Pausanias, 8.11.
26 Strabo, *Geography*, 3.3.
27 The ancient Greek meal was divided into two parts, the cereal base or *sitos* and the relish or opson. The cereal base, as mentioned in the paper, could be any kind of cooked grain be it bread, gruel, or mash, while the relish was something added to provide variation in texture and taste, and could be anything from meat or fish to vegetables, depending on the economic means of the individual eater. Since the flavour for the dish was not coming out of the sitos but rather from the opson, the slighter more bitter flavour of acorn-based flour would likely not have been that perceptible if substituted for grain based flour.
28 Pausanias, 8.1.

Amaranth: Food of the Gods, or Seed of the Devil?

David C. Sutton

Whilst not quite attaining the wonder-food status of quinoa, the seed of the beautiful tropical plant known in Spanish as *amaranto* and in English as amaranth has in recent years gained a high reputation for its healthy properties (vitamin content, protein quality, gluten-free digestibility, and antioxidant value in particular) as well as for its pleasant sesame-like flavour.[1]

This attractive, tasty, purple-ripening Mexican food has, however, a distant history unconnected with its nutritional value and linked with bloodthirsty and horrifying practices, and its consumption and use were consequently forbidden and punished by the Spanish colonial occupiers of Mexico, from the time of Hernán Cortés onwards.

The food history of the amaranth seed begins with its special status in the diet and the ritual of pre-Aztec and then Aztec Mexico, and ends with its emergence as a twenty-first century speciality food. In the course of this history, however, foods made from amaranth seeds are inextricably linked with challenging and disturbing traditions of human sacrifice, cannibalism, and the use of human blood in food preparation.

One of the best introductory descriptions of the plant itself has been written by Daniel K. Early:

> Amaranth is a strikingly beautiful and easy-to-grow plant that bears dense clusters of tiny red, green, or purple flowers atop its central stalk and at the ends of its branches. Both the small, saucer-shaped seeds produced by these flowerheads and the plant's green or purple leaves are tasty and of high nutritional value. In fact, the seeds of domesticated species contain about 16 per-cent protein – more than is found in wheat, rice, or maize – and the quality of the protein is excellent, on a par with cow's milk. Amaranth leaves, which are lance-like in shape and about two inches long, compare favourably to spinach in nutritive worth and are especially rich in calcium and vitamin A.[2]

Like many foods that have now become staples and favourites all around the world, amaranth is indigenous to Mexico.[3] Archaeological research has demonstrated that it was an essential component in the Mexican diet for the long pre-Aztec period (from approximately 5000 BCE to 1400 CE), and then was adopted as an important and typical food within the comparatively short-lived period of Aztec dominance – as part of the Aztec diet and as part of the Aztec ritual.

Amaranth: Food of the Gods, or Seed of the Devil?

There was clearly an aura about the amaranth plant which gave it a religious or magical significance in many of the Mesoamerican cultures, and the Mexican scholar Eduardo Espitia Rangel has plausibly suggested that (in cultures where sun-worship was widespread), the magical connotations would have been linked to the way in which the plant, before seeding, ripens to a dramatically rich red-purple colour.[4]

Botanical Character, Earliest Cultivation, Ancient Mexico

Mexican scholars distinguish, in discussing all those Mexican foodstuffs that have now become worldwide staples, between the date of first cultivation and the date of first domestication. The scholarly consensus is that wild forms of both maize and amaranth were first cultivated in Mexico around 9000 years ago, but there is scholarly debate about exactly when domesticated (cross-bred and improved) maize and amaranth began to appear, perhaps two millennia later.

Botanically, amaranth is clearly a seed and not a cereal, although it is sometimes characterized as a 'pseudocereal'. Here are two brief botanical descriptions:

> From a botanical point of view, amaranth is assigned to the family of the *dicotyledonous Amaranthaceae*. Even if it produces cereal-like starch-rich seeds, it is not assigned to the cereals.[5]

> Amaranth is not a true cereal grain. It comes not from a grass but from a broad-leafed plant with multiple seed heads. The heads of the amaranth plant are packed with thousands of seeds. The seeds are tiny, about the size of millet, and their color ranges from purple to yellow. [...] The harvesting of the seed is labor intensive; thus, amaranth is expensive.[6]

A detailed nutritional description gives a very positive assessment of amaranth:

> Amaranth is characterized by an excellent nutritional composition and therefore shows a high nutritional value. [... T]he protein content of amaranth is generally higher than in wheat. [...] Of the proteins, 65% are located in the germ and seed coat, and 35% in the starch-rich perisperm. Amaranth does not contain gluten and is therefore suitable for diets of persons with celiac disease. [...] The composition of amino acids is outstanding. Lysine, the limiting amino acid in cereals compared to the reference protein of the FAO, can be found in high quantity. The content of lysine in amaranth protein is comparable with that in soybeans, which has one of the highest quality plant proteins. The high content of arginine and histidine, which are essential amino acids for infants, also makes amaranth valuable for infant nutrition.[7]

Already these botanical descriptions begin to indicate why this ancient Mexican seed could be so highly regarded in the twenty-first century, and can now be seen as such an exciting food prospect for the future.

Seeds

The day-to-day foods of ordinary people (outside the priesthood or palace life) in Ancient Mexico were maize porridge (sweetened with honey or spiced with capsicums), stuffed tortillas, various types of gourd (*ayoconetl, ayotli* or *tamalayotli* in Nahuatl), amaranth, sage, beans, and sauces made from chillies or *tomatl* berries. Occasional meat came from wild birds and iguanas. Drinks included brewed cocoa and a fermented drink known as *pulque*, made from cactus juice. The foods of the elite included many types of roasted meat and fish, boiled stews, Maguey worms, with drinks and flavourings including cocoa, honey, and vanilla.[8] The rich also enjoyed fermented drinks, but drunkenness at banquets was strongly discouraged. Amaranth had its part in the day-to-day food of both rich and poor in pre-Aztec Mesoamerica, but became increasingly closely associated with religious ritual, ceremonial foods, and, especially, oven-baked religious images.

The Society of the Aztecs

In the fourteenth century AD, the fearsome Aztecs arrived in the central valley of Mexico, and established their city of Tenochtitlán, where Mexico City stands today. In less than two hundred years they built the most powerful empire in Mesoamerica. They demonstrated their supremacy over their conquered neighbours by demanding tribute from them, and engaged in both human sacrifice and cannibalism, capturing defeated enemy soldiers alive in order to kill and eat them in their religious ceremonies.[9]

As a result of these practices, Aztec society has been very harshly judged by European historians from the sixteenth to the twentieth centuries. More recently, however, a more sympathetic interpretation has begun to emerge, for which one of the strongest statements, by Caroline Dodds Pennock, was recently published by the BBC:

> It's true that human sacrifice – something we struggle to understand – was central to religious practice in Tenochtitlán. But one of the most remarkable things about the Aztec people is that they were not dehumanised by the brutal rituals of sacrifice. These were compassionate, sophisticated, and very familiar people. They loved music, poetry and flowers, and were highly educated – with universal schooling provided for both boys and girls – and treasured close emotional ties with their families. This was a culture in which children were welcomed with joy, and women and men parented together, with fathers raising their sons and women their daughters. It was a place where domestic violence was not condoned, and where women inherited property equally with their brothers. But this was also a place in which capricious and all-powerful gods demanded constant feeding with human blood to prevent the world from coming to an end.[10]

Aztec culture continued many of the practices of earlier Mexican societies, and developed and extended some of them, including human sacrifice, cannibalism, and ritual use of amaranth. Ceremonial human sacrifice has been confirmed by archaeologists as part of

Amaranth: Food of the Gods, or Seed of the Devil?

the civilization of Teotihuacan, for example, over a thousand years before the coming of the Aztecs and the building of their great city of Tenochtitlán. There is also strong evidence in the archaeology of Teotihuacan for the widespread use of amaranth, and for ritual and ceremonial cannibalism, required by the religious and social structures of the city. One scholar, Annabeth Headrick, has memorably described Teotihuacan cannibalism almost two thousand years ago as 'a civic event'.[11]

Aztec religion, like its predecessors in Mexico, contained a strong sense of a blood-debt owed by humans to the gods, and this seems to have been linked to a constant fear that the gods would withdraw their favour, that the rains would fail, that the sun would fail to rise in the sky, and so on. The gods had to be regularly propitiated with blood-gifts.

Their conquests, their demands for tributes, their ruthless cruelty towards the conquered, and their abductions of victims naturally bred a fear and hatred of the Aztecs amongst the other peoples of Mesoamerica; this fear would later be exploited by Cortés with great political skill.

The typical tributes demanded by the Aztecs, instead of or in addition to abducted victims, were reported to include: maize, cocoa, amaranth, sage, pepper, salt, ornamental feathers, animal skins, cochineal dye, precious metals, paper, cotton, and slaves.[12]

Aztec society was sophisticated and highly structured, based on complex calendar calculations and astronomical observations. It was dominated by religious rules, festivals, beliefs, and practices, and was also extremely urban in its nature. Around 1515, the population of Tenochtitlán, including its satellite town of Tlatelolco, was in excess of 200,000 – more than five times the size of the contemporary London of King Henry VIII.

Amaranth, Human Sacrifice, and Cannibalism in Mexico

In both pre-Aztec and Aztec-era societies, the use of the amaranth seed was very frequently linked to religion and ritual. Cakes made of amaranth mixed with human heart-blood formed a characteristic part of Mesoamerican ritual worship. Whilst the cakes could sometimes be biscuit-sized, on other occasions they could be shaped into huge sacrificial images, as described by Cortés himself: 'The figures of the idols in which these people believe are very much larger than the body of a big man. They are made of dough from all the seeds and vegetables which they eat, ground and mixed together, and bound with the blood of human hearts which those priests tear out while still beating.'[13] In some rituals and some recipes, the human blood may be replaced by honey (and the amaranth cakes eaten in Mexico today are, fortunately, bound exclusively with honey), which has led to some debate among Mexican writers about the frequency of use of either blood or honey. There is no explaining away, however, the regular use of human blood in Aztec religious cake-making.

The practices of human sacrifice, use of blood in cookery, and cannibalism of human body-parts clearly involve a set of religious beliefs which have their own coherent inner logic. For example, the Spanish priest Father Bernardino de Sahagún (1499-1590), who was engaged in Mesoamerican ethnography as well as missionary work for many decades, reports that an Aztec warrior would call a captured enemy his son, and that the reclassification as 'flesh of his flesh' then entitled him to kill and eat the captive.[14]

The Revulsion of the Spanish Invaders

Some of the earliest Spanish invaders were presented with peace offerings of specially prepared food, one of which was amaranth seed mixed with human blood. Cortés himself reports receiving a peace-offering of this sort on his first encounter with the Tlaxcaltecs, who could not be sure whether he was a mighty invading king or some sort of god, and approached him thus: 'Lord, here are five slaves; if you are an implacable god who eats flesh and blood, eat them and we will bring you more; if you are a benevolent god, here are some incense and some feathers; if you are a man, take these wildfowl, this bread and these cherries.'[15]

Although the Spanish themselves were capable of the most savage cruelty and punishments, for which the Spanish Inquisition (founded in 1478) has become a universal symbol, the different forms of cruelty they witnessed in Aztec religion filled them with dread and revulsion. Cannibalism, human sacrifice, and blood-debt to the gods, in particular, seemed to them to be the most barbaric of religious conventions.

In addition to their revulsion at the death-rituals themselves, the Spanish were also deeply offended by the similarities between the cannibalistic practices using amaranth and their own religious practices, especially their Holy Communion. Curiously (and with a blinkered Euro-centrism), they imagined that the Aztecs had created a disrespectful and horrible parody of the Holy Communion, as Sophie Coe has described: 'For whatever reason many Aztec ceremonies involved making an image of the god with ground amaranth, or maize and amaranth, made into a dough with honey or blood. The image was then worshipped, broken up, and eaten by the worshipers, a practice which the Spaniards regarded as a blasphemous parody of communion.'[16]

Numerous Spanish accounts indicate their outrage that the virtuous symbolic cannibalism of the Holy Communion ('Take, eat, this is my body ...') was apparently being mocked and parodied by the real cannibalism of blood-and-amaranth cakes, in a Mexican version of altar bread. This response may have been complicated or exacerbated by the contemporary Roman Catholic doctrine of transubstantiation, which holds that the Eucharistic bread and wine are literally converted into the body and blood of Jesus Christ before being consumed.

More General Reflections on Cannibalism and Ritual

Cannibalism is one of the most controversial topics in food history, and many food historians are prevented by natural revulsion from considering cannibalism as a fundamental factor in the history of meat-eating. This section includes some more

Amaranth: Food of the Gods, or Seed of the Devil?

general reflections on cannibalism, ritual, and meat-eating in human history, and the elements of religious symbolism which are very often part of cannibalistic practices.[17]

It is generally recognized that there are three types of cannibalism, which may be described as emergency, gustatory, and ritual. Emergency cannibalism, usually reported in dramatic tales of plane crashes or shipwrecks, or in pitiful historical circumstances of famine or siege, has no direct relevance to the Aztecs, but the question of whether their cannibalism was principally gustatory (and a pursuit of missing protein) or principally ritualistic, as part of their religious beliefs, has led to debate and disagreement.

In several essays, Michael Harner has developed the theory that a primary factor in Aztec cannibalism was over-population in Mesoamerica leading to protein shortage, with the result that for many people under Aztec rule the best available meat was human meat – which was also found to be sweet-flavoured and attractive.[18] Certainly King Carlos V of Spain seemed to be of this view, and he ordered Cortés, as a matter of urgency, to draw up plans to introduce beef-cattle into Mexico in order to provide the Aztecs with an alternative protein source. The theory has been robustly (and, I would say, conclusively) contested, however, by Bernard Ortiz de Montellano, who makes a case for the cannibalism having been ritualistic and religious: in summary, there is scant evidence, if any, for Aztec protein shortages; and in any case the consumption of human flesh and blood was mainly by the priests and the nobility, not by the poorer people who may have been hungry.[19]

There is, in fact, a very strong historical case for cannibalism, when it is by choice, being almost always religious or symbolic in nature. Gustatory cannibalism, within historical time, is generally associated with perversion or psychosis, although things may have been different in pre-historical time. I have suggested elsewhere that the obsessive interest in cannibalism and human sacrifice in the Old Testament may reflect a backward look to a half-remembered time when such practices were more common in the Near East and not yet subject to taboo.[20]

What is striking, for example, in the story of the two women arguing their case before King Jehoram in the Book of Kings, is the casual acceptance of cannibalism as normal:

> And the king said unto her, What aileth thee? And she answered, This woman said unto me, Give thy son, that we may eat him to day, and we will eat my son to morrow.
>
> So we boiled my son, and did eat him: and I said unto her on the next day, Give thy son, that we may eat him: and she hath hid her son. (II Kings 6:28-29)

There is a similar normalization of eating human flesh and drinking human blood in the story of Pope Innocent VIII, as he lay dying in July 1492, when three healthy youths in Rome had their blood let for the pope to drink – 'still fresh and hot'. (Unfortunately, the operation was followed by the death not only of the pope but also of the three boys.)[21]

We recall also that there are many religions, ancient and modern, in which 'eating the god' (the famous phrase of Sir James George Frazer) plays an essential part – from pre-Aztec religions through to Christianity. In Christianity, the quintessence comes at John 6:57 ('Whoever eats me shall live'), and the essential idea survives through to the thinking of the twelfth-century pilgrims who went to Canterbury, where they drank water which was mixed with the blood of Thomas à Becket.

It is also an important part of the secular histories of butchery and meat-eating that primitive peoples believed that they could absorb the characteristics of the animal whose flesh they ate. Royal lion-hunts provide a striking early historical example of this rationale for meat-eating; others come with the dried alpaca hearts eaten by high-altitude dwellers in the Andes, the European literature around hunting and eating the meat of the ferocious wild boar – and, in a more domestic and modern context, we can adduce the saying 'as strong as an ox' and its link through to the modern-day 'Nourishing meat' advertisement theme.

The Prohibition or Suppression of Amaranth

Numerous sources indicate that, as a result of their revulsion, the Spanish introduced a severely enforced legal ban on the growing, producing, and cooking of amaranth. Certainly, the priest Diego Durán included amaranth in his list of forbidden foods, as one to be particularly shunned. Internet sources are unanimous that amaranth was banned by the Spanish conquerors, but equally unanimously fail to provide any documentary evidence.[22] The more measured assessment of Daniel K. Early is preferable:

> No historical evidence has been found that the Spaniards prohibited the cultivation of amaranth itself, but they certainly waged a repressive campaign against this 'idolatry,' in which amaranth played a central role. In 1525 the Church began a systematic campaign to stamp out any vestiges of pre-Columbian religious practice, and six years later a zealous bishop claimed to have destroyed twenty thousand idols and five hundred shrines. Not only idols and shrines were destroyed. Traditional worshippers were whipped, sentenced to labor for monasteries, or executed outright.[23]

Whilst evidence for a formal legal ban is lacking, there are several accounts which graphically describe the way in which the Spanish persecuted the religious practices associated with the amaranth seed – considering amaranth as a diabolical food, regularly linked to horrifying rituals and sacrifices, regularly baked using human heart-blood as a binding agent, and often seen as a wicked and malicious parody of their own Christian Eucharist. To the Spanish, amaranth was the seed of the devil.

The Near-Disappearance of Amaranth, 1525-1975

As a seed-crop and a staple, amaranth suffered devastating setbacks from the Spanish persecution of Aztec religious practices. The close association of amaranth with human sacrifice and especially the use of human blood in cake and biscuit cookery led to an ostracizing of the seed and a fear of any form of use or growing of it.

Amaranth: Food of the Gods, or Seed of the Devil?

In the urban areas most closely controlled by the Spanish, amaranth virtually disappeared. It is clear, however, that in the more remote and rural parts of Mexico, amaranth cultivation never came to an end, even if it sometimes had to be clandestine. And some of the special regard for amaranth also survived, both in respect of the splendour of the plant and the deeper significance of the cakes and biscuits made with it.

Here is one account of the period of decline, published in 1984:

> [...] with the collapse of Indian cultures following the conquest, amaranth fell into disuse. In the Americas it survived only in small pockets of cultivation in scattered mountain areas of Mexico and the Andes. Corn and beans became two of the leading crops that feed the world, while grain amaranth faded into obscurity and today is largely forgotten. The Spanish conquest had ended amaranth's use as a staple of the New World and slowed the spread into world agriculture of a highly nutritious food.[24]

As a result, descriptions of amaranth in the twentieth and twenty-first centuries convey a sense of re-emergence, renaissance, or comeback. A widely noticed article with a bio-genetic theme, by Jonathan B. Tucker, published in 1986, was entitled 'Amaranth: The Once and Future Crop',[25] and other scholars, writing more recently, have similarly used the word 'resilience' to describe the survival of amaranth, meaning both culturally resilient and genetically resilient: 'amaranth, once closely connected to Amerindian civilization and culture, almost disappeared after being banned by the Spanish Conquistadors but has since demonstrated the diversity of its genus and its resilience'.[26]

Re-Emergence as a Modern-Day Super-Food

From the 1970s onwards, amaranth has been rehabilitated, first in Mexico and then in other parts of the world. It has become one of the many products marketed in the twenty-first century as a 'miracle food', with the additional feature, historically rooted, that it is also regarded as a source of *alegría*, a food of happiness.

From the 1970s, nutritionists began to publish studies which advocated wider planting and use of amaranth for a variety of good reasons, ranging from the quality of the protein in the seed (which began to be compared with the protein quality of soy beans) to its richness in omega fatty acids and its gluten-free baking potential.

Twenty-first century publicity in favour of amaranth has used slogans such as 'Amaranth: paleo-friendly seed vs. harmful grain', and its claimed qualities have been enumerated in a different promotion as follows:

TOP 10 BENEFITS OF AMARANTH

Straight-up nutrition: Amaranth is a complete protein and contains more minerals than most vegetables.

Immune System Support: This is the only grain that contains vitamin C. It's also high in vitamin E and other antioxidants.

Weight Loss Assistance: Amaranth is 15% protein, which lowers insulin levels and triggers a hormone that suppresses your appetite.

Heart Help: Amaranth balances cholesterol and is an excellent source of omega fatty acids. Also the potassium helps with blood pressure.

Bone Health and Development: The high calcium content, as well as other minerals in amaranth make it excellent for bone health.

Digestive Support: The high fiber content of the whole grain allows for smooth digestion and ensures that your body is able to use the nutrients you're taking in.

Vision Care: High levels of carotenoids and antioxidants in amaranth support eye health.

Neural Tube Defect Prevention: Amaranth is high in folate, which can reduce the risk of birth defects early in pregnancy.

Hair care: Amaranth contains lysine, an amino acid that is excellent for healthy hair growth and for preventing baldness.

Cellular Oxygenation: Amaranth is high in squalene, which can prevent disease by getting oxygen into cells and stopping mutations.[27]

This entertainingly overloaded list is taken from an advertisement, and thus has no medical standing (especially in respect of cell mutation, birth defects, and avoiding baldness!), but it demonstrates how amaranth is beginning to be marketed as an omni-benevolent wonder-food.

Two more subjective factors have also helped with the recent re-emergence of amaranth. First, it has a very nice taste, makes very nice biscuits, and combines especially well with honey. Second, it has a strong and historically based connection with happiness. *Alegría*, the Spanish word for joy, is traditionally a confection of amaranth and honey that continues to be very popular in Latin American countries including Mexico and Colombia. (Regrettably, in Colombia millet is increasingly used instead of amaranth, and in the USA too many *alegría* recipes add chocolate or molasses.)

Conclusion: Out of Mexico

In 1992 the University of Arizona Press published a book evocatively entitled *Chilies to Chocolate: Food the Americas Gave the World* (cited in the Notes below for the contributions by Alan Davidson and Daniel K. Early). Amaranth is beginning to take its rightful place amongst the wonderful Mexican and Mesoamerican foods that have so enriched the diets of Europe and North America.

Many foods of Mexican origin have become staples in European cuisine to the extent that their origins are generally forgotten. Non-specialists struggle to recall exactly which beans are of Mexican origin and which have had a much longer European history. The sharp *tomatl* berry has evolved into the sweet Mediterranean tomato. Chocolate is a universal comfort food; peanuts and pecans have become similarly everyday in many households.

Amaranth: Food of the Gods, or Seed of the Devil?

Maize and beans have become crucial international staples. Turkeys, sweet potatoes, and avocados are no longer exotic foods. It may be that amaranth has finally set aside its extraordinary and brutal blood-soaked history, and is ready to become one of the new healthy food staples of the twenty-first century.

Notes

1. See, for example, Jean L. Marx, 'Speaking of Science: Amaranth: A Comeback for the Food of the Aztecs', *Science*, 198.4312 (7 October 1977), 40; Cristina Barros and Marco Buenrostro, *Amaranto: fuente maravillosa de sabor y salud* (Mexico City: Grijalbo, 1997); Ricardo Ortiz, *El amaranto: historia y perspectivas* (Mexico City: Editorial Yug, 1997); Luis Alberto Vargas and María de la Luz del Valle Berrocal, 'El nuevo reventón del amaranto', *Arqueología Mexicana*, 23.138 (March-April 2016), 59-63.
2. Daniel K. Early, 'The Renaissance of Amaranth', in *Chilies to Chocolate: Food the Americas Gave the World*, ed. by Nelson Foster and Linda S. Cordell (Tucson: University of Arizona Press, 1992), p. 16.
3. For example, tomato, potato, sweet potato, chilli pepper, butter beans (lima), chocolate, maize, vanilla, pecans, peanuts, papaya and avocado. See Alan Davidson, 'Europeans' Wary Encounter with Tomato, Potatoes and Other New World Foods', in *Chilies to Chocolate: Food the Americas Gave the World*, pp. 1-15.
4. Eduardo Espitia Rangel, 'Etnología del amaranto', *Archeología Mexicana*, 23.138 (March-April 2016), 64-70. See also the article which gave this essay its title: 'Amaranth: Food of the Gods', *Manataka American Indian Council* <https://www.manataka.org/page1688.html> [accessed 22 February 2019].
5. Emmerich Berghofer and Regine Schoenlechner, 'Grain Amaranth', in *Pseudocereals and Less Common Cereals: Grain Properties and Utilization Potential*, ed. by Peter S. Belton and John R. N. Taylor (Berlin: Springer, 2002), pp. 219-260 (p. 221).
6. Christopher S. Kilham, *The Whole Food Bible: How to Select & Prepare Safe, Healthful Foods* (London: Addison-Wesley, 1991), p. 24. For more detailed descriptions, see Josefina C. Morales Guerrero, Norma Vázquez Mata, and Ricardo Bressani Castiglioni, *El amaranto: características físicas, químicas, toxicológicas y funcionales y aporte nutricio* (Mexico City: Instituto Nacional de Ciencias Médicas y Nutrición "Salvador Zubirán", 2009).
7. Berghofer and Schoenlechner, p. 226.
8. Sophie D. Coe, *America's First Cuisines* (Austin: University of Texas Press, 1994), especially pp. 9-65; Reay Tannahill, *Food in History*, new edn (New York: Three Rivers Press, 1988), pp. 208-10; Jacqueline de Durand-Forest, *Les Aztèques* (Paris: Les Belles Lettres, 2008), pp. 24, 206-07.
9. Janet Long-Solís and Luis Alberto Vargas, *Food Culture in Mexico* (Westport, CT: Greenwood Press, 2005), p. 3 and passim.
10. Caroline Dodds Pennock, 'In Search of the Real Aztecs.' *BBC World Histories*, 7 (December 2017-January 2018), 40-47 (p. 42).
11. Annabeth Headrick, *The Teotihuacan Trinity: The Socio-Political Structure of an Ancient Mesoamerican City* (Austin: University of Texas Press, 2007; e-book, 2013). On the importance of amaranth at Teotihuacan, online sources are mostly in Spanish (searching on 'Teotihuacan amaranto').
12. Durand-Forest, p. 93.
13. Anthony Pagden, *Hernan Cortes: Letters from Mexico* (New Haven: Yale University Press, 1986), p. 107.
14. Michel Graulich, *Le sacrifice humain chez les Aztèques* (Paris: Fayard, 2005), p. 43.
15. Graulich, p. 135.
16. Coe, p. 91.
17. For the ritual and symbolic significance of human sacrifice and cannibalism in pre-Hispanic Mexico, this essay draws upon the work of J. M. G. Le Clézio, *Le Rêve mexicain; ou, la Pensée interrompue* (Paris: Gallimard, 1988). See also my e-book: David C. Sutton, *Rich Food Poor Food: Stories of the Great Divide in Food History, from Champagne and Turbot to Salt Cod, Gooseberries and Meat from Cats* (Chapelfields

Press, 2017), Chapter Seven. For a more jovial account, see Gary Allen and Ken Albala, *Human Cuisine* (Charleston: Booksurge, 2008).
18 See, for example, Michael Harner, 'The Enigma of Aztec Sacrifice', *Natural History*, 86 (1977), 46-51.
19 See, for example, Bernard R. Ortiz de Montellano, 'Aztec Cannibalism: An Ecological Necessity?', *Science, 200* (1978), 611-17 and 'Counting Skulls: Comment on the Aztec Cannibalism Theory of Harner-Harris', *American Anthropologist*, 85 (1983), 403-06.
20 Sutton, Chapter Seven.
21 Richard Sugg, *Mummies, Cannibals and Vampires: The History of Corpse Medicine from the Renaissance to the Victorians*, 2nd edn (London: Routledge, 2016), p. 24.
22 As an example of the untrustworthiness of Google as a source of research, a search on 'Amaranth banned by the conquistadors' retrieves very many hits, but most of them duplicate phraseology and many of them derive from a typically poorly-sourced Wikipedia article.
23 Early, p. 25.
24 *Amaranth: Modern Prospects for an Ancient Crop. Report of an Ad Hoc Panel of the Advisory Committee on Technology Innovation* […] (Washington: National Academy Press, 1984), p. 1.
25 Jonathan B. Tucker: 'Amaranth: The Once and Future Crop', *BioScience*, 36.1 (January 1986), 9-13.
26 *Caribbean Globalizations, 1492 to the Present Day*, ed. by Eva Sansavior and Richard Scholar (Liverpool: Liverpool University Press, 2015), p. 25.
27 Advertisement published by Activation, 2017.

The English Quest for Novelty: Kitchen Garden Seeds from Abroad from the Sixteenth to the Early Eighteenth Centuries

Malcolm Thick

Writing in the 1570s, the chronicler Holinshed thought that during his lifetime much more interest had been shown in eating vegetables and salads by all classes in English society. They were to be found both at the tables of 'poore commons' and of 'delicate merchants, gentlemen and the nobilitie, who make their provision yearlie for new seeds out of strange countries'.[1] This theme of imported seeds runs through the history of English kitchen gardening from the sixteenth to the eighteenth centuries, and indeed continues today. Gardening is supposed to be a restful occupation, but in my experience kitchen gardeners are a restless bunch, ever looking for new types of vegetables or new variants of those already in their gardens. They are egged on by cooks who demand novelty, and ultimately by consumers. Of course, in many cases the same person embodies all these roles. Motives are, and were in the past, mixed; some want new and exciting tastes, others are nostalgic for vegetables and salads they have sampled abroad, for some it is all about 'one-upmanship', and others are just addicted to novelty.

In the sixteenth century the trade in garden seeds was rudimentary. Domestically-grown seeds, and some imported by general merchants, were purchased by itinerant seed sellers and hawked around the London markets and taken round the country by pedlars. Many seeds sold in this way were of poor quality, and the seed sellers were bitterly denounced: Sir Hugh Plat condemned 'these petit coseners' and 'lying and forswearing Huswives' who sold seeds in Cheapside, and a contemporary of his, Richard Gardiner, was withering in his description of 'the great and abominable falsehoode of those sortes of people which sell Garden seedes […] those Catterpillers'.[2]

As Holinshed pointed out, those who could obtained their exotic seeds direct from agents abroad. Amongst the nobility, he doubtless had in mind men such as Robert Dudley, Earl of Leicester, who in 1584 sought a French gardener who had Italian connections and would 'bring with him all manner of sedes the best you can procure among the Italians, as well for herbs and salletts as for all kind of rare floers beside sedes for myllons collyflorry and such lyke asparagus & all sorts of Radyshe'.[3] He may also have known John Gerard, a London apothecary principally remembered for his

Herbal of 1597, who was also a noted gardener. Gerard relied on many correspondents and acquaintances for exotic seeds and plants. One such was Nicholas Lete, a Levant merchant who was made English consul in Algiers in 1623. Lete was both a merchant and a plant enthusiast. Gerard wrote of the 'Swollen Colewart' (presumably kohlrabi):

> which I received from a worshipfull merchant of London master Nicholas Lete, who brought the seed thereof out of France; who is greatly in love with rare and faire floures & plants, for which he doth carefully send into Syria, having a servant there at Aleppo, and in many other countries, for which my selfe and likewise the whole land are much bound unto him.

Lete is also remembered for introducing a double yellow rose from Constantinople.[4]

Contemporary with Gerard, Gardiner, and Plat was the Italian religious exile Giacomo Castelvetro. Fleeing from the Inquisition in Venice, he ended his days teaching Italian and writing in English noble households until his death in 1616. Castelvetro was an enthusiast for the vegetables of his native Italy, producing a 1614 treatise, *The Fruit, Herbs and Vegetables of Italy*, and explaining in the introduction,

> I often reflect upon the variety of good things to eat which have been introduced into this noble country of yours over the past fifty years. The vast influx of so many refugees from the evils and cruelties of the Roman Inquisition has led to the introduction of delights previously considered inedible, worthless or even poisonous. Yet I am amazed that so few of these delicious and health-giving plants are being grown to be eaten. Through ignorance or indifference, it seems to me that they are cultivated less for the table than for show by those who want to boast of their exotic plants and well-stocked gardens.
>
> This moves me to write down all that I can remember of the names of the herbs, fruits and plants we eat in Italy, my civilised homeland, and to explain how to prepare them, either raw or cooked, for the table, so that the English no longer need be deprived through lack of information of the delights of growing and eating them.

Unfortunately, he wrote in Italian, and it was not until comparatively recently that his enthusiastic little book was translated. Nevertheless, Castelvetro did his best to introduce Italian vegetables to England, sending home long lists of seeds he wanted sent from Venice.[5]

Castelvetro was a friend of Sir Henry Wotton, sometime Ambassador to Venice. Wotton was interested enough in Italian vegetables to send packets of seeds to his friend, the royal gardener, John Tradescant the elder, who then passed some to his friend, the apothecary, gardener, and writer John Parkinson. (Tradescant, I might add, made his contribution to the influx of Mediterranean plants, going as a volunteer on a punitive expedition against Algerian pirates and bringing back a new type of apricot.) Parkinson records in 1629:

The English Quest for Novelty: Kitchen Garden Seeds from Abroad

> The sweete Cardus Fenell being sent by Sir Henrey Wotton to John Tradescant, had likewise a large direction with it how to dresse it; for they use to white it after it hath been transplanted for their uses, which by reason of the sweetnesse by nature, and the tendernesse by art, causeth it to be the more delightfull to the taste, especially with them that are accustomed to feede on greene herbes.

Wotton is obviously a lover of Florence fennel and goes into detail as to how it should be prepared for the table. Parkinson himself was keen to promote well-flavoured vegetables and herbs, and a food historian has recently noticed his many references to 'those that take delight in eating of herbs' in his herbal, suggesting that there was an upsurge of interest amongst the gentry in edible vegetables at this time. In his herbal Parkinson describes many other Italian imports as well. For instance, out of '[s]o great diversitie of Lettice'[... t]he Romane red Lettice is the best and greatest of all the rest. For Iohn Tradescant that first, as I thinke, brought it into England, and sowed it, did write unto mee, that after one of them had been bound and whited, when the refuse was cut away, the rest weighed seventeen ounces'. (Both the fennel and Roman lettuce were blanched, and the preference of Italians for blanched salads is a recurring theme.) Parkinson part-financed a plant collector to find useful new plants in Spain, but on one occasion he found Italian vegetables close to home; he was introduced to 'sweet parsley' by the Italian ambassador in his London garden.[6]

John Evelyn, a gentleman of many interests, toured Italy in the 1640s, and, although there are few hints of his interest in Italian food in his diary of that time, his passion for vegetables and salads, from Italy and elsewhere, shines through his work *Acetaria, a discourse of sallets*, of 1699. He wrote of fresh salads:

> ready to hand, and easily dress'd; requiring neither Fire, Cost, or Attendance, to boil, roast, and prepare them [...] indeed the more frugal Italians and French, to this Day, accept and gather Ogni Verdura, any thing almost that's Green and Tender, to the very Tops of Nettles; so as every Hedge affords a Sallet (not unagreeable) season'd with its proper Oxybaphon of Vinegar, salt, oyl, &c. which doubtless gives it both the Relish and Name of Salad.

Evelyn wrote with approval of broccoli from Naples; sweet fennel from Bolognia ('the Italians eat the blanch'd Stalk [...] all Winter long'); celery which he said had recently come over from Italy; and other simple Italian salads such as one 'of Scalions, Cives, and Chibbols only season'd with Oyl and Pepper'. Evelyn, like Plat and Castelvetro, was an importer of culinary ideas.[7]

Alongside the introduction of plants and seeds from abroad by gentlemen amateurs, England was developing in the seventeenth century a commercial retail seed trade supplied both from home production and abroad. Seeds were at first sold by London general merchants, grocers, and the like as well as pedlars and hawkers, but in the second half of the seventeenth century there was some specialization in garden seeds. Judging from surviving seed catalogues, the late John Harvey thought there were three major London firms in 1688, five in 1730, and at least a dozen in 1760, by which time there were also some provincial seed merchants. Certainly by the 1680s newspaper advertisements for imported seeds were common enough for readers to appreciate a spoof advertisement for foreign 'Sedition Seeds' in a satirical anti-Catholic pamphlet. In 1692 it was recorded that 450 pounds of garden seeds had been imported through the port of London in just one month, from mid-April to mid-May.[8]

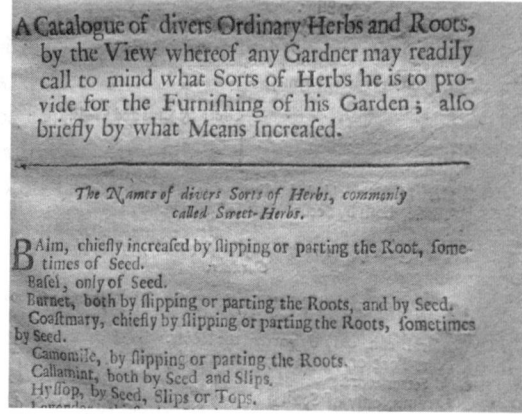

Figure 1: Part of nurseryman and seedsman Leonard Gurle's catalogue inserted into his friend Leonard Meager's English Gardener, *1704.*

The seed trade developed a distinctive mode of business in the seventeenth and eighteenth centuries. All the major firms were based in London because: they relied heavily on imported seeds and London was the predominant English port; seeds were light and could be easily sent to customers all over the country by post or carrier; the middle classes and gentry, their main customers, either lived in London or its suburbs, or visited the Capital for business and pleasure; and customers nationwide could be kept informed about the range of seeds available by catalogues posted to them. The early catalogues were simple broadsides, printed with seed lists on one side, but these developed into booklets as the range of seeds increased, and some merchants went further and produced books describing how to grow the seeds advertised and even how to dress the vegetables and salads for the table. These catalogues usually did not include prices for the seeds; instead, they were *aides memoire* of the seeds available from which customers could compile their annual orders.[9] Some seed firms' advertising efforts were helped by writers of gardening books who included seedsmen's and nurserymen's lists in their works. Leonard Meager included the list of his friend the nurseryman Leonard Gurle in a book of 1704; Thomas Langford inserted part of the Brompton Park nursery catalogue in a book dated 1696; and in 1726 Benjamin Whitmill wrote that the seeds listed in his book could be obtained from 'Mrs Arabella Fuller, at the Three Crowns and Naked Boy, over against the New Church in the Strand'. Her predecessor in the business, Edward Fuller, had his list included in the third edition of John Worlidge's gardening book of 1688.[10]

The reliance on new imported varieties of vegetable and salad seeds can be demonstrated by examining a couple of seed catalogues. An early one – the broadside of William Lucas dated 1677 – has four varieties of cabbage, two of which, the Russia and the Dutch, are foreign in origin. Of his eight varieties of lettuce, three, the Roman,

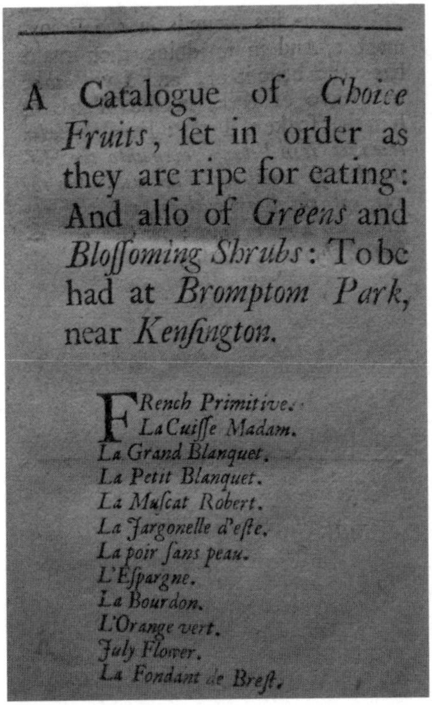

The English Quest for Novelty: Kitchen Garden Seeds from Abroad

> A Catalogue of Choice Fruits, set in order as they are ripe for eating: And also of Greens and Blossoming Shrubs: To be had at Bromptom Park, near Kensington.
>
> French Primitive.
> La Cuisse Madam.
> La Grand Blanquet.
> La Petit Blanquet.
> La Muscat Robert.
> La Jargonelle d'este.
> La poir sans peau.
> L'Espargne.
> La Bourdon.
> L'Orange vert.
> July Flower.
> La Fondant de Brest.

Figure 2: Part of the Brompton Park Nursery catalogue included in T. Langford's Plain And Full Instructions *etc, 1696.*

Arabian, and Savoy, are foreign. A list from a London seedsman of the 1720s contains seven types of cabbage, including Dutch, Red Dutch, Brown Dutch, and Russia. The list has eleven varieties of lettuce, most of them of foreign origin and half from the Mediterranean: Versailles, Brazil, Cos, Aleppo, Silesia, Black Spanish, Genoa, and Brown Dutch. By 1782 a nurseryman in a small Dorset town could offer sixteen types of Lettuce seed, including five types of Cos, as well as Silesia, Brown Dutch, Roman Cabbage, and Egyptian Green.[11]

One of the increasing numbers of seed firms in the eighteenth century was that of Stephen Switzer, who started out as a gardener and garden designer. He operated from a stall in Westminster Hall (then a fashionable shopping area) from the 1720s. Switzer was an entrepreneur who saw the potential of a seed-business in the West End, but he had to contend with 'some very il Will conceived against me by some of my Brother Seedsmen, on Account, (as I suppose, of my being a Gard'ner, and not a Seedsman bred)'. Some of the envy of rivals was probably because Switzer was an astute businessman and skilful advertiser in an age when this art was reaching some sophistication.[12]

In 1728 he published *A compendious method for raising Italian broccoli, Spanish cardoon, celeriac, finochi, and other foreign seeds*, part of a small collection of pamphlets entitled *The Country Gentleman's Companion* which went through five further editions to 1735.[13] This work was essentially an advertisement for Switzer's new and most fashionable vegetable seeds, the four in the title all being Italian salad-crops. With the exception of celeriac 'which is in great Esteem about Naples; but the Seed is imported to us from Alexandria', a port in modern day Syria, all the seeds originated in Italy. Broccoli he describes as 'a Kind of Italian Kele, or Colewort, which grows on the Sea-Coasts about Naples, and other Places in Italy; from whence the best Seed is yearly exported, that which is saved in England being little worth'. The imported seed could however, be unreliable, Switzer explains:

> The greatest Difficulty that attends this Affair in the getting Seeds from abroad, is, the great Cheat that those People, who gather it on the Sea-side, put upon the

A
CATALOGUE
OF
Seeds, Fruit and Foreſt Trees, Shrubs, Flowers, &c. *Sold by* S. SWITZER, *at the* Flower-Pot, *over-againſt the* Court of Common-Pleas *in* Weſtminſter Hall; *or at his Garden on* Millbank, Weſtminſter; *with the Seaſons of Sowing and Planting,* &c.

CLASS I.
PEASE.

HOTSPUR, beginning or middle of October and February; and for the laſt Crops, the middle of May
Eſſex Roadings, for a general Crop, the firſt ſown in February, the laſt the middle or later end of May
Dwarf Edgers, once a Month, from February to the middle or latter end of May

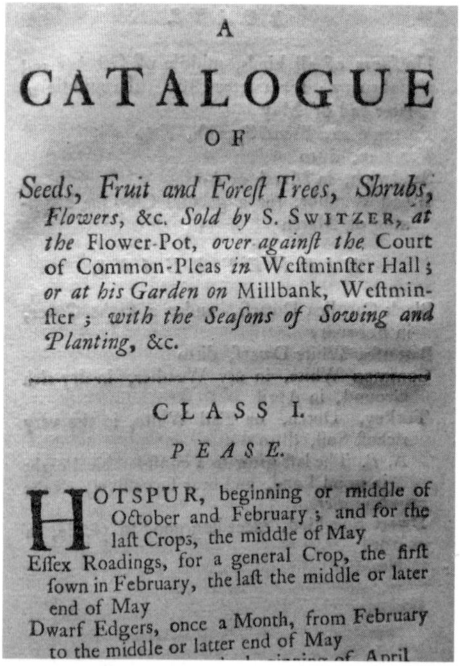

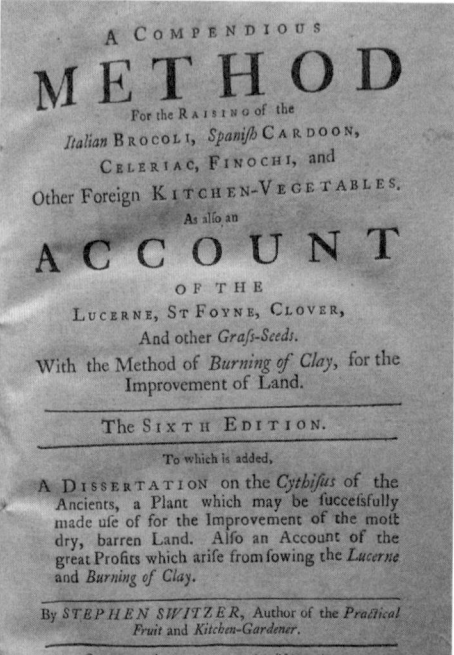

Figure 3: Switzer's seed catalogue at the rear of his pamphlet on Italian salad crops.

A COMPENDIOUS
METHOD
For the RAISING of the
Italian BROCOLI, *Spaniſh* CARDOON,
CELERIAC, FINOCHI, and
Other Foreign KITCHEN-VEGETABLES.
As alſo an
ACCOUNT
OF THE
LUCERNE, ST FOYNE, CLOVER,
And other *Graſs-Seeds.*
With the Method of *Burning of Clay,* for the Improvement of Land.

The SIXTH EDITION.

To which is added,
A DISSERTATION on the *Cythiſus* of the Ancients, a Plant which may be ſucceſsfully made uſe of for the Improvement of the moſt dry, barren Land. Alſo an Account of the great Profits which ariſe from ſowing the *Lucerne* and *Burning of Clay.*

By *STEPHEN SWITZER,* Author of the *Practical Fruit* and *Kitchen-Gardener.*

Figure 4: A Compendious Method of raising Italian Brocoli etc. *1735. The sixth edition of Stephen Switzer's advertising pamphlet.*

Merchants and consequently upon us here, has been a great Hindrance to using it for this Year: For though I saw the Bag just brought from the Water-side and mark'd with an Italian Mark and Character, and saw the Bill of Parcels, &c in the Importer's own Hands, yet when it came up, it was nothing else but Turneps; so little Faith is to be found amongst those Collectors of Seeds, who no doubt think it no Sin to cheat Hereticks.

Switzer gives an impression of disorganized and disreputable Italian producers, but seed production may have been more advanced than he admits: there were Italian seed firms in the eighteenth century. Switzer bought his Italian seed wholesale from a London overseas merchant, a 'Gentleman in the City, who has long been a great Importer of all curious Seeds' although beans of 'The Venetian Kind, I have within these two Years had from a Captain who came from thence', and he obtained lettuce seed (and celeriac) from 'Turkey merchants'.[14]

Switzer's hastily produced work makes great play of how good to eat these vegetables are, and of their novelty, while at the same time downplaying any difficulties of cultivation in our climate. Broccoli was:

a Sallad that has been some Time amongst us; but our not knowing how to manage it, has brought a kind of Disreputation upon it, though there have been, and are still, many Advocates for it and, if well managed, it is, in my humble Opinion, next to the true Asparagus, the best boil'd Winter Sallad we have, at least much better than any other kind of Sprouts that grow, and is in Season at such Time, when nothing else equal to it can be got.

Of celeriac he opines, 'Those who have eat it abroad say, that it is much better then Common Celery, as it grows thicker and smaller and eats much shorter, and has a more exalted taste than that has. [… A]nd if it be no other than what is commonly known by the Name of Italian Celery, it is, in my humble Opinion, much to be preferr'd to the common Sort.' Of the Spanish cardoon, he writes, 'I think when it is well whiten'd, it eats much better in Soups then Celery does; and being stew'd in a Pan, eats a great deal shorter, perfectly melting in a Man's Mouth.' Finally, on finochi or Italian fennel:

> It has been but a few Years amongst us, and really in the hands of very few; the Right Honourable the Earl of Peterborough being almost the only one that has brought it over, or knows its Virtues and Uses; but it is a Plant of such wonderful Properties in refining the Blood, exhilarating the Spirits, and strengthening the Stomach, that I am sanguine enough to believe, that were it possible that there were Virtues in any one Plant in nature capable of introducing Immortality among Mankind, this would do it. This Plant, if […] eat in a Morning, or indeed at any Time of the Day, with Bread and Butter, Oil and a little Vinegar, as you do Celery, is (I humbly conceive) one of the wholesomest Sallads in the World.

He concludes that these vegetables will contribute, 'if moderately us'd, to Life and Pleasure itself'.[15]

Switzer's pamphlet may give the impression that we are now well into a commercial phase of seed imports from Italy, largely in the hands of English agents in ports such as Livorno and Naples, with big importers in London supplying retail seedsmen like Switzer. He, and fellow seedsmen, followed – and led – fashion in garden crops, part of what has been termed the 'Consumer Revolution' in eighteenth-century England, when clothes, household goods, luxuries, food and drink, and many more goods were increasingly subject to fashion, and consequently bought for ostentatious display. But the amateur importer was by no means eclipsed, which we may verify from within the pamphlet itself. Note Switzer's remark that 'the Right Honourable the Earl of Peterborough' was almost the only one who had previously imported and understood the use of Florence fennel. Charles Mordaunt, the third earl, was a soldier and diplomat who had travelled extensively in Italy and fought in Spain. Retiring to his house at Parsons Green, just outside London, he became a keen gardener. He was a friend of another amateur gardener, Alexander Pope, who wrote of him, 'He, whose Lightning pierc'd the Iberian Lines, / now forms my Quincunx, and now ranks my Vines'. (Appropriately, Peterborough died in Lisbon 'of a Flux, by eating grapes'.)[16]

In discussing celeriac Switzer admitted that he had not seen the vegetable growing and thought it might be what was then known as Italian celery. His incorrect assumption was challenged in 1728 by the gardener Thomas Knowlton, who wrote to tell him exactly what the plant was and how to grow it. Switzer inserted the letter in later editions of his pamphlet. Knowlton had been gardener to James Brydges, Duke of Chandos at Cannons, in Edgeware, another suburb of London. The Duke was a keen fruit and vegetable gardener, obtaining exotics such as pineapples, avocado pear, coffee, pawpaws, star apples, and guavas from the West Indies for his garden and, significantly, 'Messrs Harriman of Leghorn supplied, among other things, Broccoli seed and Fennel, and Evergreen Oak acorns'. Switzer also mentions that 'a Person who was for some Years gardener to the British Embassy at Constantinople' had given him advice on broccoli. Of an alternative to that vegetable, Murcian Kale, he wrote 'several Gentlemen who have eaten it in Portugal [...] think it] much sweeter than Brocoli itself [.... I] had some of the Seeds this Year from the Reverend Mr Sims, Chaplain to the British Factory' (i.e. merchant community in Lisbon).[17]

The Crown was also interested in new vegetables from Portugal. In 1775 the British Consul in Lisbon was asked to seek 'such seeds of Plants or Legumes as may be for the Improvement of His Majesty's Kitchen Gardens'. He replied that there was not much to send apart from some melon pumpkin seeds, Moroccan beans, and 'cabbages of Murcia'. He would send these and 'whatsoever else I shall be able to learn may possibly be of use in an English Kitchen Garden'.[18]

The delight some of Switzer's customers took in imported varieties of vegetable was reflected in a more general increase in demand for such foods from the London gentry. A gardening colleague of Switzer's, Richard Bradley, a prolific writer and Professor of Botany at Cambridge, estimated in 1726 that 'it is not rare to see Bills from Fruiterers and Herb-shops, of one Winter's standing, to amount to Sixty, Eighty, an Hundred, and some-times an Hundred and Fifty Pounds, where the families are large'. Bradley is talking of rich Londoners, but even so these are high figures. They reflect the high prices paid in London either for ordinary vegetables grown out of season, or for fashionable vegetables, cauliflowers, asparagus, spinach, mushrooms, and the like, as well as the Italian imports I have discussed. Novelty was vital: Bradley complained (echoing Catelvetro), 'We have great variety of Lettuce, many of which are more esteemed for their Rarity than for their Goodness.' There has always been an element of ostentation in vegetable gardening – Sir Hugh Plat heard that an Italian gardener in London presented the Lord Mayor with fresh salads at Christmas 1584 and more than a century later Sir Nathaniel Gould's gardener proudly presented his master with a brace of cucumbers on New Year's Day 1722.[19]

The fashion for new vegetable and salad crops was the reason that Switzer was importuned to write his pamphlet in haste by gentlemen customers: they wanted to know how to handle imported Italian vegetables. This need was now pressing in the case of broccoli which, according to Richard Bradley in 1721, 'has been cultivated privately in

The English Quest for Novelty: Kitchen Garden Seeds from Abroad

some few gardens in England for about three years'. He too had been asked to draw up, 'for a Person of Honour', a pamphlet 'concerning their Use, and Method of preparing them for the Table [...] with some other things proper for a curious Kitchen Gardener', although he does not appear to have done so. Bradley adds that the seed of purple broccoli could be had 'at the Crown, an Italian gardener's, behind Buckingham House' so Switzer was not the only commercial broccoli-seed seller at this time. If you were a provincial gentleman, obtaining fashionable seed was much harder: a correspondent wrote to Bradley in September 1721 from Newcastle-upon-Tyne asking if he could obtain broccoli seed for him from the aforementioned Italian gardener, or from one of the 'Gentlemen, who have them every Year from Italy'.[20]

For every gentleman desperate for advice, however, there was one with experience of exotic vegetables willing to share knowledge. The additions and amendments to later editions of Switzer's pamphlet prove that the amateur importers of Italian vegetables seeds had much to teach him. In the 1732 edition he reported of sweet fennel: 'A nobleman, very curious in Gardening, tells me, he plants his Finochi Seeds in straight Lines, at about ten or twelve Inches asunder', another 'Noble Lord, who has raised a great deal of Finochi for several Years past' gave advice, as did 'An Ingenious Gentleman of Brumpton [who] has for several Years past preserved it all Year'. Finally, he writes, 'Since the second Edition of this pamphlet came out, I find Gentlemen differ as to the Methods eating of Finochi; some chuse to eat it green, other white.' We can imagine enthusiasts for these exotic food plants gathering at Switzer's shop in Westminster Hall to discuss the finer points of growing and eating Italian and other vegetables, with Switzer's pamphlet becoming in its later editions like a Wikipedia entry, with new facts and corrections inserted in each edition.[21]

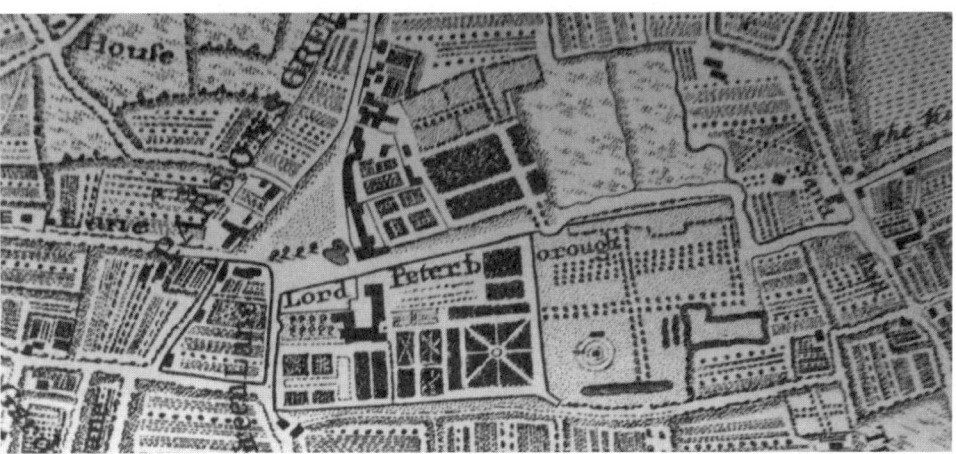

Figure 5: Lord Peterborough's garden at Parsons Green, near London, showing that it was in the 1740s almost surrounded by market gardens. John Rocque, An Exact Survey of the Cities of London and Westminster, *1741-1746.*

Seeds

I have concentrated here on novel vegetables and salads imported principally from abroad, most notably from Italy to England, up to the 1730s. Italian fruit was also prized, and I am sure much could be said about attempts to bring in fruit trees from Italy. I have sought to demonstrate that, although commercial seed imports became more important in the early seventeenth century, the lively interest of some gentlemen in their gardens (and the produce therefrom) led some to continue to import seed directly via friends and acquaintances. Indeed, the commercial seedsmen and the garden-loving gentlemen were inextricably linked: Switzer was at various times a commercial nurseryman, seedsman, gardener to the gentry, and garden designer. He talked on easy terms with his gentry customers. Indeed, many gentlemen near London lived next to commercial gardeners – John Rocque's map of London and environs published in the 1740s depicts Lord Peterborough's house and gardens at Parsons Green bordered by market gardens with the nursery garden of Rocque's brother Bartholomew very close at hand. It is no wonder that gardening innovations, including new types of imported vegetables and fruits, passed from commercial to private gardens and vice versa.[22]

Seed especially was light and easy to transport from abroad – the difficulty was in growing it in an alien soil and climate. But hope springs eternal, and no doubt gentlemen who had travelled to the Mediterranean, especially to Italy, and sampled the delights of the garden produce there were very keen to reproduce Italian salads to impress their friends and recreate the meals they remembered. In doing so they contributed to the great expansion of plant varieties cultivated in English gardens, from about 200 in 1550 to an estimated 18,000 in 1839.[23]

Notes

1. Qtd. in Alicia Amherst, *A History of Gardening in England* (London: Quaritch, 1895), p.132.
2. Qtd. in Malcolm Thick, 'Garden Seeds in England before the Late Eighteenth Century: II. The Trade in Seeds to 1760', *Agricultural History Review*, 38.II (1990), 106-07.
3. Qtd. in David Jacques, 'The Place of Kenilworth in Garden History', in *The Elizabethan Garden at Kenilworth Castle*, ed. by Anna Keay and John Watkins (London: English Heritage, 2013), p. 11.
4. British Library, Sloane MS, SL 2210, f.141; SL 2216, f.158; John Gerard, *The Herbal* (London: Adam Islip,1633), p. 314; Robert H. Jeffers, *The Friends of John Gerard* (Falls Village, CT: Herb Grower Press, 1967), p. 62; Eleanour Sinclair Rhode, *Garden-Craft in the Bible and Other Essays* (New York: Books for Libraries Press, 1967), pp. 126-27.
5. Giacomo Castelvetro, *The Fruit, Herbs and Vegetables of Italy*, trans. by Gillian Riley (London: Viking, 1989), pp. 10, 15, 25, 49.
6. Castelvetro, p. 9; Joan Thirsk, *Food in Early Modern England* (London: Continuum, 2007), pp. 68-72; John Parkinson, *Paradisi in Sole* (London: Tho. Cotes, 1629), pp. 498, 490, 502.
7. John Evelyn, *Acetaria, a discourse of Sallets* (London: B.Took, 1699), pp. 5, 16, 25, 48, 63.
8. Thick, pp. 106-09, 113; John Harvey, *Early Nurserymen* (London: Phillimore, 1974), pp. 5-7; John Houghton, *A Collection for the Improvement of Husbandry and Trade, no. 15* (London: 18 May 1692)
9. See Thick.
10. John Worlidge, *Systema horti-culturae* (London: Thos. Dring, 1688); Leonard Meager, *The English Gardener* (London: M. Wotton, 1704), pp. 48-51; Benjamin Whitmill, *The Complete Seedsman*

(London: W. Mears, 1726), f. A1.
11 John Harvey, *Early Gardening Catalogues* (London: Phillimore, 1972), pp. 65-74; Stephen Switzer, *The Country Gentlemen's Companion* (London: T. Astley, 1732), pp. 58-60; John Harvey, 'Introduction'. T*he Georgian Garden* (Wimborne: Dovecoat Press 1983); Kent Archives Office, U269; E21.
12 Troy Bickham, 'Eating the Empire: Intersections of Food, Cookery and Imperialism in Eighteenth-Century Britain', *Past & Present,* 198 (February 2008), pp. 82-83.
13 Blanche Henrey, *British Botanical and Horticultural Literature before 1800* (Oxford: Oxford University Press, 1975), III, p.125.
14 Switzer, pp. v, 1, 2, 5, 8, 21, 22.
15 Switzer, pp. v-vii, 13.
16 Switzer, pp. vii, 10; Gigliola Pagano De Divitiis, *English Merchants in Seventeenth-Century Italy* (Cambridge: Cambridge University Press, 1990), pp. 114, 121. A quincunx is pattern of planting five trees symmetrically, repeated over an orchard.
17 Switzer, pp. 1-2, 9-10, 19; Blanche Henrey, *No Ordinary Gardener, Thomas Knowlton, 1691-1781* (London: British Museum, 1986), pp. 43-44.
18 National Archives, SP 81/39/79, f.186.
19 BL, SL 2210, 189a; Richard Bradley, *General Treatise of Husbandry and Gardening* (London: J.Peele, 1721-1724), II, p. 246.
20 Bradley, I, pp. 43, 283.
21 Switzer, pp. 6, 12.
22 John Rocque, *An Exact Survey of the Cities of London and Westminster, 1741-1746.*
23 N. McKendrick, J. Brewer, and J.H. Plumb, *The Birth of Consumer Society: The Commercialization of Eighteenth-Century England* (London: HarperCollins, 1982), p. 326.

Seeds

Seed-Time: Back-to-the-Land Sex and Politics at the Fin de Siècle

Kate Thomas

The Fellowship of the New Life was a socialist, free-thinking group founded in 1883 that is now little thought of because it quickly produced an offshoot organization that eclipsed it in fame and longevity: the Fabian Society, established in 1884. Most accounts of the split have tended to characterize the Fabians as more political, public, and pragmatic in contradistinction to the Fellowship members' focus on a more inward, mystical, or 'ethical' approach to life. Some recent scholarship has, however, argued that this might be a false dichotomy; along with prompts from new materialist and 'plant life' theory, this offers new reasons to examine nineteenth-century socialist back-to-the-land projects.[1]

There is also strong reason to study germinal radical groups that grew into more mainstream organizations; it follows the logic of their own metaphors. The root of the word 'radical' means 'root', in the botanical sense. The term 'grass-root', when used by left-wing political movements, both invokes age-old concepts of the 'commons' and expresses the potentialities of botanical, non-hierarchical, mass growth. George Bernard Shaw, who joined the Fabians, mocked Fellowship members as people 'that wanted to sit among the dandelions' instead of 'organiz[ing] the docks'. On one level, it's a simple critique of dreamers versus doers. But why does Shaw reach for dandelions to level his charge? Why does he snigger at plant life as if it were inert and a partner to inaction? After all, Shaw would himself later celebrate the 'fierce energy concentrated in an acorn', and the Fellowship was acorn to the Fabian Oak.[2] The figurative associations of the two different plant forms are, however, signally different. The oak invokes gravitas, national and familial chauvinisms; in contrast, Shaw caricatures the dandelion as an effeminate and commonplace weed.[3] But if Shaw affected to crush the field flower beneath his heel, one Fellowship member was ready to grant it philosophical appreciation. In an essay on weeds, writer and gay rights activist Edward Carpenter calls dandelions 'handsome' and admires them for being able to 'hold their own in the struggle'.[4] Carpenter refuses Shaw's machismo scorn, resignifying the dandelion as dashing, not outcast, and wearing it with a gay pride.

As any gardener will attest, it is Carpenter's characterization of the dandelion as a tough adversary that rings more true. Its root system is tenacious and – as many a child

Seed-Time: Back-to-the-Land Sex and Politics at the Fin de Siècle

knows – its seed-delivery system peculiarly designed for wide and mass broadcasting. Its leaves, too, turn the plant into a nutritious vegetable, widely available for foraging. In a poem titled 'The First Dandelion', Carpenter's friend and lover, Walt Whitman, portrays that plant as democratic and free, he writes, from 'artifice of fashion, business, politics'.[5] Carpenter (who was greatly influenced not only by Whitman, but also by Henry David Thoreau) and his comrades in the Fellowship did indeed favour Nature over the commerce of the world.[6] Less interested in the import-export activities that would have gone on at Bernard Shaw's 'docks', the Fellowship described themselves in their manifesto as united around the objective of '[t]he cultivation of a perfect character in each and all'.[7] The agrarian associations of the term 'cultivation' were amplified in the title of the Fellowship's quarterly journal, *Seed-Time*.[8] This cultivation, and these seeds, were both metaphorical and literal: the Fellowship drew together interests that ranged from socialist reform, feminism, and communal living to free love, gay rights, manual labour, and vegetarianism.

The original Fellowship had been formed by Thomas Davidson, a Scottish schoolmaster, who had also spent time in North America. He and another founder, Percival Chubb, pursued transatlantic reformist careers while other London-based members maintained the activities and growth of the Fellowship, including launching the quarterly journal. Other fellowship members included the sexologist Havelock Ellis; the feminist Edith Lees; authors Arthur Ransom, Edith Nesbit, Katharine Bradley, and Olive Schreiner; and vegetarian and free-love activists Henry and Kate Salt. They also shared interests in pacificism, anti-vivisectionism, self-sufficiency, and communal living. When Edward Carpenter set up a farming community in a village called Millthorpe outside Sheffield, it showed how the seeds of change included, for many Fellowship members, planting actual seeds. That Millthorpe was also a gay commune, visited by those questing for sexual freedom, reveals a fin-de-siècle interrelation of polymorphous sexual attachments and sustainable plant-based eating.[9]

Improper Objects: Carpenter's Socialist Seed

Victorian interest in flowers is well-documented.[10] Less explored is the way that theories of evolution 'opened up' the seed for new consideration. In his 1869 study of myths, *The Queen of the Air*, John Ruskin had rejected what he saw as Charles Darwin's undue emphasis on reproduction, arguing 'the flower is the end or proper object of the seed, not the seed of the flower'.[11] Ruskin's discomfort is clearly with the sexiness of seed, and he insists on a singular 'proper object', an effort to neuter its polymorphous fruitfulness. But for others, the multiplicity contained in the seed was not threatening, but instead a source of fascination. After the turn of the century, Virginia Woolf wrote of seeds as 'germs of what might have been, had one's life been different' ('A Sketch of the Past').[12] Woolf's perfect-infinitive focus on the seed as archive of difference and possibility echoes Darwin's work on how 'strongly-marked differences occasionally appear in the young of the same litter, and in seedlings from the same seed-capsule'.[13] Both Woolf and Darwin regarded the seed as a repository of difference and variation-of-kind. Oscar Wilde also found the seed to be a compelling agent of variation because of its capacity to cross borders of nation and century, and then take root in an altogether different time and place. In a poem titled 'Athanasia' he dramatizes the finding of an ancient seed found in the grip of a mummified Egyptian girl:

> But when they had unloosed the linen band
> > Which swathed the Egyptian's body – lo! Was found
> Closed in the wasted hollow of her hand
> > A little seed, which sown in English ground
> Did wondrous snow of starry blossoms bear
> And spread rich odours through our spring-tide air.[14]

The dominant imagery of these lines is of enclosure and release: the seed is 'closed in'; the linen wraps are 'unloosed'; the blossoms then 'spread' their perfume. The seed is found doubly entombed, in both the burial pyramid and the 'hollow' of the hand. It seems fully and resonantly 'wasted,' but it then not only finds new life in new soil, but it then also has the power to revitalize that new environment: this is an Orientalist fantasy that England can be infused with that which is eastern and 'wondrous'.[15] The 'rich odours' of this plant life hybridizes the air that the English will breathe, releasing not only vitality, but intimations of immortality; the athanasia flower derives its name from the Greek: 'without' (a-) 'death' (Thanatos).[16] Wilde and other fin-de-siècle queer writers commonly turned to ancient cultures in an effort to loosen the bands of Victorian sexual and aesthetic conventions, and in this poem the portable, transported seed acts as an epistemic and ethnic agent provocateur. And the transit that the seed experiences, its nomadic undertakings, might be as important as its genetic content. As Michael Marder proposes in *Plant-Thinking: A Philosophy of Vegetal Life*, the wandering seed 'portends the beauty of what is unpredictable, unknown, discrete, discontinuous, and non-reproducible even in the middle of the reproductive cycle'.[17] We would do well to remember that the root of the word 'queer' is 'quer', meaning 'to cross'; the process of crossing borders can engage a queer, non-linear kind of reproduction. And this is what Wilde imagines; the immortality the seed embodies casts the petty strife and cares of the current age into irrelevance. The seed has such metamorphosing power that the plant it produces becomes, as in a myth, a reincarnation or offspring of the dead Egyptian girl. One of the borders it opens up is between plant-kind and human-kind.

Edward Carpenter held a similar romance of the seed, and a related aversion to mummification. 'Man has to undo the wrappings and mummydom of centuries,' he wrote, exposing himself to 'the light of the sun'.[18] His friend and Fellowship comrade Henry Salt explicated Carpenter's simple life pro-vitality philosophy further: 'The "return to nature," then, which Mr. Carpenter advocates as the cure for our present distraction, does not imply anything so foolish as a return to mere barbarism. It is a plea for a simple unencumbered life – for less luxury, less worldliness, less respectability, less 'mummydom' in general; for more freedom, more courage, more fresh air, more careless enjoyment of existence.'[19] Another member of the Fellowship, Herbert Rix, published a similar anti-materialist, pro-nature essay in Issue Two of the fellowship's journal, *Seed-Time*. 'The Return to Nature', subtitled 'An Address delivered to the New Fellowship on the Occasion of a Country Excursion', again engages the image of the revivified mummy; our return to nature, Rix tells us, is 'when the dead heart begins to beat again, when some prophet's touch unseals those eyes'. The worldly goods we pursue are false fruits that cause us to waste away: 'trifles [...] ornaments [...] and crinkum-crankums in general [...] feed neither the body nor the soul'. Rix rails against consumerist appetites for 'silk dresses, diamond rings, and hot-house fruits!' – all, of course, commodities derived from press-ganging nature's resources into over-stimulated, strip-mined, unseasonal forms of production. Why 'imprison' ourselves in this world of industrial production, he asks, when 'every May-time the hawthorn whitens for us, and the blackbird whistles, and the king-cups fill the meadows with their golden glory'.[20] Rix's hailing of nature is, perhaps, undercut by the robust androcentrism of imagining that birds sing and plants bloom 'for us'. And when we remember the occasion of this essay is the day trip of the mostly upper-class Fellowship members, who will, after their return to Nature, return to London, we can certainly see that the Fellowship's vision could not always encompass those whose lives were structured by May-times and meadows.

But 'returning to nature' also required understanding the returns within nature, and an understanding that Nature is not all fresh air and sunlight. In his 1904 essay 'The Art of Creation' Carpenter writes:

> And now, at this time of year, there are lying and being buried in the great Earth thousands and thousands of millions of seeds of all kinds of plants and trees, which during the long winter will slumber there like little dream-images in the brain of the great globe, waiting for their awakening. And when the Spring comes with the needful conditions, they will push forward towards their expression and materialization in the outer world, even as every thought presses towards its manifestation in us.[21]

Carpenter's prose swells with urgency and agency, figuring the seed as a pod of energy that is ready to join a cosmic project. For Wilde, the slumbering seed was much more careless of consciousness; it does its work of awakening desire by stealth or seduction. It changes the world not by changing minds, but by infiltrating the senses. For Carpenter, thought is more leading. Indeed, he analogizes seeds as thoughts. His project is one of self-determination and self-realization, which he makes clear in a footnote to the passage: 'Who knows but what our brains in the same way are full of tiny atoms – seed-atoms of desire and purpose – which lie there silent and compressed, till conditions liberate them to long trains of action in the drama of humanity?' There's a charm to the way Carpenter buries this question in a footnote; seed-like, it repeats the material, in only slightly different form, of the body of his text. If the emphasis is different, it might derive from the crisp sibilance of the phrase 'silent and compressed'. Just as Wilde's poem had focused on enclosure then release, Carpenter envisions the moment that these 'seed-atoms' will be 'liberated'. Then, their silence and compression will, it implies, burst with a power that has intensified from being pent-up.

We must see the figurations from these queer writers as expressions of the relations of the closet, relations that Eve Kosofsky Sedgwick glosses as 'the relations of the known and unknown, the explicit and the inexplicit'.[22] Wilde and Carpenter are, after all, the two first English writers to articulate a modern philosophy of gay rights. Wilde defended gay culture on the witness stand, and Carpenter wrote repeatedly in defence of the love he called 'homogenic' and the people he called 'Uranian' or the 'intermediate sex'. Wilde and Carpenter spoke in the love that dared not speak its name, and in so doing, awakened, emboldened, disseminated unrealized or half-realized desires in others: the novelist E.M. Forster recalls visiting Millthorpe in 1912, and Carpenter's lover George Merrill touching him. 'He made a profound impression on me,' Forster recalled, 'and touched a creative spring.'[23] Forster's words echo Carpenter's seed philosophy: Forster's creativity was dormant and needed release.

Carpenter's writing is crammed with imagery related to the idea of seed-potential and to enclosure and release, all of it petitioning for cultures of vitality to win over cultures more enamored of the death drive. A passionate walker, Carpenter introduced the Indian-style sandal to England, complaining that shoes felt like 'leather coffins'.[24] For Carpenter, the sandal was a reanimating liberation from pinched English formality.[25] That the freedom he sought felt like nothing less than resurrection is something he again turned to the cycles of plant life to understand. In *Towards Democracy*, the 1883 prose poem that raised him to literary prominence, he considers the cyclical entombments and resurrections of plants: 'Age after age, under the Earth, hidden, the womb of the dead generations arising to life again, myriads of seeds, chrysalids, pupae, cysts, rootlets, transparent white bulbs of souls in Hades, by faith working many miracles, thrills of magnetism through the whole vast frame, summer heat and winter cold and the kiss of the living air'.[26] Carpenter follows this subterranean tableau of dormancy with a hellish scape of superterranean city life, a jostling, 'money-grubbing' crowd that seethes not with life force but its man-made opposite. What is needed is the 'touch of nature', and liberation from the 'prison life of Custom'. Carpenter recognizes that nature is, as Tennyson had already declared it, 'red in tooth and claw'; the seeds and chrysalids underground must withstand 'death and decay and weakness and prostration and poisonous inbreaths' as part of their life cycle (34). But he also posits the land as a source of special solace for the outcast: 'Earth alone regards the faces of them that are oppressed [...] the stones in the wintry fields are become confidants, and the ground is sown with compressed thought, like seeds' (52). Suffering has, he writes a few pages on, 'compressed thought and purpose into one – til they are harder than rock' (53). This is a geology in which oppression becomes compression, which promises to then burst free with revolutionary force.

Biographer Sheila Rowbotham notices Carpenter's repeated use of the trope of the 'chrysalis'. She also points out that he later turned to Whitman to borrow the term 'exfoliation' to describe the importance of casting off the husks of conventional life, revealing the 'unknown, the about-to-be' and the 'immanent'.[27] Whitman himself used seed imagery very similar to Carpenter's. In 'Song of the Universal,' in *Leaves of Grass*, he writes:

> In this broad earth of ours,
> Amid the measureless grossness and the slag,
> Enclosed and safe within its central heart,
> Nestles the seed perfection.

Whitman turns the trope slightly, to find safety and comfort rather than imprisonment in the subterranean seclusion experienced by the seed. It also provides a kind of punctuation to the 'broad ... measureless' commerce of earth, the litany of commas giving way to a seed-like full stop.[28] Kirsten Harris also spots how the symbolism of the seed is shared between Whitman and Carpenter, lyrically describing how, for Carpenter, '[t]he seed is both what is first and what is last'. The seed is, she writes, a 'major metaphor' developed across Carpenter's oeuvre, pointing out that it was even something of a meta-metaphor for him; he understood his own writing via the language of germination and dissemination, at one point describing *Towards Democracy* as the 'star-point and kernal' of his later work. 'Exfoliation', therefore, was the prequel to the unfurling of new life, a small destruction that would initiate creation. 'Carpenter strongly believed,' Harris writes, 'that he and his readers lived on the cusp of progressive evolutionary change, in the time of the "husk": the oppressive conditions of the nineteenth century would ultimately prove to be generative, even as they were destroyed. That humanity might direct its development along a less worthy course was inconceivable.'[29]

Inconceivable, perhaps. But European 'world' wars and their genocides were, of course, around the corner of history. By celebrating the life force of the seed, and its capacities to overthrow a world order, Carpenter's philosophy brought him close to some theories of vital force and will-to-power that would, several decades later, be pressed into the service of fascism. Friedrich Nietzsche's thought held some attraction for Carpenter: he admired Nietzsche's irruptive opposition to weak adherence to old codes and institutions, but he ultimately rejected the philosophy, not sure of 'whither it is going to lead', and repelled by the way Nietzsche turns 'the worship of Force almost into a formula'.[30] It is nonetheless worth exploring how and when Carpenter's plant-thinking looks politically perilous, and the peril seems greatest – as the theorists Gilles Deleuze and Félix Guattari could have advised him – when he writes of roots.[31] In 'The Art of Creation', Carpenter writes of how our lives 'spring again and again from a mental root which we recognize as our real selves' and says that this is exactly how trees work, too, shaping themselves to an 'Idea': 'A dominant Idea informs the life of the Tree; persisting, it forms the tree. You may snip the leaves as much as you like to a certain pattern, but they will only grow in their own shape' (28-29). Even a snipped-off twig, he attests, 'will have within it the pervading character or purpose' that will regenerate if the twig is planted. Even if you 'cut the tree down root and branch, and burn it, but if there is left a single seed, within that seed in an almost invisible point lurks the formative ideal, which under proper conditions will again spring into life and expression' (29). This is a botanical model of latency and potency, persistence and triumph, that could tip easily toward the Nietzschean ideal of 'Beyond-men'.

In the end, however, Carpenter resisted Nietzsche's anti-democracies with vigour. It is the 'Common Life' that Carpenter seeks, and when he compares the seed to the 'compressed Desire or Need [...] lurking in the human breast', it is about connecting everyone into a civic unity that is not totalitarian but instead allows 'recognition of Individual Affection and Expression'.[32] And although Carpenter takes up a root-tree model, I would argue that he manages – in the end – to keep it turned away from patriarchal, class-striated, and hetero-biological family trees. Consider the following passage: 'Look at the huge network of Railways, now like an immense Tree, with endless branches encircling the globe. Once that Tree slept in the form of a little compressed Thought or feeling in the breast of George Stephenson, the collier-lad, and unbeknown and invisible to any but himself' (29). Carpenter's simile shifts him from talking about trees to talking about railways. And the way he deploys the simile confuses which is the tenor and which is the vehicle, the two components of any simile or metaphor. The tenor, or subject, of the simile seems to be 'Railways', which are like 'an immense Tree', making this 'Tree' the vehicle. But the entire passage is more about trees than trains, and of course a train is, ontologically speaking, a vehicle. Carpenter's simile is as circular, or compressed, as the seed. Why? First, Stephenson's 'feeling in the breast' was literally deeply buried – underground – because of his early, working-class labouring life: Carpenter reminds us that Stephenson started his working life in the coal mines (he was also illiterate until he was eighteen). In addition, Carpenter reaches for the simile of the railway because of the erotics it held for him; he met his working-class lover George Merrill on a train in 1891, and, like Whitman, Carpenter appreciated the cross-class cruising, the 'chatting and chafing' enabled on public transport.[33] Trains acted as what Michel Foucault calls 'heterotopias' – non-hegemonic spaces of otherness – for what Carpenter calls 'homogenic' love.[34] To turn the branches of the tree into the branch lines of a railway, and back again, is therefore a series of metamorphoses that allows queer and cross-class love to spring into being. Shaw had critiqued Carpenter and his comrades for neglecting the 'docks', but we see here that Carpenter can think about their kin, the railways, with a dexterity that can admit, rather than stigmatize, queer desire and kinship. When Shaw casts the docks as the heteronormative and therefore virtuous opposite of lazy, gay dandelions, he rejects the possibilities of communion between nature and commerce, upper and lower classes, and homo and hetero models of human love that Carpenter so easily claims.

Seed-Time: Back-to-the-Land Sex and Politics at the Fin de Siècle

Notes

1. For an excellent re-evaluation of the Fellowship's history and pejorative pigeonholing of its socialism as 'ethical,' see Kevin Manton, 'The Fellowship of the New Life: English Ethical Socialism Reconsidered', *History of Political Thought*, 24.2 (Summer 2003), 282-304. Manton shows that the Fellowship felt 'people had become crucially and artificially alienated from the natural world' and urged recognition that 'all life is interconnected' (291). See also Stephen Yeo, 'The New Life: The Religion of Socialism in Britain 1883-1896', *History Workshop Journal*, IV (1977).
2. George Bernard Shaw, *The Works of George Bernard Shaw* (London: Constable, 1931), XXII, p. 161.
3. When Oscar Wilde had toured North America, lecturing about aestheticism in order to promote Gilbert and Sullivan's upcoming satire of the decadence, *Patience*, a sunflower was a key accessory to his look. His sunflower joined and was an exaggerated example of the curious trope in which yellow flowers signal triviality; a trope that reaches back to Shakespeare's 'primrose path of dalliance'. Cowslips, too: they appear in Elizabeth Barrett Browning's 'The Cry of the Children' and Sonnet 33 in *Sonnets from the Portuguese* as embodiments of childish innocence and freedom.
4. Carpenter, 'Weeds: A Study of Human and Vegetable Life', *Sketches from Life* (London: George Allen, 1908), p. 232. This essay dramatizes the antagonism between the human gardener and weeds, ultimately arriving at admiration for the life-form's potential to overwhelm the civilization about which Carpenter is so dubious. For more on this essay, see Kate Thomas 'Vegetable Love: Michael Field's Queer Ecology', *Michael Field Centenary Conference Essays*, ed. by Sarah Parker and Ana Parejo Vadilla (Charlottesville: University of Virginia Press, 2019).
5. Walt Whitman, 'The First Dandelion'. First published 12 March 1888, it was subsequently included in the 'deathbed' edition of *Leaves of Grass*. The poem's humble subject echoes one of the plant life/literature word plays of the collection's title: 'grass' was the term given by publishers to literary works of minor value.
6. Whitman was very interested to learn about Carpenter's farming commune at Millthorpe. Carpenter wrote to Whitman: 'We are gardening about two acres; fruit, flowers and vegetables; have about two and a half acres grass and about the same quantity part wheat for ourselves and part oats for the horse' (qtd. in Chushichi Tsuzuki, *Edward Carpenter: Prophet of Human Fellowship* (Cambridge: Cambridge University Press, 1980), p. 50).
7. Rod Preece points out that whereas Carpenter and other Fellowship members 'believed society needed greatly reduced consumption [...] Shaw himself was a high consumer of material goods' (*Animal Sensibility and Inclusive Justice in the Age of Bernard Shaw* (Vancouver: University of British Columbia Press, 2011), p. 218).
8. Started in July 1889, this journal was called *The Sower* for its first issue, and was subsequently known as *Seed-Time*.
9. The seed has continued as a powerful trope for socialist and anarchist thinking. Anarchist theorist Colin Ward read Ignazio Silone's novel *The Seed Beneath the Snow* (1941) while on a train from London to Orkney. He subsequently deployed the metaphor in the opening lines of his 1973 theoretical work *Anarchy in Action*: 'a society which organizes itself without authority, is always in existence, like a seed beneath the snow' ((London: Allen & Unwin), p. 11). Ward David Goodway re-cites the image in his 2006 history, *Anarchist Seeds Beneath the Snow; Left-Libertarian Thought and British Writers from William Morris to Colin Ward* (Liverpool: Liverpool University Press).
10. See, for example, Debra Mancoff, *The Pre-Raphaelite Language of Flowers* (Munich: Prestel Verlag, 2012); Jack Goody, 'The Secret Language of Flowers', *Yale Journal of Criticism*, 3 (1990), 133-52; Sabine Haass, '"Speaking Flowers and Floral Emblems": The Victorian Language of Flowers', in *Word and Visual Imagination: Studies in the Interaction of English Literature and the Visual Arts*, ed. by Karl Josef Höltgen, Peter M. Daly, and Wolfgang Lottes (Erlangen: Universität-Bibliothek, 1988), pp. 241-68. For a queer theorization of nineteenth-century representations of flowers, see Alison Syme, *A Touch of Blossom: John Singer Sargent and the Queer Flora of Fin-de-Siècle Art* (University Park: The Pennsylvania State University Press, 2010).

11 John Ruskin, *The Queen of the Air* (London: George Allen, 1869; repr. Rahway, NJ: Merchon, 2006), p. 98.
12 Virginia Woolf, 'A Sketch of the Past', in *Virginia Woolf: Moments of Being*, ed. by Jeanne Schulkind (San Diego: Harcourt, 1985) pp. 61-160 (p. 135). Woolf's conceptualization of the seed as a portal into other lives was perhaps best captured by Judy Chicago's plate for her, in Chicago's 1978 feminist art installation *The Dinner Party*. Woolf's plate has a core of seeds, surrounded by curved petals. The petals are labial and also reminiscent of the pages of a book. The seeds are both clitoral and expressive of the immanence and fruitfulness of Woolf's work. And Chicago's concept, of giving women 'a place at the dining table', was particularly resonant for Woolf, who repeatedly turned to food to make her gender critiques; for Woolf, the prunes served at a women's college, or the labour of bread-making, were important vehicles for talking about the difficulty of being a woman writer and artist.
13 Charles Darwin, *The Origin of Species* (New York, P.F. Collier, 1909), p. 27.
14 Oscar Wilde, 'Athanasia', in *The Complete Poems of Oscar Wilde* (New York: Doubleday, Page, 1923), pp. 108-111 (p. 108). Wilde's poem is just one manifestation of the nineteenth-century mania for germinating, that is to say imagining the germination, of seeds taken from Egyptian tombs. Wilde's friend Bram Stoker recalls being proudly shown a 'mummy flower' by Tennyson: 'In the garden, Tennyson pointed out to us some blue flowering pea which had been reared from seed found in the hand of a mummy' (*Personal Reminiscences of Henry Irving* (London: W. Heinemann, 1907), p. 139). For more on Victorian myths about the germination of Egyptian seed, see Gabriel Moshenska, 'Esoteric Egyptology, Seed Science and the Myth of Mummy Wheat', *Open Library of Humanities*, 3.1 (2017), pp. 1-42.
15 It should be remembered that Wilde's father, Sir William Wilde, was an Egyptologist. For more on Oscar Wilde and Orientalism, see Jeff Nunokawa, *Tame Passions of Wilde: The Styles of Manageable Desire* (Princeton: Princeton UP, 2003).
16 Wilde repeatedly explored the capacity to be carried away, and to another time, by fragrance. The opening lines of *The Picture of Dorian Gray* – that novel of temporal warping – read: 'The studio was filled with the rich odour of roses' and later in the novel, Lord Henry says 'There are moments when the odour of lilas blanc passes suddenly across me, and I have to live my strangest month of my life over again' ((London: Penguin, 1891), p. 5).
17 Michael Marder, *Plant-Thinking: A Philosophy of Vegetal Life* (New York: Columbia University Press, 2013), p. 143.
18 Edward Carpenter, *Civilisation: Its Cause and Cure* (London: George Allen, 1921), p. 27. Another Fellowship member, Katharine Bradley, also wrote about throwing off mummy-wrappings. 'The Mummy Invokes His Soul', which was written with her lover, Edith Cooper, under the shared name of Michael Field, is a highly sensuous sonnet in which a mummy waits, in death, for her lover to reanimate her. The mummy begs, 'my flesh be fanned/With thy fresh breath,' and desires an orgasmic disintegration of self: 'for I lust/To break apart, delicious, loosening sand' (in *The Penguin Book of English Verse*, ed. by Paul Keegan (London: Penguin, 2000), p. 826)
19 Henry Salt, 'Edward Carpenter's Writings', *The Pioneer* (London: E. W. Allen, January 1891).
20 Herbert Rix, 'The Return to Nature', *Seed-Time*, 2 (1890), 3-4.
21 Edward Carpenter, 'The Art of Creation', in *Art of Creation or Essays on The Self & Its Powers* (London: George Allen, 1904), p. 30. Subsequent references are cited parenthetically in the text.
22 Eve Kosofksy Sedgwick, *The Epistemology of the Closet* (Berkeley: University of California Press, 1990), p. 3.
23 E.M. Forster, 'Terminal Note', in *Maurice* (New York: Norton, 1971), p. 249.
24 Qtd. in Tsuzuki, p. 64. Carpenter made a pair for George Bernard Shaw, but they didn't fit and made his feet bleed. Sandal-wearing was just one element of Carpenter's commitment to dress reform that included him making a 'Saxon tunic' of his own design which prompted an intervention from his friends, anxious that beskirted and bare-legged public appearances pushed the limits of his already-infamous eccentricity.
25 It should also be remembered that the act of walking was used as political protest by many radical

groups like the Fellowship of the New Life at this time. Walkers would assert the 'freedom to roam' and demonstrate resistance to land enclosure.

26 Edward Carpenter, *Towards Democracy* (London: John Heywood, 1883), p. 33. Subsequent references are cited parenthetically in the text.
27 Sheila Rowbotham, *Edward Carpenter: A Life of Liberty and Love* (London: Verso, 2008), pp. 145, 71.
28 Michael Moon provides wonderful historical contextualization to Whitmanian figurations of seed. He points out that nineteenth-century America was in the grip of a 'national preoccupation' with the 'waste' of America's 'seed,' meaning both the country's promise and potential and the 'reproductive secretions' of its male citizens' (*Disseminating Whitman: Revision and Corporeality in Leaves of Grass* (Cambridge, MA: Harvard University Press, 1991), p. 18).
29 Kirsten Harris, *Walt Whitman and British Socialism: 'The Love of Comrades'* (New York: Routledge, 2016), pp. 43, 45.
30 In an essay titled 'The New Morality', which Carpenter added to his 1920 edition of *Civilisation: Its Cause and Cure*, Carpenter writes that Nietzsche had a 'healthy reaction' against the weaknesses of Christianity, such as 'somewhat spooney Altruism' (p. 247). But in the same breath, Carpenter critiques Nietzsche's concept of the will to power for having no investment in 'common source of life' and therefore tending towards self-destruction (p. 248). 'The truth is,' Carpenter writes, 'that Nietzsche never really penetrated to the realization of that farther state of consciousness in which the deep underlying unity of man with Nature and his fellows is perceived and felt' (p. 248).
31 In *A Thousand Plateaus*, volume 2 of *Capitalism and Schizophrenia*, Deleuze and Guattari counter the cultural and political dominance of the trope of the tree, proposing the non-hierarchizing model of the rhizome instead: 'As a model for culture, the rhizome resists the organizational structure of the root-tree system which charts causality along chronological lines and looks for the original source of 'things' and looks towards the pinnacle or conclusion of those 'things.' A rhizome, on the other hand, is characterized by 'ceaselessly established connections between semiotic chains, organizations of power, and circumstances relative to the arts, sciences, and social struggles' (trans. by Brian Massumi (London: Continuum, 1987), p. 8).
32 Rowbotham, p. 410.
33 Rowbotham, p. 179. When Merrill moved into Carpenter's home at Millthorpe, Sheffield, in 1898, Carpenter memorialized his arrival in the poem 'Hafiz to the Cupbearer'. The central metaphor is that of transit; Hafiz/Carpenter meets Merrill who is 'With hesitant step emerging' from 'crowded footways' and the poem ends 'Let us go/A spell of life along the road together'.
34 It should also be remembered that railways provided Carpenter with financial freedom. His father, Charles Carpenter, died in April 1882, leaving a fortune that was in large part derived from overseas railway investments (Rowbotham, p. 71).

Seeds

'Throw away your *gogo*'s seed': The Centrality of Traditional Seed in KwaZulu-Natal, South Africa

Jaci van Niekerk and Rachel Wynberg

'Seeds are the very basis of human society and have been for all of human history. Until very recently, farming and seed breeding were undertaken by farmers on their own land, season after season. However, we are now witnessing the separation of these two interdependent activities, with seed breeding increasingly being privatised and farmers becoming increasingly dependent on seed varieties made available to them at the discretion of seed companies.'

Elfrieda Pschorn-Strauss (ACB 2012)

The Context: Increasing Restrictions on Farmers' Rights

Millions of small-scale farmers on the African continent highly value the seeds of their traditional crops, ensuring their viability through upholding the age-old practices of saving, using, selling, exchanging, and replanting seed. These practices, an important component of 'farmers' rights', underpin food security and sovereignty and also contribute to the conservation of agricultural biodiversity.[1]

However, the diversity represented by traditional crops, and the accompanying promise their genetic material holds for adaptation to environmental change, is under threat from multiple fronts. Arguably the most significant of these is embodied by the cooperation between multinational agricultural-input companies, development programmes, and African governments which pave the way for the introduction of industrial agriculture, replete with chemical inputs and modern seed varieties.

Such interventions are responsible for displacing traditional varieties and disrupting farmer-led seed systems, also undermining the ability of small-scale farmers to define their own food and agricultural priorities (GRAIN 2014; Fischer and others 2015; Patel and others 2015). These approaches are supported by legal interventions which increase restrictions on seed saving and exchange, stimulated by pressures on countries to adopt systems based on the 1991 version of the International Convention for the Protection of New Varieties of Plants (UPOV 1991), an international agreement stemming from the World Trade Organization's Trade Related Aspects of Intellectual Property Rights (TRIPS) Agreement (ACB 2012). African governments are being pressured into adopting UPOV 1991, which strengthens protection of the ownership of new plant varieties by commercial plant breeders, often through trade agreements with Northern countries, as well as regional harmonization of plant variety protection (PVP) policies and laws (ACB 2012; GRAIN 2015).

In Eastern and Southern Africa, harmonization has increased rapidly among the twenty-one member states of the Common Market for Eastern and Southern Africa (COMESA), since the COMESA Seed Trade Harmonization Regulations were approved in 2014 (ACB 2018). In several nations, the effect of harmonization is being felt on the ground: for instance, in Malawi it became illegal to display farmer saved seed at seed fairs in 2017 (Food Tank 2017), and in South Africa, the current definition for 'selling seed' in the new seed bills about to be enacted includes sharing or exchanging seed, thus criminalizing these acts (ACB 2016).

Civil society organizations and continent-wide networks such as the African Biodiversity Network (ABN) and the Alliance for Food Sovereignty in Africa (AFSA) are raising alarms over the development of new seed laws that aim to advance the trade in seed across national borders and expand markets for commercial seed (ACB 2018). They claim that these developments do not take into account that the majority of the continent's seed is managed by small-scale farmers, and they highlight barriers to small-scale farmers' participation in PVP schemes such as high costs and stringent certification schemes (ACB 2018).

South Africa: A Highly Dualistic Agricultural Landscape

Located at the southernmost point of the continent, South Africa is widely regarded as a gateway to African markets. The highly dualistic nature of agriculture in South Africa is largely the result of historic decisions taken during the apartheid regime. Presently, 95% of marketed output is grown on mostly white-owned commercial farms, covering approximately 80% of agricultural land, whilst the remaining arable land is cultivated by some 2.3 million black, small-scale farmers operating at subsistence or non-commercial level (Aliber and Hart 2009; Greenberg 2015).

Plans for rural transformation are underway, but the government's overriding desire is to establish a cohort of black commercial farmers, with very little support going towards small-scale farmers who do not wish to plant hybrid or genetically modified (GM) seed (van Niekerk and Wynberg 2017). In fact, farmers who continue to grow traditional seed have been told by agricultural extension officers to '[t]hrow away your *gogo*'s [grandmother's] seed', a strong indication of the impact that support from multinational seed companies such as Monsanto and Syngenta have on the officers' training.

It is among these farmers, often located in remote places where the industrial agricultural model has not yet fully penetrated, or where NGOs have lent support for the revival of traditional crops, that the custodians of traditional seeds are found. We set out to explore the socio-cultural value of saving and sharing traditional seeds among seed custodian farmers in South Africa, and partnered to do so with the NGO Biowatch.[2] Research was undertaken in northern KwaZulu-Natal Province in 2011 and

2014, involving sixty semi-structured interviews held with small-scale farmers (fifty-eight of whom were women). The interviews were supplemented with focus group discussions and participatory activities such as mapping seed flows within farmers' communities and collaborative exercises outlining threats and remedies relating to farmers' traditional seed.

Findings
This section synthesizes the findings from the two studies.

Female, Life-Long Farmers Inhabiting Marginal Lands
Northern KwaZulu-Natal was once known as KwaZulu, one of the apartheid government's rural homelands – marginal lands where large numbers of black people were compelled to live. Into the present time, cultivation of crops here mostly consists of rain-fed subsistence farming on communally owned lands under the governance of traditional authorities (Houston and Mbele 2011).

The areas where this study was conducted are home to low average incomes, high rates of unemployment, and low levels of service delivery. In fact, farmers at one site received no municipal services, instead relying on wood for cooking and heating, and collecting water from streams or communal taps.

The farmers who participated in this study were almost all women and described their farming experience as dating back 'to birth'. Apart from the proceeds of selling excess produce, farmers relied on government child grants and pensions as sources of income. The majority of farmers supported households with more than five members; and were aged between forty and sixty. Only four respondents had completed high school, most having attained some primary or secondary training, while nineteen respondents had not had any schooling.

A Diverse Range of Traditional Crops and Vegetables
In this paper we use the term 'traditional crops' to refer to farmers' varieties or landraces passed on within families or communities for generations. With input from farmers, Biowatch had developed a list of crops which each household should grow in order to be food secure (see Figure 1). This list contains a mixture of grains, legumes, and cucurbits. Their seeds were saved by almost all respondents in 2011, although in 2014 some farmers had not managed to save seed of all of these varieties due to a prolonged drought.

Although this crop list reflects the diversity between varieties, it does not indicate the significant variety within certain species; for instance, some farmers saved the seed of five different types of beans whilst others had three different varieties of pumpkin seeds in their household seed banks. Maize, too, was differentiated: some farmers saved white, red, variegated, and yellow maize separately. Furthermore, the list does not capture the diversity of vegetable seed and propagating material from a wealth of other species which are also saved for replanting, such as sweet potatoes, spinach, peas, butternut, bananas, sunflowers, potatoes, okra, papayas, sugar cane, coffee beans, and chillies.

The Centrality of Traditional Seed in KwaZulu-Natal

Employing free listing as a method for determining the most prominent or salient crops yielded similar results across the sites. The most salient crops were maize and jugo beans (also known as Bambara nuts), whilst those with the lowest score were sorghum and sweet sorghum. These findings accord with the testimony from farmers regarding the value of their traditional seeds, described below.

Traditional crop	Botanical name	Family	Zulu name
GRAINS			
Maize	*Zea mays*	Poaceae	*ummbila*
Sorghum	*Sorghum bicolor*	Poaceae	*amabele*
Sweet sorghum	*Sorghum spp.*	Poaceae	*imfe*
Pearl millet	*Pennisetum glaucum*	Poaceae	*unyawothi*
Finger millet	*Eleusine coracana*	Poaceae	*uphoko*
LEGUMES			
Mung bean	*Vigna radiata*	Fabaceae	*umngomeni*
Cow pea	*Vigna unguiculata*	Fabaceae	*imbumba*
Jugo bean	*Vigna subterranea*	Fabaceae	*izindlubu*
Peanut	*Arachis hypogea*	Fabaceae	*amakinati*
Bean	*Phaseolus vulgaris*	Fabaceae	*ubhontshisi*
CUCURBITS			
Sweet watermelon	*Citrullus spp.*	Cucurbitaceae	*ikhabe*
Pumpkin	*Cucurbita maxima*	Cucurbitaceae	*amathanga*
Calabash	*Lagenaria spp.*	Cucurbitaceae	*amaswela*
Watermelon	*Citrillus lanatus*	Cucurbitaceae	*ubhece*
OTHERS			
Sesame	*Sesamum spp.*	Pedaliaceae	*udonca*
Zulu potato	*Solenostemon rotundifolius*	Lamiaceae	*amatabhane*
Amadumbe	*Colocasia esculenta*	Araceae	*amadumbe*
Cassava	*Manihot esculenta*	Euphorbiaceae	Umdumbula

Figure 1. Traditional crops commonly grown in the study sites.

Multiple Values Attached to Traditional Crops

Farmers listed a variety of reasons for preferring traditional crops (these are summarized in Figure 2). Farmers perceived their crops to be hardy, producing good yields, having drought resistance and high nutritional value. Traditional crops also conferred social and economic benefits, encouraging self-sufficiency and enhancing social cohesion, as well as precluding the need to spend money on agricultural inputs and seeds. Culturally, traditional seeds fulfilled multiple roles, with farmers emphasizing that they saw themselves as the custodians of the seed, taking care of them on behalf of their ancestors, and thereby protecting them for the future. One farmer said of her maize seed:

> They produce a lot of food if I cultivate them. I have never had any problems with it. I do not use anything else when I cultivate it. I only pour manure. One cob of mealies (maize) from these seeds makes me very happy. It makes me very happy because I can fill three to four or even five bags when I harvest. Even if I doubt that I will get five bags, with my seeds I do get them. I am proud of it.

Another farmer commented on the health and nutritional value of traditional crops: 'There is goodness in them – no chemicals are added; when you eat them you become powerful and they protect you from diseases.' Another lauded the financial benefits of seed saving, and praised the quality of seed which was not contaminated by chemicals: 'It is important to keep traditional seeds because most of the time it helps us save money, we do not have the need to buy seeds from the shop and you can keep it for a very long time and it will last forever. Since we do not use fertilizer, it stays in a good condition.'

Attribute	Farmers' perception
Physical	Crops grown from traditional seeds are hardier than shop-bought crops. Traditional seeds last a long time in storage without the need for chemical applications.
Environmental	Crops easily withstand the area's hot summers and dry winters. Good yields. Don't need much water.
Health/nutrition	High nutritional value. Not contaminated with chemical additives. No added salt or sugar needed when cooking. Keeps children healthy and adults live a long, vigorous life. Planting crops keeps one fit.
Financial	Saving seed means seed does not have to be bought every season. Exchanging seed precludes the need to pay for seed. Not having to buy fertilizers and pesticides saves money.
Social	Historical ties – seeds are passed on from one generation to the next. Seed saving encourages self-sufficiency. Sharing traditional seed enhances social cohesion. Eating food one has cultivated imparts a sense of pride.
Cultural	Seeds were being taken care of on behalf of the ancestors. Seed from the household of a person in mourning cannot be removed until certain rituals have been performed and a specific period of time has passed. Seeds are associated with marriage rituals: in certain communities seed accompanied newly married women to their husband's family home or, in other communities, seeds were not allowed to travel with a newly married woman to her in-laws' homestead.

Figure 2. Farmers' perceptions of the value of traditional crops and their seeds.

Beans were also valued for their good yields and ability to withstand both drought and heavy rains. As one farmer remarked, 'What I like about this seed is that it grows a lot and when it rains those who know it say that water cannot penetrate it easily because it locks up. That's why I always carry it.'

The Benefits of Saving One's Own Seed

Farmers commented that seed saving encouraged self-reliance – an attribute they considered important to pass on to the next generation. Many respondents stressed the importance of being ready to plant one's own seed as soon as the rains came. Several remarked that they did not want to 'disturb' or rely on neighbours when the planting season came, while others disliked store-bought seed, one farmer stating that she 'could not rely on it' and another questioning its quality. By saving one's own seed, a farmer remarked, 'one was guaranteed that the seeds were not [chemically] treated.'

Seed saving, along with the enhanced food security it delivers, was also credited for forging stronger kinship ties, or fostering social cohesion at the household level. In the words of one farmer who was teaching her grandchildren about this 'treasure' of the home: 'It keeps the home happy when there is plenty of food, no need to buy, no need to quarrel about money spent or money for food.' Asked why she liked growing traditional crops, another farmer responded, 'if people are hungry there is no concrete [social cohesion], it [growing traditional crops] makes the concrete needed at home. It [growing traditional crops] makes children responsible; they will know how to look after themselves.'

Being the seed saver at a homestead also bestowed respect, as reported by one farmer: 'kids respect my authority and I have dignity and status as I am seen as the head of the household by my extended family because I have the seeds.'

Sources of Traditional Seed: The Value of Seed Exchanges in Resource-Poor Settings

Different modes of seed exchange were found in the study sites. The majority of farmers exchanged seed, either for the seed of varieties they did not have themselves or for vegetables. Around a third of respondents gave seed away, mostly to neighbours and relatives, but also to other Biowatch project members, members of the Zulu royal household, and to those community members who did not have any seed of their own. A third mode of seed exchange was described: a 'loan' where seed was shared with someone with the expectation that it be returned after the next successful harvest.

Seed exchange acted as a form of 'insurance' in bad years, according to one farmer: 'If I am sick and cannot plant this year I know a trusted friend, neighbour, or co-farmer will plant it, then I can get seed from her the next season.' Farmers expressed strong opinions about who was allowed to use their seed, favouring those who farmed themselves: 'I say it is only for those who are enthusiastic about ploughing ["ploughing" is a synonym for "farming" in isiZulu] and cultivating. They must be able to multiply it so that I can go and ask for it from them if I have run out.' Others noted that those who used their seed had to be aware of the inextricable traditional value embedded within it.

Besides seed exchange, farmers sometimes had to buy seed too. Some respondents reported buying seed from village markets, hawkers, or formal outlets in towns. This seemed to be closely correlated to the distance between the farmers and the nearest town – those living closer to towns were more likely to buy seed than those situated in remote areas.

A number of older farmers expressed the view that seed should not be sold; some said that in the past this would have amounted to theft. Others underlined the value of sharing seed in times of scarcity, and highlighted the sense of social cohesion seed sharing fosters: 'Sometimes I don't have enough, then I can go to my neighbour. It maintains neighbourhood and family relations. If you buy from a shop there is no relationship between family members and others.'

Discussion

This study serves to highlight the numerous values attached to seed saving at the household level and exchanging traditional seed with, in the main, fellow farmers. At an individual level, both activities foster self-reliance and independence; at the community level, these actions enhance social cohesion and trust. In resource-poor settings, these features, along with the food security benefits and cash-sparing advantages of seed saving, are of great significance for the well-being of smallholders and the sustainability of their livelihoods.

Farmer-Led Seed Systems – Accessible, Cheap, and Trustworthy

Seeds play important roles in farming productivity, nutrition, and the resilience of small-scale farmers; this study has shown that having one's own seed to plant in rain-fed agriculture systems circumvents issues related to access (Kusena 2017). Similarly Coomes found that 'access to planting material is important not only for sustained and timely crop production but also for crop diversification and on-farm experimentation' among traditional societies in Amazonia (2010: 328). Findings from this study also accord with an investigation into farmer-led seed systems in Tanzania, which identified their strengths as their 'availability, affordability, and timeliness' (Mkindi 2015: 2).

Growing a diversity of crops has strong implications for household food security, as this practice spreads the risk of crop failure (Richards and others 2009). Farmers in the study frequently noted the high nutritional value of their crops, believing this to be related to the chemical-free environment they were grown in. A reliable seed supply thus strengthens livelihoods and food security (Helicke 2015). The significance of these benefits is particularly germane in the face of seed laws which restrict seed saving and exchange of commercial varieties, and prevent the sale of uncertified seed (De Jonge 2014; Haugen 2015).

In resource-poor settings, being seed secure and practicing agroecology can free up precious cash reserves for other necessities. Farmers in this study praised their seeds' good performance in low-input farming systems. Not having to buy seeds every year, nor needing to purchase expensive agricultural inputs such as chemical fertilizers and pesticides, contrasts starkly with the high-input agricultural model advocated by programmes such as the Alliance for a Green Revolution in Africa (AGRA).

By exchanging seed via 'social relations of trust' (Badstue and others 2007: 1586), farmers invest in a future crop which they know they can rely on as they may already know the seeds' characteristics, or would be able to learn more at low cost. Respondents expressed dissatisfaction with seed bought from agricultural dealers; therefore they did not experience the same sense of trust that they had in the provenance of seed acquired through social networks.

Challenges Related to Seed Saving

Farmers experienced two main threats to saving seed successfully, changing weather patterns and inappropriate support from agricultural extension officers. The effects of the long-term drought in KwaZulu-Natal were clearly observed during the 2014 field work period, as farmers had far fewer seeds and less diversity in their household seed banks than in the preceding data collection phase. Modified weather patterns, particularly shifts in rainfall periods – as reported in the study site – were also found in Zimbabwe, Peru, and Vietnam in a meta-study undertaken by Oxfam-Novib and others (2013) which involved more than 12,000 respondents.

Some believe that traditional farming systems such as those practiced in the study areas will provide a measure of resilience in the face of climate change by including 'crop diversification, maintaining local genetic diversity, animal integration, soil organic management, water conservation and harvesting' (Altieri and others 2015: 869). Such diverse and dynamic systems are certain to be more resilient to environmental change than industrial agriculture which relies on monocrops and a limited range of seeds.

Findings also emphasize the importance of external interventions in an area where extension support is very low. Farmers associated with Biowatch have reported that the agricultural extension services that they received from government were both minimal and inappropriate, as extension officers recommended industrial agricultural practices which they did not wish to implement. Farmers recounted that in the past, extension officers had donated bags of hybrid maize seeds to them; however not wanting to plant these chemically treated seeds, the farmers fed them to their chickens instead. The training of agricultural extension officers in South Africa is skewed towards promoting the industrial agriculture model, leaving farmers who prefer to practice sustainable agriculture such as agroecology, organic production, or permaculture with little option but to forgo their services, often relying on NGOs instead (De Satgé 2008).

Conclusion

South Africa's long history of commercially-oriented agriculture has resulted in small-scale farming being viewed as 'backward' or undeveloped. These views are further entrenched by the seed industry which markets their modern seed varieties as superior to traditional seeds – modern varieties are supposed to mature faster and herbicides are intended to spare farmers the chore of weeding. These technological 'fixes', accompanied by laws which elevate plant breeders' rights above those of farmers, do not take into account the considerable social, cultural, and economic benefits which seed saving and exchange bring to farmer-led agricultural systems.

Traditional seeds are well-adapted to local niche conditions as a result of generations of selection by small-scale farmers. These farmers select for a variety of traits, including good yields in local conditions, thus enabling themselves to manage risk better and be more autonomous. In a future where climate change is a given, adaptive traits such as stress resistance and improved productivity in different soils and micro-climates will be vital. In this scenario the value of a diverse variety of traditional crops escalates, particularly the need for diversity for the sake of seed, food, and nutrition security. This is especially true in the face of pressure to conform to a model which relies on a very narrow genetic pool, making farmers vulnerable to disease and famine.

Our research has shown that household seed saving is highly valued by the small-scale farmers in the study sites, and when combined with seed exchanges, diversity – and therefore resilience – is advanced. We argue that small-scale farmers in South Africa, as well as in the rest of the continent, should be recognized for their invaluable contribution to maintaining agrobiodiversity by being given support which contributes to strengthening their seed systems within supportive policy and legislative contexts.

Acknowledgements

This research forms part of work conducted by the Seed and Knowledge Initiative (SKI), a long-term multi-sectoral collaboration in southern Africa with a vision of a future where small-holder farmers are empowered to secure seed and food sovereignty on all levels. We further acknowledge the financial support of the Centre for International Governance Innovation in Canada and the South African National Research Foundation.

Notes

1. Farmers' rights consist of the customary rights that farmers have had as stewards of agro-biodiversity since the dawn of agriculture to save, grow, share, develop, and maintain plant varieties; of their legitimate right to be rewarded and supported for their contribution to the global pool of genetic resources as well as to the development of commercial varieties of plants; and to participate in decision making on issues that may affect these rights (working definition from the Fridtjof Nansen Institute).
2. Established in 1999, Biowatch works with small-holder farmers, other civil society organizations and government to ensure that people have control over their food, agricultural processes natural resources, within a bio-diverse, agroecological, and sustainable system. For more, visit <www.biowatch.org.za>.

References

ACB. 2012. *Harmonisation of Africa's Seeds Laws: A Recipe for Disaster. Players, Motives and Dynamics* (Johannesburg: African Centre for Biodiversity).

ACB. 2016. *Integration of Small-Scale Farmers into Formal Seed Production in South Africa. A Scoping Report* (Johannesburg: African Centre for Biodiversity).

ACB. 2018. *Status Report on the SADC, COMESA and EAC Harmonised Seed Trade Regulations: Where Does This Leave the Regions' Smallholder Farmers?* (Johannesburg: African Centre for Biodiversity).

Aliber, M., and T. Hart. 2009. 'Should Subsistence Agriculture Be Supported as a Strategy to Address Rural Food Insecurity?', *Agrekon*, 48.4: 434-58.

Altieri, M.A., and others. 2015. 'Agroecology and the Design of Climate Change-Resilient Farming Systems', *Agronomy for Sustainable Development*, 35: 869-90.

Badstue, L. B., and others. 2007. 'The Dynamics of Farmers' Maize Seed Supply Practices in the Central Valleys of Oaxaca, Mexico', *World Development*, 35.9: 1579-93.

Coomes, O.T. 2010. 'Of Stakes, Stems, and Cuttings: The Importance of Local Seed Systems in Traditional Amazonian Societies', *The Professional Geographer*, 62.3: 323-34.

De Jonge, B. 2014. 'Plant Variety Protection in Sub-Saharan Africa: Balancing Commercial and Smallholder Farmers' Interests', *Journal of Politics and Law*, 7.3: 100-11.

De Satgé, R., and others. 2008. *Extension and Small Holder Agriculture: Key Issues from a Review of the Literature* (Cape Town: Phuhlisani Solutions).

Fischer, K., J. Van Den Berg, and C. Mutengwa. 2015. 'Is Bt Maize Effective in Improving South African Smallholder Agriculture?', *South African Journal of Science*, 111.1-2: 1-2.

Food Tank. 2017. 'Did Monsanto Write Malawi's Seed Policy?' <https://foodtank.com/news/2017/08/monsanto-malawis-seed-policy> [accessed November 16, 2018].

GRAIN. 2015. *UPOV 91 and Other Seed Laws: A Basic Primer on How Companies Intend to Control and Monopolise Seeds*.

GRAIN. 2014. *Hungry for Land: Small Farmers Feed the World with Less than a Quarter of All Farmland*.

Greenberg, S. 2015. 'Agrarian Reform and South Africa's Agro-Food System', *The Journal of Peasant Studies*, 42.5: 957-79.

Haugen, H.M. 2015. 'Inappropriate Processes and Unbalanced Outcomes: Plant Variety Protection in Africa Goes Beyond UPOV 1991 Requirements', *The Journal of World Intellectual Property*, 18.5: 196-216.

Helicke, N.A. 2015. 'Seed Exchange Networks and Food System Resilience in the United States', *Journal of Environmental Studies and Sciences*, 5.4: 636-49.

Houston, G.F., and T. Mbele. 2011. *KwaZulu-Natal History of Traditional Leadership Project* (Durban: Human Sciences Research Council).

Kusena, K., R. Wynberg, and C. Mujaju. 2017. 'Do Smallholder Farmer-Led Seed Systems Have the Capacity to Supply Good-Quality, Fungal-Free Sorghum Seed?', *Agriculture and Food Security*, 6: 52.

Lewis, V., and P.M. Mulvany. 1997. *A Typology of Community Seedbanks. NRI Project A0595* (Chatham: National Resources Institute).

Mkindi, A.R. 2015. *Farmers' Seed Sovereignty Is Under Threat. Policy Paper 3* (Berlin: Rosa Luxemburg Foundation).

Oxfam Novib, ANDES, CTDT, SEARICE, and CGN-WUR 2013. *Building on Farmers' Perception and Traditional Knowledge: Biodiversity Management for Climate Change Adaptation Strategies. Briefing Paper* (The Hague: Oxfam Novib).

Patel, R., and others. 2015. 'Cook, Eat, Man, Woman: Understanding the New Alliance for Food Security and Nutrition, Nutritionism and its Alternatives from Malawi', *The Journal of Peasant Studies*, 42.1: 21-44.

van Niekerk, J. and R. Wynberg. 2017. 'Traditional Seed and Exchange Systems Cement Social Relations and Provide a Safety Net: A Case Study from KwaZulu-Natal, South Africa', *Agroecology and Sustainable Food Systems*, 41.9-10: 1099-1123.

Worede, M. 2011. 'Establishing a Community Seed Supply System: Community Seed Bank Complexes in Africa', in *Climate Change and Food Systems Resilience in Sub-Saharan Africa*, ed. by Lim Li Ching, Sue Edwards, and Nadia El-Hage Scialabba (Rome: Food and Agriculture Organization of the United Nations).

Seeds

Mustard in the Talmudic Literature

Susan Weingarten

Seeds, Zera'im, is the name of the first of the six books of the Mishnah, and the Palestinian Talmud which comments on it. This book deals mostly with the religious rules concerning agriculture and agricultural produce in the Roman province of *Syria-Palaestina*, or as the rabbis called it, the Land of Israel. There is such a large amount of material there that it would be impossible to deal with it in one short Symposium paper, so I have therefore chosen to give a taste of one particular seed: mustard. Mustard appears over two hundred times in the talmudic literature, in *Seeds* and elsewhere.

The talmudic sources were written between the third and seventh centuries CE, so inevitably there are problems of identification of the various different mustards referred to in late antiquity by the generic Hebrew name of *ḥardal*, a term whose origin is unknown.[1] It is not mentioned in the Hebrew Bible, although it does appear in the New Testament. There are three main types of mustard today: white/yellow *Sinapis alba*, black *Brassica nigra*, and brown or Indian *Brassica juncea*. These colours refer to those of the seeds or seed pods, which also vary in potency. The talmudic literature, in contrast, uses different categories: wild mustard and cultivated mustard (Mishnah [=M] Kilayim i, 5), and plain mustard and Egyptian mustard (MKilayim i, 2). There is no consensus among modern scholars on which varieties are which. Both white and black mustard commonly grow wild in Israel/Palestine today, although white mustard (which has reddish-brown seeds) is more common. Mustards belong to the family of the *brassicaceae* (*cruciferae*), and there is a tendency for cross-fertilisation with other members of the cabbage family. So perhaps it is not surprising that modern 'scientific' descriptions of these plants do not agree with each other either: *Brassica nigra*, for example, is said to vary between 40 cm and 80 cm in height (*NatureGate*) or 1 m and 1.5 m (*Analytical Flora of Israel*), and Alan Davidson tells us it can even reach 3.5 m.[2] Is there a misprint here? Does the height depend on the amount of sun or rain? Or does it refer to distant lands where mustard is now grown – such as Canada, which presently supplies most of the world's mustard? It is not clear.

Many of the talmudic discussions of mustard are devoted to agricultural aspects. Mustard was sown as a border plant surrounding fields of vegetables, its bright yellow flowers and height (whatever that was) serving to differentiate it from the crop of lower plants: 'They must not flank a field of grain with mustard or safflower, but they may flank a field of vegetables with mustard or safflower.'[3] Mustard was also sown as patches in fields – perhaps planted at different times to ripen differentially – as well:

'If a man wants to lay out his field in patches each with a different crop, he may lay out 24 patches [...] and sow it any way he wants. If in a field of grain there was only one patch or two, he may sow them with mustard, but if three he may not sow them with mustard since it might appear like a field of mustard.'[4]

The rabbis distinguished between 'seeds' and 'vegetables': 'Not every kind of seed may be sown in a garden bed, but any kind of vegetable may be sown in it. Mustard and small beans are considered a kind of seed and large beans a vegetable.'[5] Mustard also appears among seeds in the Rehov inscription, a list of plants quoted from the fourth to fifth century Palestinian Talmud [=PT] Demai 22c (found on a late antique synagogue floor mosaic in northern Israel), telling local people what to do about plants in the sabbatical year, when it was forbidden to cultivate the soil. The list of seeds included:

> Black nigella
> Sesame
> Mustard
> Rice
> Cumin
> Lupines [...].[6]

Elsewhere the PT puts mustard seeds in the context of a list of foods going from the largest to the smallest: 'He filled up with citrons, pomegranates, walnuts, hazelnuts, peppercorns, sesame, mustard.'[7]

Mustard was also planted for its green leaves which were used cooked or soaked (*shluq*: PTMaaserot 48d) or pickled (*kavush* Tosefta [=Tos] Maaserot iii, 7). If it was intended as a vegetable in this way, it was not liable to tithing, as it would have been had it been planted for its seeds, which was more usual, but the rabbis were lenient if a farmer changed his mind about his mustard crop. Another source from the Tosefta (Maaser Sheni i, 13) talks about 'arum and mustard and lupines and all those pickled, whether sweetened or not'. The mustard here appears between the category of arum, whose poisonous leaves were pickled or soaked before they could be eaten, and the lupines, whose poisonous seeds were soaked in seven changes of water before their dangerous alkaloids could be leached away. It is thus not clear whether the source is referring to the leaves like the arum or the seeds like the lupines, or maybe both.

I look at 'sweetening' mustard below. The seeds were, of course, used as spice, either whole or ground up. I have not found evidence in the talmudic sources of them being used for oil.

Mustard seeds are tiny: they are used in the talmudic sources (and in Indian sources too) to signify the smallest measurable quantity of things – such as drops of blood that communicated impurity (BTBerakhot 31a).[8] Perhaps the reddish-brown colour of the seeds of wild white mustard contributed to this use as well. Their small size meant that they could behave almost like a liquid – filling up the spaces in an otherwise full basket of gourds or cucumbers (BTShabbat 153b). The Mishnah tells us that there were special sieves for mustard: 'It is permitted to strain wine through a cloth [...] and put an egg into a mustard sieve [on the Sabbath]' (MShabbat xx.2).

Commenting on this practice, the Palestinian Talmud (Shabbat 17c) makes it clear that putting the egg into the mustard sieve was in order to separate the yolk from the white: 'You can *separate* an egg in a mustard sieve [on the Sabbath]'. I originally thought that this must refer to a sieve which was used to separate the seeds from the pods. However it became clear that this may well not have been the case, as we shall see below. In my experience, extracting mustard seeds from their pods must be done after the plant has dried out in the field for two or three months, by which time the pods no longer need to be pounded hard to break them up, but shatter at the slightest touch, scattering the seeds widely. There is a somewhat unclear source in PTShevi'it 38c: 'Rabbi Shimon ben Laqish was in Huqoq, and he saw them rolling (*megalgelim*) mustard: some of it fell and they did not pick it up'. It is clear that this source refers to some sort of activity connected to mustard, which could be collecting the green plant to use as green manure, or to cook or pickle it; collecting the dry plant to separate the seeds; or some sort of operation to produce the seeds or oil from them. Scholars disagree, however about the explanation of 'rolling'.[9] Some think it refers to a wheel-and-bucket system for watering the growing mustard, while others think it refers to rolling up sheaves of mustard plants, or twisting the plant out of the ground. Rolling it as sheaves, with the brittle stalks coming out of the stem at an angle, would break off and lose many of the pods and hence the seeds. But at the ancient ruined village identified as the site of the Huqoq mentioned in the source there are some unusual agricultural installations not found elsewhere: like wine vats, but semi-circular rather than rectangular, with a much steeper incline, together with a subsidiary trough at the bottom. These have been proposed as floors for crushing the mustard pods by rolling stones or poles over them, then catching the seeds in the deeper trough at the bottom, or possibly making mustard oil from them. There is a discussion of bundles of mustard in the Babylonian Talmud, which asks whether it is permitted to crush them and use them for food on a festival. The answer is yes, but this comes from Babylonia and may not be related to what happened in Huqoq in the Land of Israel: 'The host of Rav, son of R. Hanan had bunches of mustard-stalks [and] he asked him: Is it permissible to crush this on the festival and eat it? He could not answer. He went to Raba who replied: You may rub ears of corn together and crumble pods on a festival.'[10] Crumbling pods by hand is not easy, as the pods are covered with tiny spikes, but perhaps people in antiquity had harder, more weather-beaten skin than we do in the twenty-first century.

The fact that tall plants could grow from such tiny seeds was a subject of wonder at the powers of the Creator: the New Testament (Matthew 13:31-32; Mark 4:30-32; Luke 13:18-19) quotes the parable of the tiny mustard-seed which grew into a tree with birds nesting in its branches as an image of the potential for growth of the Kingdom of Heaven. This is, of course, a miraculous exaggeration: no mustard ever grows into such a large plant that birds could nest in its branches. However, this Christian parable about the Kingdom of Heaven is paralleled and contrasted by a Jewish talmudic story which extolls the produce of the earthly Land of Israel, exaggerating its enormous fertility, in the past, present, and the Time to Come, when the righteous dead will be resurrected. In this account of the miraculous Land of Milk and Honey, milk drips from the over-full udders of sheep and goats and combines in streams with the honey dripping from the dates and figs, and a rabbi walks three miles in honey up to his ankles. Cornfields grow as high as a palm tree, cabbages grow so large that people can climb up and down their stalks – and mustard, as in the NT parable, grows into trees. These are large enough to shade buildings: 'In Sihin there was one stalk of mustard which had three branches. One fell off and it was large enough to cover a booth […] and they found three measures of mustard seed on it. Rabbi Shimon b. Halafta said: I had a single stalk of mustard and I used to go up it like someone goes up a fig tree.'[11] The story is repeated in the Babylonian Talmud, by which time the yield of the mustard plant has increased three-fold to nine measures, and the source adds: 'Rabbi Simeon b. Tahlifa said: Our father left us a cabbage stalk and we went up and down it with a ladder.'[12] This early precursor of Jack and the Beanstalk would also seem to hint at Jacob's ladder bridging heaven and earth. Recently this image of the tiny mustard-seed with huge potential for growth has been taken up by modern followers of Kabbalah.

Turning now to culinary aspects of mustard, Alan Davidson notes that very sharp mustard is a particularly English taste: the French, Dutch, Germans, and Italians prefer their mustard tamed by the addition of vinegar, wine or fruit juices which react with the chemicals found in the mustard, and it is common to add honey, sugar, etc.[13] Late antique Jews were also non-English in their taste for mustard: we have already seen that they preferred to 'sweeten' it: 'You sweeten mustard with coals' (Tos Betzah iii 15).

'Sweetening' here appears to refer to a process by which the sharpness was reduced by roasting the seeds over hot coals, as is common today in Indian cookery. Presumably this was done in some sort of dish laid on top of the coals, although Columella adds coals on top of the mustard, after it has been soaked, squeezed out, and pounded, as we shall see below.[14]

Later talmudic sources discuss this in theological terms: 'Everything which was created during the first six days of the Creation of the World needs something doing to it: like mustard which has to be sweetened, lupines which need to be sweetened, wheat which needs to be milled – and even Man has to be corrected [by circumcision].'[15] It is not clear whether 'sweetening' may also have meant what it would mean today. Lupines, as noted above, are sweetened by soaking in many changes of water to remove their bitterness. Could 'sweetening' in the talmudic sources also refer to the process whereby honey was added to ground-up mustard-seeds to make a sauce? Whatever this was called, there is certainly evidence that it took place. The Tosefta (Shabbat xiv 13) tells us: 'Mustard which has been ground before the Sabbath, you bring honey and add it to it, and you may mix it but not beat it.' The Babylonian Talmud (Shabbat 140a) commenting on this ruling is slightly different:

> If mustard seed is kneaded on Sabbath eve, then [on Sabbath] morning, Rab said: One must crush it with a utensil, but not by hand […]. Said Samuel to

him: He must crush it by hand, but not with a utensil [...]. R. Eleazar said: Both the one and the other are forbidden; while R. Yohanan ruled: Both the one and the other are permitted. [After further discussion and examples], Mar Zutra said: The law is not as all these opinions. but as the following which was stated: If mustard is kneaded on the eve of the Sabbath, in the morning you may crush it both by hand or with a utensil; you may pour honey into it, yet you must not beat it up but may mix them [...].

We may compare this with the recipe for mustard found in the first-century agricultural Roman writer Columella:

> Carefully cleanse and sift mustard-seed then wash in cold water and when it has been well cleaned leave it in water for two hours. Next take it out and after it has been squeezed in the hands, throw it into a new or thoroughly cleaned mortar and pound it with pestles. When it has been pounded, collect the whole mash in the middle of the mortar and compress it with the flat of the hand. After you have compressed it, scarify it, and after placing a few live coals pour water mixed with nitre on it in order to eliminate any bitterness and paleness from it. Then immediately lift up the mortar so that all the moisture may be drained away, and after this add sharp white vinegar and mix it with the pestle and strain it [.... For guests add crushed almonds and pine kernels].

Unlike the talmudic passage, where the rabbis are concerned with what is and is not permitted on the Sabbath in preparing mustard, Columella is concerned only with how to make mustard sauce, and he gives us all the details. We note the stress here on working with the pestle and mortar as well as with the hands in preparing mustard, and the fact that it is left to soak. All of these actions are mentioned (or implied) in the BT source above. What is missing is the honey: Columella 'sweetens' his mustard with coals. The Babylonian Talmud has further details about kneading mustard before the Sabbath, and both it and the Palestinian Tosefta talk about mixing the honey with the mustard, and not beating it. A similar recipe to the talmudic one can be found in a tenth-century Arabic cookery book from Baghdad of the Caliphs by Ibn Sayyar al- Warrāq, contemporary with the generation of rabbinic commentators on the Babylonian Talmud who were known as the *ge'onim*. The recipe gives a number of versions, but this is the nearest to our talmudic mustard:

> Take mustard seeds, pick them over to remove any small wood chips [...] twigs and any other impurities. Put them in a small mortar and pound them finely [...]. Add an equal amount of walnuts to the seeds and continue pounding. Then pour as much vinegar as you like and strain the mixture in a fine sieve. You will get mustard that is like white sea foam. Take the foam only and add to it a little salt and serve. With what's left make *sinab* sauce with pounded raisins. If you prefer, sweeten it with sugar.

Mustard in the Talmudic Literature

This recipe has almost all the elements of the talmudic recipe: pounding mustard seeds and whipping for a long time, and the alternative version recommends kneading the pounded mustard with [pounded] walnuts. Beating or whipping is forbidden by the Talmud, which would seem to imply it was normative except on the Sabbath. The honey is missing – but there are raisins and sugar instead (as well as nuts and vinegar).

Only Columella of the ancient sources mentions the necessity of pre-soaking the seeds: presumably this was otherwise taken for granted. But it is stressed by the excellent modern work called *The Compleat Mustard*.[16] However, I have found no modern works that mention the mustard foam of the ancient recipes. Presumably this is because, in my experience, soaking cultivated varieties of mustard produces only a slightly sticky liquid, and the modern authors must have used cultivated seeds. The wild mustard seeds I gathered, in contrast, produced a thick jelly after soaking, which could then be forced through a sieve together with the ground mustard seeds. The resulting mass was easily whipped to a whiteish foam, just as fenugreek jelly can be whipped into *hilbe*.[17] The fact that the talmudic sources we saw above describe the use of mustard sieves to separate eggs, which would mean that the liquid jelly of the egg white passes through the sieve, confirms this picture.

In another place the Palestinian Talmud (Shabbat 17c) talks about a 'lump' of mustard: 'A lump [*gush*] of mustard: R Yossi in the name of R Eliezer says you may pound it by hand but not with an instrument, but [...] R Yohanan in the name of R Yannai [said] you may pound it either by hand or with an instrument.' The rabbis are disagreeing here whether it is permitted to break up a lump of mustard on the Sabbath, and if so, how to do it. But what is the significance of this 'lump' of mustard? We saw Columella's instructions for compressing mustard mash in the mortar. Perhaps this can be seen as the 'lump' of our Talmudic source. If so, it was a wet one with no sweetener. But mustard is also found dried in lumps in a fourteenth-century Arab cookbook from Egypt, the *Kanz al-fawā'id fī tanwī'al-mawā'id*, (=*Kanz*).[18] It is clear from this cookbook that the mustard was stored like this for convenience, then broken up and liquid added. In fact, the recipe book (no. 483) suggests drying mustard in a lump for the convenience of travellers. Vinegar and sugar were added when it was reconstituted. Fourteenth-century Egypt may seem a long way chronologically and geographically from our talmudic sources, but we may note that the *Kanz* does share the same recipe for making mustard we saw above in al-Warrāq, although the *Kanz* has another sixteen mustard sauce recipes! This may be because there are many fish recipes in the *Kanz*, and since in the Galenic medical view fish were cold and wet, they needed to be counteracted by something hot and dry – like mustard. There are a number of fish recipes in al-Warrāq as well, and in at least two cases they include ready-made mustard sauce.

In any case, honey-flavoured mustard sauce appears to have been extremely desirable in the talmudic literature. There is an interesting contrast here to mustard-flavoured honey, which was to be avoided. It was necessary to keep mustard away from bees – implying that honey from mustard flowers tastes unpleasant.[19]

Flour was also used in making mustard sauces, but it is not clear whether this was a desirable ingredient or not: the Mishnah is merely concerned that the wet mixture is liable to ferment, and so should not be used on Passover when leavened dough foods are forbidden.[20]

The most desirable of all foods, according to the talmudic literature, was tongue with mustard. The talmudic literature tells us that this was the food given by the patriarch Abraham to the three angels who visited him to tell him that his wife Sarah was pregnant with their son. The biblical account of this meeting has Abraham telling Sarah to hurry to make bread for the guests, while he himself goes to the herd to fetch a calf. The rabbis wonder aloud why there should be three terms describing the calf – young, tender, and good – and they explain that there were in fact three calves. But why three calves for only three angels? Their answer is that Abraham wanted to serve their tongues – with mustard. Tongue with mustard appears on a number of occasions in the talmudic literature as the best possible food: it was the food of kings and priests: 'R. Hisda said: The priestly dues may be eaten only roasted and with mustard. What is the reason? Because Scripture says: For a consecrated portion (Numbers 18: 8), ie this is a mark of eminence, [and must therefore be eaten] as kings take their food.'[21] The priests were entitled to the priestly dues, their own portions of any animal ritually slaughtered: the stomach, the right foreleg and the 'cheeks.' These last are defined in MHullin 10,4: 'What are the cheeks? From the joint of the jawbone to the protrusion of the windpipe.'[22]

This definition is elaborated on by BTHullin 134b, quoting Palestinian rabbis of the Mishnah period: 'Our rabbis taught: why does it say the cheeks? — To include the wool on the head of sheep and the hair of the beard of goats.' Thus 'cheeks', according to the rabbis of the Mishnah, meant not just the cheeks but also the whole of the lower jaw and what it contained, down to the protrusion in the windpipe, with the outer 'beard' of the sheep or goat. The lower jaw, of course, contained the tongue, which was considered a very desirable portion of meat. There are some very interesting parallels here with Greek pagan sacrificial practice.[23] The tongue (and foreleg) was seen by Greek pagan priests as their special portion – in Aristophanes' *Peace* (fifth century BCE), a soothsayer appears at the first whiff of roasted sacrificial meat and clamours to be given the tongue. And the Greeks actually had a word for the cheeks/lower jaw: in a Greek papyrus from Oxyrhyncus in Roman Egypt dated to the late second or early third century CE, there is a cook's monthly meat bill, detailing the cuts of meat bought, including a *glossopogonion*, literally a 'bearded tongue'.[24] The editors of the papyrus interpret this to mean 'half a head with the tongue', that is, the lower jaw of, say, a sheep or goat, with its hairy, beard-like covering. This is exactly the rabbis' definition of the priests' portion of 'cheeks' we saw above. In another place in BT Hullin 133a, the rabbis discuss the etiquette of giving and receiving the desired tongue, and it is clear that eating it with mustard makes it even more desirable:

> Raba and R. Safra once visited the house of Mar Yuhna the son of R. Hana b. Adda [...] and he prepared for them a three-year-old calf. Thereupon Raba said to the [priestly] attendant: 'Give me the priestly dues, for I want to eat the tongue with mustard,' He gave them to him. Raba ate it, but R. Safra would not eat it.

Mustard in the Talmudic Literature

[The continuation of this source makes it clear that Raba was subject to divine censure for this greedy behaviour].

Thus there are very interesting parallels here with classical Greek sacrificial practice. But the seasoning is different. Greek practice (if we can rely on the evidence of Aristophanes' satirical work) seems to have been to sprinkle the tongue with salt and then to douse the roast meat in libation wine. Jewish practice was to roast it, with mustard, and not to douse it in wine. Perhaps we can also see similarities in the behaviour of the priests greedily seeking their tongue: the Greek soothsayer satirised by Aristophanes who eventually goes off with a beating, as compared with the Babylonian Talmud's picture of Raba, the priestly rabbi who is too eager to get his tongue and incurs divine censure. The BT then clarifies that it is proper to be eager to give the portion, but not to be eager to get it. Both Jews and Greeks must have resented their priests' eagerness for their desirable portions.

In what form the mustard was eaten with the tongue is unclear. Were the mustard seeds roasted with the roast meat? Or was the roast tongue dipped into mustard sauce? Mustard sauce was used as a dip for fish in the Byzantine *Dietary Calendar* attributed to Hierophilus the Sophist, possibly from the seventh century.[25] And around this time Christians in Antioch in Syria were apparently eating sausages, if not tongue, dipped into mustard, if we can make any real deductions from the *Life* of Saint Symeon, written in Greek in the seventh century by Leontius, in Cyprus.[26] This saint was called *salos*, the fool, because he hid his holiness under a guise of madness, going round doing crazy acts in order to attract attention: he steals food, defecates in public, bathes in the women's baths, etc. One of his crazy acts is to take a string of sausages and wear them draped round himself like an *orarion*, a churchman's stole, a strip of material worn round the neck, with the ends dangling in front. It is these sausages that Symeon dips into a pot of mustard, eating them all day long. Sausages with mustard have a long history in classical sources – there is a recipe for a mustard sauce for *farcimina* in the *Apicius* collection, and mustard is also an ingredient in Apician sauces eaten with crane, duck, flamingo, chicken, piglet, boar, hare, lobster, salted mullet, scorpion fish, moray, and eels.[27] Returning to Symeon, people mock him, so he smears his mustard on the eyes of a man with eye disease, who is nearly burned to death. Symeon recommends him to wash off the mustard with vinegar. Vinegar does indeed slow the enzymes in mustard and reduce its pungency, but adding yet another sharp foodstuff to the mustard would have seemed crazy to the sufferer, and in the story he opts to go to a doctor instead.[28] The doctor succeeds in blinding him completely, so he returns screaming to the saint, who heals him, and as a result he honours God.

Rabbinical opinion in Jewish Babylonia on medical uses of mustard claimed that it was good for the heart if taken regularly once a month, but taking it every day was dangerous (BT Berakhot 40a). And a pregnant woman who eats mustard is in danger of having neglectful children (BT Ketubot 60b).

Looking at mustard and the way it was used in the talmudic literature, and comparing this with classical, Christian, and Arab sources as well as archaeological evidence and reconstructionist experiments can thus contribute a little more to our picture of foodways in the Ancient Near East, even if some questions remain unanswered.

Notes

1. For a brief explanation of the talmudic literature, see my paper 'Nuts for the Children: The Evidence of the Talmudic Literature', *Nurture: Proceedings of the 2003 Oxford Symposium on Food and Cookery*, ed. by R. Hosking (Bristol: FootWork, 2004), p. 264.
2. 'Black Mustard', NatureGate <http://www.luontoportti.com/suomi/en/kukkakasvit/black-mustard> [accessed 22 March 2019]; A. Davidson, *Oxford Companion to Food*, 2nd edn, ed. by T. Jaine (Oxford: Oxford University Press, 2006), p. 527.
3. MKilayim ii, 8 and see also MKilayim ii 5, which talks of surrounding small vegetable beds with mustard.
4. MKilayim ii, 9, and see also Tos Kilayim ii, 5.
5. MKilayim iii, 2.
6. Y. Sussmann, 'A Halakhic Inscription from the Beth-Shean Valley,' *Tarbiz*, 43 (1974), 88-158 (Heb.); Y. Sussmann, 'The Inscription in the Synagogue at Rehob', in *Ancient Synagogues Revealed*, ed. by L. I. Levine (Jerusalem: Israel Exploration Society, 1981), pp.146-51; *Jerusalem Talmud: Masekhet Shevi'it*, ed. by Yehudah Feliks, 2nd edn (Jerusalem: Mas Press, 2001), II, pp. 447-56 (Heb.).
7. PTNazir 51c. These must be the large citrons (*etrogim*) known today as Yemenite ones.
8. They are not, of course, the smallest seeds. On India, see A. Dalby, *Dangerous Tastes: The Story of Spices* (Berkeley: University of California Press, 2002).
9. See Y. Tepper and Y. Tepper, *The Agriculture of Mustard in Jewish Galilee in the Time of the Mishnah and the Talmud* (Jerusalem: 2009) (Heb.). I am grateful to Yotam Tepper for providing this information.
10. BT Betzah 12b.
11. JTPeah 20b. It is interesting that climbing the mustard plant is here compared to climbing a fig tree: could there be a reference here to the man in the gospel of Luke 19.1-10 who climbed a sycamore fig tree to get sight of Jesus?
12. BT Ketubot 111b.
13. Davidson.
14. De re rustica xii, 57.
15. Midrash Genesis Rabbah Genesis 11.
16. R. Man and R. Weir, *The Compleat Mustard* (London: Constable, 1988).
17. H. McGee, *On Food and Cooking: The Science and Lore of the Kitchen* (New York: Scribner, 2004), pp. 417-18.
18. N. Nasrallah, 'Recipe [for mustard condiment] good to use at home and while travelling', *Treasure Trove of Benefits and Variety at the Table: A Fourteenth-Century Egyptian Cookbook* (Leiden: Brill, 2017), p. 315.
19. MBavaBatra ii 10; see also BTBava Batra 18a.
20. M Pesahim ii 8.
21. BTHullin 132b.
22. MHullin x,4.
23. See on this S. Hitch, 'Sacrifice', in *A Companion to Food in the Ancient World*, ed. by J. Wilkins and R. Nadeau (Chichester: John Wiley, 2015), pp. 337-47 (especially p. 339).
24. POxy 108, dated to the twenty-fourth year of either Caracalla or Commodus.
25. A. Dalby, *Flavours of Byzantium* (Totnes: Prospect Books, 2003), pp. 167, 229: Mustard dip: *embamma dia sinepi*.
26. D. Krueger, *Symeon the Holy Fool: Leontius' Life and the Late Antique City* (Berkeley: University of California Press, 1996).
27. Apicius 2.5.2, etc. Columella's recipe for mustard sauce gives no indication of what it was eaten with.
28. McGee, p. 416.

Karakılçık Wheat and its Promise for a Better Food World

Zafer Yenal

Introduction

This paper tells the story of the rise to local popularity of a long forgotten heirloom (ancient) wheat variety, *Karakılçık* wheat. Karakılçık wheat, literally black-awn wheat, is a sturdy wheat whose bread is most delicious. The story begins six years ago, with a Seferihisar municipal official coming upon this little-known wheat variety bagged away in the musty cellar of an old farmer living in the remote mountain village of Gödence, Seferihisar. In the story of Karakilcik, a regional seed conservation and distribution centre (Can Yücel Tohum Merkezi) and the Seferihisar Municipality are both important actors: the former in producing the seed and the latter for making it popular. Focusing on the case of a single heirloom wheat variety allows us to consider the ability of local/regional food movements and food solidarity initiatives to challenge the growing corporate power over our food chain.

Turkey is no exception to the growing interest in heirloom wheat varieties and other food products. In Turkey heirloom wheat seeds are used mainly for bread making or *bulgur* (cracked wheat). *Siyez, kavlica, iza* are some of the more popular heirloom wheat varieties or wheat landraces (as agronomists call them) that readily come to mind that have found their way onto market shelves and, as a result, become familiar to middle-class customers in the last several years, especially in big cities such as Istanbul, Ankara, and Izmir.[1] Breads and other food products made with these types of wheat are considered healthier and more nutritious. Karakılçık wheat is relatively less well known: its prominence is currently limited to Seferihisar and Izmir's hinterland. Karakılçık is a curious case that deserves a closer look particularly for two reasons. Firstly, the institutional context in which Karakılçık was rediscovered and made available to farmers after decades of neglect is quite illuminating. It lays bare the lengthy, often arduous, and innovative process through which now-forgotten or marginalized crops, especially those with significant potential to contribute to a more socially and ecologically sustainable and healthy food world, can be brought to daylight. Secondly, it shows how the fate of seed preservation projects is tied to larger questions of land ownership, the nature of trade in agricultural markets, and collective action that involves many parties ranging from local governments to NGOs to local solidarity networks.

In the first part of this paper, I will situate Karakılçık wheat in the larger historical trajectory of wheat landraces in Turkey. In the second part I will introduce the Can Yücel Seed Centre founded by the Seferihisar Municipality, which plays a vital role in the discovery and dissemination of local seed varieties in the region. Lastly, I will focus on Karakılçık wheat and analyze the major tensions and turning points in its recent history. This paper draws upon site visits to Seferihisar and the Can Yücel Seed Centre in the past four years. During these visits I had the chance to observe life in many villages and to conduct interviews with farmers, municipality officials, academics, and local residents. I also surveyed the existing literature on Karakılçık wheat.

Wheat Landraces in Turkey

Wheat is economically, nutritionally, and culturally very important in Turkey. It is the fundamental staple crop. Around twenty-five million tonnes of wheat are produced on an area larger than seven million hectares in present-day Turkey. Substantial portions of the wheat produced are used for baking bread, the main staple of the country. Annual wheat consumption in the form of bread and other wheat products (such as pasta, *bulgur, tarhana, keshkek*, etc.) is one of the highest in the world at twenty kilograms per capita. Bread symbolizes survival and sacredness, and even small increases in bread prices result in significant popular disputes from time to time.[2]

As in most countries in the world, wheat agriculture in Turkey largely relies on the high-yielding hybrid seed varieties that began to dominate the agricultural sector after the 1960s. After World War II, capital- and fossil fuel-intensive agriculture became increasingly common in Turkey. Previously uncultivated land was brought under cultivation with the help of imported tractors. High yielding varieties of seeds were introduced and adopted through several research programs sponsored by the Rockefeller Foundation, one of the main institutions that played a leading role in the process known as the 'Green Revolution', the dissemination of modern agricultural technologies across the world after the 1960s. These programs became particularly effective for wheat production, and genetic innovations resulted in increasing use of chemical fertilizers, pesticides, and herbicides in wheat farming. Consequently, agricultural productivity began to increase through mechanization, irrigation projects, chemical innovations, and seed improvement. All these changes led to the swift commodification and commercialization of agriculture, and an increasing number of growers oriented their activities towards the market rather than subsistence farming. To be more competitive many farmers abandoned traditional landraces that they and their ancestors had cultivated for decades, if not for centuries, and instead adopted 'Mexican wheats', as they were called by many back then.

The gradual substitution of traditional landraces by modern hybrid seeds in wheat farming within the context of the 'Green Revolution' in Turkey has strong parallels in other peripheral countries, especially in Asia and Latin America. What makes the Turkish case even more striking and perhaps tragic is that wheat landraces endemic to

Karakılçık Wheat and its Promise for a Better Food World

Turkey have historically constituted a fertile germplasm pool for the rest of the world, a pool that modern-day advances in plant genetics has relied upon.[3] Many gene traits that were used in various hybridization techniques to come up with disease-resistant and fertilizer-responsive varieties of commercial modern seeds originated in Turkey:

> Turkey is the centre of origin and domestication for many crop species [...]. Diverse geological and climatic conditions of Turkey have given rise to unique plant species represented nowhere else in the world. Over 30% of 8,800 species found in the country are endemic to Turkey [...]. The country is the centre of origin and a source of genetic diversity for globally important plants, which were first domesticated from wild species and still exist in Turkey. In fact, Turkey's importance in relation to progenitor species, such as wheat, barley, oats, lentil chickpea, apple and pear, used in Mediterranean and temperate agricultural systems is virtually unprecedented [...]. Wheat landraces are one of the most important genetic resources for Turkey. The archaeological findings have shown that Eastern Mediterranean regions surrounding the rivers Tigris and Euphrates were the first places, where wheat was processed.[4]

Not surprisingly, wheat diversity in Turkey has attracted the attention of scientists for a long time. For example, Mirza Gökgöl, a leading agro-ecological plant scientist, agronomist, and breeder, collected and evaluated many crop varieties (mostly wheat) and their wild relatives for their basic characteristics from 1929 to 1955. For him, not only diverse climatic and geological conditions but also the fact that Anatolia has been on the crossroads of extensive migration which involved seed transfers between Central Asia and other regions played a major role in the enrichment of crop varieties in Asia Minor. He identified about 18,000 types of wheat and singled out 256 endemic varieties.[5] Obviously the plant collection that Gökgöl compiled and studied was invaluable for understanding genetic variation in food crops. It was unprecedented both in terms of content and extent, but '[t]ragically, this invaluable collection was not given sufficient attention after Gökgöl's retirement in the 1960s [...] and it was abandoned and lost'.[6] Gökgöl's books and research articles continue to serve as important sources of reference and exploration for present-day botanists and plant scientists.

Currently only a very small portion of wheat production relies on local landraces. According to some estimates the share of landraces does not exceed 1% of total wheat production in the country and the entire amount of land on which landrace varieties (for both wheat and barley) are cultivated is around 565,312 hectares.[7] Recent studies on the availability, distribution, and genetic content of wheat landraces in Turkey clearly demonstrate that there has been a significant decline in genetic diversity in wheat, with a 75.5% reduction in morphotypes.[8]

Most producers still cultivating landrace wheat varieties in Turkey are subsistence farmers living in the mountains and remote villages, usually far from markets. Landrace cultivators have very limited connections with the grain trade. As would be expected, their cultivated lands are small in size, much lower than regional averages. A substantial number of these growers (43% for bread wheat landraces and 31% for durum wheat landraces) do not exchange seeds. In general, they use non-mechanized farming practices: hand planting and the use of primitive spreaders is quite widespread. On average, landrace wheat farmers are older than 53, and their educational levels are generally low. There are also some farmers who are cultivating with modern hybrid varieties alongside landraces. Many farmers point to excellent adaptation of landraces to cold and drought conditions, and high grain quality in terms of both storing and baking.[9]

There are two important conclusions that we can draw from these findings. First, the level of market integration for most of the landrace farmers is very low; they primarily engage in subsistence farming. Second, most belong to older generations; younger cohorts are more interested in commercial farming with modern agricultural technology, including high-yielding hybrid varieties. This shows that indigenous knowledge about local landrace types is important not only for the conservation of heirloom seed varieties but also for utilizing them in farming practices. Karakılçık wheat is one of those wheat landraces that survived in different parts of Turkey. It is generally found in northeastern and southeatern Anatolia as well as in the east Mediterranean regions. Along with Kırık and Topbaş, Karakılçık is known for its high adaptability and excellent grain qualities. It is also considered a bread wheat landrace as opposed to durum landrace, which is mainly used for cooking food products other than bread.[10]

The Can Yücel Seed Centre

The question is, then, how Karakılçık wheat could find its way to rising prominence and wider availability in Seferihisar and its surrounding regions in the recent years. To begin to respond to this question, we first need to look closely at the Can Yücel Seed Centre, which played a major role in discovering and popularizing Karakılçık cultivation in the region, and at the Seferihisar Municipality that founded the Centre.

Seferihisar is a sub-province of Izmir Province, located about thirty kilometres from Izmir, the third largest city in Turkey. In the spring, Seferihisar's air is filled with the intoxicating smell of blooming tangerines in vast orchards, in the summer its beaches offer a welcome relief to the very hot weather of the region, in late summer grapes ripen in its vineyards, and then in autumn olives ripen in its vast olive groves. Seferihisar's transformation from a small, sleepy agricultural town to a summer resort started in the 1970s with the building of summerhouses and condominiums. As is the case with many other seaside towns in this country, it was (and to an extent still is) going down the road of being an overbuilt, overcrowded summer resort where tangerine orchards may remain only in memory. Yet Seferihisar began to go through another transformation after 2009 when its mayoralty began to actively engage in policies to support the region's agricultural activities, alongside developing it as a summer destination. A major push in this direction came when, at the initiative of the mayoralty, Seferihisar was recognized as

Karakılçık Wheat and its Promise for a Better Food World

a 'Cittaslow' town in 2009. This recognition helped Seferihisar compete with the other nearby and already popular summer towns of Urla and Çeşme in attracting summer tourists from Istanbul and elsewhere.

Under the progressive mayor Tunc Soyer, who is serving his second term, the Municipality has been engaging in agricultural activities to promote the farmers and growers under its jurisdiction. Since 2009, the Municipality has been actively encouraging local tangerine and olive oil producers to organize through producer cooperatives. To increase the willingness of local producers to become cooperative members and facilitate easier access to consumer markets, the Municipality has long been involved in product certification processes. These are confined to organic products, mainly tangerines, olives, and olive oil, grown in compliance with the standards of Good Agricultural Practices.[11] The Municipality has established small-size groceries ('*seferibakkallar*') to sell packaged products offered by producer cooperatives in downtown Seferihisar and nearby places like Sığacık and Ürkmez. Apparently most of the projects that the Seferihisar Municipality has initiated had quite rightfully the intention of addressing the problems that small growers face in trying to gain access to the consumer markets.[12]

Can Yücel Tohum Merkezi, founded in 2011, is another major investment of the Seferihisar Municipality. As in many other countries, in Turkey in the past several decades we have witnessed a growing number of local initiatives and organizations formed to counter the growing domination of global food corporations in local markets by enhancing the resilience of small food producers. This seed centre is a prime example of such initiatives. It proudly carries the name of Can Yücel, a prominent Turkish poet known for his poems emphasizing social justice. This seed centre is an illuminating case for understanding the limits and the potential of what can be done by those who dream of a better, greener world which cares about concepts like ecological agriculture, food sovereignty, and social solidarity. It works with a barter system since existing legislation does not allow unregistered seed varieties to be sold in the market.[13] People often bring traditional seeds (mostly heirloom varieties) in their hands, and they can get the seeds they want from the Centre.

The last time I visited the Centre, Aylin Hanım, the director, was sorting out a straw-like pile, which, I later learned, included seeds of black radish, leek, and broccoli. In the Centre seeds are kept in jars in places that do not receive direct sunlight. Reminiscent of a primitive seed bank, the Centre holds more than a hundred seed samples from all around Turkey: Artvin corn, Çeşme melon, Birgi tomatoes, and many other varieties.[14] Right outside the tiny cottage where the Centre is located, there is a garden where they cultivate seeds to make them available in larger quantities.

Aylin Hanım said that they are working closely with various NGOs, schools, and producer organizations to propagate and widely distribute domestic heirloom seed varieties. She explained that the cost of local traditional seeds (i.e. landrace varieties) is much lower when compared to hybrid or GMO seeds in the market, and the local varieties are more resistant to diseases as well. According to Hanim, consumers have begun to become conscious of these advantages, and now they ask more often whether what they are buying are heirloom varieties. She added that there are now similar seed conservation and distribution centres in Izmir, Eskişehir, Bursa, Çanakkale, and Muğla that are actively supporting and sharing their know-how about seed conservation and distribution.

The Recent History of Karakılçık Wheat

Thanks to the collective efforts of the Centre with the local growers who supplied the Centre with initial seed source, the number of farmers producing Karakılçık wheat increased in the last two years, and breads baked with Karakılçık wheat are on sale in local markets. I will now focus on the major turning points in the journey of Karakılçık wheat from being an unknown wheat variety to being a local celebrity.

In our interview, Şevket Bey, who is leading the agricultural services in the Municipality, described the first occasion that Karakılçık wheat came to their attention:

> I was researching local seeds in preparation for our local seed festival in 2011. When I was chatting with an elderly man in Gödence village, I learned that he had a small amount of Karakılçık wheat. Until then, I only knew wheat as wheat, and had no knowledge of its varieties. This wheat was very peculiar, it did not resemble the wheat I knew before. The tufts of the wheat were different from the fringes, and it looked primitive, flattened head, etc. Altogether it was 40-50 kilograms; most of them with mold. We sorted them out individually with the old man.

Gödence, the village where our Karakılçık wheat surfaced, is a mountain village of Seferihisar with a total population of 300 people. There is a relatively old olive-oil producer cooperative, and villagers that I talked to seem to appreciate the cooperative's presence for improving the production and packaging facilities. However, they were complaining about not being able to reach urban customers. The villagers including Mustafa Bey, the *mukhtar* (village headman), talked positively about the Municipality; they particularly mentioned how useful it was that the Municipality facilitated their access to organic certification, both for olive oil and grapes. When I talked to Özcan Bey, the head of the Cooperative in Gödence, he told me about his long experience in the cooperative movement going back to the 1970s. For him, transparency and accountability were two vital elements for any collective organization to be enduring and successful.

Going over my field notes about Gödence and remembering all these interviews made me think that the discovery of Karakılçık wheat in Gödence was not accidental. The village was already an exemplary village for hosting an enduring producer cooperative for a long time – a very rare case in rural Turkey. The social and scientific activities (such as popular lectures by agronomists, festivals, etc.) that the Cooperative

Karakılçık Wheat and its Promise for a Better Food World

facilitated must have contributed to an awakening sense of the importance of local resources and indigenous knowledge. Thanks to the farmer-friendly policies of the Municipality, the villagers had already developed trust in the Municipality, and perhaps it was partly this trust that enabled the old man to share his age-old seeds with the Municipality representative.

Can Yücel Seed Centre began to cultivate Karakalçık seeds in the fall of 2011. Since then, they continued to cultivate and multiply the seeds. Just last year for the very first time they cultivated seeds for producing wheat flour that would eventually be used for bread making. The total production area is around 120 square kilometres. Interestingly, only ten square kilometres of this land belonged to the Municipality. The rest was previously uncultivated land belonging to different villagers. In other words, the Municipality convinced farmers to grow Karakılçık wheat on part of their uncultivated land.

From the interviews with the Municipality officials, I understand that persuading farmers to grow Karakılçık wheat was not easy. Nobody had a clear idea about the marketing potential of this 'new' wheat variety when made into bread. Şevket Bey, who is working as a consultant on agriculture-related projects in the Municipality, tells the rest of the story in the following way:

> Our peasants cannot adopt a product without seeing it, without touching it. So we as the municipality started to work on bread. First we brought wheat cultivation to Ulamış. It is a village located on a plain. Gödence was not conducive to expand wheat cultivation because it was a mountain village. The wheat grown in Ulamış was turned into flour by hand mills. Then, using sour yeast, we baked bread in traditional ovens. The bread made with this flour was introduced to the villagers. So the peasants understood that this crop was reputable and they were convinced to cultivate more Karakılçık wheat. Today the weekly farmers' market in Ulamış is visited by people from various parts of Izmir just to buy that bread. By the way, our municipality has two groceries. People can buy this bread from our groceries too.

I must add here that the bread comes early in the morning and quite limited in number. No customer is not allowed to buy more than one loaf. The breads sell out in about an hour.

The Municipality began a new project this year in order to support Karakılçık wheat farming and make it appealing to more farmers. Having been engaged with many agriculture-related projects over the years, the Municipality knows that one of the major difficulties that small farmers face these days is obtaining secure procurement deals. Their new undertaking is the 'Purchase Guaranteed Karakılçık Wheat Growing Project', which is intended to address this problem. Despite its surface similarity with contract farming practices, it is quite the opposite.[15] This new project prioritizes the supplier's rights, gains, and well-being rather than the buyer's. It works as follows: the Municipality provides the farmers with Karakılçık wheat seeds and guarantees that it will buy the produce at a price doubling the minimum price announced by the Soil

Products Office (the government's main procurement office for agricultural products).

Conclusion

In my paper I focused on this curious case of Karakılçık wheat, its historical and current trajectory, to better understand local food sovereignty movements and their implications not only for ancient seed preservation but also for creating viable and sustainable alternatives to corporate power. Thanks to the collective efforts of the Seed Centre and the Municipality with the local growers who supplied the Centre with initial seed source, the number of farmers producing this wheat variety has increased in the last two years.

The main takeaway from this story is the institutionalized and sustainable mechanisms and instruments that enable an ongoing relationship with small local producers and the mostly middle-class consumers. In the contemporary world, when we talk about food sovereignty, rights to food, community-supported agriculture, and alternative food networks, we often celebrate an individual cooperative, an urban garden, or a food festival. The story of Karakılçık in Seferihisar reminds us to recognize the importance of larger institutional mechanisms and structures to weave together disparate consumer or producer cooperatives and thus give them transformative power.

Notes

1. For an illuminating account of rising popularity of *siyez* wheat in Turkey, see Nurcan Atalan-Helicke, '"You can never give up *siyez* if you taste it once": Local Taste, Global Markets, and the Conservation of Einkorn, an Ancient Wheat', *Gastronomica*, 18.2 (Summer 2018), 33-45.
2. Fethiye Özberk, Alptekin Karagöz, İrfan Özberk, and Ayhan Atlı, 'Buğday Genetik Kaynaklarından Yerel ve Kültür Çeşitlerine; Türkiye'de Buğday ve Ekmek', *Tarla Bitkileri Merkez Araştırma Enstitüsü Dergisi*, 25.2 (2016), 218-33.
3. In fact, the Turkish case is not an exception. We historically observe similar patterns in germplasm transfers for many food commodities mainly between core and peripheral countries. Generally speaking, core (Northern) countries are gene-poor while peripheral (Southern) countries are gene-rich. As J.R. Kloppenburg writes, "[t]he germplasm resources of the third world have historically been considered a free good – "the common heritage of mankind"' (*First the Seed: The Political Economy of Plant Biotechnology* (Madison: University of Wisconsin Press, 1988), p. 15).
4. Mustafa Kan and others, 'Wheat Landraces Production on Farm Level in Turkey: Who Is Growing Where?', *Pakistan Journal of Agricultural Sciences,* April 2016, p. 1.
5. A. Karagöz, 'Wheat Landraces of Turkey', *Emirates Journal of Food and Agriculture*, 26.2 (2014), 149-56 (p. 150).
6. Nusret Zencirci and others, 'Mirza (Hacızade) Gökgöl (1897–1981): The Great Explorer of Wheat Genetic Resources in Turkey', *Genetic Resources and Crop Evaluation*, 65.3 (March 2018), 693-711 (p. 695).
7. Kan and others, 'Wheat Landraces Production on Farm Level in Turkey: Who Is Growing Where?'; Karagöz, p. 152.
8. A. Morgounov and others, 'Wheat Landraces Currently Grown in Turkey: Distribution, Diversity, and Use', *Crop Science*, 56 (2016), 3112-24 (p. 3120).
9. Kan and others, 'Wheat Landraces Production on Farm Level in Turkey: Who Is Growing Where?';

Morgounov and others, p. 3120.
10 Morgounov and others, p. 3116.
11 Global Partnership for Good Agricultural Practice (GLOBALGAP) is now one of the leading certification standards in the world. There are currently more than a hundred independent and accredited certification bodies affiliated with GLOBALCAP in more than eighty countries. The GAP certification system became known in Turkey in the 2000s, mainly due to marketing problems Turkish exporters encountered in European markets (Ç. Keyder and Z. Yenal, 'Agrarian Change under Globalization: Markets and Insecurity in Turkish Agriculture', *Journal of Agrarian Change* (Winter 2011), 60-86).
12 As in many other places in the world where government regulation in the agri-food sector has eroded over in the last several decades, in Turkey big buyers (such as supermarket chains, wholesalers, global food corporations) dominate the agricultural scene and are increasing their control over the supply chain. Under these conditions, smaller growers are encountering serious obstacles in marketing their produce.
13 In 2006, the government in Turkey legislated a seed law empowering a private body, the Association of Seed Growers, to regulate the seed market, to register and certify seed varieties, and to prohibit the marketing of unregistered seeds. This legislation was in line with the efforts of the World Trade Association and other global institutions which have intensively worked to institutionalize intellectual property rights in plant breeding across the world over the last several decades. One of the main outcomes of this legislation has been to keep out of the seed markets both public agencies and individual farmers who could not compete because they were not able to navigate the costly certification process. Thus, the legislation enhanced the advantages already enjoyed by transnational seed companies and the larger producers of domestic varieties, who were often tied in partnerships.
14 For an excellent essay on the current state of global seed banks, see John Seabrook, 'Sowing for Apocalypse: The Quest for a Global Seed Bank', *The New Yorker*, 27 August 2007 <https://www.newyorker.com/magazine/2007/08/27/sowing-for-apocalypse> [accessed 22 March 2019].
15 Contracts in Turkey, as everywhere in the world, often include terms and clauses that can be considered exacting for growers. The terms that the farmers have to comply with are precisely spelled out in the contracts to minimize uncertainty for the purchaser. Such precision is absent in the way the terms relating to the buyer's responsibilities and obligations are stated; stipulations regarding the pricing of the output seem to be vague and complicated, and the schedule for payment is not clear.

Contributors

Isaura Andaluz works to promote seed diversity and preservation through reviving forgotten crops. Her latest efforts are included in *Seed Sovereignty, Food Security: Woman in the Vanguard*.

Åsmund Asdal, Coordinator for the Svalbard Global Seed Vault, writes about the importance of conserving seed diversity and how frozen seeds are secured in the Arctic.

Volker Bach, a freelance translator and historical cooking instructor, is the author of *The Kitchen, Food, and Cooking in Reformation Germany*.

Hans Olav Bråtå is a Senior Researcher at Eastern Norway Research Institute, Lillehammer. He writes about the extinct naked barley 'Thorebygg' related to farmhouse ale brewing in Norway.

Adrian Bregazzi is an independent researcher living in South West England with interests in the history, culture, and theory of food.

As a Conservation Partnership Coordinator at the Royal Botanic Gardens, Kew, **Elinor Breman** works to develop and maintain Millennium Seed Bank partnerships, projects, and networks.

Anthony F. Buccini is an historical linguist and dialectologist with specialties in Germanic, Romance, and language contact. His extensive food studies publications focus primarily on the Mediterranean and Atlantic World. Buccini is a two-time winner of the Sophie Coe Prize in Food History.

Voltaire Cang is an academic researcher based in Tokyo. He researches and writes about Japan's 'intangible' heritage, including food and other cultural practices and traditions.

Currently Assistant Dean of the College of Hospitality Management, **Bel Castro** is one of the founding faculty members of Enderun Colleges in the Philippines.

Mary Margaret Chappell is an American food writer and editor who lives on the coast of Brittany in France.

A sociologist from the United States, **Renata Christen** has worked on farms, at seed companies, and with benchmarking organizations to explore how food diversity can be made accessible for all.

Len Fisher is a scientist, author, and broadcaster who won a spoof Ig Nobel prize for using physics to work out the best way to dunk a biscuit. He was a finalist in the recent

Global Challenges 'New Shape' competition to find new approaches to resolving global challenges, many of which are related to food.

Anny Gaul is a PhD candidate in the Arabic and Islamic Studies Department at Georgetown University. She also blogs at cookingwithgaul.com and works as a freelance translator.

American filmmaker **B.Z. Goldberg** grew up in Israel. His work includes co-directing *Promises*.

Peter Hertzmann is an autodidactic polymath with a strong contrarian bent who likes to provide an alternative approach about all aspects of food. His three books are *Knife Skills Illustrated: A User's Manual, A Perfect Mouthful,* and *50 Ways to Cook a Carrot*.

Elizabeth Hoover is Manning Assistant Professor of American Studies at Brown University, where she teaches and writes about Native American food sovereignty projects, environmental health, and community-based research.

A PhD candidate in Italian Studies at Rutgers University, **Èilis Kierans**'s research focuses on the relationship between food and power in women's literature.

Molly MacVeagh is a PhD student at Cornell University. She studies the relationships between twentieth-century food science, realist fiction, and changing conceptions of the body.

Lecturer in Medieval History and in Economic and Social History of the Middle Ages at the University of Bari, **Andrea Maraschi** writes about various aspects of food in medieval society.

Professor of English at the United States Naval Academy, **Mark McWilliams** has served as Editor of the Oxford Symposium on Food and Cookery since 2011.

Professor of Hospitality and Food Culture at the Federal University of Rio de Janeiro, **Myriam Melchior** writes about how modernity impacts Brazilian and Ibero-American culinary traditions.

Sandra Mian is a food engineer who works as a consultant for the food industry and home appliance manufacturers. She lives and works in Canada, Brazil, and Mexico.

Katharina Mojescik is a PhD student in Sociology at Ruhr-University Bochum. Her research focuses on the relevance of food in cultural and social transformation processes.

Contributors

She also likes to broaden her own culinary horizon by discovering new tastes and cooking techniques.

Raluca Parfentie is a former radio journalist. The author of *Bomboanele sovietice – agenți sub acoperire*, a book about the secret political life of soviet candies, she is currently a PhD student at the University of Bucharest, writing about food advertising in interwar Romania.

Jeffrey Rubel earned his undergraduate degree at Williams College in 2017; there, he studied geology and food history, focusing on the connections between scientific advancement and everyday eating. He currently resides in Boston, MA, where he works as a management consultant.

An archaeologist and anthropologist, **Kathryn Sampeck** writes about the social history of American foods and culinary practices, particularly chocolate. She is an Associate Professor at Illinois State University.

The founder of the Sioux Chef, caterer and food educator **Sean Sherman** has worked to revitalize indigenous food systems in a modern context and to make indigenous foods more broadly accessible.

Carolina Distinguished Professor at the University of South Carolina, **David Shields** restores landrace grains and heirloom vegetables to the fields and tables of the American South. He recently published *The Culinarians,* recounting the careers of 175 American chefs, caterers, and restaurateurs from 1793 to 1919.

Hanna Lise Simonsen has researched crops able to grow in extreme weather and in low quality soil on different continents.

Ray Sokolov attended the first public Symposium in 1983. His appetite for food history is undiminished. Most recently he investigated Mexican cuisine through tacos de ubre (udder) on the streets of San Miguel de Allende and indoors at all three of its Michelin-starred restaurants.

Corey Straub is a food historian based in Montreal. His research explores food, culture, and identity in Classical antiquity.

Carolina Sulis is a nutritionist and coffee specialist living in Lugano, Switzerland.

Marcella Sulis is a PhD researcher in Hospitality at University Anhembi Morumbi and professor of gastronomy at the Federal University of Rio de Janeiro.

David Sutton is a literary and archival researcher, Director of Research Projects in the University of Reading Library, member of the governing body of the International Council on Archives, and Treasurer of the Oxford Symposium. His books include *Figs* and *Rich Food, Poor Food*.

Malcolm Thick writes on food history, agricultural history, and also dabbles in the history of science. In 2010 he published *Sir Hugh Plat: The Search for Useful Knowledge in Early Modern London*, and he has also written about market gardening around early modern London.

Kate Thomas is the K. Laurence Stapleton Professor of English at Bryn Mawr College, where she teaches classes on Victorian Literature and Culture, gender and sexuality, and Food Studies. She is the author of *Postal Pleasures: Sex, Scandal, and Victorian Letters*.

Jaci van Niekerk conducts research on biodiversity and traditional knowledge, and is exploring the foodways of the local peoples of the Cederberg Mountains for her PhD.

Food researcher, journalist, and author **Ronit Vered** frequently lectures on themes relating to cuisines and identity, food and politics, the Jewish kitchen, and the flourishing of Israeli cuisine.

Susan Weingarten is a food historian and archaeologist living in Jerusalem.

Rachel Wynberg is an Associate Professor at the University of Cape Town where she has a research chair on the social and environmental dimensions of the bio-economy.

Professor of Sociology at Boğaziçi University, Istanbul, **Zafer Yenal** studies food cultures and agrarian transformations in Turkey.